UNMAPPED
COUNTRIES

Anthem Nineteenth Century Studies
Series editor: Robert Douglas-Fairhurst

UNMAPPED COUNTRIES

Biological Visions in Nineteenth Century
Literature and Culture

edited by
Anne-Julia Zwierlein

Anthem Press
London

Anthem Press
An imprint of Wimbledon Publishing Company
75-76 Blackfriars Road, London SE1 8HA
or
PO Box 9779, London SW19 7QA
www.anthempress.com

This edition first published by Anthem Press 2005

British Library Cataloguing in Publication Data
A catalogue record for this book is available from the British Library.

Library of Congress Cataloging in Publication Data
A catalog record for this book has been requested.

1 3 5 7 9 10 8 6 4 2

ISBN 1 84331 159 3 (Hbk)
ISBN 1 84331 160 7 (Pbk)

Typeset by Footprint Labs Ltd, London
www.footprintlabs.com

Printed in India

CONTENTS

LIST OF ILLUSTRATIONS

Cover Illustration. Ernst Haeckel, 1998 [1904], 'Phaeodaria. Rohrstrahlinge', in *Art Forms in Nature: One Hundred Colour Plates*, with contributions by O Breidbach and I Eibl-Eibesfeld, introd. R Hartmann, Munich, Prestel, Table 61–'Aulographis'.

ABOUT THE AUTHORS

Kirstie Blair is a Supernumerary Fellow and Tutor in English at St Peter's College, Oxford, where she teaches nineteenth and twentieth century literature. She has published several articles on Victorian literature, particularly in the fields of literature and religion and literature and medicine. Her first book, *Victorian Poetry and the Culture of the Heart*, is forthcoming in 2005.

Johan Braeckman is a Professor at the Department of Philosophy, Ghent University, and at the Faculty of Science, University of Amsterdam. His research is on evolutionary theory, philosophy of biology, bio-ethics and evolutionary psychology. He has co-authored books on science, on reproductive cloning and other issues, co-edited several books and authored a book on the development and philosophical implications of Darwin's theories.

Janet Browne is a Professor at the Wellcome Trust Centre for the History of Medicine, University College, London. She specializes in the life sciences, natural history and evolutionary biology from the seventeenth to the nineteenth century. She has published on Charles Darwin, including a two-volume biography *Voyaging* (1995), and *The Power of Place* (2002). She has also written on the history of botany and early ideas on the geography of animals and plants. Research for the academic session 2002 concentrated on the Centre's special project on medicine in literature funded by the Wellcome Trust.

Gowan Dawson is Lecturer in Victorian Literature at the University of Leicester. Previously he was a Leverhulme Research Fellow on the Science in the Nineteenth Century Periodical Project ('SciPer') at the University of Sheffield. His main research interests are in the interrelations between Victorian literature and science, as well as in the print culture of the nineteenth century. He is co-author of *Science in the Nineteenth Century Periodical: Reading the Magazine of Nature* (2004); and co-editor of *Culture and Science in the Nineteenth Century Media* (2004). He has also guest-edited, with Sally Shuttleworth, a special number of the journal *Victorian Poetry* on 'Science and Victorian Poetry' (2003), and is currently completing a book on aestheticism, obscenity and the Victorian debates over Darwin.

Marysa Demoor is a Professor of English Literature at the University of Ghent. She teaches Victorian Literature, critical theory, textual editing and gender studies. She has published widely on biography, women's writing, Andrew Lang, and Robert Louis Stevenson, and edited Henry James's letters to Lucy Clifford (1999); she has also written on female contributors to the *Athenaeum* (2000) and edited a collection of essays on the construction of writerly selves (2004).

Kate Flint is Professor of English at Rutgers, The State University of New Jersey (New Brunswick). She formerly taught at Oxford University for fifteen years. Her publications include *The Woman Reader, 1837–1914* (1993) and *The Victorians and the Visual Imagination* (2000), as well as numerous articles on nineteenth and twentieth century literature, cultural history and the history of art. She is currently completing a project entitled *The Transatlantic Indian 1780–1930*, and working on various topics connecting the senses, perception and memory in Victorian and Modernist writing.

Paul Goetsch was Professor at the English Department of Freiburg University. He is the author of books on Dickens, Hardy, the English novel 1880–1910, the short story and modern English and American drama. His most recent publications include *Monsters in English Literature: From the Romantic Age to the First World War* (2002); and *The Oral and the Written in Nineteenth Century British Fiction* (2003).

Alexandra Karl received two Bachelors from the University of Ottawa and her Masters from the University of Munich. She has worked at the National Gallery of Canada (1991–92) and at Munich's Städtische Galerie im Lenbachhaus (1994–98). She curated an exhibition of contemporary art at Lucy Cavendish College, University of Cambridge, called 'Crème de la Crème' (2000). She has won two scholarships, DAAD (Deutscher Akademischer Austauschdienst) and TIARKS (German Scholarship Fund at Cambridge University) and the Brancusi Prize for Art History. She lives in Salt Lake City, where she is finishing her doctoral dissertation for Cambridge.

Annette Kern-Stähler is Assistant Professor of English at the University of Düsseldorf. She studied English and biology at the Universities of Bonn and York, where she also received an MA in Medieval Studies. Her PhD on women and space in late-medieval England (Bonn, Münster, Oxford) was published in 2001. Other fields of interest and publications include the New English Literatures, Cultural Studies and contemporary drama.

Jürgen Meyer studied English philology and German literature at the Universities of Göttingen and Freiburg (1988–96). After various positions at the Sonderforschungsbereich 321 'Transitions and Tensions between Orality and Literacy' (Freiburg, 1992–96), he received a DFG grant for the postgraduate college 'Theory of Literature and Communication' at the University of Constance (1997–2000). Meyer teaches English literature at the Institute for English and American Studies at Martin Luther University, Halle-Wittenberg (since 2000). His doctoral thesis, *Allegorien des Wissens: Flann O'Briens* The Third Policeman *und Friedrich Dürrenmatts* Durcheinandertal *als ironische Kosmographien*, was published at Stauffenburg (2001). Current research focuses on the problem of simulacra in sixteenth-century texts. Publications include essays on E A Abbott, O Wilde, R Menasse, R Musil, F Dürrenmatt and S Rushdie.

Laura Otis is Professor of English at Emory University, and the author of *Organic Memory* (1994), *Membranes* (1999), and *Networking: Communicating with Bodies and Machines in the Nineteenth Century* (2001). Awarded a Humboldt Fellowship and a MacArthur Fellowship for her interdisciplinary studies of the nervous system, she has worked since 2000 as an occasional guest scholar at the Max Planck Institute for the History of Science in Berlin.

Carol Peaker completed a Masters degree in the History of the Book at the School of Advanced Study, University of London, before beginning a career as an art historian and art journalist. Between 1998 and 2001, she worked as the UK editor of *C International Art Magazine*, and as an arts correspondent for *The National Post* (Canada). She is also the author of *The Penguin Modern Painters: A History* (2001). Currently, she is completing a DPhil at Oxford University which examines how Russian émigré propagandists helped to direct the reception of nineteenth century Russian writers between 1885 and 1910. Her work is supported by a grant from the AHRB (Arts and Humanities Research Board).

Sally Shuttleworth is Professor of Modern English Literature at the University of Sheffield. Among her publications are *George Eliot and Nineteenth Century Science* (1984), *Charlotte Brontë and Victorian Psychology* (1996) and as co-editor, with Jenny Bourne Taylor, *Embodied Selves: An Anthology of Psychological Texts, 1830–1890* (1998). She is director of the Science in the Nineteenth Century Periodical Project, whose publications include *Science in the Nineteenth Century Periodical: Reading the Magazine of Nature* (2004); two edited volumes, *Science Serialized* (2004) and *Culture and Science in the Nineteenth Century Media* (2004), and an electronic database (http://www.sciper.leeds.ac.uk).

Charlotte Sleigh obtained her PhD from the University of Cambridge in 1999. Following this, she spent one year at the University of California at Los Angeles as a post-doctoral fellow, before taking up a permanent appointment as lecturer in the Centre for History and Cultural Studies of Science at the University of Kent. Her research covers the recent history of the life sciences, especially natural history and the place occupied by ants in human culture. She has published a number of journal articles and has one recently published book and another forthcoming. *Ant* (2003) is a general work of cultural studies, while *Six Legs Better* (forthcoming) is a history of myrmecology in the late nineteenth and early twentieth centuries.

Klaus Stierstorfer is Professor of English at the University of Münster. He studied at the Universities of Regensburg and Oxford, and received his DPhil at Oxford in 1993. Before moving to Münster in 2004, he was Professor of English at the University of Düsseldorf from 2002–2004, a Junior Research Fellow at St Cross College, Oxford, and an Assistant Professor at the University of Würzburg. His publications include *John Oxenford (1812–1877) as Farceur and Critic of Comedy* (1996); with Heinz Antor (eds), *English Literatures in International Contexts* (2000); (ed., introd., annot.), *London Assurance and Other Victorian Comedies* (2001); *Konstruktion literarischer Vergangenheit: Die englische Literaturgeschichtsschreibung von Warton bis Courthope und Ward* (2001), which is forthcoming, in an extended and revised version, in English translation in 2005.

Merle Tönnies studied at the Universities of Bochum and Oxford, completing her studies with an MA at Bochum and an MLitt (Oxon). Currently, she is Assistant Professor of English literature and Cultural Studies at the University of Bochum. She has recently completed her *Habilitation* with a thesis on the roles of women in nineteenth century British melodrama and has published widely on contemporary British drama, the Victorian Age, the consumer society and British political culture. She is the author of *Samuel Beckett's Dramatic Strategy* (1997), and has co-edited *British Literature and Culture* (1999), *Youth Identities* (2000), as well as Hanif Kureishi's *My Beautiful Launderette* (1999) and the volume *British Political Speeches* (2001). Since 2001, she has been co-editor of *anglistik & englischunterricht*.

Griet Vandermassen (Centre for Gender Studies, Department of English, University of Ghent) is a philosopher and a philologist. She is currently preparing a PhD thesis on the conflict between feminism(s) and Darwinism(s). Her main research interests are Darwinian theory, feminism, history of science, and philosophy of science. She is one of 118 collaborators in the International Sexuality Description Project, a cross-cultural survey of sex differences across 52 nations and 10 major world regions, and author of *Who's Afraid of Charles Darwin? Debating Feminism and Evolutionary Theory* (forthcoming, 2005).

Anne-Julia Zwierlein is Assistant Professor of English at the Centre for British Studies, University of Bamberg. She studied at Bonn, Oxford and Münster, and received her PhD in 2000 for *Majestick Milton: British Imperial Expansion and Transformations of* Paradise Lost, *1667–1837* (2001). She has co-edited a volume on the concept of interiority in literature (2002) and *Plotting Early Modern London: New Essays on Jacobean City Comedy* (2004). Her articles are on Shakespeare, Milton, early modern science, Paley, G H Lewes and Bulwer-Lytton, as well as Victorian medicine. She is currently preparing a book on the physiological *Bildungsroman* in the Victorian age.

PREFACE

This book documents the results of the international conference on 'Biology, Literature and Culture in the Nineteenth Century' held at the Centre for British Studies, University of Bamberg, 14–16 May 2004. I would like to express my gratitude to the Deutsche Forschungsgemeinschaft (DFG) and the British Council for generously funding this event. Special thanks go to Christa Jansohn, Director of the Centre for British Studies, for all her support, and to Christoph Houswitschka, Vice Dean of the Faculty of Languages and Literatures, for representing the university at the conference. Jürgen Krippner and Kerstin Clark were an invaluable help throughout. I am grateful to Kerstin Clark for her meticulous proofreading, and to André Schüller-Zwierlein for all his help and valuable suggestions. Most of all, I would like to thank the contributors: their academic rigour and warm-hearted collegiality made the conference an unforgettable event, and their wonderful cooperation, not least in keeping to tight deadlines, has made the present volume possible. At Anthem Press, I would like to record my sincere thanks to our editors, Tom Penn, Paolo Cabrelli, and Renu Sood, who have been very patient and supportive throughout.

Anne-Julia Zwierlein
Bamberg, December 2004

INTRODUCTION

UNMAPPED COUNTRIES: BIOLOGY, LITERATURE AND CULTURE IN THE NINETEENTH CENTURY

Anne-Julia Zwierlein

Biological Sciences in the Nineteenth Century

Bio-technology and human genetics are the dominant applied sciences in the twenty-first century; the 'irresistible rise of the biological sciences' has shaped our culture to a considerable extent.[1] Yet it was already during the nineteenth century that the cultural dominance of the natural sciences developed. Victorian science and the humanities still spoke a common language: scientific and creative writers drew on a common imagination; they shared narrative techniques, stylistic devices and topoi and often wrote about the same subjects. In the field of literary and cultural studies, interest in nineteenth century biology has never waned since Gillian Beer (*Darwin's Plots*, 1983) and George Levine (*Darwin and the Novelists*, 1988) demonstrated the intricate connections between the Victorian scientific and cultural spheres.[2] However, Beer and Levine also initiated the focus on evolutionary theory which has dominated scholarly debates ever since, the most recent example being Joseph Carroll's *Literary Darwinism: Evolution, Human Nature and Literature* (2004).[3] While evolutionary theory did have an immediate impact on nineteenth century thought, as in the dark visions of Social Darwinism or 'racial hygiene' and eugenics, it has to be remembered that at the time, many people were actually not too disquieted by Darwin's theories.[4] In gauging the development of the

biological sciences in the nineteenth century, it is vital to accord equal weight
to the perspectives of physiology, bacteriology, cell biology and neurology, with
their focus on networks of cells and nerves, as well as to the larger theoretical
background of post-Romantic organicism.[5] Auguste Comte's and Herbert
Spencer's organicism emphasized both the diachronic and the synchronic
perspective, proposing that, synchronically viewed, organic life was the relation
between an organism and its environment or 'medium', while diachronically
viewed, organic evolution, as well as embryological development and 'all
progress', involved an increasing specialization of parts, from homogeneity to
heterogeneity of structure.[6] It goes without saying that Darwin's theory of
evolution by natural selection itself combined the diachronic perspective of
species slowly evolving over centuries with the synchronic perspective of the
'struggle for existence', as well as of harmonious 'coadaptations' and mutually
beneficial living arrangements between species contemporary to each other.
Darwin emphasized that 'plants and animals, most remote in the scale of nature,
are bound together by a web of complex relations', and his metaphor of the
'entangled bank' concluding the *Origin of Species* (1859) has become famous.[7]
The present collection is, as much as a contribution to the 'Science and
Literature' debate, a plea for viewing jointly the diverse aspects of nineteenth
century biology: the 'temporal' patterns of evolution and degeneration, as well
as the 'spatial' patterns of physiology and pathology.

The term 'biology' itself, denoting the 'science of life', was introduced into
English usage in the early nineteenth century. It continued to vie for
predominance with the older term 'physiology', the science of the functions of
the living organism.[8] William Coleman classifies nineteenth century biological
thinking – roughly – as belonging to the categories of 'form', 'function' and
'transformation', grouping under 'form' anatomists, histologists and
embryologists, who studied organic form, appearance and structure; under
'function' physiologists, who studied the workings of the body (respiration,
nutrition, excretion, etc.), and under 'transformation' evolutionists, who studied
the transformations of life over vast spans of time.[9] While '[u]ntil well into
the century biology and physiology were virtually synonymous expressions',[10]
biology was increasingly used as the more inclusive term, extending to the study
of plant and animal life, while physiology remained semantically restricted to
the medical concern with the functions of the human body.

Thus, while evolutionary theory, like nineteenth century geology, cosmology
and palaeontology, foregrounded historical explanation, and concentrated on
the mechanisms of historical descent and transformation of organisms, to
another group of biologists 'historical explanation was of little interest and
probably irrelevant. Their subject was physiology.' Physiologists, probing into
the functions of the living organism, made startling progress throughout the

century, analysing the energy relationships of life and discovering the nature of the nervous impulse as well as chemical agents cooperating with the nervous system. While the different branches of physiology operated with 'a bewildering variety of vitalisms and mechanisms',[11] its lasting methodological contribution to biological science was the emphasis on experimentalism and verifiable data. Evolutionary theory did have unverifiable 'blind spots': evolutionists could argue from the – incomplete – historical record only, which caused a tendency to confuse temporal succession with causal explanation ('post hoc ergo propter hoc'), a tendency which Coleman calls the 'great intellectual prejudice of nineteenth century thought'.[12] The experimental method was to help fill in these blind spots as the twentieth century progressed, for instance with Mendel's experimental investigation of heredity and variation which inaugurated the new science of genetics. Experiment was also the core of the new cell biology, which made revolutionary discoveries from the 1830s onwards due to improved microscopes and the technique of tissue cultures. Especially important was the medical branch of cellular pathology – the development of cancer cells, for instance, was first scientifically described by Wilhelm Waldeyer in 1867. Robert Koch's germ theory of disease, published in 1879 and translated into English in 1880, was likewise developed in the laboratory. Pre-Freudian physiological psychology, a fascinating area of research which sought to define consciousness as a physiological phenomenon, had seen some of its major exponents already in mid-century with Spencer's *Principles of Psychology* (1855) and G H Lewes's *Problems of Life and Mind* (1874–9) – but that scientific branch really came into its own when physio-psychologists began to analyse states of mind experimentally towards the end of the century.[13]

The repercussions in literary discourse of these 'synchronic' biological disciplines, like the repercussions of Darwinism, were immediate and widespread. Post-Romantic theories of organicism, especially Spencer's theory of the 'Social Organism', enabled nineteenth century scientists and creative writers to see the 'social body' as an interdependent, complex mechanism. Its individual components were seen as 'coordinated' – for instance by Lewes in *The Physical Basis of Mind* (1877) – into a meaningful whole which was more than the sum of its parts. As Sally Shuttleworth has shown, his partner, George Eliot perfected the image of society's organic interdependence in a sensitive 'web of connections'.[14] Especially in *Middlemarch* (1871–2) she shows how seemingly detached elements of the social body latently influence the course of all other elements: 'there is no creature whose inward being is so strong that it is not greatly determined by what lies outside it'.[15] Also, for Spencer and others, the study of biology (and psychology) was a necessary preliminary to approaching social, philosophical and political questions; biology, as Spencer claimed in 1873, provided 'an adequate theory of the social unit – Man'.[16]

T H Huxley's 1876 essay 'On the Study of Biology' defined biology as 'the study of all phenomena exhibited by living things'; Huxley deliberately included politics, philosophy and education as legitimate fields of inquiry for the biologist.[17] Cell biology, as Laura Otis has demonstrated, offered multiple opportunities for metaphorically describing social fragmentation and cooperation, human communication and 'networking', as well as the dangers of contagion and 'invasion' by microbes.[18] Indeed, as we will see, the political relevance of scientific theories is among the most distinctive features of Victorian thinking about biology. From Spencer's ideas about the organic harmony of society to Virchow's conception of the organism as composed of countless single cells, to natural-philosophical analyses of the ant republic or socialist ideas of 'mutual aid' as a driving factor in evolution, nineteenth century political theory, literary texts and biological research are markedly interdependent.

The 'Science and Literature' Debate

In focusing on the exchange between biology, literature and culture in the nineteenth century, an exciting period when the distinction between 'professional science' and 'cultural science' was beginning to take shape,[19] this volume engages with the 'Science and Literature' strand of criticism, which has been especially productive since the mid-1980s. While deconstruction had for a while engendered a new kind of 'immanent' reading of texts, the question of cultural and scientific 'contexts' is now again at the forefront of critical discussion. Moreover, the division between science and the humanities was not as rigid in the nineteenth century as it is today: Gillian Beer has shown how Victorian scientific knowledge was generated 'between metaphors sustained in narrative',[20] how scientists quoted poets and novelists to substantiate their arguments, while poets and novelists wrote and edited magazine articles on astronomy, physics or biology. It is also important to keep in mind that while on the one hand the nineteenth century witnessed the increased professionalization and specialization of the sciences, on the other hand there was an increasing market for popularized versions of scientific knowledge. As Geoffrey Cantor and Sally Shuttleworth have recently argued in *Science Serialized: Representations of the Sciences in Nineteenth Century Periodicals* (2004), the proliferating periodical publications of the day provide an excellent model for understanding 'how scientific ideas were woven into the texture of nineteenth century cultural life'. The flexible boundaries between the arts and the sciences during that time allowed for the juxtaposition of articles on philology, physics and biology within one single periodical issue; all these were thought of as areas of 'contemporary scientific development'.[21] The crucial role of the imagination in both realms of knowledge was obvious to Victorians; the remarkable account of scientific imagination in *Middlemarch*, Chapter 16, and G H Lewes's famous dictum in *The Principles of Success in Literature* (1865) that '[n]o man ever made a discovery ... without the exercise of as much imagination as ... would have gone to the creation of a poem' are representative of the attitude of many Victorian scientists. At the level of what the traditional *ars rhetorica* would call *inventio*, literature and science may not be all that far apart, and invention or creation may come close to discovery.

On the other hand, it was in the nineteenth century that the so-called 'two cultures' debate was inaugurated: T H Huxley in 'Science and Culture' (1880) and Matthew Arnold in 'Literature and Science' (1882) anticipated the by now well-worn debate between C P Snow and F R Leavis, triggered by Snow's 1959 essay *The Two Cultures*.[22] Since then, scholars have identified anything from one to four cultures. It is important to remember, however, that when George Levine argues in *One Culture* that literature and science are 'modes of discourse within the same cultural field',[23] his shift of emphasis to the level of discourse reiterates Michel Foucault's claim that science *is* culture, partaking of the same fundamental rules of what is 'knowable' in a culture at any given time, and that we can therefore speak of a co-evolution of literature and science.[24] Foucault himself had his forerunners, of course: in the 1930s, Ludwik Fleck and Gaston Bachelard had pointed to the importance of linguistic and ideological preconditions, 'styles of thinking', for the emergence of scientific knowledge.[25] These ideas have also been followed up by the 'Narrative School' of 'Science and Literature' criticism, which, drawing on Hayden White, posits that the necessity of 'translating knowing into telling' unites science and literature,[26] as well as by the 'Rhetoric of Science' school in the wake of Alan Gross, which conceptualizes scientific activity as rhetorical invention.[27] As the German philosopher Martin Seel has recently argued, even the most distanced scientific observer cannot reject his or her own participation in the cultural mode of exchange, his subjection to the rules of communication.[28] Snow himself, when he revisited the question in *The Two Cultures: A Second Look* (1963), proposed sociology as a 'third culture' describing the common social medium in which both writers and scientists move.[29] In what is starting to look like an infinite regress, some critics have added, as a fourth culture, the meta-level of observation adopted by 'Science and Literature' critics themselves.[30] In any case, Snow's intervention, whatever its intrinsic merits, paradoxically triggered a wealth of 'Science and Literature' writing: The question, 'What conditions have to be fulfilled for a message to be accepted as "knowledge"?' has been taken up by Thomas Kuhn, whose idea of the 'paradigm shift' emphasizes that science is always also a social construction.[31] Moreover,

the issue of authority in science, productively opened up by Steven Shapin in
A Social History of Truth (1994), needs henceforth to be considered as an
indispensable framework for all investigations of nineteenth century biology.
Accordingly, this collection reflects throughout the discursive nature and the
social 'embeddedness' of the natural sciences, and also explicitly attends to
gender issues.[32]

Still, there is a significant difference in the goals and contexts of these two
types of narrative, literature and science. The fact of a shared rhetorical and
sociological dimension should not make us collapse all differences between
fictional and scientific texts – they are neither incompatible nor identical. In
1967, Roland Barthes stated: '[a]lthough science has a certain need of language
it is not, like literature, in language'.[33] The enthusiasm of postmodern literary
scholars for the indeterminacy principle and the chaos theory of modern physics,
and even for the nineteenth century entropy principle, has pointed up some
interesting alignments between elements of uncertainty in literature and
science, but has also met with severe criticism, most famously from Alan Sokal
and Jean Bricmont.[34] One essential difference between the two discourses, at
any rate, is the respective value they accord to history: 'Unlike art, science
destroys its past.'[35] According to Wolf Lepenies, literature can therefore
function as a 'store' for obsolete models of knowledge, conserving some models
of thinking, modifying them and sometimes even reintroducing them into
scientific discourse in a modified form.[36] The ancient model of the 'poetization
of knowledge' is still around, according to which literature not only adapts
knowledge, but creates independent models of reality which may then, as in
the fictional counter-worlds of dystopias and satires (see Chapter 4 by Janet
Browne; Chapter 13 by Jürgen Meyer), take on a 'corrective function' by
criticizing or subverting scientific positions.[37] Or again, literary texts – especially,
perhaps, where the realm of psychology is concerned – may also anticipate
scientific developments: they may face up to 'terrifying' realities more explicitly
than contemporary scientific texts, which sometimes appear to be more
orthodox, more willing to impose the rules of 'normality' on 'digressive' human
behaviour (see Chapter 14 by Merle Tönnies, Chapter 15 by Sally Shuttleworth).
The traffic is thus two-way: literature often expresses ideas or describes
phenomena that only later become part of scientific theory.

Unmapped Countries

Taking into account the aforementioned areas of debate, the title of this
collection not only combines the diachronic, Darwinian perspective with the
synchronic perspective of physiology and its networks of cells and nerves: it
also hints at the intricate connections between the natural sciences and the

cultural sphere and, of course, at the international context of nineteenth century British science. The contributions in this volume are by renowned experts and younger scholars in the field, affiliated to university departments of English and comparative literature, history of science, history of medicine, art history or women's studies; together they provide an excellent interdisciplinary survey of the field, while at the same time offering in-depth research into their respective special areas. The collection aims at demonstrating that the relation between literature, culture and biology in the nineteenth century is far more complex than the habitual reference to Darwin would have us believe. Correspondingly, a major emphasis in all the contributions is on the discursive constructions of 'biological reality' in the nineteenth century. The volume's title, 'Unmapped Countries', is taken from Eliot's *Daniel Deronda* (1876): 'There is a great deal of unmapped country within us which would have to be taken into account in an explanation of our gusts and storms.'[38] Any such mention in Eliot of the mysteries of the human psyche would clearly imply a reference to the unsolved problems in contemporary physiological psychology – and, by extension, in (human) biology. Some of the 'mapping' that was going on in these scientific fields during the nineteenth century will be dealt with in this volume.

The essays are grouped into three parts whose perspectives complement each other. Part I takes up some of the most important strands of the 'Science and Literature' debate, discussing the role of the imagination in science, its categories and taxonomies as well as the question of scientific authority.[39] Part II deals with evolution and degeneration, while Part III focuses on physiology and pathology as themes in nineteenth century culture and literature. Part II, 'Evolution and Degeneration', expatiates on the now established discussion of literary elements and narrative structures in Darwin's texts and, conversely, finds Darwinian patterns in literary texts.[40] It is concerned with how Darwin's theories became 'Darwinism', or even, in the words of Morse Peckham, 'Darwinisticism'.[41] One has to remember that evolutionary theory in the late nineteenth century was, in fact, a mixture of Darwin's theories on the mechanisms of natural and sexual selection, neo-Lamarckian theories of environmentalism and the inheritance of acquired characteristics, and Spencerian organicism – and that evolutionary theory could be used to accommodate almost any political line of reasoning. Part III, 'Physiology and Pathology', then looks at the repercussions in literature of physiological theories of the human and animal organism and their political and philosophical ramifications, taking into account the close connection between physiology and pathology as formulated in mid-century by Rudolf Virchow and others, namely that '[a]ll pathological formations are either degenerations, transformations, or repetitions of typical physiological structures'.[42]

The interconnections between the Parts II and III are even more important than their respective emphases; thus – to pick out a few examples – Annette Kern-Stähler's analysis of nineteenth century anthropological approaches to the evolution of the human colour sense is complemented by Kate Flint's chapter on nineteenth century discussions about the physiological basis, role and representation of the senses in Victorian science and culture. The chapter by Griet Vandermassen, Marysa Demoor and Johan Braeckman highlights nineteenth century proto-feminist rereadings of Darwin's theory of sexual selection, while Merle Tönnies' contribution looks at mid-to-late-nineteenth century medical and psychological constructions of the female – and alternative constructions in sensation novels. Paul Goetsch's chapter on evolutionary anthropology's anxieties about the 'savage within' opens up a historical dimension to the human individual in the same way that Sally Shuttleworth's contribution on nineteenth century medical explanations of childhood fears takes into account the model of inherited patterns of thought and emotion.

The Chapters

Charlotte Sleigh's opening chapter, '"This Questionable Little Book": Narrative Ambiguity in Nineteenth Century Literature of Science', tackles the problem of authority in science. Addressing science-related fictional texts by, among others, Mary Shelley, Thomas Carlyle and H G Wells, she considers how their playful and troubling approaches to narrative and 'authorial' credibility constitute literary responses to the presumed authority of science. Klaus Stierstorfer's ensuing chapter, 'Vestiges of English Literature: Robert Chambers', offers an example of a demonstrably close relation between literature and science, examining how Robert Chambers' proto-Darwinian *Vestiges of the Natural History of Creation* (1844), a scientific text permeated by literary qualities and assumptions, can be persuasively linked to the ways in which knowledge is systematized in his *History of English Language and Literature* (1836).

From Chambers' proto-Darwinism we progress, in Part II, to Darwinism proper. Gowan Dawson, in his chapter on 'Aestheticism, Immorality and the Reception of Darwinism in Victorian Britain', is concerned with the publication and reception of Darwin's *The Descent of Man* (1871), demonstrating how contemporary reviews established connections between the 'immoral' poetry of Swinburne and Darwin's theory of sexual selection. This chapter underlines some of the findings of Sleigh's opening chapter, showing how close the link was in the later nineteenth century between intellectual authority in science and the 'moral character' of its exponents. Furthermore, Dawson emphasizes that the connection between the discourses of literature and science was not necessarily a creative one (as the 'one culture' model routinely assumes), but could also – as in this case – be deleterious. Janet Browne, in 'Constructing Darwinism in Literary Culture', is concerned with post-Darwinian literature, looking at the impact of Darwin's ideas of natural selection and reproductive behaviour on late nineteenth century utopias and dystopias. She shows how literature became increasingly preoccupied with both the threat and the potential of evolutionary theory, as in Émile Zola's *Docteur Pascal* (1893–9), Wells's *The Time Machine* (1895) or Edgar Rice Burroughs' *Tarzan of the Apes* (1914). Browne's discussion of the concept of degeneration and late-nineteenth century eugenics establishes a link with Jürgen Meyer's chapter on the surgical and physiological aspects of eugenics in Part III.

Griet Vandermassen, Marysa Demoor and Johan Braeckman, in 'Close Encounters with a New Species: Darwin's Clash with the Feminists at the End of the Nineteenth Century', delve into the reception of Darwin's theories of sexual selection by proto-feminists such as Antoinette Brown Blackwell, Eliza Burt Gamble, Charlotte Perkins Gilman and Olive Schreiner. Although he claimed that female sexual choice was a driving force in evolution, Darwin remained a child of his time in describing (non-human as well as human) females as 'passive' and 'coy'. Perkins Gilman *et al.* argued that the gender hegemony forced women into a state of 'arrested development', thereby forestalling the natural course of evolution (and progress). Women had become prone to all kinds of ailments not because of inherent weakness but because of their unnatural, enforced passivity. The thematic connection with Tönnies' chapter on the oppression of women through the (male) medical discourse is striking. Carol Peaker, in 'Mutual Aid, a Factor of Peter Kropotkin's Literary Criticism', is concerned with another counter-position to Darwinism: Prince Peter Kropotkin's theory of 'mutual aid' as a driving force of evolution, which was first published in an 1890s series of articles in the English journal *Nineteenth Century*, and became increasingly popular towards the beginning of the twentieth century. Kropotkin's writings demonstrate both the close link between nineteenth century biological and political thought and the ways in which scientific knowledge was popularized in literary circles. Besides providing a scientific basis for his own theories of anarchism, the articles refuted the claim of Social Darwinists such as Huxley that as long as humans multiplied, they would engage with one another in a brutal 'struggle for existence'. Kropotkin argued that mankind would return naturally to a system of cooperation once it had discarded the corrupting shackles of government and private property.

Paul Goetsch's chapter on 'The Savage Within: Evolutionary Theory, Anthropology and the Unconscious in *Fin-de-siècle* Literature' discusses how the unconscious was imagined before Sigmund Freud – that is to say, in the languages of evolutionary theory and anthropology. Looking at, among other texts, Robert Louis Stevenson's *The Strange Case of Dr Jekyll and Mr Hyde* (1886) and Joseph Conrad's *Heart of Darkness* (1902), Goetsch discusses the themes of regression and evolutionary 'survivals', showing how Freud's theses in *Civilization and its Discontents* (1930) were prefigured in *fin-de-siècle* literature, with its inward turn, its interest in the manifestation of primitive desires and aggressions. Freud, designated the 'Darwin of mental life' by his pupil and biographer Ernest Jones, thus responded not least to evolutionary thought when he mapped the 'internal foreign territory' of the mind. Annette Kern-Stähler, in 'Homer on the Evolutionary Scale: Interrelations between Biology and Literature in the Writings of William Gladstone and Grant Allen', analyses the use made of Homer's texts by nineteenth century anthropologists as providing clues to the otherwise inaccessible workings of the human mind and sense apparatus in 'primitive' times. She concentrates on Gladstone's and Allen's inquiries into 'Homeric evidence' of the development of human sense perception, especially the colour sense, and of 'aesthetic evolution'. Alexandra Karl, in '"Naturfreund" or "Naturfeind"? Darwinism in the Early Drawings of Alfred Kubin', discusses the impact of continental 'Darwinismus', propagated by Ernst Haeckel and his disciples, on Alfred Kubin, a Symbolist artist working in *fin-de-siècle* Munich. Karl traces Kubin's artistic transformations of visual material on Darwinism, ranging from natural history illustrations to diagrams of recent dinosaur finds in the fossil record to new schematizations of the 'Entwicklungsgeschichte'. Analysing Kubin's nightmarish pictures of biological transmutation, extinction and degeneration, Karl extends the discussion from literary to pictorial 'texts'.

Part III opens with Laura Otis's chapter on 'Cells and Networks in Nineteenth Century Literature', which offers a synthesis of her former work on *Membranes* (1999) and *Networking* (2001), as well as new avenues for research. Reviewing the emergence of cell theory in the late 1830s, Otis discusses resulting scientific and literary models of identity and communication, concentrating on the competition between the model of the networked individual with that of the cellular self. Discussing scientific texts by Santiago Ramón y Cajal and Camillo Golgi as well as various literary works and literary criticism, Otis emphasizes the differences between these scientific and literary representations of selfhood, and closes with a tentative typology of science-literature relations. Kirstie Blair, in 'Contagious Sympathies: George Eliot and Rudolf Virchow', examines connections between Eliot's and Lewes's concepts of infection and contagion and those of the German scientist and founder of the cell theory, Rudolf Virchow. She shows that Virchow's heady combination of scientific discovery with philosophical and political inspiration was an important background, especially for *Middlemarch*.

Anne-Julia Zwierlein, in 'From Parasitology to Parapsychology: Parasites in Nineteenth Century Science and Literature', examines a representative choice of parasitological texts from Charles Darwin to T Spencer Cobbold, as well as fiction by Charles Dickens, George Eliot, Bram Stoker and Arthur Conan Doyle, asking how far parasites in these scientific and literary texts were seen as 'horrible' and marginal (as by John Ruskin), how far they were accepted as inevitable, and how far a purpose and function within the natural system was ascribed to them. Moralizing Victorian accounts of biological parasitism drew parallels between parasitic stagnation in the animal world and reprehensible human indolence – dangerous concepts, as their subsequent application to 'unwanted elements' in social reality all too clearly showed. The chapter closes by demonstrating how the biological phenomenon of the parasite was increasingly psychologized and interiorized in late nineteenth century literature (if not in science) – a clear link to Paul Goetsch's 'savage within', another contemporary image of the darker aspects of the human psyche. The idea of the expulsion of the 'parasite' leads directly to the question of eugenics, already discussed by Browne in Part II and taken up in Jürgen Meyer's chapter on 'Surgical Engineering in the Nineteenth Century: *Frankenstein*, *The Island of Dr Moreau*, *Flatland*'. Meyer looks at literary depictions of new surgical techniques and the concept of eugenics, demonstrating literature's 'corrective function' in that the texts often foreground the vengeance taken by science on individuals who misuse it. Analysing visions of the (failed) engineering of a perfected human race, Meyer goes on to discuss the anachronistic gulf manifesting itself in the field of surgery between creationist and evolutionary views of medicine.

Merle Tönnies, in '"Serious" Science versus "Light" Entertainment? Femininity Concepts in Nineteenth Century British Medical Discourse and Popular Fiction', takes up some of the issues discussed in Part II about proto-feminist views of Darwin from a different angle, arguing that sensation novels of the 1860s and 1870s challenged dominant medical beliefs about female behaviour and 'femininity', depicting female transgression in the areas of sexuality and criminality. Thus, Tönnies argues, these texts were able to counteract the dominant discourse of medical authority, which 'naturalized' gender hierarchies and the doctor – patient hierarchy by grounding them in the biological basis of human existence. Tönnies' chapter links up with Sally Shuttleworth's on 'Night Terrors: Medical and Literary Representations of Childhood Fear', in that both the medicalization of the female and the medicalization of the child operated to preserve the boundaries of female and childhood 'purity'. Shuttleworth looks at pre-Freudian medical, literary and physio-psychological approaches to the phenomenon of childhood fear and their discursive links to the concept of insanity, concentrating on the question posed throughout the century: whether such fears originated in the child's own mind, or had external causes. She argues that literary texts anticipated Freud in showing that the secrets of human identity were to be sought not only in racial history but also in individual 'prehistory', that is childhood. Kate Flint's concluding chapter on 'Sensuous Knowledge' discusses the representation of the senses in Victorian culture, taking into account recent critical work on sound, sight and smell, and uncovering a broader Victorian concern with the operation and socio-cultural dimension of the senses, whether in scientific works by G H Lewes, Alexander Bain and James Sully, or in the work of novelists such as Wilkie Collins, Herman Melville and George Meredith. Concluding with Lewes's concept of 'unconscious sensibility', Flint argues that today neuroscience has returned psychoanalytic study, at least in some quarters, to the same physiological basis that preoccupied its mid-nineteenth century forerunners.

PART I

Science and Literature

1

'THIS QUESTIONABLE LITTLE BOOK': NARRATIVE AMBIGUITY IN NINETEENTH CENTURY LITERATURE OF SCIENCE

Charlotte Sleigh

To no honest purpose was a man ever made or suffered to speak in the third person ... (Jeremy Bentham, *Rationale of Judicial Evidence*, Book III, Chapter X, §2)

Introduction

There has been some wonderful writing on science and literature over the last twenty years, by and large fine-grained analyses of the interaction of literature and science. The best of it makes the point that their interrelation must be seen as a two-way process. In other words, metaphors are things that are used to construct science, not just things that are inspired in literature by science.

Overviews of science and literature are, however, scarce, and I have found myself wondering how such a thing might be written. The obvious way (and this is the model employed by some books, and especially university courses) is to trace how themes of science have been echoed in the literature of their day. But this is a poor model for writing an overview, inasmuch as it tempts the reader once again to see the interaction of science and literature as one-way.

It occurred to me that a fruitful way to write a history of literature's intersection with modern science might be to focus on narrative authority: the ways in which texts invite their readers to trust or distrust the narrative perspective. Doing this, I suggest, might give a sufficiently continuous sense of the evolution of the novelistic genre while also suggesting specific work on contextualization, so that we do not lose sight of the particularities of the production and reading of any given text.[1] In other words, I propose the treatment of narrative form as a socio-historical phenomenon.

Current approaches to the study of narrative mostly stem, in one way or another, from Gérard Genette's 1972 distinction between voice ('who speaks') and focalization ('who sees'). His concept of 'voice' includes the narrator's involvement in the story, the person – normally first or third – in which it is told, the time of narration and the level of narrative embedding.[2] Thus in the work of Henry James, for example, there can be an intrusive narrative style that is focalized through the protagonist's account.[3] It has been suggested that Genette's narrator voice, the standard against which to measure other narratological elements of the text, is too close to an imputed authorial voice – the deadly sin of postmodernism. Another criticism of his work proceeds from the observation that no one has convincingly proposed any theoretical grounds upon which to label an aspect or a portion of the text as 'focalized' or 'voiced'; both, it is therefore claimed, are ungrounded interpretative manoeuvres.[4] There have also been attempts to show that there can be narratorless narrative, which would also pose problems for Genette's division.[5] Finally (in this by no means all-inclusive list), Franz Stanzel has been more concerned to find historically – or perhaps, rather, generically – typical combinations of what Genette calls voice and focalization, rather than seeking always to discriminate between them.[6]

In these poststructural approaches, a sense of how narrative (whether read or written; standpoint, voice, or neither) might be treated as a socio-historical question has by and large been lost.[7] Watt's mid-twentieth century history of the novel has had an ongoing influence, but there has been remarkably little in the same vein until recently, perhaps due to the postmodernist suspicions of grand narrative.[8] My approach is resolutely metalinguistic: a revisitation of the history of literature that is encouraged by recent history of science and its adoption of the 'history of the book'. Though primarily a historiography of material culture, this also invites us, through the evidence it provides, to discover who readers of a given text were, what they made of it, and to what extent the author was engaging in a conversation with them.[9] (It may be appropriate to treat some texts, such as newspaper editorials, as though there were authorial intention at work, while a nineteenth century reading of Milton clearly would not suit this analysis.)

Focusing on narrative authority suggestively echoes the issues of trust in testimony that were raised by Steven Shapin's *A Social History of Truth*. Shapin argued that since early modern times testimony has been an unavoidable part of scientific method, and that, correspondingly, reliance upon testimony – trust – remains a social dimension of epistemology that can never be purged from the practice of science. 'What we know about comets, icebergs and neutrinos irreducibly contains what we know of those people who speak for and about these things.'[10]

Michael McKeon, influenced by Bakhtin, has also addressed the establishment of norms of cultural credibility in the early modern period – in his case in and through the construction of the novelistic form.[11] His arguments corroborate Shapin's; McKeon's novels have the cultural function of mediating the difficult early modern issues of truth and virtue, exactly the same starting materials and processes necessary for the establishment of the 'discoveries' promulgated by Shapin's natural philosophers.

The questions I want to take from McKeon and Shapin and into the nineteenth century are: What models of trust and authority framed science in the nineteenth century? And how were these worked through in the literature of science? In my discussion of various texts, I will attempt to look for authorial efforts to impose a judgemental framework upon the reader, and the spaces in which the reader may be able to generate her own. Throughout I will use the term 'authoriality', generally used to indicate the relative presence or absence of the authorial (as opposed to narrative) voice in the text. Here the term is extended somewhat to be suggestive also of evident authorial intention, narrative authority (in terms of voice and/or focalization), and textual 'reality' or applicability/connection to the real world (not quite the same thing as realism). Like McKeon, I find that virtue (or – better in the nineteenth century context – morals) and epistemology are the key terms to conjure with. My working model compares the Benthamite standards informing some early nineteenth century thought and judgement with the more Whewellian model that later normalized scientific method, and with it, literature.

In this chapter I am purposely restricting myself to texts that have an obvious connection with science, though a lengthier study would obviously include 'non-scientific' literature as well as 'factual' accounts of science. I am also restricting myself to English-language texts read in Britain. Other themes would emerge if, for example, we were to look at French or Russian stories, with their more rigorous criteria for realism. Finally, I offer reservations over the brevity and oversimplification of my argument – due in part to its brevity, but also to the tentative stage of the research process that it reflects.

Early Century: *a posteriori* Desiderata and the Democratic Ideal

Jeremy Bentham's (1748–1832) *Rationale of Judicial Evidence*, later published 'for the use of non-lawyers as well as lawyers' had a considerable impact upon nineteenth century legal epistemology, and, for a brief time, appeared to crystallize opinions upon standards of proof within the sciences also.[12] The overarching aim of Bentham's evidential writings was, first, to assert that no evidence ought ever to be excluded from judicial consideration. Nothing was to be ruled inadmissible as unreliable, as hearsay, or for any reason. Even the evidence of 'imbeciles' (infants, the superannuated and the insane) was to be heard and considered.[13] The role of judge and jury was to exercise their judgement regarding the amount of trust that might be placed in each piece of evidence, and the force that evidence had for deciding the case as a whole. Although Bentham set out to provide guidelines regarding such judgements, his starting point was a fundamental faith in the Englishman's abilities to make them. In a deliberately domestic analogy, he compared these to the cook's tacit judgement, based on sundry factors, as to whether a leg of lamb was sufficiently cooked. Bentham did not, however, extend this same faith to the professional judiciary, whose powers of discernment he considered to be almost hopelessly blunted and spoiled by centuries of obfuscating legal tradition.

Bentham's friend and editor John Bowring (1792–1872) made the point even more strongly:

> If the discovery of truth be the end of the rules of evidence, and if sagacity consist in the adaptation of means to ends, it appeared to me that, in the line of judicature, the sagacity displayed by the sages of law was as much below the level of that displayed by an illiterate peasant or mechanic in the bosom of his family, as, in the line of physical science, the sagacity displayed by the peasant is below the sagacity displayed in the same line by a Newton.[14]

The comparison with science was important for Bowring, since he had himself been scientifically trained. Bentham did not share quite such an elevated opinion of science as Bowring's,[15] but he did most certainly subscribe to the understanding that the same principles of evidence were needed in every area of modern life and 'the whole field of human knowledge',[16] including science: 'Questions in natural philosophy, questions in natural history, questions in technology in all its branches, questions in medicine, are all questions of evidence. When we use the words *observation*, *experience* and *experiment*, what we mean is, facts observed, or supposed to be observed, by ourselves or others ... .'[17]

In their critique of extant institutions, in their preference for the discriminatory abilities of the common man over that of the judiciary, and in the timing of their publication, Bentham's suggestions about evidence were profoundly democratic. At this time, the extension of the vote and the foundation of the British Association for the Advancement of Science both represented, in however partial and flawed a manner, a broadening of the circle of those permitted to arbitrate upon the evidence of politicians and men of science: to reach their own informed opinions, if not to superimpose these upon the most powerful.[18]

Mary Shelley's *Frankenstein* (c.1818)

'Every thing must have a beginning ... and that beginning must be linked to something that went before. The Hindoos give the world an elephant to support it, but they make the elephant stand upon a tortoise.'[19] Thus Mary Shelley, in describing the generation of her story, indicates the infinity of textual regress; such tales of origin merely invite the question: *On what does the tortoise stand?*

This riddle forms the framework for the construction of Shelley's tale, which consists of stories within stories – a Russian doll of a novel. At one point, no fewer than five stories are nested within each other: Margaret Saville's trove of letters relates the tale of her brother Captain Walton, who tells the story of Victor Frankenstein, who recounts the Creature's autobiography, which includes the history of Safie (guaranteed, symmetrically enough, by another trove of letters supposed to be in the Creature's possession). While Safie's story, lying as it does at the heart of the book, provides one key to the novel, the most striking intertextuality concerns Walton and Frankenstein's narratives – a point that Shelley emphasized in her rewriting of the tale for its publication in 1831. Walton is given an increased regard for Frankenstein, bordering on hero-worship. Having heard from Victor's lips the ostensive warning to 'avoid ambition ... in science and discoveries', Walton copies his actions, not his words, and shows no sign of turning back with his near-mutinous crew.

On the one hand, this construction guides the reader in applying the novel's moral – the mortal danger in which Walton places himself reinforces the reader's need to take account of Frankenstein's tale. In fact there is a solid tradition of morals couched as stories within stories; readers or listeners familiar with the genre read them knowledgeably as such. The Bible contains many examples of dreams, warnings and parables within its once intimately known text. The story of David and the prophet Nathan (2 Samuel 12), for example, derived a large part of its force from the fact that the reader knew what was coming; nested within a larger moral text, its meaning was made all the more clear. By making layers of the text speak to each other, Shelley causes them to bear witness to one another's credibility.

An alternative reading of Shelley's nested narrative would, rather, highlight the levels of unreliability, each compounding the unreliability of the last (can we really trust Frankenstein's judgement?). In her 1831 introduction she compared the writing of her tale to the story of Columbus and the egg,[20] bathetically suggesting that its composition was merely an act of pragmatism.

Yet this apparently self-deprecating statement is slippery, for Columbus, after all, achieved something precisely on a par with Walton or Frankenstein.

This difficulty in pinning down the authoriality of Shelley's tale is perhaps the point. The reader's level of credulity determines where she will enter and exit the text; which doors she will use between stories and which will be her points of access to the real world, with their accordingly different outlooks. Perhaps in this the reader echoes Shelley's morally tergiversating response to the promises then held out by science.[21]

Thomas Carlyle's *Sartor Resartus* (1833–4)[22]

Carlyle's legal training predisposed him to ask the same kinds of questions as Bentham regarding the plausibility of evidence; science and technology, rather than law were, however, a focus for Carlyle's questioning. Having begun its life as a serious essay upon metaphors, the volume *Sartor Resartus* was directly about the power of science (in its widest sense) to describe nature.

Sartor Resartus is predicated upon a fundamental narrative unreliability, not least in that it was initially published anonymously.[23] Its account of the extraordinary Professor Teufelsdröckh [devil-dung] and his philosophy of clothes confutes normal categories of literature, being written by the 'editor', whose manuscript has apparently been subject to executive editing in the person of one 'Oliver Yorke' (Yorick?). Thus the moral and empirical distance generally assumed by the editorial perspective is utterly lost, and the reader is uncertain how to deal, for example, with an editorial apology for the revolutionary tone of the book when its contents are in fact all the editor's own. And although the book is supposedly inspired by the editor's exceptional regard for Professor Teufelsdröckh, the more words he expends, the more he 'inadvertently' gives an unsatisfactory or even adverse impression of his character and philosophy.[24]

Carlyle muddied the waters still further when *Sartor* was first published as a single volume in Great Britain. 'This questionable little book was undoubtedly written among the mountain solitudes, in 1831', he began – and the tension internal to this opening sentence sets the tone for the narrative ambiguity throughout. In it, Carlyle implies that he is *not* the author/editor, for otherwise he would not need that disingenuous qualification, 'undoubtedly'. He further appended to the text by way of preface four letters of doubtful authenticity discussing the volume; all gave highly irregular reviews, while it has recently been suggested that one is a downright forgery.[25] The book seemed so genuine, if this is not too paradoxical a judgement, that some reviewers announced in all seriousness their 'discovery' that it was, in fact, fiction. If *Frankenstein* offers the reader windows and doors between its intercalating texts and the real world, *Sartor* is a hall of mirrors.

In *Sartor Resartus*, Carlyle satirized the very German Romanticism that he had endeavoured to promote in Britain through translation. Confident as he was of the deadening effects of mechanical science, he could not bring himself to recommend this as a suitable alternative. Readers were able to extract what moral they wished. T H Huxley reportedly managed in all seriousness to derive succour for his agnosticism from *Sartor*,[26] showing the multiple levels on which the book could be read – even by one and the same reader.

Edgar Allan Poe's *Tales* (1830s–40s)

Poe's *Tales* are heirs to Shelley's *Frankenstein* and Carlyle. Poe loves to play with issues of science and authoriality. On the most accessible level of his work, Poe is keen to supplement – and even substitute – Whewell and Herschel's inductive scientific method with the powers of imagination, or, – as Eco and Sebeok put it – abductive reason.[27] Toying with the reader at a deeper level, a number of Poe's tales ('The Black Cat', 'The Maelstrom') begin with the self-defeating protestation 'I'm not mad. ...' The attentive reader may also notice that, for example, the narrator of the extraordinary events of the 'MS Found in a Bottle' admits early on that his ship is carrying a vast quantity of opium. Even this may be interpreted as encouraging the reader's Benthamite approach to science; Bentham emphasized the value of false witness in permitting judge and jury to fill in the full story.

Poe takes things a stage further than Shelley, however, in using narrative uncertainty to impugn the claims of science itself. Hiding behind the reader's discovery and acceptance of the narrator's possible unreliability, Poe then proceeds to do the same himself. He plays a game whose boundaries, unlike Shelley's, actually lie outside the book. It is possible to read one of his stories and remain hoodwinked by it until independently disabused of its plausibility at a later date. For example, generations of readers have read the patient's diagnosis proffered in 'The Facts in the Case of M Valdemar' without realizing that it is actually an impossible medical achievement, being a description that could be obtained only through an autopsy.[28]

Thus Poe takes his audience to extreme possibilities; reading what is narrated on the most unreliable authority, they are required to form their own evaluations. Like the readers of Shelley and Carlyle, they are heirs to the democratic theory of evidence propounded by Bentham.

Late Century: *a priori* Desiderata and the Moral Authoriality of Science

By mid-century there was a substantial generalized intellectual reading public. Their diet of books and journals was not, as historians have pointed out, strictly divided between science and the arts. Some have also suggested that a split between high and middlebrow literature did not emerge until comparatively late in the century.[29] Yet I suspect that norms of authoriality in the literature of science were already beginning to close down opportunities for the reader's judgement even before this division occurred. One of the chief (if unintentional) architects of this change was William Whewell (1794–1866).[30]

Whewell's work differed from that of Bentham, and from his utilitarian successor John Stuart Mill (1806–73), in that it insisted upon a major role for *a priori* considerations in the weighing of evidence.[31] No necessary truths, for Whewell, could arise purely from experience.

> ... we are often told that such a thing is *a Fact*; A FACT and not a Theory, with all the emphasis which, in speaking or writing, tone or italics or capitals can give. ... [W]hen this is urged, before we can estimate the truth, or the value of the assertion, we must ask to whom is it a Fact? what habits of thought, what previous information, what Ideas does it imply, to conceive the Fact as a Fact? ... Did not the ancients assert it as a Fact, that the earth stood still, and the stars moved? and can any Fact have stronger apparent evidence to justify persons in asserting it emphatically than this had?[32]

Whewell's two-part *The History of the Inductive Sciences, From the Earliest to the Present Time* (1837) and *The Philosophy of the Inductive Sciences, Founded Upon Their History* (1st ed. 1840) rapidly achieved the status of scientific classic; Darwin was among those allying his 'inductive' method with the methods they favourably described.[33]

In moving away from the epistemological model offered by Bentham, science managed to sever itself a little more from the Chartist associations that had tainted early work on transformism.[34] It distanced itself from the democratic epistemology that had been so well captured in ambiguously authorial narrative. The literary trend of the nineteenth century was towards the omniscient narrative, and with it came a corresponding decrease in authorial ambiguity. This rise of realism and naturalism is classically instantiated in the work of Émile Zola. Although he claimed that his characters' behaviour and his plots' outcomes were natural phenomena beyond his creative control, like the outcome of a chemical reaction, he actually permitted no indeterminacy whatsoever. Zola's debt to Bernard has been discussed elsewhere; one might also profitably compare his *oeuvre* to the performances of Michael Faraday, whose protestations of 'Look! No hands!' concealed his incredibly tight control over what was seen by his audience and what was not.[35]

This being the case, it seems somewhat confusing that the multi-perspectival work of Wilkie Collins should also have been described by Henry James in

1865 as a work of science rather than a work of art, owing to its 'massive and elaborate construction ... for the proper mastery of which ... an index and notebook were required'.[36] *The Woman in White* was famously 'told by more than one pen, as the story of an offence against the laws is told in Court by more than one witness – with the same object, in both cases', and as such it appears to be a late heir of Bentham's theory of evidence, inviting the reader to cast her light of judgement upon its judicial data.

Certainly the text contains some interesting episodes that reflect upon contemporary grounds for belief and their limitations, such as the child Jacob Postlethwaite and his sighting of a 'ghost' (actually Anne Catherick), and the doctor's refusal to take advice from a non-medical man, Count Fosco (again, the advice turns out to have been wise). But how accurate is the widely held interpretation of *The Woman in White* that it invites the reader to act as open-minded juror? Certainly there are points of disagreement between the narrators, crucially regarding the assessment of character, which cast mutual doubt upon one another.[37] Yet the overall hand of Hartright in collecting and dominating the narrative fragments perhaps makes this less of a 'you decide' novel than is sometimes suggested. The options for belief are fluid in the middle but clearly crystallized at the end.[38] In the end we trust Hartright for moral reasons, as his name suggests.

Charles Kingsley's *The Water Babies* (1863)

Kingsley's standard for scientific authority is firmly moral, not empirical.[39] It is heavy-handed in terms of narrative voice, often alluding to things that will not be mentioned in the presence of little ears (or eyes), thus setting up the narrator as an authoritative adult. There are flights of fanciful argument that 'prove', in Carrollesque manner, the existence of water babies. The real world – metaphysical as well as epistemological – is mixed with the textual, but not to shore up the romance. Quite the contrary; it is what Professors Owen, Huxley and Faraday do *not* know that is emphasized. They do not know how to look at the world as a child, implies Kingsley, open to magic. (It is worth reminding oneself at this point that Kingsley's Christian faith was by no means an anti-Humean faith in the supernatural.[40]) The punch line of the book, appearing halfway through and again at the end, is this: 'Am I in earnest? Oh dear no! Don't you know that this is a fairy tale, and all fun and pretence; and that you are not to believe one word of it, even if it is true'?[41]

Appealing to children not to do something is generally a good guarantee of their doing it; in this case there is the additional incentive of keeping a secret from the Gradgrinds and other adults of the real world. But more importantly, truth, as defined by men of science, is asserted as poor grounds for trust. This is illustrated in the natural-historical passages of Kingsley's novel, which bear

direct comparison to children's popularizations of science, most notably
Arabella Buckley's *Fairy-Land of Science* (1878). In such works, the real is
defamiliarized and made fairy-like; readers are invited to believe in the wonders
of science through the exercise of aesthetic, poetic or, – better still – moral
judgement. Tom's happy discovery of the other water babies does not occur
until he has done a good turn, thus underlining the moral logic of the story.
Even though the reader has been assured less than a page before that the book
has 'no moral whatsoever ... [in] any part ... because it is a fairy tale, you
know', she has now learned that 'fairy tales' have a logic of truth and belief
that transcends such scholarly protestations.

H G Wells's *The Time Machine* (1895)

Wells's *fin-de-siècle* tale, which, like *Frankenstein*, is a nested text, contains
subtle uncertainty due to certain oversights and hints in the narrative. Why is
the narrator unnamed? In this he is like a scientist writing a paper for *Nature*,
but in the context of the story this anonymity introduces a perturbing
ungentlemanliness. The time traveller also gives hints of untrustworthiness;
his brutish behaviour and his demands for meat ally him unpleasantly with
the Morlocks. And then again, the air-headed guests at dinner are not exactly
the reliable kind of witnesses that would make them, say, desirable judges of
Collins' text.

Over all this, Wells finally obtrudes his presence as the hidden narrative
hand, producing a moral standard of judgement just as we saw in *The
Water Babies*.

> [The Time Traveller] looked at the Medical Man. 'No. I cannot expect
> you to believe it. Take it as a lie – or a prophecy. ... Consider I have been
> speculating upon the destinies of our race until I have hatched this
> fiction. Treat my assertion of its truth as a mere stroke of art to enhance
> its interest. And taking it as a story, what do you think of it?' ... The
> Editor stood up with a sigh. 'What a pity it is you're not a writer of
> stories!' he said. ...[42]

Conan Doyle was arguably more heavy-handed in the authoriality of his
scientific fantasies. In *The Lost World* (1912), Professor Challenger's credibility
is enhanced only the more as further doubts are cast upon it. This culminates
with the loss of his evidence, which causes the scientific community to reject
his claims out of hand, but raises Challenger to the status of scientific martyr
in the mind of the reader. In this, Conan Doyle employs the narrative device
used also in the Holmes stories: a self-acknowledged ingénue narrator who
'reluctantly' comes to believe the unbelievable. The reader is pleased to be

one step ahead of the 'nice but dim' narrator; his trustworthiness means that the reader is flattered to believe or figure things out before he does. Again, this is a moral criterion for scientific credibility.

The spiritualist Challenger stories are the most heavy-handed of all. It is striking that the 'scientific' and the 'irrational' were, for Conan Doyle (and presumably a good many of his readers), framed by the same moral authoriality. 'If they hear not Moses and the prophets, neither will they be persuaded, though one rose from the dead' (Luke 16:31). In other words, no 'evidence' will convince the unenlightened, but the wise are convinced of the truth through moral considerations. This move towards a moral criterion for scientific authoriality is interesting, as it echoes the scientists' moves to subsume moral authority at the end of the nineteenth century. T H Huxley's sermonic lectures, such as 'On a Piece of Chalk', did not merely borrow from a ubiquitous genre of public oration; they reflected an actual ambition shared with his peers, and the narrative formulation in which this was couched for the 'common' audience.

Conclusion

My argument has not been that a Victorian clerk on a train reading Wilkie Collins was adjudicating on the epistemology of science but, rather, that the book's engagement with authority was a constitutive part of that cultural process. Standards of scientific credibility can never be generated internally by science; since such texts were read by men of science, by other 'makers and shakers', and by those who were disciplined (or chose) to accept that authority, they contributed to that negotiation.

Many questions remain, however. Are the texts I have discussed representative (however that quality might be defined) of the early- and late-century periods into which I have divided them? What were the exceptions, and can they be contextualized and explained without destroying the directional story I have attempted to tell? And can the directional story be extended backward into the eighteenth century, when the authority of science was in general less settled, or forward into turn-of-the-twentieth century novels, when a literary reaction to science was beginning to coalesce? On a very basic level, a survey of narrative viewpoints (first- or third-person, single or multiple) of the eighteenth and nineteenth centuries would be a useful starting point for further work.

There is also mileage in revisiting the rise of nineteenth century literary criticism, including its discussion of romance and realism. Did verisimilitude or verifiability form the better guide to reliability in a nineteenth century context, and how was this considered to be signified within a text?[43] Or are romance/realism and verisimilitude/verifiability in some senses unhelpful dualities to impose? Such questions might prompt reconsideration, for example, of David Masson's *British Novelists and Their Styles* (1859) in the context of the history of science; how were non-fictional genres of science narrated and authorialized?

Another line of questioning concerns readers. How docile or subversive *were* readers when it came to accepting authoriality? Sally Shuttleworth, in response to this chapter, has protested that readers of *The Woman in White*, for example, were actually very knowing concerning conventions of the sensation novel, and hence inventive, playful and sophisticated in their interpretation of the book. One response to this important critique is to look at reviews, as far as possible in instances where the reviewer is drawn from, or at least enters into an exchange with, the intended audience. A more challenging method would be to survey personal journals in which readings are described: a potentially fascinating history of the socially located yet intensely personal experience of reading.[44]

So far from destroying the argument here presented, however, such questions tend rather to underline the untapped historical potential that lies in a further examination of authoriality in the literature of science.

Acknowledgements

I should like to thank Rod Edmond for the helpful suggestions and kind encouragement that resulted in the writing of this chapter. I am also grateful to Sally Shuttleworth for her testing yet benevolent critique, which has provided direction for future research.

2

VESTIGES OF ENGLISH LITERATURE: ROBERT CHAMBERS

Klaus Stierstorfer

Introduction

It has by now become received wisdom, thanks to pioneering work such as Gillian Beer's,[1] that the systematizing of knowledge in nineteenth century Britain has to be studied across the dividing lines between natural science and the arts, and that such discursive delimitations are retrospective, and hence anachronistic. It will be equally uncontentious to maintain that the most innovative strategies of systematizing knowledge and understanding the world at the time had become primarily and preferably historical. Both aspects – the integrative approach to what came to be treated as the disparate domains of the arts and science, as well as the historical turn in their understanding and description – reached a first high point in Robert Chambers' polymathic work, which encompassed both science and literature, and drew on both 'scientific' and 'literary' strategies of conceptualization and presentation. Recent studies, notably by J A Secord, have highlighted the outstanding importance and merits of Chambers' *Vestiges of the Natural History of Creation* (1844) beyond its earlier categorization as a predecessor to Charles Darwin's *On the Origin of Species* (1859). In fact, the *Vestiges* could be considered the first complete history of the world from its beginnings to the present according to an evolutionary principle. It is true that Chambers certainly did not invent the idea. The tradition goes a long way back, and has many 'forerunners';[2] versions of it had been famously expounded by Lamarck and applied in Lyell's *Geology*, on which

Chambers, for his part, was to draw extensively. Chambers' achievement was to realize previous theorizings and partial stories into one, overarching narrative from the first primordial nebulae to the emergence of human beings.

While Chambers has thus become rightly celebrated for writing the first evolutionary history of the world in English, his other, earlier achievement still remains little noticed. It was also the same Scotsman, Robert Chambers, who wrote the first complete history of English literature from the beginnings to the present. When Chambers' *History of English Language and Literature* was published in 1836, it was the first work to offer, so to speak, 'the whole story'. The fact that the systematizing within a historical narrative of both literature and science was achieved by the same writer within a decade is as remarkable in its historic accomplishment as in its neglect in recent scholarship. James Secord, as today's most prominent authority on Chambers, does not even index Chambers' literary history in his monumental study of the *Vestiges*[3] and hardly mentions it *en passant*. Where Secord does refer to Chambers' work on English literature, it is almost exclusively to the later *Cyclopaedia of English Literature*,[4] and – to give another example, – the same applies to Margit Sichert's *Modern Language Quarterly* survey on 'Foundational British History'.[5] Neither Secord nor Sichert notes the importance of Chambers' first book of literary history published in 1836.

The following considerations, then, are concerned with exploring the biographical and chronological coincidence of the first complete history of English literature on the one hand and of the first complete history of the evolution of the universe on the other. The investigation starts with literary history, mainly because of the simple chronological precedence of the history of literature in Chambers' work. The historiographic problems Chambers faced and the concepts he applied in successfully tackling these difficulties – some of them inherited, some of them newly arisen in his own time – will thus form the first part of this chapter. A second step will then lead to a search for 'Vestiges of English Literature' – that is, of Chambers' work on the history of the same – in his *Vestiges of the Natural History of Creation*, thus attempting some answers to the questions: Are there, perhaps, vestiges of literary history in the natural history of creation or, was the world formed according to precepts of English literary history?

Robert Chambers, *History of English Language and Literature*

When Chambers sat down to write his literary history, he inherited a vexed dilemma from his most important sources and eighteenth century predecessors. This consisted, briefly, in the paradox that British literature was, on the one hand, perceived to partake of the general progress of civilization, of which it was sometimes seen as the highest manifestation, while on the other hand earlier vernacular traditions, variously described as 'romance' or 'Gothic', became much admired and important, but were potentially irritating in structuring historical narratives according to progressive linearity. The dilemma was already a problem, but, as I have argued elsewhere,[6] also a plot device in Thomas Warton's *History of English Poetry* (1774–81), in so far as the two traditions of romance and classicism stimulated each other, and Warton's mission could be seen as accomplished in his recuperation of the older, vernacular tradition of romance which he again brought to his readers' attention.

The dilemma became an open struggle, however, when the classicist vein was directly identified with French influence, and English writers began to look like traitors in the unstable climate of the years following the French Revolution and the Napoleonic Wars. Such contrastive plotting of English literary history was most vociferously and influentially propagated by, among others, Francis Jeffrey in the *Edinburgh Review*. According to Jeffrey, the French customs and culture which swept across Britain in the wake of the Restoration were the direct cause of a decline in English literature; worse still, the French influence could never have overcome the strong English tradition, had it not been for help that came from within Britain herself. High treason is Jeffrey's allegation, and the allegation is intimately linked to a name: John Dryden, Jeffrey's particular *bête noire*:

> [W]hen the wits and profligates of King Charles had sufficiently insulted the seriousness and virtue of their predecessors, there would probably have been a revulsion towards the accustomed taste of the nation, had not the party of the innovators been reinforced by champions of more temperance and judgement. The result seemed at one time suspended on the will of Dryden – in whose individual person the genius of the English and of the French school of literature may be said to have maintained a protracted struggle. But the evil principle prevailed.[7]

This 'evil principle' was only much later gradually overcome again, with a first dawning of recovery in Cowper, while it took, in Jeffrey's historical system, a Walter Scott and Thomas Campbell for renewed originality and British genius to return.

Francis Jeffrey had expressed these opinions in various reviews in his journal. He did not, however, try to write a history of English literature himself. Such narrative realization was, as we have seen, another two decades in coming, and when it did arrive in Robert Chambers' *History* it had nothing of Jeffrey's agonistic design and belligerence, although it drew heavily on Jeffrey's writings, as Chambers' numerous references to Jeffrey's reviews in the *Edinburgh* and elsewhere clearly indicate.[8] What were Chambers' precepts, and why had he so fundamentally changed the overall design of one of his major sources?

We can begin to solve this riddle by reflecting for a moment on what the consequences would have been if Chambers had followed Jeffrey's precepts. What kind of literary history would have resulted? Jeffrey's dismissal of what he saw as the influence of his much-reviled French classicism would have dictated a plot where the better part of two centuries of English literature, from the Restoration to his own day, would have fallen under Jeffrey's anathema, with only a gradual increase of 'acceptable' authors from Cowper onwards. The improvements in prosody and rhetorical control with which even Jeffrey credited the poets following John Dryden would have been a dead-end evolution. A massive body of texts and a substantial period of history – but, what is more, also the readers past and present who continued to treasure and enjoy the authors who belonged to those categories – would have to be presented as misguided and, ultimately, 'un-English', hence unworthy of any further attention by the readers of Chambers' history. It is obvious that even on these practical grounds Jeffrey's polemics, effective as they might have been as such, would constitute a most impracticable and awkward basis for a historical narrative about the development of English literature. Further considerations on Chambers' part were, however, to link up with these general complications.

Jeffrey's principles of anti-French and anti-classicist invective were not only impracticable as narrative strategy; they also reflected a different situation in Britain's politics and social condition. Jeffrey still wrote under the impression of the *terreur* of the French Revolution and the Napoleonic Wars, with all the fears these engendered in Britain, concerning the interior stability of British society as well as the foreign threat emanating from across the Channel. When Chambers set about his version of English literary history, the foreign danger was perceived as less acute, if not averted, and British society was in the midst of a reform process which clearly aimed at a more integrated and pacified civil society, under a common British identity ultimately transcending social divisions of – mainly – class and religion. What is more, Chambers' *History*, published in the firm's own series called 'Chambers' Educational Course', edited by William and Robert Chambers themselves, had a clear-cut social objective: providing access to educational material for those strata of society which traditionally had had few opportunities to profit from the official channels of communication and teaching. Chambers' *History* was written for use in the burgeoning mechanics institutes and other new forms of educating the better-paid workmen and lower middle classes who had some money to spend on a moderately priced book, but could never afford to go to the traditional universities (the newly founded London University was a different matter), or had been debarred from reading scholarly work because of high book prices before the arrival of new and cheaper printing and publishing methods gradually established what was to develop into the modern mass market in the course of the nineteenth century.

Ultimately, it therefore seems more plausible to say that Chambers did not have different principles dictated to him by his intention to cast his *History* into narrative form, but narrative was his chosen form precisely because of its very specific properties, which enabled him to establish principles very different from those of the literary commentators of one or two decades before. Narrative gave him the means to shape a literary history tailored to his purposes of national integration through educational enfranchisement. How, then, did his integrative approach translate into literary history?

Here, Dryden and the classicist school seem an appropriate test case to begin with. Although Chambers did take up some of Jeffrey's criticism, sometimes quoting Jeffrey directly from the *Edinburgh Review*,[9] his overall verdict was clearly on the positive side. Even Jeffrey's traitor Dryden was shown to have redeeming qualities when Chambers writes, in his general appreciation of Dryden: 'In spite of his faults, which were not small, Dryden continues to be regarded as one of the most illustrious of English poets.'[10] Chambers' strategy of negotiating a complex view on various writers and traditions is further illustrated and clarified in his comments on the Augustan poets. After quoting Jeffrey's dismissal of their classicist poetics, he gives his own opinion:

> While there is general truth in these [i.e. Jeffrey's negative] remarks, it must at the same time be observed, that the age produced several writers, who, each in his own line, may be called extraordinary. Satire, expressed in forcible and copious language, was certainly carried to its utmost pitch of excellence by Swift. The poetry of elegant and artificial life was exhibited, in a perfection never since attained, by Pope. The art of describing the manners, and discussing the morals of the passing age, was practised for the first time, and with unrivalled felicity, by Addison. And, with all the licentiousness of Congreve and Farquhar, it may be fairly said that English comedy was in their hands what it had never been before, and has scarcely in any instance been since.[11]

This passage captures Chambers' historical method in a nutshell: authors are subsumed into one overarching tradition and one integrating narrative where each writer and each mode of writing has its place and its merits; generic niches are filled by authors from different schools and with different literary virtues; different areas of literary activity have had their highlights at various times in English literary history.

If, however, Chambers' story is one of alternating poetic excellences, does this preclude any teleology in its overall conception? In a sense, Chambers found a view on Scott which helped him to square this circle. Chambers had come across Jeffrey's opinions on Scott in a review by Jeffrey on 'Ford's Dramatic Works' which Chambers also mentioned in his *History*:[12]

> [Scott] has copied every style, and borrowed from every manner that has prevailed, from the times of Chaucer to his own, – illuminating and uniting, if not harmonizing them all, by a force of colouring, and a rapidity of succession, which is not to be met with in any of his many models.[13]

Remarkably, Scott is not praised as the high point of British literature for his originality or invention of something entirely unprecedented, but attains the pinnacle of Chambers' poetics by an integrative faculty that takes up and unites all the warring traditions into one harmonious work, incorporating the whole of literary history in present perfection.

We do not know if Chambers was aware of the adventurousness of his verdict, but if it was not founded entirely on aesthetic and patriotic grounds, it certainly fitted the bill of his history's rationale. Here was a writer from the Scottish margins who could be studied by the eager readers of literary history as a showcase for everything worth reading and learning about in English literary history. That history had thus found a unifying expression and an integrative identity which was a far cry from Jeffrey's schizophrenic exclusiveness, and could be presented as an ideal image for British society as a whole.

Chambers' *History* does not, however, end with Walter Scott or, for that matter, with any 'literary' works in the narrow sense. The last pages are filled with an account of the competitive activities of two main publishers: Robert and William Chambers in Edinburgh, Charles Knight's Society for the Diffusion of Useful Knowledge in London. The focus is on various encyclopaedias, notably Chambers' *Encyclopaedia*, started as early as 1728 by Ephraim Chambers, – but in the meantime grown to an impressive array of forty volumes, which was, Chambers comments, 'a work of such magnificent proportions and embellishments, that no country but one so advanced as Britain in affluence, literature, and the arts, could have produced it'.[14] Although he does not say so explicitly, Chambers was in the same sense also referring to the *History of English Language and Literature* the reader would just then be holding in his hand. What else was it but the summary collection and appreciation of Britain's remarkable literature in a historical narrative? What critics and scholars aware of literary history, such as Robert Chambers, could see in Walter Scott was presented here in its historical detail. The influences and tradition Walter Scott had synthesized into his novelistic art could be read here in an analytic condition, so to speak, as a discrete historical narrative accounting for all the good things that had come together in the reader's present not only to shape Scott's art but also to offer a model for an integrative view of British literature and, by analogy, of British society as a whole, procuring a powerful basis for a new and inclusive British identity.

Robert Chambers, *Vestiges of the Natural History of Creation*

When Chambers' *Vestiges of the Natural History of Creation* was published eight years after the appearance of the *History of English Language and Literature*, none of his early readers would have suspected any connections – not only because the subject matter seemed so different, but also for the simple reason that *Vestiges* was printed anonymously. Guessing its author became a popular parlour game throughout the country, and the work was still listed under George Combe's name in the British Library catalogue as late as 1877.[15] But what about possible interdependences in Chambers' work itself? First of all, there are no direct indicators in Chambers' literary history that he was consciously and explicitly applying any evolutionary principles which he might have derived from studies in evolutionary science. This circumstance is all the more striking in view of the fact that Chambers' preoccupation with 'Theories of the Universe and of the Earth', goes right back to his satirical essay 'Vindication of the World and of Providence' in *Kaleidoscope*, a journal he had started at the tender age of nineteen, in 1822, which his brother William printed for him during its short life of only eight issues.[16] Conversely, however, *Vestiges* is full of literary references and linkages to literature and literary history, which suggest an almost unidirectional influence of Chambers' literary history on his evolutionary history, but not vice versa. These connections need to be explored further.

Although it is a book on natural science, *Vestiges* is replete with literary metaphors and references. Geological strata are described as 'the leaves of the *Stone Book*',[17] and a particular variety of limestone beds can form the 'chronicles' of a period,[18] while it is geology that 'chronicles' 'the great natural transactions', and it is only after the 'conclusion' of 'the wondrous chapter of the earth's history which is told by geology' that the 'creation of our own species' actually begins;[19] evolution is 'shewn in the pages of the geological record', and analogous processes of development are presented as taking place in 'countless theatres of being which are suspended in space',[20] just like the one theatre which is the earth and its history.

Chambers' extensive use of the book metaphor seems particularly striking. As Hans Blumenberg has pointed out in *Die Lesbarkeit der Welt* ('The Readability of the World'), the primacy of books, and the one Book in the shape of the Christian Bible in particular, significantly antedates the Baconian emphasis on empiricism. Modernity's turn to a supposedly direct experience of nature as reality is therefore by no means 'natural' or 'immediate', but constructed in rivalry to the authoritative distribution of knowledge and experience through books.[21] The 'scientific' method of empiricism, therefore, is a derivative phenomenon of a burgeoning book culture. Why, then, does Chambers return to the use of this metaphor in his semi-scientific treatise on evolution in what consequently would almost have to be called a postmodern gesture? In his further elaboration of this theme, Blumenberg[22] also encounters this paradox. On the one hand, he maintains, there is an old enmity between books and reality, in so far as the written text is always bent on substituting reality, presenting itself as something definitively categorized and ascertained, and thus making reality itself redundant. On the other, Blumenberg observes the surprising circumstance that, despite this rivalry, the book could become a metaphor of nature. He infers that the reasons for creating this paradox, for forcing these antithetical concepts into one metaphor, must have been important. Blumenberg finds two reasons for this. First, using the book metaphor for nature can become a strategy to subvert the authority of the one Book, the Bible. Second – and more significantly here – he sees an important impetus in the fascination of the totalizing power of the book: Books have the power to integrate the disparate, recondite, recalcitrant, alien with the familiar. Reading nature as a book presupposes an elementary unity, for which the process of reading only rediscovers the laws and links. As in Thomas Mann's *Doctor Faustus*, Blumenberg points to the sensation of the uncanny [*Unheimlichkeit*] caused by the perception of non-human nature as illiterate. Making that part of nature – and the stones of prehistory are a particularly striking instance – legible is an appropriating gesture which takes away the uncanny associations from nature and familiarizes it, humanizes it. A book, finally, signals a sense of closure and unity, of definitiveness, which makes its contents 'comprehensible', accessible to human grasp and, hence, opens it to manipulation. In its historical aspect, Blumenberg's overriding metaphor for this characteristic of perceiving nature as a book is 'evolution', in the literal sense of the word, meaning unwrapping, unfolding, *Ent-wicklung*, recalling the unfurling of an ancient scroll.

All these associations so suggestively evoked in Blumenberg's seminal study dovetail neatly as explanations of Chambers' rationale in the *Vestiges*. In a time of upheaval and uncertainty, when traditional cosmologies and strategies of systematizing the world have become highly unstable, he presents his contemporaries with the stabilizing impact of two scrolls which are unrolled in the reading process: the scroll of literary history, where readers can follow the 'evolution' of their literary, cultural and national identity; and the scroll of Creation, where readers can follow the 'evolution' of the universe. Although the latter seems the more daring and expansive enterprise, it is – not only in the publication history of Chambers' works, but also in conceptual terms – preceded by the history of the book. In Blumenberg's sense, Chambers' move was, indeed, from the book to nature.

All the propensities suggested in Blumenberg's elaborations on the book metaphor are present in Chambers' *Vestiges*. The book metaphor helped him to present the evolution of the world as a closed text which could safely be followed by his readers without the fear of losing themselves in some illiterate, unreadable wilderness. But Chambers did not only present nature as a book; he also put his own views together with the views from the various sciences on nature's evolution into book form, as one of the early reviewers in *The Examiner* (9 November 1844) was already quick to realize: 'In this small and unpretending volume we have found so many great results of knowledge and reflection, that we cannot too earnestly recommend it to the attention of thoughtful men. It is the first attempt that has been made to connect the natural sciences into a history of creation.'[23]

Just as Chambers had, in the earlier work, taken all the findings of literary scholarship, from the antiquarians to historians like Warton, and critics and reviewers like Jeffrey, to shape the narrative of his literary history, he now assembled the results of the natural sciences in a similar texture. Not surprisingly, it is, above all, Walter Scott's novelistic art which provided him with the tools to accomplish this feat. Secord comments:

> *Vestiges* stripped the Waverley novels to their essentials in nature's laws. By retaining traces of the generic conventions of historical fiction, however, the evolutionary cosmology of the Enlightenment was recast in a form appropriate for a Victorian readership. ... Hence the widespread acknowledgement among contemporary readers that the *Vestiges* read like a novel.[24]

Thus Chambers not only presented cosmological history as a book, but he also did so in book form and, what is more, in the very book form which his contemporaries found most accessible and readable, the novel. One could argue that Chambers had at least partly realized what he had presented as an impossible fantasy in his youthful satire of 1822, where he had written in his conclusion:

> We hastily close this subject with an idea of impotent nothingness: for even though we possessed the congregated talents of a world – though we had for our ink-horn the immeasurable ocean, and for our pen the enduring *stylus* of the Recording Angel – though the Chaos from which sprung the germs of the Universe were extended into immensity, thin as the sheet on which we now write, and placed before us for a scroll – and though Eternity itself were compressed into an hour, for the sake of our feeble functions – we could never sufficiently record the boundless divinity of God, or explain the interminable excellences of his Providence.[25]

In the *Vestiges*, Chambers may not have recorded the boundless divinity of God, but, instead of fantastically expanding his writing utensils to match the infinitude of the universe, he was able to compress the universe into an eminently readable history within the covers of a moderately sized and moderately priced book.

As with literary history and the antiquarian, or at least rich book collector's remoteness of its library holdings before, serving something previously arcane, uncanny, or at least inaccessible in the view of the common reader in a dish which was easily to be consumed by everyone, was the feat for which Chambers had trained in his literary history, and which he now successfully applied to the history of the world. What Secord says in the 'Prologue' to his study of the *Vestiges* holds equally true as an assessment of Chambers' literary history: 'This is a book about evolution for the people, and the evolving self-identity of "the people".'[26]

The trajectory of this evolution in the *Vestiges* is, once again, a narrative of progress. And once again, the conceptualization of this progress shares its major cues with the history of literature. It is not only Sir Walter Scott's narrative mode which is adopted, but also Scott's position in literary history as the incorporation of the progress of English literature which is taken up again in the *Vestiges*, where he reappears, together with Shakespeare, as an illustration of the highest developmental stage of animate being. Expanding Scott's universality beyond literature, Chambers writes:

> [T]o a limited number is given the finely assorted assemblage of qualities which places them on a parallel with the typical. To this may be attributed the universality which marks all the very highest brains, such as those of Shakespeare and Scott, men of whom it has been remarked that they must have possessed within themselves not only the poet, but the warrior, the statesman, and the philosopher; and who, moreover, appear to have had the mild and manly, the moral and the forcible parts of our nature in the most perfect balance.[27]

The principle of progressive accumulation of superiority which still retains the former developmental stages as valuable components was the model Chambers had used as the basis of his literary history. Here it is deployed on a much wider scale. How is this possible?

Such a widening scope, coming from Chambers' literary history can be reconstructed from the *Vestiges* as follows. First, the geniuses of Scott or Shakespeare are expanded in their ingenuity to include not only the literary merits of former and inferior writers, but also the superiority of the literary figures they write about (warriors, statesmen, philosophers). At the same time, an intimate connectedness within the human species is emphasized. The various endowments of individuals are only differently developed; discrepancies, however wide, are thus of degree, not of kind, as Chambers cogently says at one point in Vestiges: 'Thus a Cuvier and a Newton are but expansions of a clown, and the person emphatically called the wicked man, is one whose highest moral feelings are rudimental.'[28]

This scope is further widened to include all animate beings. One of the key linkages is to be found in Chambers' embryology. Eventually favouring the theory put forward by the Estonian naturalist Karl Ernst von Baer over the popular version of recapitulation theory, Chambers saw the development of foetal life as a process of branching differentiation from the general to the specific, as shown in a diagram he took from William Carpenter, one of Von Baer's first disciples in Britain.[29] Embryos share a common development before they branch off towards their particular species. The level of development attained is the higher the longer this gestation period lasts and the later the branching-off happens, so that mammals' foetuses stay in the undifferentiated state of life's gestation for the longest time, but nevertheless share in a common nature of being much as Newton and the clown do in Chambers' former example.

This overall, gradual progress is derived from unchanging and timeless laws of nature[30] ultimately originating in a deistically conceived Creator. It is the principle on which the whole universe has developed from its beginning as cosmic nebulae to the present. Starting from the surface of the earth, Chambers thus explains:

> The surface [of the earth] has also undergone a gradual progress by which it has become always more and more variegated, and thereby fitted for the residence of a higher class of animals. In pursuing the progress of the development of both plants and animals upon the globe, we have seen an advance in both cases, along the line leading to the higher forms of organization. Among the plants, we have first sea-weeds, afterwards land plants; ... In the department of zoology, we see zoophytes, radiata, mollusca, articulata, existing for ages before there were any higher forms. The first step forward gives fishes, the humblest class of the vertebrata; ... Afterwards come land animals, of which the first are reptiles ... From reptiles we advance to birds, and thence to mammalia ... .[31]

In stating this, Chambers had popularized a last step in the development of progress narratives, which had originally started with a claim to a progressive accumulation of human knowledge and civilization, as in Francis Bacon's Advancement of Learning, had then been extended – first with some difficulty and then, in Chambers' History, with great smoothness – to literary history, to include now in the Vestiges both the animate and inanimate world in one great sweep of a progressive, unitarian cosmology. Thus the idea of progress did not proceed chronologically, so to speak, but began with the human sphere and from there was gradually expanded to incorporate all kinds of being. Is there a reason for this inverted progress of progress itself?

Obviously, the world of science or civilization in general, and literature as one of its markers in particular, was not widely regarded as part of any sacred cosmology, much as progress narratives might be discussed within theological speculation. But Creation had reached its climax with humankind, and the discussion of historical patterns had a different quality after that. However, Chambers' popular expansion of the progress narrative beyond the human domain was of course hotly contested, since readers at the time saw it as an encroachment on biblical premises, where prehistoric time was clearly structured by the Creator's direct interventions. While extending progress to that domain can be understood as humanizing it by applying a pattern previously reserved for human history, the idea could backfire and lead to fears of dehumanizing the sphere of human history by linking it without clear demarcations with a pre-human past. Not surprisingly, the extension of the progress narrative to the pre-human period thus faced the strongest opposition from readings of the Bible, and any other book had to compete with that authority. Clearly, this is one important reason why the introduction of the idea of progress to that part of universal history came last, and made such a stir when it came in its popular guise in Chambers' novelistic bestseller.

As a kind of side-effect of this development of the idea of progress to be observed in Chambers' work, patterns of progress and linkage of disparate structures were therefore first tested and probed within the confines of human – and here in particular literary – history as the highest achievements of human language and human minds. It was only from this vantage point of the highest pinnacle of civilization – from minds like Shakespeare and, above all, Walter Scott – that Chambers then began to work his way through the entire history of creation, retaining and adapting many of his proven strategies to connect and integrate items from various discourses, disciplines and fields of knowledge, and infusing his narrative with a literary quality.

More importantly, the two books do not only share important concepts and narrative strategies; they can also be read as originating in very similar contexts, serving very similar cultural needs, and addressing very similar social problems. Both histories are permeated by the same symbolic and analogical values, which can ultimately be summed up in a sweeping integrative, unifying gesture and an attempt to establish connectedness where historical conceptions at the time were marked by deep rifts and chasms. These narrative or conceptual ruptures addressed by Chambers must, in turn, be read as symbolic of deep divisions in Britain's society and culture at that time.

In this sense, both the *History of English Language and Literature* and *Vestiges of the Natural History of Creation* reflect a specific moment in British cultural history. They were born of deep rifts in British society and culture, which had broken up as side-effects of processes of industrialization, heightened by fears fed through intimations of revolution and foreign threat emanating from across the Channel, and leading to a general impetus to reform. It is within this context, I would like to suggest, that Chambers' two pioneering works are most profitably read; a context which casts clearer light on his achievements than categorizing him as a successor to Warton in the area of literary history on the one hand, and as a predecessor to Darwin in the field of evolution theory, on the other. Chambers did not aim primarily at accomplishing Warton's unfinished project, with its focus on the historical integration of poetics, aesthetics and antiquarian concerns; neither was he preoccupied with path-breaking research in evolution theory. His work was, as far as its research-based grounding is concerned, derivative and far from pioneering in both sectors. What made his accomplishments in both respects so important, however, was his success in narrative integration. This success was not driven by any unmotivated scientific curiosity or sheer desire for knowledge, but originated in the reform movement of his time, and here in particular in the context of the widespread educational reforms which were so extensively on the agendas of politicians, authors, critics, publishers and many other activists of all kinds and convictions.

The fact that it was a passing moment, at least where evolutionary theory is concerned, can be seen in Darwin's writings of some dozen years later. Here the focus is much more divided between continuity or unity, and a much less optimistic view of loss and futility: much of the abundant growth is lost and redundant in the process of evolution here. Many branches die in Darwin's favourite tree metaphor: 'From the first growth of the tree, many a limb and branch has decayed and dropped off; and these lost branches of various sizes may represent those whole orders, families, and genera which have now no living representatives, and which are known to us only from having been found in a fossil state.'[32] This is what Gillian Beer calls Darwin's attempt at 'the restoration of familial ties, the discovery of a lost inheritance, the restitution of pious memory, a genealogical enterprise'.[33] In that sense, Darwin is much closer to Thomas Warton than he is to Robert Chambers. While for Chambers, past literary merits and cultural achievements remained present in their potential, now fully developed in every respect by Walter Scott, or, in evolutionary development, in the great characters and minds of Shakespeare or Scott, Warton's conception of literary history is one of loss – specifically, of the Romantic tradition – and his gesture is one of recuperation and commemoration, without breaking through to a revitalizing activation of that tradition. It was Robert Chambers who had been able to forge the linkage between progressive evolution and restitution of the relevance of the past in the present in a particularly unstable but also highly productive period in British culture.

PART II

Evolution and Degeneration

3

AESTHETICISM, IMMORALITY AND THE RECEPTION OF DARWINISM IN VICTORIAN BRITAIN

Gowan Dawson

In 1867, Charles Darwin told Alfred Russel Wallace that sexual selection was 'growing into quite a large subject', and this increasing concern with reproductive behaviour would, four years later, come to dominate *The Descent of Man*, taking up far more of the book's two volumes than the discussion of human origins.[1] Indeed, it was sex and procreation, rather than death and extinction, that was now increasingly depicted as the driving force in the evolutionary process. In the *Descent*, of course, Darwin included man in his wide-ranging account of the physical combat and aesthetic competition by which active males struggled for passive female mates. This potentially provocative inclusion of human sexual behaviour alongside that of other species was moderated, as historians have noted frequently, by the anthropomorphic – and decidedly Victorian – assumptions which Darwin brought to descriptions of the mating habits of widely different animals. The more disquieting implications of rooting human sexuality in animal behaviour, however, could not be elided entirely by Darwin's cosy anthropomorphism and frequent interludes of lush romantic rhetoric. Notwithstanding the exemplary personal reputation of its author, the *Descent*, according to a surprisingly large number of critics, transgressed both genteel standards of decency and the boundaries of acceptability common to nineteenth century scientific publishing, and the prominence given to sexuality throughout the book was considered to be not only highly distasteful but also possibly encouraging of vice and immoral behaviour.

While historians have often disregarded hostile notices of the *Descent* as the outpourings of 'cranks' whose harsh words 'could no longer hurt' Darwin,[2] in this chapter I will examine a particular aspect of the book's critical reception, and of Darwinism's position in literary culture more generally, which has not hitherto been acknowledged, but which seems to have troubled Darwin deeply. As is well known, the *Descent* was published in early 1871, just as a bloody class war was breaking out on the streets of Paris, and many reviewers furtively associated the theories expressed in Darwin's book with the contemporaneous collapse of civic and moral order in France, long regarded as a hotbed of similarly heretical sentiments. What has not previously been noted, however, is that the *Descent*'s publication, delayed as it was by Darwin's customary ill-health, also coincided with the release of Algernon Swinburne's latest collection of verse, *Songs Before Sunrise*. In fact, Darwin's book was frequently implicated not only with Swinburne's own political radicalism but also, and potentially much more harmfully, with the infamous poet's notoriety for aesthetic sensualism and flagrant sexual depravity. Such iniquitous literary connections were particularly undesirable in that they associated the *Descent* with precisely the concerns, and sexual desire and moral impropriety especially, which Darwin had deliberately endeavoured to expunge from its pages.

The study of nineteenth century science and literature has for a long time been dominated by what has come to be known as the 'one culture' model, which subsumes disciplinary differences within a unitary cultural context that facilitates the interconnection of scientific and literary discourses.[3] Implicit in this model is the assumption that such discursive interchanges are, even when they are unintended, invariably creative and productive for both scientific and literary modes of writing. To 'Victorian scientific writers', as Gillian Beer has observed, 'Literature, especially English literature, offered ... *stories* by whose means to imagine the world, and organizations which potentiated fresh relations', while 'Poetry offered particular formal resources to think with.'[4] What seems to be neglected in this positive 'one culture' model, however, is that such interconnectedness, as the example of Darwin and Swinburne in this chapter will suggest, could just as easily be dangerous and deleterious, requiring strenuous efforts to disentangle a scientific text like the *Descent* from the wrong kind of literary associations. By recognizing the adverse potential of such cross-disciplinary interconnections, moreover, we can also gain an insight into how concerns with sexual immorality became integral to the opposition to Darwinism in the 1870s and beyond.

The Imputation of Indecency

The *Descent*'s incessant focus on sexuality obliged Darwin to be scrupulously careful in the language he used, and John Murray, the book's publisher, was particularly alert to the need for discretion. Reading through Darwin's manuscript in the autumn of 1870, he even counselled that the word 'Sexual' ought not to appear in the book's title, and when Darwin proposed 'The Descent of Man & Selection according to Sex' as a compromise, Murray expressed himself 'glad' to be 'rid of an objectionable adjective' (and in the final title, of course, the specific connection between selection and sex was further diluted to merely '*in Relation to*').[5] Murray took exception to many other aspects of the *Descent*'s manuscript, and Darwin, at his publisher's behest, employed numerous rhetorical devices to tone down particular passages which, as Murray suggested, might be 'liable to the imputation of indecency'.[6] One of these devices found particular favour with Murray, who commended Darwin for 'the note which you have very properly veiled in Latin'.[7] It is unclear exactly which of the *Descent*'s numerous footnotes Murray was referring to, but at one point in the chapter on secondary sexual characteristics in man, Darwin's footnoted commentary appears, without any notice or explanation, in Latin, and the necessity of shielding general readers from what would have doubtless been considered a taboo and highly indelicate subject is, in this case, manifestly evident.

Drawing on his correspondence with Andrew Smith, a retired army surgeon who had been stationed in South Africa, Darwin described how the large 'posterior part' of 'Hottentot women ... projects in a wonderful manner', and is 'greatly admired by the men'.[8] This discussion of the local aesthetic preferences which, Darwin argued, were responsible for the different racial characteristics of humans was augmented by a footnote in Latin which referred once more to the same letter, from March 1867, in which Smith had apprised Darwin of the ideals of female beauty peculiar to the Hottentots:

> Idem illustrissimus viator dixit mihi præcinctorium vel tabulam foeminæ, quod nobis teterrimum est, quondam permagno æstimari ab hominibus in hâc gente. Nunc – res mutata est, et censent talem conformationem minime optandam esse.
> [The famous explorer told me that the very girdle or protuberance on women which we see as repulsive is thought to be of considerable value by the men of this tribe. Now, though, the case has changed and they think that such a shape is by no means desirable.][9]

Darwin distrusted his own rusty Latin and requested that his son Francis, who had recently graduated from Trinity College, Cambridge, cast a more practised eye over such passages.[10] Even veiled in an antique language that was generally the exclusive preserve of university-educated gentlemen, however, Darwin's footnote remained self-consciously vague and evasive about the precise nature of this 'præcinctorium vel tabulam [girdle or protuberance]' which was so

repellent to Western tastes, especially compared with what Smith had actually
told him in his letter, which had stated frankly:

> ... so far as the Hottentot is concerned I can with certainty say ... he
> some time ago used to value highly such of the females as had lengthened
> nymphæ [i.e. the labia minora of the vulva] but now he rather views
> these ugly developments as undesirable if not as deformities. I have
> been told of some who had them as elongated as that they were able
> during sexual intercourse to encircle the man's loins and fix him by
> them until the appetite of both was thoroughly satisfied.[11]

The disparity between the *Descent*'s demure footnote and the rather earthy
letter from a retired military man on which it was based, suggests not merely
Darwin's reluctance to refer candidly to certain areas of the female body, but
also an unwillingness to countenance the sexual dominance of Hottentot
women suggested by Smith's eyewitness account, which contrasted markedly
with the diffident coyness that was attributed to females of all species
throughout the *Descent*.

The anatomical peculiarity to which Smith referred had in fact been noted
regularly by travellers and explorers since at least the late seventeenth century,
and was described more explicitly – although again employing a sartorial
euphemism, and still partially in Latin – in J F Collingwood's translation of
Theodor Waitz's *Introduction to Anthropology* (1863) as 'the much talked-of
Hottentot apron, which ... consists of a prolongation of the *præputium clitoridis*
and of the *nymphæ*'.[12] While it was just about acceptable to mention
steatopygous females in the main text of the *Descent*, it was inevitably
impossible for Darwin even to allude to anthropological accounts of such
variations in women's genitalia – as well as men's apparent preference for
them – outside of an extremely circumspect footnote which, veiled in Latin,
was intended never to be understood by the majority of the book's readers.
Nevertheless, at pains to convince doubters such as Wallace of the
effectiveness of his theory, Darwin could not afford to disregard any evidence
that apparently supported sexual selection, even if its potential to perturb
the moral sensibilities of the *Descent*'s general audience meant that it had to
be effectively smuggled into the book in a form that would have been
meaningful only to the most erudite and specialist readers.

The strenuous endeavours of both Darwin and Murray to purge the *Descent*
of any potential impropriety have generally been regarded as an unqualified
success. The *Dublin Review*, even while acknowledging that sexual selection
was 'a subject that it is difficult to treat in any Review but a strictly scientific
one', nevertheless conceded that 'Mr Darwin handles it in a way that entirely
strips it of all offensiveness'.[13] The *Westminster Review* likewise agreed that

Darwin, 'with modesty and caution all his own, ... makes a temperate use of his discovery' of sexual selection.[14] Although the *Westminster*'s anonymous assurances regarding the *Descent*'s discretion were in fact written by William Sweetland Dallas, who was hardly impartial, having, among many other services to Darwin, compiled the book's index, historians have, for the most part, nevertheless similarly assumed that Darwin's attempts to render his evolutionary account of human origins respectable were both relatively unproblematic and largely successful. Ruth Yeazell, among many others, has even suggested that the *Descent* resembled 'a respectable Victorian novel'.[15] But this was not necessarily the experience of much of the book's original audience; readers, after all, approach texts in a multiplicity of different ways, and are notoriously resistant to authorially mandated meanings. Indeed, several reviewers of the *Descent* drew attention to the apparently unseemly tone of much that still remained even in its carefully bowdlerized pages, implying that Darwin's evolutionary tome was unsuitable reading material for all but the most worldly gentlemen.

Some, for instance, raised eyebrows at the book's apparent preoccupation with sex, and at least part of the problem was the explicitness even of Darwin's scientific language. The *Athenaeum* was simply lost for words, claiming: 'We scarcely know how to deal with Sexual Selection.' It was, the *Athenaeum* claimed, 'both a delicate and difficult subject', and, when a passage from the *Descent* dealing with the emergence of sexual dimorphism in early man was reprinted in the review, it was noted that 'we quote [it] with the omission of a few words that might displease the fastidious'. The potentially objectionable missing words were merely 'the excreta were voided through a cloaca', but the *Athenaeum*'s reprinted passage was also brought to an abrupt halt with the melodramatic aposiopesis, 'we decline to continue the extract', just as the particular section extracted from the *Descent* was about to move on to androgynous male mammals which 'possess ... rudiments of a uterus with the adjacent passage', as well as 'rudiments of mammæ'. Those readers willing to tolerate such explicit descriptions, the review advised, 'must have recourse to the book'.[16] Darwin's latest evolutionary monograph, it was clearly implied, transgressed the boundaries of acceptability even of a highbrow journal like the *Athenaeum*, and the widespread practice of general readers gaining a detailed knowledge of the latest scientific publications from periodical reviews and extracts was, in this case, considered inappropriate.[17]

An even more forthright response to the *Descent*'s apparent indecency came in the *Edinburgh Review*, which commissioned the geologist William Boyd Dawkins to take on Darwin's book. Dawkins was in fact sympathetic to many aspects of evolution, and his anonymous review seemed, at first, to warm to the *Descent*, which, it observed, was 'On every side ... raising a storm of mingled

wrath, wonder, and admiration'.[18] It was only when he came to consider the
disconcertingly dominant role of sex in Darwin's thinking that Dawkins
switched to a more abrasive rhetoric. After caustically dismissing the theory of
sexual selection as 'altogether inconsistent with known fact', Dawkins observed:

> Inferences might not unfairly be drawn from this portion of Mr Darwin's
> work, to which we cannot in this place do more than advert. But we do
> him no injustice in ascribing to him the theory of Lucretius – that Venus
> is the creative power of the world, and that the mysterious law of
> reproduction, with the passions which belong to it, is the dominant
> force of life. He appears to see nothing beyond or above it. In a heathen
> poet such doctrines appear gross and degrading, if not vicious. We know
> not how to characterise them in an English naturalist, well known for
> the purity and elevation of his own life and character.[19]

The veritable obsession with sex and its attendant passions evinced by
Darwin's book rendered Dawkins, like the *Athenaeum*'s reviewer, almost
speechless. Even while acknowledging the exemplary nature of Darwin's
own personal reputation, he insinuated that the overriding importance
that the *Descent* placed on sexual selection in evolutionary development
was as coarse and demeaning as the most lascivious philosophies of the
corrupt pagan world. The *Descent*, it was inferred, might even encourage
the same kind of corrosive sexual abandon that had long been ascribed to
the infamous Roman poet Lucretius.

Nameless Shameless Abominations

For readers of the number of the *Edinburgh* in which Dawkins's review appeared,
the brief reference to a gross and degrading heathen poet would also have had
other, and much more recent, associations. Less than a hundred pages before
Dawkins's astringent review, the *Edinburgh* for July 1871 had also carried a
similarly critical notice of Swinburne's *Songs Before Sunrise*. Since the
publication of the iconoclastic *Poems and Ballads* in 1866, Swinburne had
become infamous for his poetic treatment of pagan debauchery and vice, and
his notorious volume was widely condemned for its apotheosis of what one
reviewer called 'all the bestial delights that the subtleness of Greek depravity
was able to contrive'.[20] Five years later, the *Edinburgh*'s review of *Songs Before
Sunrise* similarly noted Swinburne's dubious 'admiration for the ancients', and
insisted that his moral perceptions were 'perverted ... even from the Greek
point of view'.[21] The close proximity of this literary notice in the *Edinburgh*
provided a context in which Dawkins's passing allusion to an indecent heathen

poet might signify not merely Lucretius, but also perhaps the most infamously transgressive writer of verse of the entire nineteenth century.

Songs Before Sunrise championed atheism, republicanism and the revolutionary politics of Giuseppe Mazzini, and many of the poems in the collection combined such democratic and heretical concerns with a mystical evolutionary pantheism. In 'Hertha', which experimented with conventional rhyme and metre while similarly reinterpreting the myth of Creation, the eponymous goddess of organic growth proclaims herself the source of an evolutionary power which ensures the continuity of all forms of life, and precedes the false hierarchical dogmas of the orthodox Christian deity:

> First life on my sources
> First drifted and swam;
> Out of me are the forces
> That save it or damn;
> Out of me man and woman, and wild-beast and bird;
> Before God was, I am.[22]

Inevitably, the *Edinburgh* considered that such verse was guilty of a wide variety of crimes, but, significantly, many of these alleged poetic transgressions closely resembled the charges that, later in the same number of the review, would be made against the *Descent*. So, while Dawkins censured Darwin's inability to see beyond the passions which belong to reproduction, Swinburne was likewise accused of acknowledging nothing beyond the animalism of physical love: 'He simply deals with the animal side of the passion – with lust instead of love – with the sensual appetite instead of the strong and pure spiritual feeling.'[23] The hostile notices of Swinburne's and Darwin's latest books carried in the July 1871 *Edinburgh* were both unsigned, and each quarterly number of the strictly anonymous review would have presented contemporary readers with a continuous single text with a particular party line that was adhered to in virtually every article. This juxtaposition of the two reviews, as well as their close verbal and thematic parallels, would inevitably tarnish Darwin's scientific theories by association with Swinburne's notorious verse.

The clear interconnections between the two reviews may actually have been deliberately intended by the *Edinburgh*'s bullish editor Henry Reeve, who oversaw the production of every article published in the journal and was notorious for constantly altering the work of his contributors. As Reeve's biographer noted: 'He not only read the articles to approve of them, very commonly in the MS., but in all cases he revised the proof slips ... thus every article that appeared in the "Review" bore, to some extent, the impress of his own mind.'[24] Significantly, Reeve also expressed similar reservations about the moral consequences of modern science in his own articles for the *Edinburgh*, and it seems likely that, in the July 1871 number, he strategically juxtaposed his contributor's notices, perhaps even making alterations which rendered the parallels between them still more conspicuous.[25] Certainly, when, in the following year, Darwin published *The Expression of the Emotions in Man and Animals*, Reeve commissioned a review from Thomas Spencer Baynes, the same reactionary polymath who had earlier penned the *Edinburgh*'s vitriolic notice of *Songs Before Sunrise*. As Reeve had perhaps anticipated, Baynes's review of *The Expression of the Emotions* identified various shortcomings in Darwin's work which were almost identical to the moral and intellectual lapses in Swinburne's verse that he had already derided in the *Edinburgh*'s pages.

Whereas Swinburne, according to Baynes's review of *Songs Before Sunrise*, exhibited 'a feverish sensuality' and 'a passion ... for reviling the higher powers and laws of the universe', Darwin likewise, as Baynes claimed in his notice of *The Expression of the Emotions*, 'engaged in the study of sensuous facts' until he had become 'relatively insensible to the phenomena and powers of the moral and spiritual universe'.[26] Similarly, Baynes's use of a scientific analogy to describe Swinburne's poems as 'molluscs rather than vertebrate ... fungoid growths rather than ... strong well-proportioned trees' inevitably associated them with the preoccupations of Darwin, who, Baynes claimed, 'dwells ... only on the lower and more animal aspects' of existence.[27] The aesthetic exploration of sensuality which, among other things, had made Swinburne's poetry so contentious could, in the adept hands of a critic such as Baynes, be made synonymous with scientific theories, like those of Darwin, that sought explanations in the material rather than the spiritual.[28]

Even Baynes's criticism of the poetic language employed by Swinburne, with its 'wild luxuriance of merely metrical diction' and 'monotony of ... rhythmical effect', resembled his objections to Darwin's scientific prose, which 'abound[s] with ... strained emphasis, [and] eager word-catching'.[29] In fact, the overblown writings of the two, according to Baynes, appealed to an almost identical audience, with Swinburne's poetry having a 'disastrous fascination for excitable but weak and unbalanced natures', while the 'sect of the Darwinian evolutionists' was 'largely recruited from the crowd of facile minds ever ready to follow the newest fashion in art or science'.[30] Indeed, Baynes, in his review of *The Expression of the Emotions*, proclaimed that

> in many circles, especially in certain sections of London, fluent conversational evolutionists are to be found whose literary culture hardly goes deeper than a slight knowledge of Mr Swinburne's poetry, and whose scientific and philosophical training is restricted to a desultory acquaintance with some of Mr Darwin's more popular works.[31]

After all the verbal and conceptual borrowings of the *Edinburgh*'s various reviews of their work, Baynes, for the first time, made the alleged connection between Swinburne and Darwin explicit. Both, he contended, were equally guilty of valorizing mere lustful desires as the highest form of love, and such trite and superficial teachings would, inevitably, seduce the shallow followers of metropolitan fashion.

Darwin was, of course, widely revered as an almost saintly scientific sage, but the *Edinburgh*'s explicit connection of his evolutionary theories with Swinburne's poetic iconoclasm was still potentially very damaging. By the early 1870s, as Rikky Rooksby has observed, Swinburne was an 'international figurehead for sexual, religious and political radicalism', and his 'very name' was 'charged with a satanic aura for the timid and conservative'.[32] He was regularly depicted in the press as a 'libidinous laureate of a pack of satyrs ... grovelling down among ... nameless shameless abominations', while his verse – much of which, it was claimed, 'could not be quoted out of Holywell Street' – was considered little better than pornography.[33] It had even been rumoured that Swinburne's 1866 volume *Poems and Ballads* was to be prosecuted for obscenity, and respectable publishers shunned any involvement with his incendiary poetry.

Still more perturbingly, some of Swinburne's most notorious poems – including 'Laus Veneris', in which the goddess Venus's 'face with all her eager hair ... cleave[s]' to her lover 'clinging as a fire that clings' – celebrated precisely the kind of sexually desirous and dangerously dominant women whose very existence Darwin, as we have seen, had been reluctant even to countenance.[34] While in the *Descent* Darwin responded apprehensively to another naturalist's description of how a male spider 'was seized by the object of his attractions, enveloped by her in a web and then devoured' with the bizarrely incongruous observation that 'the female carries her coyness to a dangerous pitch', exactly such hyperbolically voracious *femmes fatales*, like the eponymous prostitute in 'Dolores' whose 'cruel / Red mouth [is] like a venomous flower', while her

> ... ravenous teeth ... have smitten
> Through the kisses that blossom and bud,
> By the lips intertwisted and bitten
> Till the foam has a savour of blood,

were one of the most distinctive, and widely reviled, features of Swinburne's writing.[35] Such iniquitous literary associations could easily alter the way the *Descent* was read by its different audiences, negating all Darwin and Murray's careful attempts to remove any potentially indecent connotations from its pages.

'I Cannot Endure to Read a Line of Poetry'

In fact, the only nineteenth century poet that Darwin even alluded to in the *Descent* was Alfred Tennyson, the eminently respectable Poet Laureate as well as a member of the Royal Society. In order to illustrate the 'highest stage in moral culture at which we can arrive', Darwin had used the stoical words of Queen Guinevere, in the first series of *Idylls of the King* (1859), renouncing even affectionate memories of her adulterous lover Lancelot:

> Not ev'n in inmost thought to think again
> The sins that made the past so pleasant to us.[36]

One of the dominant themes of Tennyson's Arthurian epic was the struggle to 'keep down the base in man', and the *Descent*'s allusion to the bestselling poem was perhaps intended to lend an air of epic grandeur to its own evolutionary narrative of how a highly developed species like humanity had become able to 'control our thoughts'.[37] Reassuring images of man's upward ascent abounded in Tennyson's verse, and the famous lines from section CXVIII of *In Memoriam* (1850) –

> ... Arise and fly
> The reeling Faun, the sensual feast;
> Move upward, working out the beast,
> And let the ape and tiger die[,]

– had long been employed as a means of representing human evolution as a positive process involving the renunciation of man's erstwhile animalism, as they were, for instance, in John Chapman's 1861 account of the simian inhabitants of Equatorial Africa in the *Westminster*.[38] Over three decades later, the same lines would be used again for an identical purpose in Thomas Huxley's celebrated Romanes Lecture *Evolution and Ethics* (1894).[39]

But Darwin himself, according to his wife Emma, did 'not read Tennyson', and apparently would not have understood even a playful reference, in a letter from Huxley, to *Idylls of the King*.[40] Certainly, he appears to have been oblivious to the lingering hints of the destructive power of female sexuality and desire inherent in the short passage from the poem that was quoted in the *Descent*. Huxley's own wife Henrietta also complained of Darwin's 'slyly disparaging remarks on my beloved Tennyson', and protested that he had not only quoted lines from the poem 'Sea Dreams' 'without the context shockingly Owenlike', but had failed to appreciate the true merits of Tennyson's verse in a way that 'should have damaged your reputation for accuracy'.[41] In his autobiographical recollections, of course, Darwin famously claimed: 'for many years I cannot endure to read a line of poetry', and admitted that his capacity for aesthetic appreciation extended only to 'moderately good' romantic novels which 'do not end unhappily'.[42] Nevertheless, even the most superficial literary allusions, especially to the work of the Poet Laureate, could be used to denote the decency or respectability of particular scientific theories in relation to wider culture, and Helen Small has noted how, in the writings of many nineteenth century psychiatrists, 'literary reference tended to be decorative: it was a mark of accomplishment, a guarantee of the doctor's credentials as a gentlemanly physician'.[43] So, while the *Edinburgh* sought to identify the doctrines of the *Descent* with the degrading poetry of Swinburne, Darwin himself had meant them to be read as consistent with the more genteel values of Tennyson's highly regarded verse (and Swinburne later wrote a short skit alleging, in the style of contemporaneous claims that Francis Bacon had been responsible for the plays of Shakespeare, that Darwin had in fact been the author of Tennyson's poems).[44] With periodical reviewers like Baynes regularly contributing notices of both scientific and poetic publications, and frequently identifying almost identical transgressions in them, such competing literary associations could play an extremely significant role in the reception of a work like the *Descent* among non-specialist reading audiences.

It was the criticisms of the *Descent* made by the comparative anatomist St George Mivart that most annoyed Darwin, and I want to conclude briefly by suggesting how Darwin's exasperation at Mivart's censure can help to reveal his anxieties about his involvement in the particular aspects of Victorian literary culture examined in this chapter. Mivart's 1871 book *On the Genesis of Species*, Darwin complained, had been 'savage [and] contemptuous', and he suspected that, 'stimulated by theological fervour', its Catholic author had played 'not ... quite fair'.[45] But Mivart's apparent unscrupulousness only increased in the following years, and by 1873 this Darwinian apostate was twisting the knife still further by identifying his former mentor's theories with the scandalous poetry of Swinburne. Writing in the *Contemporary Review*, Mivart insisted that among Darwinian evolutionists:

> the prevailing tone of sentiment has long been increasingly Pagan, until its most hideous features reveal themselves in a living English poet, by open revilings of Christianity, amidst loathsome and revoltingly filthy verses which seem to invoke a combined worship of the old deities of lust and cruelty.[46]

It was common practice to refrain from even naming Swinburne in the pages of more decorous periodicals, and readers of the *Contemporary*, where Swinburne had for many years been the subject of persistent vilification, would no doubt have understood the nature of Mivart's malevolent insinuations.

Such an allegation, of course, connected Darwinism with the taint of wantonness, paganism, blasphemy and, above all, sexual immorality that Swinburne's name unmistakably signified at this time. Less than a year later – and this time in the pages of the *Quarterly Review* – Mivart would make these associations even more explicit, claiming: 'There is no hideous sexual criminality of Pagan days that might not be defended on the principles advocated by the [Darwinian] school.'[47] As has been much discussed by historians, this notoriously lurid and misjudged accusation so enraged Darwin that he orchestrated Mivart's ostracism from polite society, and the so-called 'Mivart episode' has long been recognized as one of the most ferocious and personal confrontations of the evolutionary debates of the nineteenth century.[48] By locating this well-known episode within the wider context of the *Descent's* interconnection with Swinburne's transgressive poetics, however, we can also understand Darwin's agitated response as an indication of just how deeply perturbed he was by his entanglement throughout the early 1870s with the wrong kinds of literary associations.

4

CONSTRUCTING DARWINISM IN LITERARY CULTURE

Janet Browne

The question of what lies in store for humanity has worried any number of Western writers and thinkers since Antiquity. Not all of them speculated about the medical or biological future. Many authors were embedded in religious and philosophical contexts that sought moral guidance for the soul's salvation, or promoted stoicism in the face of adversity, and dwelled on heavenly expectations rather than actual times to come.[1] Nevertheless, over the centuries the prospect for improved human health has provoked endless conjecture.[2] In particular, during the late nineteenth century both the threat and the potential of evolutionary theory became increasingly relevant across a broad spectrum of thought. Charles Darwin's work and the wider transformations associated with evolutionary ideas are specially noted for having had a marked impact on creative literature of all kinds at that time.[3] This chapter will single out some of Darwin's influence on the developing genre of utopian and dystopian fiction, and consider the actual extent of that influence. It seems likely that the impact of natural selection theory was probably less direct than is commonly assumed. From the literary side, it hardly needs to be said that utopian and dystopian fiction is not so much about the future as it is about the present. It pursues a wide variety of literary, social and political aims, among which the sciences play a substantial, though not exclusive, role. As such, this form of literature naturally reflected increasingly concrete views about the role that biology and medicine were thought to play in European and American society from Darwin's day up to around 1910 or so.[4] In literature, as in science, it will be argued that questions about the human condition and our future – questions that were once usually discussed in terms of spirituality – were increasingly perceived as part of biology.

Darwin and Wallace's theory of evolution by natural selection, published in 1858 and 1859, needs little introduction except to say that at the start it meshed fluently with Victorian notions of competition and progress across the realms of society, technology, politics and culture, while also stimulating great controversy about our origins and relationship with the divine force of the Christian Bible.[5] Benjamin Disraeli's satirical question 'Is man an ape or an angel?' reflected genuine anxieties among his contemporaries.[6] By the end of the nineteenth century, however, this sense of progress was in tatters, fiercely overthrown by the strongest intellects of the day, and apparently supported by medical and social statistics relating to the decline of the human race through alcoholism, disease, crime, prostitution, urban overpopulation, lax moral values, drugs, war and ever more secularization and political instability.[7] Human evolution, seemingly, was moving in the wrong direction.

Fear of degeneration was clearly a very significant organizing principle here – an important turn-of-the-century theme that literary scholars have explored in depth in complex and rewarding novels published by Hardy, Zola, Mann, Wells and others.[8] But before turning to the problem of imagining the future in the works of serious, canonical authors like these, there is opportunity to mention a small and relatively obscure genre of post-Darwinian fiction that relates very closely to contemporary perceptions of evolutionary change. A handful of slight and journalistic writings captures something of the dread felt by ordinary Victorians when they were forced to contemplate the prospect for humanity. These authors focus on the human species being replaced by apes.

Even though apes were not mentioned by Darwin as possible ancestors for humans in his *Origin of Species*, they were, nevertheless, a prominent topic of Victorian debate from 1860 onwards, encouraged by inflammatory polemic from Thomas Henry Huxley and others.[9] Huxley's long-running argument with Richard Owen at the British Museum, for example, spilled over into public contests in the British Association for the Advancement of Science, and across a wide variety of literary spaces such as the *Westminster Review* and the *Athenaeum*. One widely broadcast aspect of this debate hinged on Paul Du Chaillu's spectacular introduction of gorilla skins and specimens in 1861 [Figure 1].[10] Du Chaillu's popular lectures, his dramatic displays of stuffed skins, his colourful book of adventures published by John Murray in 1863, and the ensuing controversy over his claim that gorillas were ferocious, untameable beasts of the jungle brought the notion of ape ancestry to the forefront of Victorian consciousness. In fact, contemporary excitement about the gorilla is an excellent way to explore shifts in human self-perception during the decades following Darwin and Wallace's evolutionary proposals – not least

Figure 1. Paul Du Chaillu brought the skins of gorillas to Britain in 1861. This illustration from his book *Explorations and Adventures in Equatorial Africa* (London, 1861) worried Victorians about their ancestry from apes. Courtesy of the Syndics of Cambridge University Library.

because the animal became properly known to the developed world only at much the same time as Darwin's *Origin of Species* was published. Its history was closely tied up with the reception of evolutionary theory, and featured very widely in the literature of the day as a likely ancestor for humans, simultaneously terrifying, amusing and revolting to many Victorians. These ape-ancestry debates ranged far and wide, moving from classification theory and the finer points of simian anatomy to the history of anthropology, philosophy of language, human spirituality, intellect and moral behaviour, even feeding into the commercial marketplace as a surge in evolutionary freaks and hairy individuals renamed themselves Darwinian 'missing links', and stepped on to the stage in popular venues across Europe and North America. Julia Pastrana, the ape-woman, was one of the most famous [Figure 2].[11] She toured Europe in 1862. By the time of her death in 1865, she had become so marketable an exhibit that her manager-husband embalmed her body and continued the displays for a number of years thereafter. Of course there was a long tradition, reaching back at least to medieval times, of freak-show display, and of using apes in art as a symbol of folly and perverted humanity.[12] Similar symbolism also underlay the British and American caricatures produced in the 1870s that poked fun at Darwinism and ape ancestry [Figure 3].[13] Nevertheless, the existence of such a large number of different cultural responses to evolutionary thought indicates that the notion of real physical links between apes and humans provided many opportunities to reflect anew on man's place in nature. With the publication of Darwin's *Descent of Man* in 1871, these issues acquired intense literary and cultural relevance.[14]

Figure 2. Julia Pastrana toured Europe in the 1860s, advertising herself as the 'Baboon-Woman'. Wellcome Library London.

Figure 3. 'The Lion of the Season', *Punch* 40, 1861, p. 213. Darwin's theories were widely caricatured after the *Descent of Man* was published in 1871. Wellcome Library London.

Two contemporary dramatizations describe a future in which humans have been succeeded by apelike species. One anonymous tract called *The Fall of Man, or The Loves of the Gorillas, A Popular Scientific Lecture upon the Darwinian Theory of Development by Sexual Selection, by a Learned Gorilla* (1871, authored by the Shakespearian scholar Richard Grant White), reverses the evolutionary tree, and satirizes feeble and foolish human beings as if they were the primitive extinct ancestors of sophisticated gorillas. The book is archly dedicated to Charles Darwin, and is set in the African jungle. It is narrated by an explorer who has apparently overheard a lecture by a gorilla. The gorilla explains the curious habits of humans, who are long dead, to a large assembly of other gorillas – evidently an allusion to the British Association meetings and equivalent functions overseas. The publisher, Sampson Low (Sampson Low, Marsden & Co.), of Fleet Street, London, specialized in social commentaries and realist fiction, including well-known authors such as R D Blackmore, Harriet Beecher Stowe, Charles Reade, Oliver Wendell Holmes, Ralph Waldo Emerson, Victor Hugo, Wilkie Collins, Harrison Ainsworth, Charles Dickens and H M Stanley, whose *In Darkest Africa* (1890) was one of the biggest, as well as one of the most successful, enterprises the firm ever undertook. *The Fall of Man* begins with an allusion to Stanley's search for David Livingstone.[15] The engraved frontispiece of gorillas [Figure 4] – with its explicit reference to Raphael's cherubs in the Sistine Chapel, and by implication, to the heights

Figure 4. Engraved title page of *The Fall of Man, or The Loves of the Gorillas*, London and New York, 1871, by Richard Grant White. British Library.

of Western culture – was probably drawn by the New York publisher of this text, George Washington Carleton, an artist and caricaturist before he became a publisher.[16]

Another is called *Two Missing Links* (1876), and is purportedly transcribed from an abandoned ape-language document found by the author in an ancient temple in faraway lands. It was published under the pseudonym Jonas Potterkin, alias 'W. A. B.', who might possibly be William Alfred Browne, author of various Civil Service examination manuals and geographical instruction booklets.[17] Browne was the author of *The Merchants' Handbook* (1867), in which economic issues of the day are discussed. *Two Missing Links* projects a forceful attack on contemporary Victorian society, especially related to wealth, the law of property, money-grasping lawyers, alcohol and Parliament. In this brave new world, humans have died out because of selfish indulgence and arrogance, leaving sensible, egalitarian apes in charge. The apes regard themselves as having descended from a 'race of inferior and degraded type' called by them 'Homokins'. The homokins are white-skinned, hairless individuals, 'walking always erect on their lower limbs'.

A third work published in Chicago in 1894 by the radical theological writer Austin Bierbower, is *From Monkey to Man*, a saga of origins about the emergence of a race intermediate between apes and humans, which discovers morals and family life, but is eventually defeated and overtaken by warlike humans.[18] Bierbower's mind turned on futurist philosophical and religious topics with a eugenic twist. A large part of the story echoes the Christian biblical narrative. The female missing link shown here, for example, is depicted meeting a snake in the jungle [Figure 5]. The ape-people are industrious, courageous in war, grave and reflective, generous, liberal, humble and disdainful of servility. The humans who overrun them convert Eden into a land of strife.[19]

There is much in these texts that fits into the classic utopian mould first set out by Thomas More in 1516. Using outsiders or visitors to comment on the familiar is an old but effective trick.[20] Often the narrator is a traveller who somehow leaves a record of the tale, a constant reworking of the ancient theme of the *Odyssey*. The geographic setting is typically an unknown island or an isolated spot in the jungle – sometimes the moon, as in Cyrano de Bergerac's *L'Autre Monde* (1656); or another planet, as in *Planet of the Apes* (1968). It is very common for authors to reverse key characteristics to reinforce absurdity, or enlarge or reduce certain aspects of life, as in *Gulliver's Travels* (1726). A frequent theme is the biblical framework of survival and repopulation – two people, or sometimes a handful more, survive a catastrophe or expulsion, and found a new race. Most importantly, such writings are frequently presented as autobiography, giving the allure of personal testimony, sometimes even offered as a 'scientific' anthropology or ethnography, feeding into a well-established

Figure 5. 'Soshee's mother encounters the snake'. Austin Bierbower, *From Monkey to Man*, Chicago, 1894, facing p. 11. British Library.

Victorian interest in travel literature and the exotic, and bestowing the same authoritative tone of voice displayed by the men (and more rarely, women) who had genuinely encountered strange new places. The parallels with geographical literature are notable. Much of the travel writing relating to geographical exploration from the 1550s onwards, for example, was as fantastical as any fantasy, and drew on many of the same motifs. First-person narration gave personal validation to the text, for a geographical author invariably claimed to be a witness to the facts related.[21] This sense of personal verification – of personal 'discovery' – became a crucial ingredient in the developing genre of scientific writing that emerged during the scientific revolution. Notions of scientific 'witnessing', and its corollary 'trustworthiness', became essential.[22] Lengthy descriptions of practical details about the voyage were thus important in establishing the author's veracity, and in many respects resemble the elaborate framing devices that usually accompany utopian fiction. In geographical literature, there was plenty of scope for making moralizing comparisons with one's own country, and room for political and religious comment. And as Mary Baine Campbell remarks, observations that would later come to be called ethnographic made some of their first appearances in forms of literature where the dividing line between fact and fiction was thin.[23] While these little ape-man books hardly count as prescriptive utopian literature,

they reflect in part many of the longstanding preoccupations of authors coming
face to face with new issues, here represented by Darwinism.

What of the future in other, more canonical texts? Imaginative literature
about humanity's power to transform the world commonly goes hand in hand
with disillusion and powerful critiques of the author's own society. The word
utopia entered the English language with More's book satirizing Tudor society –
an amalgamation of the Greek *ou* (not) with *topos* (place). This kind of satirical
commentary went on to flourish in the eighteenth century, when social prophets
looked forward and back, with profound doubts about what might constitute
a perfect society. Early-nineteenth century writings embraced the newly
scientific and industrial world, typified by Benjamin Disraeli's dystopia *The
Voyage of Captain Popanilla* (1827), whose main target was Benthamite
utilitarianism and competition as an end in itself, or John Trotter's *Travels to
Phrenologasto* (1829), which attacked phrenology's claims to understand human
behaviour. Later on, doubts about the current medical, scientific and
technological context were expressed in Edward Bellamy's socialist story *Looking
Backward* (1887); the buried beast in man was revealed in *Dr Jekyll and
Mr Hyde* (1886); and contemporary gender issues were exposed by Charlotte
Perkins Gilman in the female utopia of *Herland* (1915), or Sarah Grand's
syphilitic dystopia *The Heavenly Twins* (1893). Visions of the future in *The
Time Machine* (1895) and *Brave New World* (1932) were ambivalent and cynical.
Broadly speaking, all these novels carried obvious elements of warning.

Furthermore, disease and degeneration frequently stood as metaphors for
important issues. Sometimes this took the form of the literary trope that
society is sick at heart. Often it supplied the means to investigate the response
of a community to some perceived threat. The health/disease dichotomy
became a standard way of symbolizing the difference between an ordered
inside and disorder outside, the normal and the pathological, the usual and
the 'other'. Plato, for example, did not include doctors in his *Republic*. He
said it would be best if the unhealthy were left to die. Similar eugenic and
sanitarian sentiments were high on the agenda of most utopian writers. In
such scenarios it was often civilization itself that was thought to undermine
vitality and breed sickness. Alternatively, in looking forward to future
perfection, mankind would perhaps be so healthy that physicians would not
be necessary. This is the case in *Gulliver's Travels*, where the Houyhnhnms
have no concept of disease, or in *Herland*, where the women display classical
physical perfection.[24] Then again, the presence or absence of good health
could be used to indicate personality, social class or national origin. The
existence of some marked physical debility might signal social difference, or
that the individual is to be regarded as an outcast.

The idea of degeneration, then, was an important source of imagery for authors in the late nineteenth and early twentieth centuries. Not all of this imagery drew directly on Darwinian ideas. Indeed, a strong case might be made for understanding the ethos of the degeneration movement as essentially social and environmental in character, only loosely linked to contemporary ideas about natural selection. The key point is, rather, that degenerative literature drew extensively on science for its justification. The propertied classes in Europe and North America worried about crime, poor public health, declining national fitness, loss of imperial status and the future of the human race. Darwinists, to be sure, backed this up with hereditarian notions about the transmission of innate traits from generation to generation, and supported by the new discipline of eugenics initiated by Francis Galton, loudly asserted that humans were deteriorating [Figure 6].[25] Many felt that natural selection had stopped working in the human domain, and that medical science and public health policies were deliberately preserving the 'unfit': those who would, in a state of nature, be removed from the reproductive population. These anxieties interlaced with prejudice against decadent artists, criminals, militant 'new women', neurotics, drunkards, the insane and homosexuals. Such ideas were assimilated and

Figure 6. Eugenics poster, n.d. Reproduced by permission of the Galton Institute London. From the Eugenics Society Archives in the Contemporary Medical Archives Centre, Wellcome Library London.

deployed by writers in different ways. 'Degeneration' as a concept enabled many to articulate their hostility to the deviant, the diseased or the subversive.

It should not be forgotten, however, that another sub-genre arose in response to changing currents in biology. This was the tale of prehistory, the adventure story set in the remotest conceivable human past. In many ways, this type of tale blended well with those that explored degenerative themes. Sometimes the 'wild man' or feral-child theme was reworked as an imaginative response, however muddled, to the nineteenth century discovery of fossilized human remains such as the skull of Neanderthal Man. Sometimes authors took their heroes back into the ancestral past through the use of hallucinogenic drugs, or by sending them on a long journey to unexplored lands where an isolated prehistoric community is discovered. Jules Verne dispatched his voyagers to the centre of the earth; Arthur Conan Doyle propelled them into a lost world. The colourful and conventional historical romance had been a popular genre for a long time, at least since the days of Sir Walter Scott's *Ivanhoe* (1819) and Bulwer Lytton's *The Last Days of Pompeii* (1834), and there were French-language precedents – for example, an 1861 novel called *Paris avant les hommes* by Pierre Boitard. But in the English-speaking world, the tale of prehistory really got under way in the 1880s, inspired by the sciences of evolutionary archaeology and palaeontology. The ape-tales discussed here seem to fit very broadly into this genre as a form of retro-utopianism, invoking an idyllic return to the prehistoric past.

By contrast, Zola's novel *Docteur Pascal* (1893) is well known for openly discussing some of the main degenerative concerns of the day. Dr Pascal has given up his regular medical practice in order to investigate his own genealogy. He studies his ancestors' frequent instances of insanity and, to his mother's chagrin, monitors the 'mad' family members who are still alive, rather than conveniently hiding them away as a family embarrassment. He devises a serum (an 'elixir') from sheeps' brains, hoping that an injection of this substance will restore the nervous mental matter that he believes is lacking in his patients. One of the injections kills a man, and this failure leads Pascal to question the fundamental rationale of medicine. He ponders whether he ought instead to allow fate to take its course – in essence, whether doctors should interfere with natural events like disease at all: '*I doubt,* I tremble at the thought of my twentieth century alchemy, and end by believing that it is wiser, healthier not to thwart the natural evolution.'[26]

Zola's novels are sometimes read as literary equivalents to the hereditarian ideas of Cesare Lombroso and J B Morel. The latter, in his *Traité des dégénérescences de l'espèce humaine* (1857), systematically viewed insanity, alcoholism and criminality as hereditary disorders that led to sterility, imbecility and the extinction of the family line in a few generations. Evolutionary ideas, combined with fear of racial or national degeneration, increased the persuasiveness of these notions during the last decades of the nineteenth century. And *Docteur Pascal* certainly reflects Zola's interest in hereditary insanity and medical worries about degeneration. All the novels in the Rougon-Macquart series share a preoccupation with human type and its deterioration – what Zola called *la bête humaine*. Here and there it seems as if he were metaphorically exploring Lombroso's contemporary reworking of the idea of atavism, reversion to the beast.[27] The novel *L'assommoir* deals with the degenerative effects of alcoholism through the generations, *Thérèse Raquin* with unleashed sexuality. In *Docteur Pascal*, Zola examines very clear-sightedly the hereditary nature of mental illness, and whether it can be tempered at all by treatment or social and environmental factors. Another aspect of *Docteur Pascal* that reflects contemporary French medical research was the elixir that Pascal used to restore mental energy, derived from animal extracts. Hormones as such were not defined at that time, although the suggestion that extracts or macerations from the ovary and testes could have striking effects on the human body had been verified in the eighteenth century. When Zola was writing, this was one of the most exciting areas of experimental medical research. In 1889 the French physiologist Charles-Edouard Brown-Sequard was using extracts from horse testicles – first on himself, then on his patients – to restore vitality and virility. An elderly man who self-injected testicular extracts under Brown-Sequard's supervision famously improved his health and vigour. Interestingly, Zola's ideas in the round are therefore not as hereditarian as might be expected if he were a complete Darwinian. Instead, Zola regards the environment as an important degenerative factor that combines with human nature to spawn immorality and corruption. In modern terms, he is interested in the way environment interacts with heredity: whether one can rein in the other. Purely Darwinian tropes are relatively scarce in his work.

H G Wells's *The Time Machine* (1895) reiterates some of these concerns. Far into the future, the time traveller encounters human evolution run wild. Mankind has diversified into two: the surface-dwelling, effete race of Eloi, and the subterranean, meat-eating Morlocks. The narrator recoils from the discovery that the Morlocks prey on the Eloi for sustenance. Then the time machine takes him further forward to discover that the Earth is dying, barren except for grotesque crab-like beings and poisonous vegetation. As Wells's contemporary, William Thompson (Lord Kelvin) argued, the new theory of entropy dictated that the sun, the source of life, must come to a physical end. The time traveller returns to tell his astonishing tale to a party of assembled guests before embarking on one more journey, maybe never to return. Wells draws no moral, but the message is clear: Mankind as it was understood at the time, was doomed.

In his fiction Wells liked to project his protagonists to a distant standpoint – the moon, the future – where they could observe and comment on the normal world as outsiders. For Wells, the Eloi and the Morlocks were no doubt symbols of good and evil, supremacy and inferiority – or, more obviously, representatives of the elite, educated classes and the mob. Contemporary concepts of the mob were taking shape at that time, on occasion exacerbated by actual riots in London's streets [Figure 7]. And Wells, whose 'A Story of the Stone Age' (1897) envisages the crucial moment in human evolution as the invention of a 'new club' – a better means to cut and kill – certainly seems to have felt that fierce biological drives underlay modern society. The undoubted biological success of the Morlocks can be read either as Darwinism writ large or as Marx's victory of the proletariat.[28] But while the central tenet of Darwinism is principally natural selection and the extinction of the unfit, Wells, like Zola, also calls on non-Darwinian environmentalism. The social divisions of his day, he seems to be saying, if not corrected, will lead to a divided and disastrous future. Furthermore, Wells seems to envisage evolution as narrowing down. The wide diversity of the evolutionary past has become redundant. Race becomes binary, consisting of only Eloi or Morlocks, and the further the time traveller moves into the future, the more basic the inhabitants of the planet become, until they appear like 'foul, slow-stirring monsters'. Evolution, for Wells, does not necessarily result in progress.

Turning from degeneration to manly physical perfection, and from Europe to North America, some seventeen years later Edgar Rice Burroughs tapped

Figure 7. 'The Mob in St James' Street'. Unattributed illustration in *The Graphic*, February 13, 1886. British Library.

into a rich vein of the American psyche with the first *Tarzan* story in 1912.[29] Burroughs may have been influenced by Hendrika, the baboon-woman in Rider Haggard's earlier novel *Allan's Wife* (1889). Little more than comic-strip fantasy, his idea generated scores of sequels and spin-offs. Burroughs became extremely wealthy by making Tarzan one of the first registered trademarks in the world of entertainment.

The resourceful main character is the child of English aristocrats – the heir to the title and estates of Lord Greystoke. He is orphaned deep in the African jungle, and raised by a fierce she-ape. Tarzan grows up to be a man with the strength and courage of his fellow apes, a magnificent physique and the character of an English gentleman. In time, his intelligence makes him Lord of the Jungle. He learns to read and write, but cannot speak. Then civilized men enter the forest, and Tarzan is forced to choose between two worlds. Improbably, he meets a beautiful American woman, Jane Porter, and saves her from wild beasts. They are separated and, through a series of even more improbable events, he meets a Frenchman who teaches him about civilization. Thus equipped, Tarzan ventures forth to Baltimore to claim Jane. This, the first book in the series, ends with Tarzan honourably renouncing Jane and his inheritance so that she can marry the man to whom she is engaged – who turns out to be Tarzan's cousin, the new Lord Greystoke. Throughout, Burroughs emphasizes the virility, masculinity and near-godly abilities of his jungle hero. Sublimated sexuality, racial superiority and the frontier spirit are uppermost.

It is a book that is very much a product of its age: replete with bloodthirsty natives, effete aristocrats, murderous sailors, self-involved academics and a bulky, swooning American Negress; and haunted by roaring beasts with no regard to proper geographical location. A pulp masterpiece, it is of great interest for its stereotypical view of male perfection, and for contributing materially to the codification of that stereotype in Anglo-American culture. The imagery of manly physical perfection played an important role in American society at the turn of the century, in much the same way as the notion of 'muscular Christianity' was widespread in the fiction of nineteenth century England [Figures 8 and 9].[30] For Burroughs it evoked an earlier, less troubled time of pioneers pushing across America, dependent on their own ability to tame nature – an ideology underpinned by Social Darwinism and survival of the fittest. For Burroughs, it was civilization that created weaklings. Male and female bodies in this text therefore signify nationality, social position and race. It is unclear whether Burroughs was a eugenist and believed in controlled breeding for better bodies. Despite this his books encouraged jingoism about racial superiority supported by Darwinian principles of selection.

Figure 8. Front cover to an Italian edition of Edgar Rice Burroughs, *Tarzan the Untamable*. Illustration by F Fabbi, 1935. Mary Evans Picture Library.

Figure 9. Max Enger in classical pose, unattributed photograph from *La Culture Physique*, 1904. Wellcome Library London.

The authors discussed here concentrated on the most varied and extraordinary possibilities for the human race. They explored a range of alternative existences as seen from a contemporary perspective, including the extinction of life far in the future, the impossibility of reversing human decline, the senselessness of medical endeavour, and the possibility that we are little else but reconstituted apes, possessing an apeish inner nature that will come to predominate in the years ahead. While the cautionary and disheartening emotions behind these visions could surely have been experienced at almost any period in history, and no doubt do lie behind some of the most famous early projections of future worlds, it seems that the actual shape of these futuristic constructions, and the biological imagery that these authors employed, could have come about only in a late-nineteenth century Darwinian context, a context in which biology was already appropriating – or even demolishing – traditional intellectual domains like theology, and becoming the most authoritative medium for thinking about the human condition. Discussion and debate about natural selection and ancestry in an increasingly secular world threw the emphasis on to the future in particularly biologistic ways.

The bonds between biology, medicine and literature are therefore apparent in many areas. At root, each discipline tries to understand the human condition. A focus on futuristic literature in the post-Darwinian Anglophone world – in this case, texts that play with ideas of evolution and degeneration – allows consideration of the creative interplay between author and source materials, between popular science, imagination, real-life experience and the form in which these come together in print. Looking for connections between creative literature and biology opens the door to appreciating the personal, social, ethical, scientific and medical complexity of history in culture.

5

CLOSE ENCOUNTERS WITH A NEW SPECIES: DARWIN'S CLASH WITH THE FEMINISTS AT THE END OF THE NINETEENTH CENTURY

Griet Vandermassen, Marysa Demoor and Johan Braeckman

... with the dawn of scientific investigation it might have been hoped that the prejudices resulting from lower conditions of human society would disappear ... When, however, we turn to the most advanced scientific writers of the present century, we find that the prejudices which throughout thousands of years have been gathering strength are by no means eradicated. (Eliza Burt Gamble, *The Evolution of Woman*, 1894, p. vii)

When the American feminist Eliza Burt Gamble published *The Evolution of Woman: An Inquiry into the Dogma of her Inferiority to Man* (1894),[1] she was one in a long line of Victorian women intellectuals who decried the use of evolutionary theory to argue for female inferiority. Ever since the publication of Charles Darwin's *On the Origin of Species* (1859), evolutionary arguments justifying women's subordination had been circulating. Although Darwin himself barely mentioned human evolution in the *Origin*, and only briefly touched upon the subject of sexual selection, others were quite happy to expand on his theories and apply them to the 'woman question', defined by Helen

THE DARWINIAN THEORY—VARIATION FROM ENVIRONMENT.

Figure 10. Everard Hopkins, 'The Darwinian Theory – Variation from Environment'. *Punch*, June 18, 1892, p. 291.

Watterson in 1895 as 'first, the question as to woman's right to live in the world on the same terms as a man does ... and, second, the question as to woman's competence to do so'.[2]

This chapter attempts to address three issues. First, it wants to look at the ways in which Victorian scientists and intellectuals appropriated evolutionary theory to pronounce upon women's capabilities and women's rights. Second, it will glance at the disparate reactions of women intellectuals to the frequent undermining of feminist demands under the guise of scientific authority. And third, it will try to determine the role Darwin played in all of this.

Male Scientists on Female Inferiority

When it came to gender, many Victorian scientists were unable to think beyond the principle of separate male and female spheres that had emerged in the late eighteenth century, although they might hold progressive ideas on other subjects. The Victorian period was a time of 'hyperbolic gender difference',[3] with women and men seen not as part of a continuum, but as polar opposites. The view of man as an essentially competitive being, having to struggle in the amoral world in order to provide for his family, and of woman as an essentially caring, domestic being making home a peaceful place where he can come to rest, led scientists in their theories and in the interpretation of their 'evidence'.

When Darwin published his *Origin* in 1859, he did this in a social climate in which the woman question had become a matter of public concern. Property rights for married women, the right to education, and, in the mid-1860s, the franchise, were continuously debated by educated Anglo-American men and women. In this climate, with so much at stake in gender terms, Darwin's pronouncements on sex could hardly be neutrally received. Although the *Origin* does not speak out on humans, it does present the preliminaries of the theory of sexual selection as fully elaborated later in *The Descent of Man* (1871). Sexual selection, the reproductive competition between members of one sex, usually the males, for members of the other sex, leads to increasing gender specialization, Darwin argued. Some of his supporters immediately started teasing out the implications of this theory for human males and females. Not surprisingly perhaps, they generally tended to interpret it as evidence that women were, indeed, biologically inferior to men. By combining the findings from the new social anthropology with evolutionary theory, they 'demonstrated' that the subordination of women was a hallmark of civilization, since primitive societies were characterized by a near-equality of the sexes. The philosopher Herbert Spencer played an important role in this linking of anthropology and evolutionary theory. In *First Principles* (1862) evolution – and, hence, increasing gender difference – became a prescription. Feminist claims were misguided, in his view, since they hindered evolution.[4]

Many other influential works of the 1860s could be named in the same context. There is Carl Vogt's *Lectures on Man*,[5] which claimed that the development of woman's brain was stuck at the level of the child and the 'savage'; or Thomas Huxley's widely read essay 'Emancipation – Black and White' (1865). Huxley ambiguously defended women's right to education, because even then it would still be men who carried the day. Still – and unusually for male scientists in those days – the focus of his essay was much more on the necessity of equal rights for both sexes than on the bar that nature might have put to their equality:

> We reply, emancipate girls. Recognize the fact that they share the senses, perceptions, feelings, reasoning powers, emotions, of boys, and that the mind of the average girl is less different from that of the average boy, than the mind of one boy is from that of another; so that whatever argument justifies a given education for all boys justifies its application to girls as well.[6]

Although he agreed with the conviction of his times that women and 'primitive' people had smaller and simpler brains than white men did, Huxley was less sexist and racist than most of his male contemporaries. If we set him against his Victorian background, we might even call him a feminist.[7]

Darwin was influenced by the work of these and other authors. In the *Descent* he refers, for instance, to Vogt for his claim that women are physiologically and mentally more childlike than men. Writing about sexual selection in humans, he forsakes his usual scientific carefulness, drawing largely on anthropological accounts by fellow Victorians and, just like them, letting prejudice and Victorian values pervade his views. He writes unabashedly that, as a result of sexual selection, man has become superior to woman. Because our prehistoric male ancestors had to compete with rival males and had to hunt, as well as to defend females and children, they have inevitably become stronger and more intelligent than women: 'The chief distinction in the intellectual powers of the two sexes is shown by man's attaining to a higher eminence, in whatever he takes up, than can woman – whether requiring deep thought, reason, or imagination, or merely the use of the senses and hands.'[8] This bias in Darwin's sexual selection theory does not imply, however, that the whole theory is an ideological, patriarchal construct.[9] First, in proposing the importance of female choice of a sexual partner in many species, Darwin contravened the expectations of his male contemporaries regarding female agency – and, indeed, most of them rejected the idea of sexual selection.[10] '[I]ts valid action has to be proved', *The Quarterly Review* wrote.[11] '[W]e cannot refrain from an expression of regret that so vain a parade should have been made of the presumed effects of sexual selection', *The Athenaeum* countered.[12] Second, and most important, the theory of sexual selection had much more to offer to women than first thought. Since its major revival in the 1970s, and with the correction of male prejudice by (often women) biologists, its refined, modernized version has proved very fruitful scientifically, and an indispensable theoretical instrument for understanding the ultimate roots of gender difference.[13]

The publication of the *Descent* in turn lent a scientific aura to the large number of studies of the mental and moral differences between men and women that appeared in the 1870s and 1880s, such as comparative psychologist George Romanes's essay 'Mental Differences between Men and Women' (1887), and the highly influential *The Evolution of Sex* (1889) by the Scottish biologists Patrick Geddes and J. Arthur Thomson. The high degree of speculation, the heavy reliance on folk wisdom and the ideological bent of their theories make these and other late-Victorian works on sex differences decidedly unscientific to modern eyes, but, as historian of science Cynthia Russett explains, psychology at that time was still in its infancy, only just beginning to acquire some experimental and clinical grounding.[14] A comment such as that made by Romanes that 'it must take many centuries for heredity to produce the missing five ounces of the female brain'[15] was perfectly legitimate to most Victorians.[16]

Victorian Women Reply

In the nineteenth century, the influence of the social subordination of women seems to have been so strong that it was hard for people to question the premise that a person is so radically determined by his or her sex, and so radically different from the other sex, that women and men necessarily have to occupy separate spheres. Most Victorian women viewed the existing gender roles as entirely natural – as shown, for instance, by the many women who were willing to fight against female suffrage. They argued that women were too ignorant and too weak for that task and insisted, moreover, that getting embroiled in politics would impair women's typically feminine moral sensibilities.[17]

Those who demanded increased opportunities for women, such as Florence Nightingale, the British antivivisectionist Frances Power Cobbe, feminist freethinker Harriet Martineau and the British journalist Eliza Lynn Linton, often viewed this enlarged female role within the confines of the biologically determined female sphere: that of teaching, medicine and social service.[18] Julia Wedgwood, suffragette and Darwin's niece, took a similar view, asking to give the natural feminine qualities, such as a taste for beauty and a feeling of responsibility for the young, their due respect, because without women, men would not be able to learn these qualities.[19] George Eliot, an ardent Darwinian, was concerned with the cultural and intellectual restrictions to which women were subjected, but she was not a feminist, and her female characters did not reflect her personal life as an independent woman.[20] In her later novels Eliot applied sexual selection theory in her own idiosyncratic way: it is often the women, not the men, who choose their partner and make their choices. Strong women characters such as Dorothea Brooke in *Middlemarch* and Gwendolen Harleth in *Daniel Deronda* determine the course of their lives, even if they sometimes err. Eliot wanted to demonstrate that although humanity as a species is governed by the laws of evolution, individual human beings are to some extent unpredictable. This is a crucial modification of the then predominant essentialist notions about women. By comparison, we might look at the views held by Iosefa Ioteyko, a Polish feminist residing in Belgium, some three decades later. Ioteyko made a scathing analysis of the inconsistencies in the evolutionary explanation of presumed female intellectual inferiority as advanced by the Belgian child psychologist Medard Schuyten. The finding of greater intellectual variability in men than in women, for instance – a finding then generally regarded as 'proof' that males were the more active element – tells us nothing about the average man's intellect, Ioteyko argues. Espousing sexual difference, she makes a plea for regarding the sexes as equivalent.[21] In 1862, Clémence Royer, a Frenchwoman living in Geneva, provided the first French translation of the *Origin*, supplying it with a long anticlerical preface and rewriting parts to fit her own ideas – to Darwin's great dismay.[22] Being the major disseminator of Darwinian ideas to a French-speaking audience, she was also highly critical of the male-dominated scientific establishment. 'Up until now,' she declared in 1874, 'science ... has too often considered woman as an absolutely passive being, without instincts or passions or her own interests; as a purely plastic material capable of taking any form given her without resistance ... Woman is not made like this.'[23]

Our apelike ancestry was cunningly played out by feminist women writers to advance their cause. Whereas Henry Rider Haggard's dazzling and immortal queen Ayesha shrivels into a monkey at the end of *She* (1886) – seemingly entailing the message that, fundamentally, feminist demands for power and equality are absurd – monkeys served more undermining purposes in the work of the Spanish Emilia Pardo Bazán and the British Marie Corelli. Through her fiction and her essays, Pardo Bazán, the most important woman writer of nineteenth century Spain, tried to instil a feminist consciousness in her readers. In one of her splendid, surprisingly modern short stories, 'Piña' (1890), she uses the behaviour of the monkeys Piña and Coco to draw attention to the problem of physical violence against women – a problem that was rarely addressed in those days. In 'The Oldest Story' (1893) she offers a delightful revision of the story of Genesis, suggesting that woman's subordination is not divinely or biologically ordained, but the result of her having been brainwashed into believing that she is inferior.[24] In her essay 'Coward Adam', popular writer Marie Corelli scorns men for blaming their own lack of will on women, just as Adam did with Eve when she, unselfish as she was, wanted to share her apple with him. 'She *had* thought him a man, – and when he suddenly changes into a monkey, she doesn't understand it.'[25] But Woman, superior as she is, is now beginning to claim her rights. She should take care not to want to imitate Man, who is but a vain animal who wants to be admired: 'Like the peacock, he struts forward and spreads out his glittering tail.'[26]

Women Rewriting Darwin

Most feminists thus seem to have been content to argue that women's qualities were not inferior to men's, just different and complementary, and to ask that these qualities should be equally valued in society. Feminists who made evolutionary theory a source of radical liberation for women were few. In what follows we will concentrate on the work of four feminists who reinterpreted the work of Darwin, Spencer and other evolutionists to more subversive ends: Antoinette Brown Blackwell (1825–1921), Eliza Burt Gamble (1841–1920), Charlotte Perkins Gilman (1860–1935) and Olive Schreiner (1855–1920).[27]

It is important to add that these women did not draw on the work of Darwin alone. Evolutionary theory in the late nineteenth century was, to many people, a mixture of the work of Darwin, who stressed the primacy of the mechanisms of natural and sexual selection, neo-Lamarckian theories, explaining evolution by the inheritance of acquired characteristics, and the work of Spencer, who was more a Lamarckian than a Darwinian. Spencer also thought that evolution inevitably entailed progress and that, therefore, it was our duty not to thwart its course. Those who wanted to apply evolution to social behaviour could thus pick and choose from these and other theories the aspects that appealed to them ideologically, then construct their own theoretical framework. Furthermore, there was Darwin's own ambivalence in his writings on sexual selection, as well as the fact that, strictly speaking, Darwinian theory can be used to accommodate almost *any* political line of reasoning. Indeed, in the late nineteenth century it appealed to socialists as much as to defenders of *laissez-faire*. It just depends on what elements you prefer to focus on in Darwinian theory: cooperation or competition.

A number of feminists and social radicals, such as Alfred Russel Wallace,[28] argued that the subjugation of women was thwarting sexual selection, since women were no longer in a position to choose their mates freely; therefore the future of humanity was endangered. This was the course taken by Charlotte Perkins Gilman in her bestseller *Women and Economics* (1898), and in her subsequent *The Home: Its Work and Influence* (1903). Olive Schreiner, a socialist like Gilman, developed a similar line of argument in *Woman and Labour* (1911), a book that was also widely acclaimed.[29] Both authors emphasized the values of love, altruism and cooperation in the evolution of our species, and both twisted the conventional biological wisdom of their time to their own ends.

Woman, Gilman argued, is the natural worker, because of her motherhood. When man started subjugating her, she could no longer choose her own marriage partner, and hence could no longer do what she had always done: improve the race by going for the right marriage. Her subjugation was a necessary step in human evolution, however, because it was through this process that man learned to love and to take care of his family. And because of his passion and energy, the race could reach a higher stage in intellectual and cultural evolution. Now, however, this process has become deleterious, because woman, by being dependent on the male, has been forced to overdevelop her femininity, and has become weak and ignorant as a result. She is in a state of arrested development: since she is overprotected and shielded from external stimuli, natural selection can no longer act on her:

Man, in supporting woman, has become her economic environment ... [I]n her position of economic dependence in the sex-relation, sex-distinction is with her not only a means of attracting a mate, as with all creatures, but a means of getting her livelihood, as is the case with no other creature under heaven. Because of the economic dependence of the human female on her mate, she is modified to sex to an excessive degree.[30]

Under these circumstances, woman can no longer develop the common humanity that she shares with the male. The women's movement, according to Gilman, is an evolutionary sign that the time has come to restore the proper role of women as workers and sexual selectors. In *The Home* she cleverly deconstructs all the myths about traditional home life, showing that it is harmful to both women and men, and advancing a passionate plea for the professionalizing of the household, which she considers 'savage'.[31] Only when they are freed from domestic tasks will women be happy.[32]

Like Gilman, Schreiner argues that it is unnatural for women not to step out into the world to work. Women have always been natural labourers – they were the ones who fed and nurtured the race, whereas men fought. But men have robbed them of their ancient domain of social labour, making woman's condition today that of a parasite. Woman is reduced 'to the passive exercise of her sex functions alone'.[33] It is as a result of not being able to exercise all her human functions that woman is restless and prone to all kinds of ailments, not because she is inherently biologically weak.

Quite rightly Schreiner has concluded that when it comes to inherent psychological differences between the sexes, 'it is exactly as we approach the sphere of sexual and reproductive activity, with those emotions and instincts connected directly with sex and the reproduction of the race, that a difference does appear'.[34] Therefore it is obligatory that women should be able to defend the interests of their sex when it comes to matters of sexuality, such as prostitution and adultery, because men will not do it for them. And, for the sake of humanity, all opportunities should be open to women, because only then can man and woman progress together, as they should.

Whereas many of their contemporaries interpreted nature as sanctioning traditional sex roles, Gilman and Schreiner came to the opposite conclusion. Their arguments drew heavily on the neo-Lamarckian supposition that social change would effect biological change and on other ideas which we now know to be wrong, such as the progressist belief that humans are inevitably advancing towards higher civilization. But what is important is that they taught their public that the evolutionary wisdom of the time did not necessarily imply that feminist aspirations were 'unnatural'.

Less influential was the work of two of their precursors: Antoinette Brown Blackwell and Eliza Burt Gamble. Especially in the case of Blackwell this is a pity, for not only was she the first woman to provide an elaborated critique of Darwin's sexual selection theory; her line of reasoning was also the most scientifically sound. Her book *The Sexes Throughout Nature* (1875), which appeared four years after the *Descent*, starts by pointing out that a scientist tends to see everything in the light of his own convictions, and that, therefore, scientific theories should always be scrutinized by others before being accepted as true. The problem with Darwin's and Spencer's theories is that their views are limited by their sex: females have fallen out of perspective. Blackwell then proceeds to analyse some of Darwin's and Spencer's arguments and evidence, and to identify instances of male bias in their line of reasoning. For all male secondary sexual characteristics that Darwin describes, there are equally important corresponding traits in females. The net effect of these complementations leads to sexual equality. The precise character of these complementary characteristics is advanced more as a hypothesis. As she says, the facts need careful investigation: 'Let science investigate the whole subject quantitatively. It may be found, process for process, in detail and in totality, that the average woman is equal to the average man. By all means let the sexes be studied mathematically.'[35] In evolution Blackwell finds a basis for demanding more freedom for women because women cannot exercise all their evolved human faculties within the confines of the home.

The Sexes Throughout Nature is primarily a critique and a deconstruction; it does not really offer a new theory. It is more narrowly aimed at the field of evolutionary biology than the other books considered here, and less a work of social philosophy. To be sure, Blackwell, too, makes excursions into the realms of ideology – for example, when she says that evolution dictates that men, not women, should prepare the food. And, like the others, she is very Victorian in her tentative description of male and female qualities, women having 'risen above' the 'animal sexual passions' that still predominate in men.

Darwin does not seem to have read this book; and in 1894, when the second major feminist attack on his theories of female inferiority, *The Evolution of Woman* by Eliza Gamble, was published, he had already been dead for twelve years. This book did not cause much of a stir either. Attempts like these to radicalize sexual selection theory received little attention from feminists and Darwinians alike.[36] Yet Gamble's book was the first ever defence of female *superiority* based on Darwinian arguments – this was probably why it got mixed reviews.[37] In her subversive interpretation of Darwin's sexual selection theory, Gamble argues that his evidence shows the existence of female superiority on all levels of organization. The female, she says, is more stable than the male, and has no need for conspicuous and useless ornamentation like the males of so many species. Therefore she has more energy for the development of a higher intelligence, and a more refined physiological and mental structure. It is in her that, thanks to her maternal instincts, the social instinct and the moral sense originated. The male principle, by contrast, is destructive and egoistic. If women were freed from the unnatural restrictions imposed upon them by men, they would reemerge as the dominant sex, and sexual choice would once again become their prerogative, as it was in prehistoric times.

Historian of science Evelleen Richards has argued that feminists like Blackwell and Gamble were trapped by their belief in science once a biological basis for mental differences between the sexes had been established. The only recourse left to them was to challenge claims about female inferiority, rather than to dispute the innateness of these differences.[38] Whereas it is certainly true that these women (and men) were caught up in a Victorian world-view, and that their views might be called 'biological determinist', leaving hardly any room for environmental influences, the unarticulated assumptions behind this kind of argument are disputable. Surely the well-established role of culture and socialization in human behaviour does not preclude the role of biological factors. Indeed, the evidence for an interactionist framework is by now overwhelming.[39]

Darwin and Women's Emancipation

Darwin very probably would not have been convinced by Gamble's arguments. Yet his views were much more congenial to feminist aspirations than those of many of his contemporaries. Indeed, Darwin was not a typical Victorian patriarch at all. Thus he supported the vote for women, a view which was adamantly opposed by some prominent intellectual women under the leadership of Mary Humphry Ward. He also advocated education for women. '[I]mprove the women (double influence) & mankind must improve', he had written in his notebook in 1838. And when, many years later, women were admitted to the 'Little-Go' and Tripos examinations at Cambridge – although they could not get a degree – he reacted with enthusiasm.[40] Yet certain presuppositions about women's mental capabilities were probably too deeply ingrained – even for the gentle Darwin – to allow for rebuttal. Moreover, Darwin seems to have been rather conservative in other respects: he opposed contraceptives for fear of female promiscuity, and he liked 'real women': pretty, soft and caring creatures; he did not long for self-assured intellectual equals.[41] His interpretation of the appropriation of female sexual choice by men in modern societies as a sign of evolutionary progress also testifies to his male bias.

In short, Darwin succeeded in being a revolutionary *as well as* an old fogey. The fact that evolutionary views of female inferiority became so widespread in late-Victorian society can, however, hardly be blamed on him. Scientists, both real and phoney, had tried throughout the century to prove the inferiority of the female sex on the basis of so-called scientific observations (lighter brains, the influence of female reproductive organs etc.). Darwin's theory merely compounded those viewpoints, and was used and abused thereafter by antifeminists to serve their own purpose.

Many feminists would probably stand perplexed at the Australian feminist Elizabeth Wilson's urge that they should 'find 12$ to buy a copy of *The Origin of Species*, as it may turn out to be one of the most important feminist texts you will read'.[42] Although this is an overstatement, it has a certain truth to it. Darwin's theory of evolution is, after all, essentially a theory of becoming, of variation and change, of the constant interaction between an organism and its environment, of the ways in which we are all sites of identity and difference. Darwin might not have meant his theory to be feminist, but neither did he mean it to be antifeminist. He just wanted to understand the workings of nature. And we, knowing now where he seems to have been wrong or prejudiced, can only try to learn from his insights as well as his mistakes.

Acknowledgements

We would like to thank Laura Otis for bringing the work of Emilia Pardo Bazán to our attention.

MUTUAL AID, A FACTOR OF PETER KROPOTKIN'S LITERARY CRITICISM

Carol Peaker

'Of no man in Europe are more diverse opinions held than of Prince Kropotkin', wrote Edith Sellers in *The Contemporary Review* in 1894:

> To one section of society he is the Red Flag personified; to another he is the Sermon on the Mount incarnate. Some even of those who know him well are convinced that by nature he is a poet, and that he passes his days indulging in beautiful dreams; others, equally well able to judge, maintain that he is a scientist pure and simple, with no thought beyond the verification of his theories; others again declare that he is a revolutionist of the most dangerous type, one whose sole aim in life is the destruction of everything the orthodox hold dear.[1]

Today Kropotkin's reputation has achieved some consolidation. He is widely recognized as a Russian aristocrat who relinquished privilege and fortune to become Europe's leading anarchist theorist; the successor to Proudhon and Bakunin; and 'one of the fiercest opponents of all governments and national states' in the late nineteenth and early twentieth centuries.[2] It is not surprising, however, that to Edith Sellers in the *Contemporary Review* and to other commentators at the *fin de siècle*, Kropotkin defied easy classification. Besides his articles and books on anarchy, intellectuals in Britain (where he settled in 1886) would also have come across his writings on geology, chemistry, Ibsen, prison conditions in Siberia, and his childhood as the tsar's page. In the 1890s, a Londoner might have signed up for one of his evening courses in biology at the University of London.[3] In 1901, an American might have attended one of the eight lectures he gave to packed theatres, while visiting Boston, on the subject of Russian literature. As much at ease preaching anarchist-socialism to Russian Jewish refugees at grimy workers' meetings in East London as he was accepting toasts made in his honour at the prestigious Royal Geographical Society,[4] Kropotkin was indeed a man with diverse talents.

Notwithstanding the staggering range of his intellectual output, however, whether he was discussing metaphysics, espousing revolution or pillorying Zola, Kropotkin seemed always to express a holistic and contiguous vision of the world. Like Comte's Positivism, Spencer's Synthetic Philosophy, or Marx's communism, Kropotkin's anarchism was concerned with the unity of *all* realms of human life – from the physiological to the cultural to the ethical to the political. In this chapter, I sketch out some of the links between Kropotkin's ideas about biology, history, social reconstruction and aesthetics. In particular, I demonstrate that Kropotkin's theory of human sociability and altruism, as expressed in his book *Mutual Aid, a Factor of Evolution*, not only provides the basis to his entire theory of anarchism (as has been suggested by several Kropotkin scholars),[5] but also lies at the heart of his aesthetics and his literary criticism.

Kropotkin's Evolutionary Narrative

In February 1888, Kropotkin read an article in *Nineteenth Century* by Thomas Huxley entitled 'The Struggle for Existence: A Programme'. The piece vexed him greatly. Responding to the overpopulation and squalor of 1880s England, Huxley put forward the case for a Malthusian concept of the natural world as a ceaseless competition among too many animals for too few resources. In this struggle, only the fittest survive. 'From the point of view of the moralist,' Huxley writes, 'the animal is on about the same level as a gladiator's show. The creatures are fairly well treated, and set to fight – whereby the strongest, the swiftest, and the cunningest live to fight another day.'[6] Huxley proposes that without the state to counterbalance man's innate competitive instincts, humankind is little different from the animal kingdom:

> [A]mong primitive men, the weakest and stupidest went to the wall, while the toughest and shrewdest, those who were best fitted to cope with their circumstances, but not the best in any other sense, survived. Life was a continual free fight, and beyond the limited and temporary relations of the family, the Hobbesian war of each against all was the normal state of existence.[7]

To Kropotkin, Huxley's understanding of evolutionary processes was 'atrocious' – not least because, by arguing that in the 'struggle for life' one must either fight or perish, it created a biological underpinning for the ideologies behind the capitalist state and imperialism.[8] As he comments in his *Memoirs*, '[t]here is no infamy in civilized society or in the relations of the whites towards the so-called lower races, or of the "strong" towards the "weak", which would not have found its excuse in this formula.'[9] Clearly, if Huxley's doctrine were true, the anarchist conception of a society based on voluntary agreement was jeopardized. Over the next six years, Kropotkin developed a countervailing evolutionary narrative in a series of articles which appeared in *Nineteenth Century*. In 1902, these articles were expanded and published in *Mutual Aid, a Factor of Evolution*.

So what does Kropotkin mean by mutual aid? In contradistinction to Huxley's gladiator's show, Kropotkin sees in the animal world infinite signs of sociability, kindness and cooperation. He talks about the lack of self-interest among bees in their hives and ants in their colonies. He quotes the then famous observation of Captain Stansbury, who, on his journey to Utah, discovered a blind pelican being kept alive by other pelicans upon fish 'which had to be brought from a distance of thirty miles'.[10] He describes his own experience at Brighton Aquarium, where he stood watching in astonishment as big Molucca crabs attempted to set to rights a comrade which had landed on its back.[11] To Kropotkin, the mainspring of mutual aid is animal sociability: a sociability he sees in the mass migrations of birds, the 'villages' of beaver lodges along the banks of rivers and lakes, and the huddling together of sheep for mutual warmth. It is this sociability which makes identification among members of a species possible, and leads to cooperation and compassion. And it is a species' facility for cooperation, not mutual struggle, that makes it strong. Providing an alternative reading of Darwinian evolution, Kropotkin notes: 'the fittest are not the physically strongest, nor the cunningest, but those who learn to combine so as mutually to support each other, strong and weak alike, for the welfare of the community'.[12]

Unlike Huxley, then, for whom the state was constructed by man as a necessary defence against the destructive effects of mutual struggle, Kropotkin establishes society and cooperation as traits *anterior* to man's appearance on the evolutionary timeline, and places moral development on a continuum with animal sociability. As he turns to humans, Kropotkin argues that mutual aid has existed since the earliest epoch: 'savages' lived in small clans and tribes, sharing food and caring for one another; their successors, the 'Barbarians', formed communities or villages, where land was owned and tilled in common, and poor families were aided by their better-off neighbours.[13] A highpoint in human social evolution was the medieval city, where community, mutual support and common aims found expression in craftsmen's guilds, co-jurations and fraternities. In modern times, mutual aid could also be seen in workers' unions, the organization of socialist newspapers, and the fishermen's Lifeboat Association, whose crews consisted of volunteers ready to sacrifice their lives for the rescue of complete strangers.[14]

What impedes the growth of the mutual-aid principle and the progressive evolution of humankind in Kropotkin's own epoch is the centralized military state. (And this is the crux of Kropotkin's anarchist philosophy.) As the European state began consolidating its power in the fifteenth century, it gradually stamped out the guilds and mutual-aid institutions of the Middle Ages. Centralized authorities endorsed the systematic seizure of common lands, removed the people's agency, replaced community with competition, and forced labour into a condition of degradation.[15] By the late nineteenth century, the result is a largely dehumanized society in which 'every one for himself, and the State for all' was the fashionable individualistic creed of the day:[16] 'while in a savage land, among the Hottentots, it would be scandalous to eat without having loudly called out thrice whether there is not somebody wanting to share the food, all that a respectable citizen has to do now is to pay the poor tax and to let the starving starve'.[17]

While Kropotkin clearly regards mutual aid as a primal instinct and sees in his own age manifold signs of a decaying society, he nonetheless believes in evolutionary progress. Yet his formulation of history suggests that it follows a cyclical rather than a linear design. During each stage in man's social evolution – from the tribal clan to the medieval guild – the principle of mutual aid is elaborated, resulting in a more complex and variegated society. This forward movement, however, is punctuated with periods in which mutual-aid institutions are 'invaded by parasitic growths, and thus become hindrances to progress'.[18] The principle of mutual aid lies dormant until it is resurrected by means of popular revolt, leading to further progress: 'Each time', Kropotkin writes, '... that an attempt to return to this old principle was made, its fundamental idea itself was widened. ... It was also refined'.[19] For Kropotkin, revolt, in the form of popular movements, is a manifestation of the repressed instinct of mutual aid striving to reassert man's natural cooperative tendency. By claiming revolutions through the ages as agents of evolutionary progress, Kropotkin thus inverts Huxley's portrayal of anarchy and rebellion as signs of an atavistic regression towards 'chaos' and 'the brute struggle for existence'.[20]

While Kropotkin never once uses the word 'anarchism' in *Mutual Aid*, the book's relentless antistatist message marked it instantly as an anarchist classic,[21] and so it has remained. Its message is clear: if humankind is to evolve in a positive direction, what is needed is an anarchist revolution – the reorganization of society along lines which offer the fewest impediments to the further development of mutual aid in all spheres of life. The connections he makes between social renewal and biological evolution evoke the neo-Lamarckian conception of the evolutionary mechanism, to which he (and many others at the *fin de siècle*) subscribed.[22] In this system, the action of the environment upon parents directly affected the traits inherited by their offspring. Kropotkin evidently believes that a society with mutual-aid institutions will – by improving the morale and well-being of the greater population – result in the inheritance of better traits. As he concludes *Mutual Aid*: '[i]n [mutual aid's] wide extension, even at the present time, we … see the best guarantee of a still loftier evolution of our race'.[23] Like the ants and termites who have 'renounced the "Hobbesian war", and … are the better for it',[24] so too will humanity, once it has renounced competition and egotistic individualism, find both life and progeny improved.

Kropotkin's Aesthetic Narrative

Kropotkin was by no means alone in drawing connections between socio-economic conditions and the production of art. Indeed, in arguing that both good and bad art are environmentally determined, he was preceded by William Morris, John Ruskin, Oscar Wilde, Max Nordau and many others. The criticism of these figures and the general ethos of 1890s London, in which Kropotkin fashioned the bulk of his social theory, contributed much to his own ideas about aesthetic progress and decay. Morris's idealization of a medieval past, Ruskin's belief that great art was simply incompatible with any viciousness of intent, Wilde's emphasis on the artist's need for freedom from the tyranny of the marketplace, Nordau's fears of cultural as well as biological degeneration – all these threads find their way into Kropotkin's own views about art. Also present in Kropotkin's aesthetics are signs of his Russian heritage: in particular, the theory of 'social command' in art as elaborated by the nineteenth century literary critics Belinsky, Dobrolyubov and Chernyshevsky. Nor can we ignore the influence of Marx's ideas about art, though Marxism, as a whole, was a theory Kropotkin decried. Yet underlying Kropotkin's aesthetics is the principle of mutual aid – its presence in society fostering artistic creativity, its absence leading to an art which is hollow. Mutual aid also figures in Kropotkin's conception of revolutionary art – an art whose virtue lies in its capacity for eliciting sympathy with the downtrodden, and awakening man's consciousness of the mechanisms of oppression.

Kropotkin's reading of cultural history in *Mutual Aid* follows the same pattern as his evolutionary narrative. His theory is that good art can be produced only in a society in which there are cooperative institutions, shared values and plenty of scope for the expression of the 'communal genius'. In the two chapters in the book he devotes to the medieval city, he draws a direct line between the instinct of sociability, the organization of the city into guilds and brotherhoods, and the creative realization of the communal genius in architecture:

> Mediaeval architecture attained its grandeur ... because it was born out of a grand idea. Like Greek art, it sprang out of a conception of brotherhood and unity fostered by the city. ... A cathedral or a communal house symbolized the grandeur of an organism of which every mason and stone-cutter was the builder, and a mediaeval building appears – not as a solitary effort to which thousands of slaves would have contributed the share assigned them by one man's imagination; all the city contributed to it. The lofty bell-tower rose upon a structure, grand in itself, in which the life of the city was throbbing. ...[25]

Kropotkin takes care to emphasize that such 'grand results' found their inspiration 'not in the genius of individual heroes, not in the mighty organization of huge States or the political capacities of their rulers', but in guilds – mutual-aid institutions of common aspiration and shared labour.[26] In an earlier work of anarchist propaganda, *The Conquest of Bread*, Kropotkin discovers the same 'grand idea', the same unity between artist and citizen, in Renaissance churches.[27] Nor does the mutual-aid principle only vivify the decorative arts or architecture, 'a social art above all'.[28] It is present in the poetry of Dante and the language of the Bible.[29] And it can also be discovered in the medieval Russian sagas, which are 'imbued with a communal spirit ... characteristic of Russian popular life'.[30]

Contrasted with this *living* art, which manifests the cooperative ideal both in its execution and in its sentiment, is the stultified, languishing art which is produced in the conditions manufactured by the centralized state. Kropotkin derides contemporary architecture for containing nothing of 'the people': the Paris iron tower, he says, is 'a meaningless scaffold'; London's Tower Bridge is 'a sham structure in stone intended to conceal the ugliness of an iron frame'.[31] In *The Conquest of Bread*, he echoes Europe's widespread despair with the age's art: 'From all sides we hear lamentations about the decadence of art'; today 'art seems to fly from civilisation!' and 'inspiration frequents artists' studios less than ever'.[32] The explanation he gives for this degeneration in art is the demise of sociability, that necessary precursor to mutual aid and an art which expresses a collective intelligence. In the centralized state, '[t]he town is a chance agglomeration of people who do not know one another, who have no common interest, save that of enriching themselves at the expense of one another'.[33] Art is produced not for use and appreciation by the public but for the self-aggrandizement of the artist, whose highest hope is to have one of his canvases hung in a gilded frame in 'a museum, a sort of old curiosity shop'.[34] Art in Kropotkin's day is motivated by competition, not cooperation. It is no longer a vivifying ideal, but a commodity.

Perpetuating this dismal state of affairs, of course, is the insidious ideology of the capitalist state, which pervades all cultural production: history books, annals and scientific tracts, as well as poetry and fiction. It is from these deadly tomes, rather than from life, that the bourgeois artist (alienated through privilege from his labouring brothers), draws his inspiration. Yet their 'predilection for the most dramatic aspects of history' means that these books contain but a one-sided view of reality: 'They hand down to posterity the most minute descriptions of every war, every battle and skirmish, every contest and act of violence ... but they hardly bear any trace of the countless acts of mutual support and devotion which ... makes the very essence of our daily life – our social instincts and manners.'[35] In *Mutual Aid*, Kropotkin complains of the painters and poets infected with this spirit, who direct their attention not to their fellow man, but towards 'the sort of heroism which promotes the idea of the State':

> ... they admire the Roman hero, or the soldier in the battle, while they pass by the fisherman's heroism, hardly paying attention to it. The poet and the painter might, of course, be taken by the beauty of the human heart in itself; but both seldom know the life of the poorer classes, and while they can sing or paint the Roman or the military hero in conventional surroundings, they can neither sing nor paint impressively the hero who acts in those modest surroundings which they ignore. If they venture to do so, they produce a mere piece of rhetoric.[36]

'Heroic' art and literature do not strike one as being central features of the nineteenth century canon, and Kropotkin does not furnish any examples. He may have been referring to French Neoclassicism or state-sponsored poetry: Tennyson's *Ode on the Death of the Duke of Wellington* comes to mind. In any event, it is clear that to Kropotkin, art about wars and heroes feeds the same elitist myth, the same cult of individualism, as Huxley's interpretation of the 'survival of the fittest'. It strengthens the notion of history as a perpetual struggle, glorifies the conqueror, and reinforces the idea of the exceptional individual as the true and necessary agent in human history.

In *The Conquest of Bread*, Kropotkin describes a future post-revolutionary society in which all art would express the communality of labour and ideals. In this utopia, even the production of literature would be a collective endeavour, no longer compromised by the crass dictates of the marketplace. Poets would be compositors and typesetters, and printers would know how to write: 'all having become producers, all having received an education that enables them to cultivate science or art, and all having leisure to do so – men would combine to publish the works of their choice, by contributing each his share of manual work'.[37] In this mutual-aid society, where art and industry would be linked 'by a thousand intermediate degrees', 'the works of … artists who will have lived the life of the people, like the great artists of the past, will not be destined for sale. They will be an integrant [sic] part of a living whole that would not be complete without them, any more than they would be complete without it.'[38]

In the meantime, however, there is only one way artists can reinject the principle of mutual aid into art. In a tract written during his early, rabble-rousing days as a propagandist, Kropotkin appeals to artists everywhere: 'You poets, painters, sculptors, musicians, if you understand your true mission and the very interests of art itself, come and place your pen, your pencil, your chisel, your ideas at the service of the revolution.' Art, he advises, should poke holes in the ideological fabric of the centralized state by performing the function of social criticism. It should 'show the people what is ugly in present-day life', while indicating 'the causes of that ugliness', and teach us 'what a rational life might be if it did not have to stumble at every pace because of the ineptitude and the ignominies of the present social order'.[39] In a society where mutual aid is not permitted to flourish, art must have an educative and moral role. But it must also work to reintegrate society, to overcome the divisions and mutual alienation that have grown up out of the state system. Kropotkin urges artists to join the revolution not as 'masters', but as 'comrades in the struggle, not to govern, but to draw … inspiration from a new environment, not so much to teach as to conceive the aspirations of the masses, fathom and formulate them, then … with the full vitality of youth, to incorporate them into life itself'.[40] Only by operating in the 'service of society' can art express 'the communal genius', and usurp the ideology of the oppressive state.

Mutual Aid and Kropotkin's Literary Criticism

How art which is invested with the principle of mutual aid can advance revolutionary aims is more fully developed in Kropotkin's *Ideals and Realities in Russian Literature* (1905). This volume, the outcome of a series of lectures Kropotkin delivered on the subject in 1901 at the Lowell Institute in Boston, represented a lifetime engagement with literature. As a child in Russia, Kropotkin copied out by hand the second book of Gogol's *Dead Souls* for illicit circulation. He also started up a 'monthly review' (with two subscribers, himself and his tutor) in which he published verses, and his own novelettes – often with social themes. In his youth he assiduously studied the writings of radical Russian critics, who then, as now, were regarded as the intellectual forebears of the Russian revolutionary movement. Having lived in a repressive autocracy where censorship was draconian, Kropotkin was well attuned to literature's potential to inflict small lashes on the legitimizing ideologies of the state. It is no surprise that in *Ideals and Realities*, Kropotkin identifies the nineteenth century Russian realist tradition as the model to date for progressive or revolutionary art.

According to Kropotkin, Russian realism both expresses and, in so doing, extends the principle of mutual aid by engaging in social inquiry: the investigation of all realms of Russian social life and the pressing political questions of the day. The Russian realist addresses subjects like '[t]he evils of serfdom ... the struggle between the tiller of the soil and growing commercialism; the effects of factories upon village life, the great cooperative fisheries, ... slum life and tramp life'.[41] In the course of his investigations, he attempts to penetrate the fabric of society, to expose the underlying relations between classes, and to reveal the impact of social conditions upon man and of man upon his social environment. 'A good work of art', Kropotkin affirms, 'gives material for discussing nearly the whole of mutual relations in a society of a given type'. Kropotkin ascribes to the poet a role equal to that of the scientist. Both push forward mankind's comprehension of reality: '[I]n the last analysis every economical and social question is also a question of psychology of both the individual and the social aggregation. It cannot be resolved by arithmetic alone. Therefore, in social science, as in human psychology, the poet often sees his way better than the physiologist. At any rate, he too has his voice in the matter'.[42]

Such investigation promotes mutual aid on all sorts of levels. For one, it uplifts writers by bringing them into contact with people who are not part of their inherited social milieu – writers like the novelist Uspensky, who grew up in a large industrial town in the family of a small functionary, but realized, after making an ethnographical study of the villagers of Northern Russia, the 'moral forces of land cultivation and communal life, and of what free labour on a free soil might be'.[43] The incorporation of fisherman, peasant, factory worker or slum-dweller into mainstream literature also constructs a bond of sympathy between the privileged reader and the downtrodden. It provides a form of sociability, if only in the abstract. In short, it lays the psychological foundations for future acts of mutual aid. In practical terms it can accomplish a great deal. As Kropotkin writes,

> ... the novels of Grigorovitch exercised a profound influence on a whole generation. They made us love the peasants and feel how heavy was the indebtedness towards them which weighed upon us – the educated part of society. They powerfully contributed towards creating a general feeling in favour of the serfs, without which the abolition of serfdom would have certainly been delayed for many years to come.[44]

Social inquiry in literature also challenges the legitimizing state ideologies of 'mutual struggle' and competition. Literature which investigates the common man readjusts our understanding of the forces behind history, shifting the emphasis away from the hero or military general as history's principal mover, and empowering the 'shapeless crowd'. In a chapter on folk-novelists, Kropotkin extols the merits of the folk poet Ryeshétnikoff, whose fiction contains no heroes whatsoever: no 'demoniacal characters', no 'Richard III, in a fustian jacket', no 'Cordelia', not 'even a Dickens' "Nell"'. Ryeshétnikoff's men and women are exactly like thousands of other poor men and women. But by virtue of their astonishing feats of endurance in the course of their daily struggle for the next crust of bread, Ryeshétnikoff proves that they are *all* Titans in their own right.[45] In his discussion of *War and Peace*, Kropotkin praises Tolstoy for portraying Napoleon as an 'ordinary' man, and showing that 'the success of an army depends infinitely more upon its number of [brave artillery officers] than upon the genius of its higher commanders'.[46] Kropotkin, above all, exalts Gorky for his sketches, not of heroes, but of 'the most ordinary tramps or slum-dwellers'; men and women who are truly 'submerged', and who yet exhibit the most extraordinary individuality, strength and spirit.[47] The sort of lowly heroes Kropotkin finds in Russian literature are no mere losers in the gladiatorial arena, but future citizens of an anarchist utopia. Neither are they degenerate proletarians or regressive 'primitive' races living on the outskirts of Christian civilization in need of governmental policing. Kropotkin's workers, soldiers, peasantry, and mountain Cossacks are a vitalizing and moral force, dreaming of the day when 'we, once "the poor", shall vanish, after having enriched the Croesuses with the richness of the spirit and the power of life'.[48]

Needless to say, the sort of social inquiry Kropotkin sees dominating Russian literature is not at all like the 'anatomical' works of French Naturalists like Zola. Russian authors dispel illusions, whereas the French Naturalists merely produce a skewed vision of reality, limiting their 'observations to the lowest aspects of life only'. 'Degeneracy', writes Kropotkin, 'is not the sole nor dominant feature of modern society, if we look at it as a whole. Consequently, the artist who limits his observations to the lowest and most degenerate aspects only, and not for a special purpose, does not make us understand that he explores only one small corner of life.'[49] Nor do Russian writers confine their realism to exacting pictorial reproductions of the world around them. In his early tract 'To the Young', Kropotkin derides those artists (again presumably French) who 'strive to represent a drop of dew on a leaf like a photograph but in colour, or to imitate the muscles of a cow's rump, or to represent meticulously … the suffocating mud of a sewer or the boudoir of a lady of love', thinking all the while that they have realized a new art form.[50] Russian writers, in contrast, employ the same inductive-deductive method which Kropotkin sees in *Modern Science and Anarchism* as engendering a 'universal awakening of thought'. They look *below* the surface of reality to reveal ontological truths about society's inner structure and dynamic. Zola is to Tolstoy what a photograph album is to *The Origin of Species*.

What allows Russian authors to promote higher ideals while remaining true to scientific reasoning is their concern for the well-being of humanity. In *Modern Science and Anarchism*, Kropotkin states that the anarchist-scientist must always have in mind the question: '*What social forms best guarantee in such and such societies, and in humanity at large, the greatest amount of happiness, and therefore the greatest sum of vitality?*'[51] In *Ideals and Realities* he finds this concern everywhere: 'for us,' he writes, 'realism must have a more elevated back-cloth'; the Russian poet must always have in mind '[a] higher aspiration, [and] noble ideas which can help to make us better'. Kropotkin points to Gogol as an early practitioner of this form of idealistic realism: Art, in Gogol's conception, is a torch-bearer which indicates a higher ideal. 'His art was pure realism, but it was imbued with the desire of making for mankind something good and great.'[52]

If the practice of this realism with higher aims promotes mutual aid in real life, it also has a snowball effect within the literary canon. Much of Kropotkin's book traces the ever-increasing presence of mutual aid in Russian literature and, correspondingly, the progressive evolution of Russian novelistic and dramatic forms. Pushkin, by adopting the language of the people, frees Russian literature from its Classical tethers; Gogol introduces the social element into the canon; early folk novelists bring educated society into direct intercourse with the toiling masses; the later folk novelists introduce a higher conception concerning the duties of art in the representation of the poor; Tolstoy and Gorky reveal the artificialities of so-called civilized life. At each stage of Russian realism's development, more and more holes are pierced in the ideological fabric of the state. But it is also clear in *Ideals and Realities* that the Russian canon is only a half-trodden pathway to a much higher ideal for art. The literature of Russia, Kropotkin suggests, is not yet equivalent to birdsong, the medieval spires of Nuremberg, or the basilica of the Renaissance. Despite its high-minded social aims, it cannot shake off its bourgeois roots. It was written largely by the rich for the rich. 'Take the mass of excellent works that have been mentioned in this book,' writes Kropotkin. 'How very few of them will ever become accessible to a large public!' Towards the end of *Ideals and Realities*, Kropotkin calls for a new art: an art grounded in common assent and positive faith, an art which speaks to and for all. What is 'really wanted', he writes, is 'truly great Art, which, notwithstanding its depth and its lofty flight, will penetrate into every peasant's hut and inspire everyone with higher conceptions of thought and life'.[53]

7

THE SAVAGE WITHIN: EVOLUTIONARY THEORY, ANTHROPOLOGY AND THE UNCONSCIOUS IN *FIN-DE-SIÈCLE* LITERATURE

Paul Goetsch

Introduction

In *The Unconscious Before Freud*, L L Whyte argues: '... the idea of unconscious mental processes was, in many of its aspects, conceivable around 1700, topical around 1800, and became effective around 1900'.[1] This thesis is supported by developments in English literature. Although the unconscious mind has fascinated writers since Antiquity, it was the Gothic novelists and the Romantic poets who concerned themselves with unconscious mental processes – 'whatever they be: organic or personal tendencies or needs, memories, processes of mimicry, emotions, motives, intentions, policies, beliefs, assumptions, thoughts, or dishonesties'.[2] This interest abated somewhat during the period of Victorian realism. It was, however, given a new lease of life at the end of the nineteenth century, as the revival of Gothic fiction indicates.[3] This was due to various factors: for instance, new studies in psychiatry and psychology, the contemporary fad of the occult and the widespread belief that civilization was only a thin veneer easily disrupted by irrational forces in man, the beast or savage within.

In this chapter, I will discuss one of these factors: evolutionary anthropology. Since the relationship between Darwinism and Victorian literature has been well documented,[4] I will confine myself to describing how evolutionary anthropology influenced writers' treatment and interpretation of the unconscious. In any study of the relationship between contemporary thought and the depiction of the unconscious, two caveats are necessary. Writers respond imaginatively, and often highly selectively, and eclectically, to scientific theories and ideas. Normally they are more interested in achieving narrative effects than in reproducing scientific assumptions faithfully. Besides, they cross over into unconscious territory far more easily than psychologists would allow; when they plumb the depths of the unconscious, their works are often more remarkable for their 'shallowness' than anything else.[5] Lacan, for one, warns against a blurring of the difference between the popular and the Freudian unconscious: 'Freud's unconscious is not at all the romantic unconscious of imaginative creation. It is not the locus of the divinities of the night.'[6]

In this study, the popular or literary unconscious will be the centre of attention. After a brief introduction to evolutionary anthropology, I will show how contemporary ideas influenced the narrative conventions of dealing with the unconscious.

Evolutionary Anthropology

The Darwinian revolution had a great impact on anthropology and ethnology. It effected 'a shift from traditional ethnological, comparative philological, or historical orientation towards a more systematically "developmental" point of view'.[7] This manifested itself in the socio-cultural evolutionism advocated by Lubbock, Tylor and others.

Accepting the Darwinian assumption of the antiquity of man, the Victorian anthropologists gathered data from contemporary and older cultures. Wherever evidence was scarce, they reasoned backward from modern times, for instance, by comparing contemporary indigenes with prehistoric men and women. Searching for universals, they constructed a pattern of evolution according to which all cultures had progressed from so-called savagery to civilization.

John Lubbock maintains in *Origin of Civilization* (1870) that 'the human mind, in its upward progress, everywhere passes through the same or similar phases'. Since man, even in the savage state, does not act without reason, Lubbock posits that the most distinct races of man have 'independently raised themselves' from 'utter barbarism', to develop 'higher and better ideas as to Marriage, Relationships, Law, Religion, etc'.[8]

Sharing Lubbock's belief in progress, in *Primitive Culture* (1871) E B Tylor attempts to reconstruct the evolution of civilization by analysing the so-called survivals, those 'processes, customs, opinions and so forth, which have been carried on by force of habit into a new state of society from that in which they had their original home'.[9] Tylor compares his study of the details of culture with Darwin's research on the species of plants and animals, and argues that traces of various stages of evolution can be found in the present. Human development, he believes, results from the 'exercise of purely human faculties in purely human ways', and can therefore be described as mental evolution.[10]

Tylor's *Primitive Culture* proved highly influential. So did the doctrine of survivals, which was developed further by John MacLennan and others. Consequently, folklore, myths, ancient social customs and institutions were taken seriously as evidence of the progress of civilization. At the same time, contemporary 'savages' were no longer marginalized as 'the degenerate offshoots, the waifs and strays of mankind'.[11] Instead, they were treated as representatives of the distant past of civilization. While this integration of 'savages' into the evolution of civilization was an advance on older views, the Eurocentric bias of evolutionary anthropology had problematic implications. Stocking observes:

> In the beginning, black savages and white savages had been psychologically one. But while white savages were busily acquiring superior brains in the course of cultural progress, dark-skinned savages had remained back near the beginning ... their assumed inferiority of culture and capacity now reduced them to the status of missing links in the evolutionary chain. Their cultural focus, although at the centre of anthropological attention, had still only a subordinate interest. One studied these forms not for themselves, or in terms of the meaning they might have to the people who created them, but in order to cast light on the processes by which the ape had developed into the British gentleman.[12]

This implicit racism, which came out into the open in a number of works written by Social Darwinists and imperialists, was only one of several problematic aspects of evolutionary anthropology. Other problems included its emphasis on universals and neglect of cultural differences, its progressive direction and, last but not least, the terminology of 'savagery' and 'primitivism'.[13]

Of these limitations late-Victorian writers were, if at all, only partly aware. They knew, however, that the model of progressive evolution had been challenged by some Darwinists as well as by cultural pessimists. As H G Wells put it: '... human nature has not changed in any significant way from the "Stone" age'.[14] Moreover, writers were familiar with contemporary worries and fears concerning the rapid modernization of England, the degeneration of people's health, the atavism of criminals and others. In this context, they found some of the ideas of the cultural evolutionists useful when depicting both the external social world and the psychic reality of their characters.

Traditional Representations of the Unconscious

Traditionally, the difficulties in representing the unconscious have been overcome with the help of a number of narrative devices: these include mapping the unconscious metaphorically and concentrating on mental states such as reveries, dreams and nightmares, introducing fantastic plot elements that seem to open up an irrational world, and employing characters who mirror what goes on in the protagonist's psyche.[15]

The unconscious is usually defined as a dark *terra incognita*, hardly accessible to the light of reason. Ever since the Renaissance, the exploration of unknown countries has been compared to a journey into the unconscious. In *Religio Medici* (1642), Thomas Browne speaks of the 'Cosmography of my self', and asserts: '... wee carry with us the wonders, we seake without us: There is all Africa, and her prodigies in us; we are that bold and adventurous piece of nature, which he that studies, wisely, learns in a compendium, what others labour at in a divided piece and endless volume.'[16]

In 1804, the German writer Jean Paul identified the unconscious not only as the seat of passions and emotions but also as the home of the creative imagination: 'The unconsciousness is really the largest realm in our minds, and just on account of this unconsciousness, the inner Africa, whose unknown boundaries may extend far away.'[17] When late-Victorian writers dealt with the influence of colonial settings on the representatives of the West, they were drawn to the traditional concept of inner Africa.

In *Heart of Darkness* (1899), the doctor who examines Marlow before the latter leaves for Africa predicts the action's direction when he says that the changes which travellers to Africa undergo take place on the inside. Consequently, Marlow's journey into the jungle is also one into the self, or an archetypal 'night journey into the unconscious'.[18] The impenetrability of the jungle can be associated with the resistance of the unconscious to the light of reason. Marlow's geographical and moral disorientation is expressed by his fever and the nightmarish features of his journey, while the unsettling influence of the environment points to temptations from within. A number of characters illuminate Marlow's psychic development. The most important one is Kurtz, who, for Marlow, is not so much a real person as a voice, a shade, a double with whom he has to struggle if he does not wish to succumb to the wilderness without or the irrational within.

Other popular spatial concepts were the urban labyrinth, underworld, or nocturnal city. This symbolism was made available to late-Victorian writers in works such as *Oliver Twist* (1837–9) and *Bleak House* (1852–3), in later urban Gothic fiction,[19] and in various late-Victorian studies of the London slums. The East End, in particular, appeared to contemporary social critics as Britain's Africa, as a place where one ran the risk of going native. Whereas a naturalist like George Gissing focused on the external social reality of London's slums (*The Nether World*, 1889), Robert Louis Stevenson saw Mr Hyde's excursions into Soho and the East End rather as illustrations of mental states and processes (*The Strange Case of Dr Jekyll and Mr Hyde*, 1886). Soho, for instance, is said to resemble 'a district of some city in a nightmare'.[20] References to uncanny, frightening events abound. Late at night, respectable gentlemen appear in unlikely places. The self-division of Dr Jekyll corresponds to the dualistic character of his house, and the contrasting images of daytime and nocturnal London.

While Stevenson and Conrad, like other *fin-de-siècle* writers, resort to traditional techniques of representing the unconscious, they also use insights from evolutionary anthropology to characterize their unknown countries.

Anthropologizing the Unconscious: Stevenson

Stevenson's debt to contemporary thought is evident in his description of Mr Hyde. Dr Jekyll's second self is a horrifying and revolting creature that seems at home in nocturnal London, invades Mr Utterson's dreams, and comes alive not only after Jekyll has taken the drug, but also later when Jekyll lies in bed asleep. Repeatedly, Stevenson tells the reader that as a monster Hyde defies classification. Nevertheless, he draws upon four discourses to circumscribe his nature.

In moral and religious terms, Hyde represents evil and is likened to the devil. Jekyll desperately tries to lay the burden of blame on Hyde, but he is forced to admit that, due to the 'perennial war' among his 'members',[21] he dwelt with pleasure on the idea of separating these elements and acquiring a second self for a while.

Stevenson's characterization of Hyde also invokes Darwinian discourse. At the end of *The Descent of Man* (1871), Darwin argues that 'with all his noble qualities ... Man still bears in his bodily frame the indelible stamp of his lowly origin'. And yet he asserts that man may hope 'for a still higher destiny in the distant future'.[22] Stevenson challenged this optimism. He once called man an 'ennobled lemur', and wrote: '... nowadays the pride of man denies in vain his kinship with the original dust. He stands no longer like a thing apart.'[23] In *The Strange Case*, Stevenson attributes 'apelike' fury, spite and tricks to Hyde, comparing his movements in the laboratory to those of a monkey and his dismal screech to 'mere animal terror'. For Jekyll, Hyde is the animal within him, which is 'drinking pleasure with bestial avidity from any degree of torture to another', and 'licking the chops of memory' afterwards.[24]

As an animal-like being that pursues unnamed pleasures and disregards other people's needs, Hyde also resembles a savage. Utterson speculates that Hyde might be 'something troglodytic'. Stevenson mentions Hyde's snarling 'savage laughter', and compares his indifference to Jekyll to the way a mountain bandit remembers 'the cavern in which he conceals himself from pursuit'. In this context, one of Hyde's most striking characteristics is that he provokes savage reactions in others. The fact that he tramples on a girl like a Juggernaut, transforms the women who gather quickly in the street into wild 'harpies' who are ready to lynch him. Both Enfield and a doctor who has been called to the scene quell their desire to kill Hyde, and threaten to ruin his reputation instead.[25]

Since Hyde centres on 'self',[26] he is a pre-social barbarian rather than a 'savage' who represents the first stage of civilization's evolution. In *Prehistoric Times* (1865), a book written before his evolutionist turn, John Lubbock defines the barbarian as follows: '... the true savage is neither free nor noble; he is a slave to his own wants, his own passions; ... hunger always stares him in the face, and often drives him to the dreadful alternative of cannibalism or death'.[27] Thanks to Jekyll's money, Hyde does not go hungry, but he is no doubt the slave of his wants and lusts. Some of his actions – trampling on a child, murdering Sir Danvers, and smiting a woman who offers him a box of matches – recall the features which Herbert Spencer associated with the moral character of primitive man or the inferior races: 'impulsiveness', the 'sudden ... passing of a single passion into the conduct it prompts', frequently brutal behaviour to women, a thoughtless absorption in the present, lack of restraint, justice and mercy.[28] Spencer's *First Principles* (1862–99) may also have been an important source for Stevenson's account of Jekyll's transformation into Hyde.[29] By taking the drug, Jekyll shakes 'the very fortress of his identity', and releases the 'lower elements' in his 'soul' – that is, dwarfish, selfish Hyde, the embodiment of man's primitive ancestors.[30]

A fourth kind of discourse Stevenson taps for his portrayal of Hyde is the medico-criminological one.[31] Utterson, his clerk and Dr Lanyon call Jekyll's sanity into question. For the greater part of the story, however, it is Hyde who is linked to both crime and insanity. Like Lombroso's criminals, he is branded as an outsider because of his physical appearance (even though his deformities remain undefined). Eager to distance himself from his second self, Jekyll registers Hyde's crime against the girl with disgust, and declares that 'no man morally sane could have been guilty of that crime upon so pitiful a provocation'.[32] A witness to the murder of Sir Danvers testifies that Hyde resembled a madman in his sudden outbreak of anger.

Discussing hatred and anger, Darwin states in *The Expression of the Emotions in Man and Animals* (1872):

> Dr Maudsley, after detailing various animal-like traits in idiots, asks, whether these are not due to the reappearance of primitive instincts. ... He adds, that as every human brain passes, in the course of its development, through the same stages as those occurring in the lower vertebrate animals, and as the brain of an idiot is in arrested condition, we may presume that it 'will manifest its most primitive functions, and no higher functions'. Dr Maudsley thinks that the same view may be extended to the brain in its degenerated condition in some insane patients: and asks, whence come 'the savage snarl, the destructive disposition, the obscene language, the wild howl, the offensive habits, displayed by some of the insane? Why should a human being, deprived of his reason, ever become so brutal in character, as some do, unless he has the brute nature within him?' The question must ... be answered in the affirmative.[33]

Darwin's statement conveniently illustrates that the discourses Stevenson employs are closely related to each other. As a monster, Hyde resembles an ape or other beasts, an ignoble savage, or a criminal and madman. These negative evaluations point to a 'strong conservative strain' in the story,[34] a revulsion from the findings propagated by contemporary evolutionists. This revulsion is expressed most dramatically when Jekyll, at the very moment of his transformation into Hyde, notices that his hand is turning 'corded and hairy'.[35]

Obviously, Stevenson does not share the evolutionist belief in moral progress. He shows Jekyll's regression to primitivism and the resulting disintegration of his personality. Although Jekyll, Utterson and the other narrators attempt to impose a moral framework on the action, they never quite succeed. All the bachelor gentlemen in the story lead double lives, and seek pleasure in odd places and at odd times.[36] For instance, one may well wonder why Sir Danvers accosts Hyde on a London street late at night. Even the minor characters – the women-harpies mentioned above, the woman who solicits Hyde in the middle of the night, and the girl who is sent for the doctor at three o'clock in the morning – point to facets of urban life which Stevenson hesitates to unveil fully.

Like Wilde's *The Picture of Dorian Gray* (1890), Stevenson's story is triggered off by the assumption that social conventions stand in the way of individual development, and enforce a problematic repression of one's emotions and instincts. Since Dr Jekyll does not wish to stifle his 'gaiety of disposition' completely, he begins to lead a double life early on in his professional career.

Out of a sense of shame, and because of his social ambitions, he keeps his 'irregularities' a secret.[37] In the course of time, he seems to reach a limit beyond which his constitution can no longer 'comply with the demands of civilization'.[38] He is persuaded of the duality of man's nature, and experiments on himself. At first he experiences the transformations into Hyde as liberating: 'I felt younger, lighter, happier in body; within I was conscious of a heady recklessness, a current of disordered sensual images running like a mill race in my fancy, a solution of the bonds of obligation, an unknown but not an innocent freedom of the soul'.[39] In *Civilization and its Discontents* (1930), Freud traces the 'urge for freedom' that is directed against the 'demands of civilization' back to the remains of people's 'original personality, which is still untamed by civilization'.

After a while, Jekyll feels shocked at the development of his second self. In Freud's terminology, Jekyll now pays a price for the advance of civilization: 'a loss of happiness through the heightening of the sense of guilt'.[40]

> The pleasures which I made haste to seek in my disguise were ... undignified; I could scarce use a harder term. But in the hands of Edward Hyde they soon began to turn towards the monstrous. ... This familiar that I called out of my own soul, and sent forth alone to do his good pleasure, was a being inherently malign and villainous ... .[41]

Finally, the ego is no longer master in its own house. Whether Hyde kills Jekyll or Jekyll commits suicide is left open; the story ends with the mutual destruction of both parts of the personality. This outcome strongly suggests that Jekyll's experimental self-division is the 'original crime' that costs him his humanity.[42]

The Strange Case exemplifies how evolutionary anthropology and related disciplines were put to effective use in Gothic fiction. Stevenson's story anticipated and influenced novels such as *The Picture of Dorian Gray*, *Dracula* (1897) and *The Hound of the Baskervilles* (1902). While *Heart of Darkness* is not entirely without Gothic traits, it deals with evolutionary theory and anthropology more extensively and systematically. Hence it clearly reflects what Griffith has called the anthropological dilemma: the fact that anthropology undermined the very idea of progress which it had set out to propagate.[43]

Anthropologizing the Unconscious: Conrad

In a famous passage, Conrad describes Marlow's river journey as follows:

> Going up that river was like travelling back to the earliest beginnings of the world, when vegetation rioted on the earth and the big trees were kings. An empty stream, a great silence, an impenetrable forest. The air

was warm, thick, heavy, sluggish. There was no joy in the brilliance of sunshine. The long stretches of the waterway ran on, deserted, with the gloom of overshadowed distances. On silvery sandbanks hippos and alligators sunned themselves side by side.[44]

This journey to origins seems to have been inspired by Darwin's revelation that the world is 'infinitely larger, wilder and less anthropocentric' than had previously been assumed.[45] Conrad's description also responds to the vastness of the timescale that evolutionists had insisted on in their studies of the history of the earth, the development of species and the progress of civilization. In this connection, a brief comparison with Thomas Hardy, another writer steeped in evolutionary theory, may help to define Conrad's approach more precisely.

Like Thomas Hardy in *Tess of the d'Urbervilles* (1891), Conrad moves freely between the present, earlier historical periods and prehistoric times. He suggests parallels between modern colonialism and the Roman conquest of England and compares modern London to Central Africa. Like Hardy, he draws upon socio-cultural evolutionism to articulate his views on civilization, primitive life and progress. In *Tess*, Hardy takes his point of departure from Tylor's hypothesis that the European peasantry constitutes a link between primitive and modern civilized man. He patiently depicts traditional ways of life, cultural survivals and the impact of modernization.[46] Conrad's approach is different. It is true that he provides sufficient details from his experiences in Africa and his reading to anchor his story in the colonial history of the Congo in the 1880s and 1890s. Yet he is not particularly interested in documenting long-term processes. One reason for this is his radical critique of colonialism. Whereas Hardy records the gradual erosion of agricultural communities in Wessex, Conrad focuses on the disastrous results of imperialism. He fails to discover functioning traditional societies in Africa. Instead, he observes that tribal societies have been destroyed by slavery and the colonial exploitation of the native workforce. Marlow passes many abandoned villages, and comes across many uprooted migrant workers as well as starving or dead Africans. The only tribes he mentions have been relocated to the camps near Kurtz's station. Marlow is appalled by the heads on the stakes under Kurtz's windows, by the unspeakable rites the savages and Kurtz engage in, and by the Africans' utter subservience to Kurtz's rule. Above all, he is shocked at the fact that Kurtz allows himself to be revered as a god, and has thus 'entered into a final state of self-deception'.[47] Kurtz has not assisted the Africans in advancing on the ladder of evolution. Instead, he has taken them a few steps farther down with him.[48] He has disrupted their culture, and sacrificed his humanitarian ideals to his greed for ivory, his desire for power and – as the presence of his black mistress suggests – his sexual lust. Symbolically, he has been transformed into a ravenous mouth that seeks to devour the earth and all its inhabitants.[49] The emissary of light, civilization and imperialism is unmasked as a cannibal.

In this connection, Conrad mentions time and again that Kurtz has succumbed not so much to the influence of the foreign environment as to the primitive darkness within his psyche.[50] As Marlow states: 'I tried to break the spell – the heavy, mute spell of the wilderness – that seemed to draw him to its pitiless breast by the awakening of forgotten and brutal instincts, by the memory of gratified and monstrous passions.'[51]

Conrad's story, then, focuses on the confrontation of Europeans with stereotyped Blacks, the wilderness and themselves. Marlow's journey is to a large extent a surrealistic and symbolic one. The Congo is never mentioned by name, but is simply identified as a serpentine river. Likewise, Central Africa is more or less reduced to a jungle, a stream and a few colonial stations. Many allusions to Homer, Virgil and Dante characterize the country as an underworld, a Hades or an Inferno. Ultimately, the heart of darkness is a symbolic setting that can be located not only in Africa and European countries, but also in the human psyche.[52] It is a place where the beat of the drum is at times confounded with the beating of one's heart.[53] Like Wells's *The Island of Dr Moreau* (1896), Conrad's evolutionary story shows representatives of European civilization regressing to earlier stages of social and mental evolution. One of them, Kurtz, degenerates morally and psychologically; the other, Marlow, succeeds in returning to civilization, but has learned to question its principles.

Conrad's debt to evolutionary anthropology has been well documented.[54] So has the influence of contemporary discourses of degeneration, imperialism and racism. The controversy initiated by Chinua Achebe's charge that Conrad was a racist has not yet subsided.[55] To my mind, Conrad criticizes both the concept of progressive evolution and modern imperialism. He demonstrates that binary oppositions such as savage culture/civilization, whiteness/blackness, European/African are highly questionable. In doing so, however, he does not simply reverse the usual patterns, so that 'darkness means truth, whiteness means falsehood'.[56] Nor does he, as some of his defenders suggest, completely subvert the discourses of which he makes use. Like Marlow, Conrad reproduces racist stereotypes and questionable Spencerian and other evolutionist notions; he remains caught in the discourses which he partly deconstructs.[57]

Marlow's journey into Africa and the unconscious is a journey through an epistemological and linguistic crisis.[58] During this crisis, the Eurocentric terms, definitions and values with which Marlow is familiar are rendered problematic. This is reflected by his changing images for Africans. Especially at the beginning of his journey, Marlow romanticizes the natives, and seems to assume that they are well adapted to their primeval environment. Later, he regards them as cannibals and barbarians, and is inclined to follow pre-Darwinian anthropology in treating them as pre-social Stone Age 'primitives'. The more he realizes how undisciplined and immoral the invaders from Europe are, the more he sympathizes with the victims of colonialism. He recognizes his fundamental kinship with the Africans. In the terminology of socio-cultural evolutionism, he also acknowledges their potential for higher development.[59] For instance, he attributes restraint, one of his key values, to his helmsman and other cannibals. On the other hand, he realizes that Kurtz, as well as he himself, is capable of jettisoning European values altogether.[60] By interpreting Kurtz's last words, 'The horror! The horror!', as a moral victory over the forces of darkness, Marlow embraces civilization as a sustaining fiction or illusion,[61] even though he has learned that very little separates civilized men from barbarians, or individual consciousness from the darkness within.

The group of gentlemen to whom Marlow addresses his account resembles that of Stevenson's *The Strange Case*. But what Marlow has to offer is not only a cautionary tale about civilization and its discontents. Marlow and, more radically, Conrad doubt that civilization is a dependable stay against chaos and darkness. Marlow attacks the complacency of his friends, who are 'moored with two good addresses, like a hulk with two anchors, a butcher round one corner, a policeman round another, excellent appetites and temperature normal'. Thus, he hopes to drive home the point that the civilized self is a cultural construct.[62] Both Marlow and Conrad foreground the violence with which civilized people set out to colonize and subject others, and they associate the savage within the European chiefly, though not exclusively, with what Freud called 'the aggressive or destructive instincts'.[63] From this perspective, Kurtz anticipates Freud's 1933 comments on the motives of men going to war:

A lust for aggression and destructiveness is certainly among them: the countless cruelties in history and in our everyday lives vouch for its existence and its strength. The satisfaction of these destructive impulses is of course facilitated by their admixture with others of an erotic and idealistic kind. When we read of the atrocities of the past, it sometimes seems as though the idealistic motives served only as an excuse for the destructive appetites; and sometimes ... it seems as though the idealistic motives had pushed themselves forward in consciousness, while the destructive ones lent them an unconscious reinforcement. Both may be true.[64]

Conclusion

Evolutionary anthropology and its offshoots – Spencerian sociology, Social Darwinism, degeneration theory – exerted a great influence on realists and naturalists. They provided explanations for social conflicts, and phenomena such as crime and the coexistence of civilized and atavistic traits in modern society.

At the same time, evolutionary anthropology encouraged writers to leave realism behind and explore the psychic reality of characters in Gothic fiction, fantasies, evolutionary romances and other genres. Judging from the works of Stevenson, Conrad and other authors, socio-cultural evolutionism made writers emphasize the archaic content of the unconscious – that is, primitive desires and aggressions. It helped writers to account for atavistic regressions and the self-destructive potential within human beings. Apart from Kurtz and Dr Jekyll, Hardy's Tess and Conrad's Winnie Verloc (*The Secret Agent*, 1907), both of whom become guilty of murder, may be mentioned as examples.

Evolutionary anthropology also stimulated writers to explore the need as well as the dangers of self-discipline and restraint. While criticizing civilization and its demands, the late-Victorian authors were still too much under the influence of negative evaluations of primitive life by Darwin and others to romanticize primitivism as an alternative way of life. It is true that Hardy stresses the therapeutic value of Tess's immersion in the agricultural community at Talbothays, but he then shows that she cannot fully return to a state which she has outgrown mentally and psychically. She is alienated both from society and from nature. Dorian Gray may play the hedonist and give in to his libidinal wishes even more than Stevenson's Hyde, but he ultimately destroys himself, too.

All in all, evolutionary anthropology promoted an inward turn in late-Victorian fiction that can be regarded as an important step in the direction of the stream-of-consciousness novel and the reception of Sigmund Freud in modernist fiction. If the *fin-de-siècle* writers seem to have anticipated Freud in some respects, this is largely due to the fact that Freud, whom Ernest Jones once lauded as the Darwin of mental life, also responded to evolutionary thought when he began to map the 'internal foreign territory' of the mind.[65]

8

HOMER ON THE EVOLUTIONARY SCALE: INTERRELATIONS BETWEEN BIOLOGY AND LITERATURE IN THE WRITINGS OF WILLIAM GLADSTONE AND GRANT ALLEN

Annette Kern-Stähler

Did Homer see red? Not 'red' as in the charging bull incensed by the toreador's red cloth; but was he physically able to see the full spectrum of the colours of the rainbow? Or, if he was blind, as legend has it, one may wonder whether his contemporaries were so too? The question may seem purely academic – or not even that, in our day. Yet in the nineteenth century, the origin of the colour sense was an intriguing mystery in whose solution scientists and philologists alike engaged. Indeed, the question of origins (of nations, of species, or of languages) was a predominant concern of the imaginative mind, and in their retrospective activities, philologists and evolutionary biologists shared a common interest. The 'new' comparative philology, which provided a genealogical model of language, in particular lent itself to comparisons with the Darwinian theory of evolution. Scholars of both fields assumed divergent speciation from a common progenitor, as represented (in both areas) by the branching tree, and both focused on relics of the past – be they words or fossils.[1] Linguistic forms shared by a set of contemporaneous languages are to the comparative philologist what common characteristics of species are to the evolutionary biologist, and fragments of dead languages are to the comparative philologist what fossils are to the evolutionist.

However, the interrelations between both disciplines went deeper in that literature, for obvious reasons the subject of philological scrutiny, became the source material also for the anthropological inquiry into the otherwise mostly inaccessible past of human ideas. As early as 1835, Richard Garnett, in his review of some of the lexicographical landmarks of his time, highlighted the usefulness of the new philology to this end, which he ascribed to the assumption that 'a scientific acquaintance with a language cannot fail to throw some light on the origin, history and condition of those who speak or spoke it'.[2] A repository of language, literature was consequently considered well qualified to remedy the inadequacy of material evidence for the exploration of the history of processes in the human mind.

Considered to be among the oldest surviving corpora of literature, the Iliad and the Odyssey quite naturally enjoyed much attention in the academic search for origins. Both poems proved to be invaluable, for instance, for the historical analysis of the development of human sense perception, a subject which ranked high on the academic agenda, not least because of its ramifications with a view to determining the place of humankind in nature. Among the sensory perceptions, the colour sense was the most controversial. Goethe, in his Farbenlehre (1810), observed: 'There has always been a certain danger in discoursing upon colours; to such an extent that one of our predecessors even dares to utter: If one shows a red cloth to a bull, it will become enraged; but the philosopher, if one even talks about colour, begins to rave.'[3]

Given its status as evidence of the historical development of human sense perceptions, it is not surprising that the battle of colours was also fought over classical literature. It is my purpose to explore in this chapter a particular skirmish in this larger battle. My interest is focused less on the merit of the arguments exchanged than on the interrelations of biology and literature inherent to the scholarly texts in question, which discuss the Homeric poems as an illustration of a stage in the development of human sense perceptions. In the first part, I will concern myself with a particular debate about the Homeric use of colour epithets engaged in by William Gladstone and Grant Allen. Their discussion of the development of human colour perception, enacted in various publications between 1858 and 1884, is a particularly intriguing example of the interrelations between biology and literature in the nineteenth century. In the second part I propose to inquire into the interactions of the two fields in questions of aesthetics as they appear in Grant Allen's evolution of aestheticism.

The Development of the Colour Sense

Research into the perception of colours, among humans and animals, made remarkable progress in the nineteenth century. This is witnessed, for instance, by the discovery of the light-sensitive pigments and of the cells responsible for colour vision, on which Hermann von Helmholtz based his theory of trichromacy (1866).[4] The colour perception of children and of those referred to as the 'native uncivilised races', who were deemed to represent an earlier stage of culture, and thus considered relics of the past, was taken to approximate early stages in the development of the human colour sense left behind by the more progressive races.[5] When it came to the development of human colour vision, however, physiology needed, above all, the assistance of philology: early literature, which yields insights into the anthropological past, proved to be an invaluable aid. As such it had been advanced by the German philologist Lazarus Geiger, addressing an assembly of German naturalists in Frankfurt in September 1867 on the question of the development of the human colour sense: 'We may be able', Geiger explained,

> to deduce from geological findings an idea of the skeleton and probably also the entire exterior aspect of an extinct animal species; from the fragments of a cranium we may be able to draw conclusions as to the imperfect human race of primordial times: but it may be nigh on impossible to infer, from looking at it, anything about the way the head may have thought whose fragments have survived in the Neanderthal as a puzzle to the present. Fortunately, the history of human ideas also has its primordial relics, its deposits and fossils of a different kind: they offer knowledge more instructive than one should be inclined to believe: carefully pursued, they lead to results which are probably unexpected but, as I believe, for all that no less reliable.[6]

Geiger's deliberations were elaborated upon by the German ophthalmologist Hugo Magnus, who published his findings in 1877.[7] In his tract on the historical development of the colour sense, Magnus held that the question at which point in time the human retina was able to perceive colour could not be studied in the field of medicine, but involved the study of earlier literature. The results might then be used by medicine for physiological explanations.[8] Earlier literature, then, was considered as valuable proof of the historical development of human sense perception. The *Iliad* and the *Odyssey* were, to Magnus, 'instructive' as to determining the stage of development of the colour sense in Homer's time, and he suggested that philologists and scientists 'shake hands'.[9]

While physiologists thus ventured into the field of literature, many philologists, Magnus complained, in their analyses of literature neglected to consider physiological explanations for the scarcity of colour terms.[10] Exceptions to this were the aforementioned Lazarus Geiger and William Gladstone, both of whom were praised by Magnus for their approaches to literature, and both of whom contributed to the debate about the historical development of the colour sense.[11]

Apart from his career as a statesman, William Ewart Gladstone is known to literary historians for his influential work on Homer,[12] about whose personal identity as the writer of both the *Iliad* and the *Odyssey* he felt certain.[13] Not much concerned with the poet's 'reputed blindness',[14] Gladstone, in several of his publications, dealt with Homer's perception of colours as attested to by the colour terms used in his epics. Gladstone proposed that, while Homer's retina was exceptionally sensitive to light and dark,[15] his 'perceptions of the prismatic colours, or colours of the rainbow ... were, as a general rule, vague and indeterminate'.[16] In a painstaking exercise of drawing up a statistics of colour for extended portions of the *Iliad* and the *Odyssey*,[17] he attempts to show that apart from the words for red and orange (*eruthros* and *xanthos*), Homer does not use any true colour epithets, and that the words which might at first seem to be epithets of colour are, in fact, either figurative words, borrowed from natural objects, such as wine-colour and rose-colour,[18] or, more often, epithets of light and dark, such as *chloros* (denoting paleness and, as such, a light epithet)[19] and *porphureos* (applied as an image of darkness).[20] From the paucity of colour epithets in Homer's poems, Gladstone concludes that 'the organ of colour was but partially developed among the Greeks of his age'.[21] Homer's poems thus are interpreted by Gladstone as evidence for the historical development of the human colour sense. In fact, he considers them to be 'the most important magazine of information' on the 'imperfect conception of colour in early times'.[22]

It might have been expected that between the first publication of his theory in 1858, as part of his *Studies on Homer and the Homeric Age*, and his essay on the colour sense of 1877, the publications of Darwin's *Origin of Species* (1859) and *Descent of Man* (1871), or of Huxley's *Evidences as to Man's Place in Nature* (1863), might have had an impact on Gladstone's theory. Darwin's work, and the burgeoning research on social insects by John Lubbock and others, had confronted common assumptions as to the place of man in nature: they had challenged the belief that the mind, language and emotions (such as homesickness, jealousy and gratitude) and their expressions were characteristics unique to humankind.[23] However, as the secularist George William Foote complained in the *Freethinker* in 1885, Gladstone could still continue to write as if Darwin never existed.[24] Instead, Gladstone made use of German publications of the kind the rationalist Edward Clodd was later to refer to as 'Teutonic theories of the development of the colour sense within historical epochs'. 'These theories', Clodd continued, 'were supported, on purely philological grounds, by Mr Gladstone, and others equally conservative, who welcomed and backed arguments, good, bad, or indifferent, against the inclusion of man, "body, soul and spirit," as a product of evolution'.[25] And indeed, colour perception, to Gladstone, was clearly a human characteristic.

In his essay on 'The Colour Sense', Gladstone explicitly refers to two works by the aforementioned Hugo Magnus, who worked *inter alia* on the basis of historical research by the philologist Lazarus Geiger and Gladstone's earlier work.[26] Magnus does not explain the development of the colour sense by natural, or sexual, selection, advanced by Darwin as the driving force of evolution.[27] Instead, his theory is clearly informed by Lamarck's theory of the inheritance of acquired characteristics. According to Magnus, to start with, human beings were blind to colour.[28] Through the incessant action of a light stimulus, and frequent and sustained employment of the eye, the retina acquired increasing susceptibility (corresponding to Lamarck's first law), the modifications of which are then transmitted to the progeny (corresponding to Lamarck's second law).[29] Magnus believed that in the progressive education of the human eye, colours were successively disclosed to it in the order of 'their wealth in light' – starting with the colour richest in light, corresponding to prismatic red, and finally arriving at those corresponding to prismatic blue and violet.[30]

Where, now, does Homer stand in this history of the development of the human eye? Magnus assigns him to the second stage of perception, at which only the most luminous of colours, the red, orange and yellow of the Newtonian scale, are discerned.[31] To Gladstone, this seemed too far-reaching; according to his research, Homer could perceive only red and orange,[32] a restriction which (to Gladstone's mind) makes his talent even more remarkable: 'If without the lengthened history ... of long hereditary development of the organs, he has achieved his present results, what would he have accomplished had he been possessed of the vast and varied apparatus of all kinds which we enjoy!'[33]

Gladstone's theory was contested upon its publication.[34] Alfred Wallace, for one, disputes the classicist's interpretation of the scarcity of colour terms in Homer's poems, and asserts that they cannot be 'held to prove so recent an origin for colour-sensations as they would at first sight appear to do, because we have seen that both flowers and fruits have become diversely coloured in adaptation to the visual powers of insects, birds, and mammals'.[35] Foremost among those taking issue with Gladstone's interpretation was Grant Allen, man of letters and of science and popularizer of Darwin's theory of evolution, which he publicized in many of his writings.[36] At the time, Allen himself was engaged in writing a book on the origin and development of the colour sense, and promptly responded to Gladstone's essay with a contribution in the journal *Mind* entitled 'Development of the Sense of Colour'.[37] Allen's own theory, which has had great impact on biologists and has only very recently been challenged,[38] was inspired by the dazzling colours of tropical fruits in Jamaica.[39] In his book, Allen endeavoured to show that the colour sense in humans is not a recent acquisition but derived from our fruit-eating ancestors, that it has not evolved recently but can be placed 'far lower down the animal scale'. 'In no other way', he argues, 'can we account for the varied hues of flowers, fruits, insects, birds and mammals, all of which seem to have been developed as allurements for the eye, guiding it towards food or the opposite sex'; nor for the protective colouring among plants and animals,[40] as observed by Darwin and Wallace;[41] or for the distinction between colours even among what to Allen and his contemporaries are the 'native uncivilised races'.[42] Allen sums up the development of the colour sense at the end of his book *The Colour Sense*:

> Insects produce flowers. Flowers produce the colour sense in insects. The colour sense produces a taste for colour. The taste for colour produces butterflies and brilliant bees. Birds and mammals produce fruits. Fruits produce a taste for colour in birds and mammals. The taste for colour produces the external hues of humming-birds, parrots and monkeys. Man's frugivorous ancestry produces in him a similar taste and that taste produces the final result of human chromatic arts.[43]

Allen thereby shows once more that the 'apparent distinction between man and the lower animals, like all the other artificial distinctions whereby man seeks to hide the community of origin between himself and the brutes, fades away to a great extent upon closer consideration'.[44] Whereas Magnus had praised Gladstone for considering physiological explanations in his analysis of literature, Allen criticizes him for having disregarded recent scientific discoveries of both cones and rods in humans and mammals, of the preference of frogs for blue, and of the colour sense among bees and butterflies,[45] which have 'metamorphosed the world'.[46]

Allen's explanation for the scarcity of colour epithets in Homeric ballads differs markedly from Gladstone's. Allen argues that the missing colour epithets in Homer's poems depend not on dichromic vision but upon an insufficiency of language. He contends that brightly coloured objects such as butterflies, flowers and birds were of little importance to the warrior. Rather, the objects Homer needed to describe, such as arms, sky, earth, clouds and sea, show variations concerning light and shade, but are 'indefinitely coloured'. Language, Allen asserts, is indicative not of the perception of the language users, but of their 'need for intercommunication'.[47] It grows rich in colour with the use of dyed cloth; describing colours became important to manufacturers and artists, whose vocabulary shows the greatest variation concerning colour terms. Until the necessity arises, 'language does not keep pace with perception', as W. Robertson Smith puts it in a comment on Gladstone written independently of Allen's some weeks earlier;[48] Wallace, too, ascribes the use of only few colour terms in Homer to the lack of 'a precise *nomenclature* of colours'.[49] By 1880, Magnus, too, realized that the increasing complexity of colour terminology does not necessarily reflect the physiological development of colour perception.[50]

The more complex civilization grew, as a corollary of human evolution, the more the need for colour epithets increased.[51] Important to Allen, and to other critics of Gladstone, was the insight that literary texts could not be considered evidence for the actual sense perception, but were to be considered rather as documents of cultural evolution: they illustrate the process of an increasing significance placed on colours.[52] Allen, broadening his scope, discerns a similar process in the evolution of the aesthetic sense, which exhibits pertinent parallels to the development of the colour sense, to which it seems to be intricately linked. Again, Allen interprets literature as illustration of the evolutionary process. Moreover, literature is treated as a product of the evolutionary process, and appears at the same time to propel this very process.

Aesthetic Evolution

As with the origin of the taste for colour – which he finds, is not restricted to humankind, but traceable 'far lower down the animal scale' – Grant Allen contends that the aesthetic taste for form and symmetry, and the love of music, are not the prerogative of man either, but are also displayed among insects, birds and mammals.[53] He discovers proof of these senses of visual and auditory beauty in, for instance, 'the gracefully spiral horns of the Koodoo antelope', and the 'outpoured song of the ... nightingale',[54] which he understands as 'aesthetic products' of sexual selection.[55] From these observations Allen develops his theory of aesthetic evolution, published in 1880, in which he traces the evolution of man's delight in nature and scenery.[56] 'The facts on which Mr Darwin bases his theory of sexual selection', Allen expounds, 'become of the first importance for the aesthetic philosopher, because they are really the only solid evidence for the existence of a love for beauty in the infra-human world.'[57] They are also the basis for the evolution of human aesthetic feeling. Particular to humankind, however, is the ability and the obvious need to augment their natural beauty by adding personal decoration: pieces of bone, for instance, or shells and stones as ornaments worn by palaeolithic humans. According to Allen, this ability forms the link to the aesthetic feeling for nature and scenery, for 'beauty for its own sake alone', specific to humankind, which he considers to be the climax of aesthetic evolution.[58]

Retrospectively, Allen observes four early levels in the evolution of human aesthetic perception. From love of personal decoration (the first level of aesthetic development), man progresses via admiration of weapons and domestic utensils (the second and third levels) to delight in the beauty of architecture and the decoration of the home (the fourth level). Nature, in these early levels, is, however, only ever referred to as an obstacle to man and is not admired as such. From this early, 'anthropinistic' stage, at which all aesthetic feeling is 'gathered mainly around the personality of man or woman', human aesthetic feeling gradually evolves in a process of apanthropinization, 'a gradual regression or concentric widening of aesthetic feeling around this fixed point',[59] and advances to the appreciation of beauty in nature.[60]

Once again, it is literature which provides the data for this deduction. To Allen, poetry in particular lends itself to the analysis of aesthetic development, because, as he says, it is 'aesthetic feeling crystallised into words'.[61] Accordingly, he traces the progress of aesthetic feeling from Homer via Horace to Virgil, and, after a decline in the Middle Ages, to the 'welling emotions of a Wordsworth',[62] until, in his own day, it 'probably reaches the furthest development that it has ever yet attained'.[63] Allen describes Homer, although he has not yet transcended the anthropinistic stage, as having advanced up to the fourth level of aesthetic development: in so far as he refers to human beauty (for example in Helen, Briseis, Hera) and personal decoration (the first level); to utensils, weapons and works of primitive art, such as the wrought figures on Achilles' shield (the second and third levels); and to the palaces of Priam and of the Phaeacians (the fourth level).[64]

Allen, however, does not use only the content of literature to argue for the evolution of aesthetics. Another illustration of his theory may be found in the generic development of literature, for its evolution, in his view, parallels the progress from the anthropinistic to the apanthropinistic stage, from concerns with human interest alone to those of scenery, of landscapes, of nature:

> All primaeval literary works consist of a legend, a story historical or mythical, the tale of what some man or some god has done. To the very end, novels, plays and biography, the most human in their interest, are the favourite forms of literature. Poetry at first is all epic or narrative: lyric and descriptive verse only come in at a much later point of evolution, and are seldom thoroughly relished by any but the most cultivated.[65]

Thus, evolution brings forth new genres. However, Allen describes this process as bidirectional, because he perceives literature conversely to take an active part in the evolution of human aesthetic feeling, too. Beauty in art, he argues, prepared the human mind for the appreciation of beauty in nature; art can 'educate and strengthen the aesthetic faculties of the mass',[66] and aesthetic values mediated through literature intensify the attachment to the real object.[67] As an example, Allen cites the aesthetic transformation of the daisy in poetry and in everyday life: 'the figure', he says, 'which it [i.e. the daisy] takes in literature re-enacts upon the feelings with which we regard it in the actuality', and he concludes: 'With the reading class, memories of Wordsworth and Burns and Tennyson cling about every individual daisy.'[68] Finally, still referring to the example of the daisy, Allen sums up the bidirectional relation of the evolution of aesthetics:

> The daisy is admitted as a component of poetry because it is a flower, pink and white and yellow, pretty, symmetrical, graceful, familiar, and domestic. Poetry is all made up of such pretty objects, strung into a beautiful framework of metre, and connected by a thread of narrative or abstract lyrical thought. And then, in consequence, we love the objects themselves all the better, because of the good company in which we have so often found them.[69]

Conclusion

Science, as has often been pointed out, 'shapes ... our sense of what it means to be human'.[70] A taste for beauty, be it in colour, music, or form and symmetry, was long conceived to be man's exclusive possession. In the quest for the origin of human sense perceptions, which should be considered as partaking in the larger debate about the continuity between animal and human mentality, literature turned out to be indispensable. Gladstone takes Homer's poems as evidence of an early stage in the development of colour sense in historical times. Allen, on the other hand, who shares Darwin's conviction that 'man possesses the same senses as the lower animals',[71] takes literature as an indication of an insufficient colour terminology. As he endeavoured to show in several publications, the germs of the taste for beauty can be found among animals. To both Allen and Gladstone, literature serves as invaluable source material. The interrelations between literature and evolutionary biology have been shown to be more intricate in that insights into the evolution of aestheticism are transferred on to literary history: genres appear to have evolved in correspondence to the progress from the anthropinistic to the apanthropinistic stage in aesthetic evolution. Moreover, literature takes an active part in the evolution of the aesthetic sense: the appreciation of an object in art paves the way for the aesthetic appreciation of the object in nature.

There seems to be no doubt, then, that Homer saw red. Yet, had he witnessed a bull fight and made it the subject of an epic, his description of the toreador's cloth as being red were to be credited not only to the susceptibility of his eye but, according to Allen, also to the fact that the red cloth is an indispensable utensil to get the bull going. It seems a pity that this epic was never written, because it might have explained the aesthetic allure of many a tourist's souvenir of a red toreador's cloth.

9

'NATURFREUND' OR 'NATURFEIND'? DARWINISM IN THE EARLY DRAWINGS OF ALFRED KUBIN

Alexandra Karl

The artists of Germany's Symbolist era were productive during that country's most extensive period of science dissemination; their imagery was concurrent with the popularization of Darwinism. This is evident in several works of visual art created during this time. For instance, in the *oeuvre* of Alfred Kubin (1877–1959) we encounter many subjects which resonate with man-animal dialectics inspired by Darwinism. In particular, the process of transmutation inspired a new pantheon of subjects, and our analysis of them confirms the central role that Darwinism played in Kubin's graphic works. Despite this fact, other aspects of Kubin's production conspire to undermine this reading, and present a more contradictory, incongruous picture. Most immediately, his *Naturbild* proffers a less-than-Darwinian philosophy of nature, as it draws on strains of Romanticism as well as the artist's personal philosophy and personality. As we will see, Kubin's Darwinism is further complicated by the conditions under which it was acquired, as well as his referencing of the science illustration of the day.

Alfred Kubin came to Munich in 1898 to study art, though lessons in a private studio and at the *Akademie der schönen Künste* were soon abandoned. Around this time he began a series of black-and-white ink drawings which he continued to work on until 1904, when they were superseded by new artistic interests.[1] He experimented with tempera and gouache in his *Untersee* paintings, and continued to draw, albeit in a lighter, scribblier style. While many of his later drawings illustrated works of literature,[2] Kubin pursued his own literary interests with equal passion. In 1909, several early text fragments culminated in the publication of a work of Expressionist writing, *Die andere Seite*, for which he is best known.[3] During this time, his talents both as writer and as philosopher manifested themselves,[4] and he was known as a magician, wizard, seer, oddball [*Sonderling*], *Traumkünstler* and *Einzelphänomen*. He became involved to varying degrees with Munich's new movements in Modernism, exhibited with *Phalanx* and the Berlin and Viennese Secessions, and was a founding member of the *Neue Künstlervereinigung München* as well as *Der Blaue Reiter*.

The drawings created before 1904 (henceforth referred to as the *Frühwerk*) constitute both an autonomous and anomalous phase in Kubin's *oeuvre*. Generally speaking, the works demonstrate a dark and pessimistic world view. They are characterized by obscure and murky atmospheric effects which are achieved by spray and wash techniques; these serve as an antidote to the cheerful palettes of his Modernist contemporaries. Above all, a profound sense of doom and dread is conveyed, as themes such as carnage, misogyny, plague, paedophilia, rape and torture are rendered with frightening potency. For this reason Kubin's subject matter has been called a chamber of horrors or *Schreckenskammer*. Paul Klee declared that Kubin was 'most alive in the depiction of destruction,'[5] and Kandinsky wrote in his treatise *On the Spiritual in Art*: 'With irrepressible force one is drawn into the blood-curdling atmosphere of the savage void. This power streams forth from Kubin's drawings, and also from the pages of his novel.'[6]

Kubin's *Frühwerk* is difficult to contextualize. This is because his images are more evocative of post-war sentiments; indeed it would be more logical to assume that the senselessness of human nature so vividly conveyed was conceived shortly after World War One or Two, particularly since many works are suggestive of the Holocaust. Most accounts however attribute Kubin's subject matter to a nihilistic resignation grounded in his life experiences. These consist of a series of cataclysmic events outlined in Kubin's autobiographies which shattered the innocence and happiness of his youth and laid the groundwork for a pessimistic disposition. When Kubin was ten, his mother died of tuberculosis, an event followed two years later by the death of his stepmother. Kubin was subsequently raised by an implacable, at times abusive, father. During this time he was raped by an older pregnant woman. These events, coupled with rejection at school and in the military, led Kubin to a nervous breakdown and his first suicide attempt at age 19. A more interesting reaction is registered when Kubin is faced with the death of his Munich fiancée Emmy Bayer in 1903. Now operating under the guise of a Munich decadent, Kubin capitalized on the event by manufacturing a second suicide letter, which has been described as a work of 'literary-philosophical self-stylization.'[7] Remarkably, scholarship by Andreas Geyer has revealed that the resulting suicide letter was appropriated from Philipp Mailänder's *Philosophie der Erlösung* (1876) and authored two months after Bayer's death, during which time the 'bereaved' Kubin was courting his new fiancée, Hedwig Gründler.

Kubin's turbulent adolescence and his pessimistic *Weltanschauung* acquired new impetus upon his 1898 descent into bohemian Schwabing. By his own accounts, he pursued 'an existence like Murgen's *Gypsy Life*' which involved drinking, frequenting prostitutes and otherwise becoming a more permanent fixture in café society.[8] During this time, he was described as 'a delicate youth, always dressed in black, with a pale boyish face, which looked strained and shy, like a young wolf forced out of the hollow and into the light.'[9] Clearly there is an histrionic element to this character; it is parodied in *Simplicissimus* as *Der große Eduard*,[10] and Kubin even fancies himself 'wrapped up in a violet velvet cloak, drinking absinth from a mouse's skull to promote [his] fantasies'.[11] Kubin was exposed during this time to a collection of artists who had a profound effect on him; they included Hieronymus Bosch, Pieter Bruegel the Elder, James Ensor, Francisco Goya, Jean Ignace Isidore Grandville, Henry de Groux, Max Klinger, Eduard Munch, Felicien Rops and Odilon Redon. Such influences were then augmented by a concerted study of (philosophical) works by Friedrich Nietzsche, Arthur Schopenhauer, Otto Weininger, Johann Jakob Bachofen, Julius Bahnsen, Salomo 'Mynona' Friedländer (pseudonym opposite of 'anonym') and Ludwig Klages: all of whom contributed various strains of pessimism, fatalism and misogyny to Kubin's artistic production.

Throughout the scholarship on Kubin, all these factors are presented as central influences in the establishment of his creative process, and are pivotal in explicating the nihilistic and 'bloodcurdling' flavour of his subject matter. Selected works from the *Frühwerk*, however, deviate from these sources, and appear to draw their inspiration from the scientific revolutions contemporary to and predating Kubin. It is certainly in these works that critics have observed a 'horror before the abyss of existence, [and] a primeval feeling of Angst'.[12] More specifically, several works suggest that notions of degeneracy are based on a vision of nature which postulates Darwinism as its *modus operandi*.[13] Here, nature appears to have been reduced to a handful of basically Darwinian mechanisms, including competition, extinction and transmutation. For instance, forces of competition are conveyed through antagonistic relationships in which animals struggle in *Battles of the Sexes* or *Survivals of the Fittest*.[14] Moreover, many animal subjects are perpetually condemned to adversarial roles with humans, where the demise of mankind is always the outcome of this *Battle of the Species*. In many of these works, animal subjects become gigantic, horrific forces of nature, threatening to extinguish vulnerable Man. In their exaggerated, super-inflated states, they are oblivious to any human presence – and it is this blindness which underscores mankind's volatility and futility of purpose. Indeed, unlike more popular genres which feature animals seething with rage, Kubin's protagonists are often disturbingly lucid and emotionally detached, suggesting a more disquieting side to evolutionary competition.[15]

Themes of extinction also permeate many works, in which naturally occurring phenomena such as plague and illness are rendered with great intensity.[16] These sentiments are exemplified in a work from 1902–3 entitled *Swarm Spirits* (*Schwarmgeister*) [Figure 11], which features an unidentified primordial organism which swerves up through the sky with its own busy momentum, evoking a swarm of locusts. Within the figure are hundreds of tiny individual people, who spin, tumble and fumble within the general confines of a 'primeval bird or snake'. The image evokes those scientific theories which emerged throughout the nineteenth century, articulating new and demeaning relationships between the individual and the natural world. Evolutionary theory implied particularly derogatory notions of individuals, whose lives were helplessly subordinate to the laws of nature and to the goals of the group, the herd and the species. So wrote Wilhelm Bölsche in 1887:

> Sometimes one feels obliged to call nature cruel, due to the crude means it employs in the struggle for existence for the creation of a new species of animal or plant. The cradle of progress, which is new in the spiritual life of mankind, is in that sense the most brutal Procrustean bed that can altogether be imagined. The individual here is no longer valid.[17]

Figure 11. Alfred Kubin, *Swarm Spirits* (*Schwarmgeister*) (c.1902–3). Private Collection. Reproduced in A Hoberg, ed., 1990, *Alfred Kubin 1877–1959*, Munich, Spangenberg, p. 101. Courtesy of Leopold Museum, Vienna.

This giant bird snake, with its large avian head and simple snake body, has no precedent in visual art traditions. Few creatures from the animal kingdom offer concrete sources. The creature evokes a primeval vertebrate; indeed, there is morphological resemblance to the 'Zeuglodon' animal [Figure 12]. Possessing the head and flippers of a seal, the ribs of a manatee, the shoulder blades of a whale, and vertebrae unique ('onion-structured') to itself, the Zeuglodon fossils are abundant in the Gulf of Mexico and the southern states of the USA. These creatures typically measured 50–70 feet, yet a gargantuan specimen measuring over twice that length toured Europe in 1846 at the initiative of a Dr Albert Koch. Measuring 114 feet in length, the mythical Hydrarchos (or water king) was a sensation. Its remains were eventually sold for a small fortune to the Museum of Dresden, after which it was established that the creature consisted of composite fossilized vertebrae compiled from arbitrary animals, long since known. Although the scandal took place over thirty years before Kubin's birth, the story of the Hydrarchos, as well as its illustration, is recounted in his copy of *Wunderglaube und Wirklichkeit*, and must be considered a source to the image.

With this in mind, it seems no coincidence that Kubin chose the skeleton of an *extinct* vertebrate as a vehicle or symbol for the human race. For Kubin's conception of mankind's destiny shares the fate of the Hydrarchos: extinction. In many of his early text fragments, the fate of the world leads to only one thing: 'Death, nothingness, is the fate of the world, [and all] those individual forces which together constitute the world. Each expires unconditionally [along] a predestined route – like a machine ... Indeed, look how not only we, but everything leads to annihilation.'[18] Andreas Geyer observes how

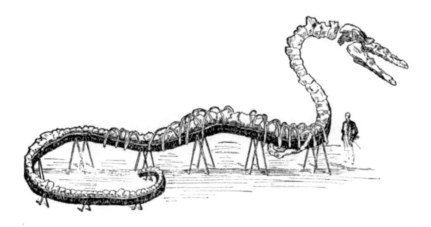

Figure 12. Unknown artist, *Hydrarchos*. In F Otto, 1899, *Wunderglaube und Wirklichkeit*, Leipzig.

early text fragments by Kubin also place an evolutionary spin on definitions of Mankind, and are expressed in Darwinian terms: 'In a journal entry, Kubin refers to the "stupidity and baseness of people" and later to the "unbelievable narrow-mindedness of this sordid race".'[19] These descriptions, as well as the drawing's content, convey a notion of man as not just submerged in nature, as would have been the case with the Romantics' Natural Man, but, rather, defeated and consumed by it. The principle at work here is extinction in the evolutionary sense.

Beyond Kubin's interest in extinction, the notion of transmutation becomes a central, governing principle in many of his creations, and the indelible factor which characterizes them. Transmutation is the process by which a species acquires new characteristics or traits, and transforms, evolves or morphs into a different creature altogether. In Kubin's graphic work, this becomes a force of distortion and disfiguration, transforming his subjects into monstrous beings which simultaneously subsume several taxonomic categories. Now of course, in the theory of evolution, this is a process which takes place gradually over centuries and millennia. In the artist's imagination, however, the process is perpetually condensed to become an immediate, spontaneous experience, whereby mutants not only transgress taxonomic boundaries but remain frozen or trapped in the transitory, intermediary moment. In *Digression (Abweg)* [Figure 13], a man's head tapers down into the body of a snake, the dualism of which signifies the disparate realms of the marine and the terrestrial which his body bridges. Likewise, *The Last Adventure (Das letzte Abendteuer)* [Figure 14]

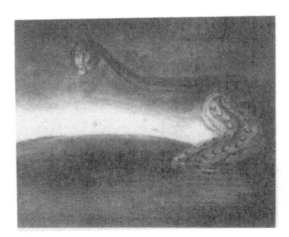

Figure 13. Alfred Kubin, *Digression (Abweg)*. Undated. Reprinted in C Brockhaus, 1977, *Alfred Kubin: Das zeichnerische Frühwerk bis 1904*. Staatliche Kunsthalle Baden-Baden, p. 6. Courtesy of the Graphische Sammlung Wien (Albertina). No. 33557.

Figure 14. Alfred Kubin, *The Last Adventure (Das letzte Abendteuer)* (c.1900–1). Reproduced in A Hoberg, ed., 1990, *Alfred Kubin 1877–1959*, Munich, Spangenberg. Catalogue No. 47. Courtesy of Leopold Museum, Vienna.

features a devolved female subject, half-woman, half-worm, who forms a new breed of *femme fatale* for her unfortunate suitor.

In many works, the process of transmutation exerts its influence upon the human body. We see this in a drawing from 1900 called *The Monster (Der Unhold)* [Figure 15],[20] where a naked, long-haired figure bites down into a smaller, female body. It has already been suggested that the composition has been adapted from Goya's *Saturn*, which was widely available in print at the time. From Goya's image, however, Kubin made several changes to the subject's physique. His legs are just barely longer than his arms; his forehead has been widened, as has his nose – modifications which typify the simian rather than the human form. The subject also possesses a minuscule underdeveloped tail, which was considered to be a remnant of man's primate ancestry. We also see a pair of grotesque feet, which are in the process of transforming from a prehensile or gripping state – what a critic called *Bierhände* – but have not yet become the fully developed feet of *homo erectus*. By making these changes, Kubin transformed Goya's *Saturn* into a monster with contemporary intonations: the Neanderthal. With this in mind, we can ascertain that another source for Kubin's monster, alongside Goya's *Saturn*, was probably Gabriel von Max's *Family of the Ape People* (1894) [Figure 16], which illustrated Ernst Haeckel's *Natürliche Schöpfungsgeschichte* (1898). Kubin's monster is also circumcised – an unlikely attribute for prehistoric man, and most probably the result of Kubin's anti-Semitic milieu.

Figure 15. Alfred Kubin, *The Monster (Der Unhold)* (c.1900). Reproduced in *Alfred Kubin,* Kunstmuseum Winterthur, 1986. Catalogue No. 73. Courtesy of Private Collection, Switzerland.

As well as exploring the effects of transmutation on the human body, Kubin applies this process to the animal kingdom. In a drawing from 1899 entitled *Grotesque Animal World (Groteske Tierwelt)* [Figure 17],[21] a cacophony of zoological anomalies are shown, all rendered with imaginative modifications and mutations, and assembled into a watery landscape. With such exaggerated proportions and attributes, redistributed inappropriately to absurd conclusions, Kubin has taken tremendous liberties in his rendition of the animal kingdom. Although one could attribute this phenomenon to Kubin's overactive imagination, such features are analogous to the peculiar and truly anomalous forms revealed in the fossil record. Kubin probably appropriated the composition from scientific diagrams such as Henry De La Beche's *Duria antiquior* (1830) [Figure 18].[22] Here, an antediluvian world is inhabited by both marine and amphibian life. De La Beche's image is dominated by the three stars of nineteenth century palaeontology: the plesiosaurus, the ichthyosaurus and the pterodactyl. Following the discovery of their fossils, around 1830, these creatures proceeded to dominate prehistoric visions until other creatures such as the iguanodon, the megatherium and the gigantic brontosauri of the American West were unearthed and slowly incorporated into the genre of dinosaur fantasies. The peculiar forms of these creatures resembled no animal known at that time, and represented an entirely alternate taxonomy to the

Figure 16. Gabriel von Max, *Family of the Ape People* (1894). Reproduced in E Haeckel, 1898, *Natürliche Schöpfungsgeschichte*, Table XXIX.

Figure 17. Alfred Kubin, *Grotesque Animal World* (*Groteske Tierwelt*) (1899). Reproduced in *Alfred Kubin*, Kunstmuseum Winterthur, 1986. Catalogue No. 51. Oberösterreichisches Landesmuseum Linz. Inv. No. HA 7361. Courtesy of Design and Artists Copyright Society.

Figure 18. Henry De La Beche, *Duria antiquior* (1830). Reproduced in M Rudwick, 1992, *Scenes from Deep Time: Early Pictorial Representations of the Prehistoric World*, Chicago, University of Chicago Press.

perceived natural world. Today we can only speculate as to how shocking these dinosaurs might have appeared to nineteenth century eyes. Yet the net effect has been registered by Kubin's interpretation, resulting in monsters which resemble neither living nor fossilized creatures.

Peculiar modifications also permeate a work from 1903 called *The Offspring* (*Das Gezüchte*) [Figure 19].[23] Here, in an obscure interior space, an intriguing

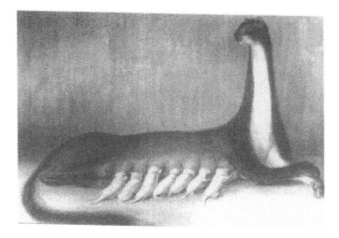

Figure 19. Alfred Kubin, *The Offspring (Das Gezüchte)* (1903). Reproduced in A Hoberg, ed., 1990, *Alfred Kubin 1877–1959*, Munich, Spangenberg. Städtische Galerie im Lenbachhaus, Kub. No. 202. Courtesy of Annegret Hoberg, Lenbachhaus.

creature reclines, revealing seven identical offspring which suckle at its breasts. In combination with the title *Das Gezüchte*, derived from the verb *züchten* (to breed), the creature's single fateful destiny is suggested. Earlier art historians have identified the creature as a member of the big-cat family. Kubin, however, has modified the animal by elongating its neck, torso and tail, thereby imbuing it with what was then described as a 'synthetic spine'. In particular, its elongated neck offers a variety of significations; its erect gesture is undeniably phallic, and indeed other works by Kubin are more explicit in this regard.[24] Lamarck also attributed a great deal of significance to an elongated neck: the giraffe's extended neck not only demonstrated the horse's ability to adapt to its environment in order to survive, but became emblematic of natural selection in general. Certainly this modification permeates many of Kubin's monsters, as several works feature this specific characteristic.[25] Kubin's awareness of the centrality of the spine to the taxonomic underpinnings of evolutionary theory is illustrated in a work from c.1898, entitled *Der Erste und der Letzte*:[26] here, an oversized vertebral column is flanked by an elderly gentleman and a Neanderthal, suggesting that this is the crucial missing link which binds these otherwise disparate characters together.

A more convincing source to *The Offspring*, however, can be seen in 'the most colossal animal on earth', the brontosaurus and brachiosaurus dinosaurs, which were unearthed around 1877 in the United States. Their giant sauropod skeletons circulated Europe towards the turn of the century, and plaster casts of *Diplodocus carnegii* (nicknamed *Dippy*) were sent to London, Berlin, Paris, St Petersburg, Barcelona and Buenos Aires. The final destination of the Carnegie gifts, incidentally, was the *Bayerische Staatssammlung* in Munich; they could have served as a source to Kubin's creature, had they not arrived only in 1934. (Assemblage was interrupted by the war; the casts were only rediscovered accidentally in the basement of the museum in 1977, still in their original thirty-three crates, with the instructions for reassemblage long lost.) There remains a final source which links Kubin's animal to this palaeontological specimen: an 1898 reconstruction of a living brontosaurus (*Apatosaurus*) completed by American artist Charles Knight [Figure 20].[27] This may have been among a cycle of paintings sent to Paris, London and Munich between 1896 and 1900 which hung in the halls of fossilized vertebrates, and could thereby have inspired Kubin's enigmatic creature.[28] In all, the creature embodies a mélange of human and animal attributes: as mother, mammal, phallus, dinosaur and mutant vertebrate, the net sum of these references surpasses categories of the hybrid or the hermaphroditic. The creature has lost all meaning as a big cat, and has simply become a conglomeration of biological and evolutionary attributes and signs.

Figure 20. Charles Knight, *Apatosaurus* (1898). Reproduced in S Massey Czerkas, and D F Glut, 1982, *Dinosaurs, Mammoths and Cavemen: The Art of Charles R Knight*, New York, E P Dutton Inc., p. 43, figure 45. Courtesy of American Museum of National History.

These examples demonstrate not only the central role that transmutation played in Kubin's graphic work, but also the multidimensional nature of his Darwinism. We encounter this most immediately in the nature of the alterations and metaphors employed, which are explicit in underscoring the implications of Darwinism – and of their impact on both the human and animal world. As we have seen, the notion of transmutation became a persistent and governing force in these works, inspiring the creation of a highly distorted pantheon of subjects. Evidently, many of Kubin's subjects were informed not only by Darwinism, but also by an acute awareness of the disciplines in which it was manifest.

It appears that Kubin's Darwinism is also buttressed by the invocation of science imagery, and we have seen how several drawings were inspired by illustrations drawn from both popular and scholarly science. These were clearly used as a template to be reworked and altered, such that new metaphors and intonations could be applied. Certainly this practice sets him apart from his colleagues, most of whom were involved in dialogues more specific to the art world. It also suggests the employment of a quasi-Darwinian *method*, seeking to invoke the implications of a new Darwinian world in the visual language in which it was originally manifest. Yet despite this impression, a distinction must be made between this reading and the actual impetus from which it stems. In a work from 1887 entitled *Landscape with Animals* (*Landschaft mit Tieren*) [Figure 21],[29] clichés such as a palm tree, a turban-wearing native and an alligator emerging ashore all indicate that this drawing has its roots in standard

Figure 21. Alfred Kubin, *Landscape with Animals (Landschaft mit Tieren)* (1887). Reproduced in A Hoberg, ed., 1990, *Alfred Kubin 1877–1959*, Munich, Spangenberg. Catalogue No. 2. Städtische Galerie im Lenbachhaus, Kub. No. 515. Courtesy of Annegret Hoberg, Lenbachhaus.

nineteenth century compositional prototypes. Here, the act of appropriation is hardly the cunning strategy of an avant-garde Darwinian, but essentially the juvenile pastime of a young boy: Kubin created the work when he was just ten years old. Kubin's fondness for copying continued throughout his adolescence. During his military convalescence in 1897, he described how he 'copied pictures from *Die Gartenlaube* to pass the time.'[30]

Not surprisingly, the dating of this practice is in keeping with Kubin's espousal of Darwinism in general. The evidence for this lies in his extensive library still housed today at the *Kubinhaus* in Zwickledt, Austria. Amid over 5,500 volumes, many are on nineteenth century popular science.[31] The vast majority however were published prior to 1898, indicating that Kubin's exposure to Darwinism – and more generally, to German *Naturgeschichte* – predates his arrival in Munich. This connection is significant, since it pertains to the narrative and sequencing of Kubin's artistic production. This supports the premise that Kubin's mature work began only after his arrival in *Kunststadt München*; it is argued that the various elements he encountered there were instrumental in precipitating his first mature body of work: the *Frühwerk*. Certainly there are several biographical facts which support this argument. One could hypothesize, for instance, that Kubin learned about Darwinism through those friends who were members of the *Friedrichshagener Dichterkreis*, and had close ties with key Darwinians such as Wilhelm Bölsche and Ernst Haeckel.[32] Alternatively, Darwinism could have been amidst the many *Lektüre*

Kubin undertook during this time in subjects such as philosophy, psychology and psychiatry; this is suggested by Andreas Geyer in his discussion of Kubin's written production.[33] Yet his library holdings indicate another scenario entirely, and demonstrate not only that Kubin learned of Darwinism at a much earlier time, but – more interestingly – that Darwinism was not a pronounced feature of Munich's avant-garde. This is corroborated by Kubin's autobiographies and extensive correspondence, which make no mention of encountering this ground-breaking discourse, nor of any contact with science popularizers or scientists. Indeed, despite the fact that Kubin wrote extensively, constantly reworking his ideas and revising his self-image, Darwinism is clearly absent from these pages.

Beyond these issues, it is also curious that while Darwinism clearly played a significant role in Kubin's graphic work, it is tempered and at times eclipsed by an altogether different philosophy of nature, which permeates his memoirs and writings, presenting a highly convoluted *Naturbild* which at once venerates and vilifies the subject. Reminiscing on his childhood years, Kubin described how he '… gave lease to all those horrible, suppressed instincts, and in any old corner of the garden, staged torture scenes on small, pitiful animals, who were so unlucky to have entered into my dominion. And I must admit that as awful as I find it today, and so often as I regretted it later, I derived deep feelings of pleasure from it.'[34] Such acts are temporarily mitigated when Kubin later expresses shame; however, this was soon forgotten. In 1906, similar practices resurfaced upon the acquisition of two chimpanzees. The first, Tip, was boxed up and shipped off to Hamburg for misbehaving. Kubin killed the other chimp (Giovanni) with a blow to the head, during an altercation in which Kubin's 'most sensitive parts' were accidentally manhandled. The unfortunate fate of these animals was subsequently repackaged as one of many charming episodes in Kubin's memoirs, *Aus meinem Leben*.[35]

Other biographical excerpts, however, stand in contrast, complicating this *Naturbild* with a warmer attitude. These testify to Kubin's early fondness for Nature and *Naturgeschichte*, and proffer a more idealized, idyllic approach. Kubin writes: 'I was always a nature lover. From my boyhood days I collected beetles and butterflies, kept reptiles, fish, birds, and was passionately devoted to observing them.'[36] Kubin also suggested an intimate relationship with nature when he reminisced: 'My greatest joy came from fairy tales; I was also involved a lot with Natural History and filled my free time with bird hunting and fishing'.[37] Later, during a sojourn in Klagenfurt: 'I enjoyed my free time with a fullness of things. I bought myself a bicycle, kept snakes and all kinds of worms in cages.'[38] Years later, his sense of awe and wonder at nature is invoked during a visit to a friend in the Bayerische Wald: 'We visited the painter R. [Reinhold] Koeppel in Waldhäuser, with hour-long hiking in the dark green [foliage], tree-on-tree, root-on-root, which aroused in us a rare exhilaration which must have [had] its secret reason in this powerful plant-life. It was inexplicably primeval, that which stirred the soul so elementally.'[39]

From such accounts a more complex picture emerges, one which oscillates between an idealized, Romantic concept of nature and a more dilapidated, derogatory one. This dialectic became most pronounced following Kubin's 1904 marriage to the widow Hedwig Gründler (née Schmitz). In 1906, the couple abandoned urban life in *Kunststadt München* and retreated to an historic *Schlößchen* [= a small castle] in the rural foothills of a remote Austrian hamlet, Zwickledt. Kubin was pleased with the honourable provenance of the property, dating back four centuries to a *Ritter* [= Knight] *von Schmelzing und Wernstein*. While admittedly it had its practical and financial advantages, the move can only be seen as a return to nature. Here, Kubin could focus on his animal collections and otherwise pursue a quieter life, 'closer to nature'. For sustenance, he kept geese, deer, swine and goats, as well as a tomcat and crow for company. He also describes how 'Here in Zwickledt we had the most beautiful aquaria, African frogs, an iguana, squirrels and dormice. Also, the collecting of beetles, the love of my youth, surfaced once again for a few years.'[40] He later stated: 'In the next three months, I ... devoted my attention to various animals, among them a lively ape, a tame deer, cats, aquaria and beetle collections, and roamed around for hours in the field and forest'.[41]

Demonstrating the polarized nature of Kubin's *Naturbild* is the fact that concurrent with these domestic changes is the emergence of a new body of

Figure 22. Alfred Kubin, *Pupated World (Verpuppte Welt)* (1906). Reproduced in A Hoberg, ed., 1990, *Alfred Kubin 1877–1959*, Munich, Spangenberg. Städtische Galerie im Lenbachhaus. Kub. No. 289. Courtesy of Annegret Hoberg, Lenbachhaus.

works, initially precipitated by Kubin's 1905 studio visit to Odilon Redon. For paradoxically, it was from the seclusion and solitude of this new rural idyll that Kubin conjured up a new vision of nature which was both enchanting and demonic: the *Untersee* works [Figure 22]. Incorporating references to both microscopes and aquaria, as well as the discoveries of marine biologists such as Carl Chun, these works feature subjects such as children's corpses and monstrous mutants, bloated and immobile, in various states of decay and growth, teetering between one life form and another.

From this, we can only conclude that however dialectical or polarized Kubin's *Naturbild* is, it appears to be grounded in a more general approach to life. For throughout Kubin's ongoing process of self-stylization, he often presented himself as an artist in conflict, torn between two irreconcilable worlds. This involved shifting between two cultural epochs: the Romantic and the Modern. He was nostalgic about the decline of the Austro-Hungarian Empire, and yet embraced the temptations of the modern metropolis. He lamented that he was born a century too late, yet he participated in Munich's most avant-garde Modernist movements. He masqueraded as an *enfant terrible*, yet he chose the conventional life of marriage and domesticity. Kubin's conception of nature clearly played itself out within the parameters of this framework, as we encounter an ongoing dilemma regarding his approach to nature: to marvel or to destroy, to venerate or to vilify?

PART III

Physiology and Pathology

10

CELLS AND NETWORKS IN NINETEENTH CENTURY LITERATURE

Laura Otis

Since I wrote about cells and networks five to ten years ago, I have had some new thoughts about how these competing nineteenth century representations of neurons inspired and drew on clashing notions of personal and national identity. In this chapter, I would like to review the arguments I made in *Membranes* and *Networking*, address some of the most valuable criticisms I have received, and discuss the implications for future studies of nineteenth century literature and science.[1]

I got the idea for *Membranes* while reading Lawrence Rothfield's book *Vital Signs*, an excellent study of the way changes in realist novels paralleled evolving medical attitudes.[2] Early in this work, Rothfield claimed that cell theory had developed out of Romantic notions of the human individual. I found this intriguing, and thought: 'You could write a whole book about this.' In 1997, when I finally had an opportunity to ask Rothfield about the relationship between cells and selves, he told me that the connection between Romantic philosophy and cell theory was common knowledge. Like most scholars of literature and science, however, I remained unsatisfied, wanting to know how the exchange of ideas took place. What philosophical and cultural ideas might make a person *want* to see cells under a microscope?

Since I left the field of neuroscience in 1986, and began studying comparative literature, I have been comparing the ways in which biologists, psychologists and literary writers represent memory, heredity and identity. The major philosophical and psychological question that has most interested me has always been how individual people form their senses of identity. When I did the research for *Membranes*, I decided to control for personality, selecting writers who were both scientists or physicians *and* literary writers, and comparing the words that they used to describe cells and individual people. The central figures were the American neurologist S Weir Mitchell, the Spanish neurobiologist Santiago Ramón y Cajal, the British storyteller Arthur Conan Doyle and the Austrian playwright and novelist Arthur Schnitzler. I also examined the scientific writing of pathologist and politician Rudolf Virchow and bacteriologist Robert Koch, and the literature of Thomas Mann, who had no formal scientific training.

In these writers' works, I discovered what I then perceived as a cultural pattern of defining healthy people, minds and nations by means of protective, semi-permeable boundaries. This attitude seemed to have evolved between 1839, when the German histologist Theodor Schwann proposed that all animals were made of cells, and the turn of the century, when writers such as Schnitzler challenged this membrane-based model of identity by showing how open and interconnected human individuals were. My experiences of contemporary culture told me that the notion of the bounded individual was still thriving in 1998, so I urged people to work towards a concept of identity based on connections and relations rather than exclusions. I must admit that when I made that plea, I was also trying to convince myself. I still cling to the concept of a discrete, bounded, responsible self that we supposedly overcame a hundred years ago, and it is possible that culturally, we still need it. Certainly our legal systems rely on a concept of individual responsibility. The American soldiers who tortured Iraqi prisoners will win little sympathy if they argue that they were just intersections of discourses.

As I was completing *Membranes*, I became increasingly aware that I was presenting only part of the picture. There were indeed nineteenth century writers, literary and scientific, who represented surrounding borders as the key elements of individual identity, but engaged in dialogue with these were others – George Eliot, for instance – who conceived of individuals as intersecting points in a social network. In *Membranes*, I had told the story with the writers emphasizing individual cells as protagonists, perhaps because of a personal affinity with their way of thinking. But as I read on, I became more and more interested in their opponents, those who envisioned nerve nets in which individuals were intersections. What motivated them? With microscopic evidence available for both points of view, why would one scientist or novelist see networks and another individual cells?

While writing *Membranes*, I had also noticed a pattern of metaphors for describing communication within a body, involving comparisons of nerves to telegraph lines. Many of the scientists investigating nerves in the mid-nineteenth century were equally interested in electricity and telegraphy, and collaborated with engineers, with the result that they talked about nerves and telegraphs in terms of each other. Historians of science such as Tim Lenoir have already documented this telecommunications – neuroscience link,[3] but I began to see something even more interesting: evidence of engineers listening to physiologists and adopting communications solutions offered by the body. I also saw literary writers developing the organic-technical comparisons made by the scientists.

So here again, I examined the way in which literary and scientific writers used language to approach the same issue: how communication occurred within a human body or a human society. Comparing an apparatus that permitted communication in a body with an apparatus that permitted communication in society made a lot of sense, but I wanted to do more than point out the mere presence of these metaphors. Far more interesting was the evidence for the motivational power of metaphors. As Lenoir has shown, the nerve – telegraph metaphors encouraged physiologists to do experiments and design instruments.

In juxtaposing these descriptions of communication, I focused on complaints about how little people could know and communicate, comparing literary writers', telegraphers' and physiologists' ideas about what could *not* be transmitted. I examined the writings of two Berlin physiologists, Hermann von Helmholtz and Emil Du Bois-Reymond, then that of the inventor Charles Babbage, and the novelists George Eliot, Bram Stoker, Mark Twain and Henry James. I found the literature by telegraphers the most interesting to analyse, such as the novel of former hotel telegrapher Ella Cheever Thayer, *Wired Love*. In this story, two operators fall in love over the wires, but have great difficulty bonding when they are physically together. Some of this literature by and for telegraph operators challenged gender roles in a fascinating way. In the story 'Playing with Fire', a tomboyish telegraph girl impersonates a man on line, only to discover that she has been writing to a man impersonating a woman.

By reading literary and scientific works in parallel, I was able to see how similar these writers' doubts and anxieties were about the limits of human communication. Writers such as Eliot saw the railway network in a positive light, as a representation of society's structure that might remind individuals of their connectedness to others, and consequently their responsibility to others.[4] But the fiction of the telegraphers showed the same skepticism as the scientists' accounts of human knowledge, in the sense of both *wissen* (knowing information) and *kennen* (being acquainted). When they are compared, the technological and organic communication systems revealed many of the same weaknesses, failing to permit a real merging of consciousness.

The criticisms that these two books have drawn over the past five years have offered some valuable insights into how literature and science may be studied in parallel.

During the past four years I have been working closely with historians of science, and their main response to my work has been that in analysing the way scientists have developed their ideas, I have assigned culture too great a role, and ignored practical, material factors such as what kinds of microscopes investigators used, what kinds of stains they employed, and what kinds of disciplinary pressures they faced. I believe that the historians are right, and I have been paying much more attention to these material factors in my current study of nineteenth century scientists.

For example, a key issue in *Membranes* was what motivates scientists. I was fascinated by why Italian neurohistologist Camillo Golgi, who invented a highly sensitive new staining technique in the 1870s, saw an interconnected network of neurons under his microscope, whereas Santiago Ramón y Cajal, who used Golgi's technique, saw individual cells that were closely intertwined. I was equally interested in why Robert Koch kept looking for the tuberculosis bacillus in 1880, even when his stains were not revealing any bacteria. I wondered why a microscopist in 1880 would continue to believe that tuberculosis was caused by bacteria, or that neurons were individual cells, if he could find no evidence for his ideas for months, even years, and respected investigators contradicted him. What would make him keep looking, opting to try one more stain? Certainly Cajal and Koch saw what they did partly because they selected, cut, stained and observed tissue more skillfully than other scientists. But even today, having learned a lot more about the history of science, I would assign culture a role. Where does scientific self-confidence come from? Why believe that there are individual cells to see? Why become a microscopist, not a plumber? Cultural and individual assumptions about the way the world works enter into all these decisions. Of course, culture can never fully account for what people see, since individual innovation and creativity play roles as important in science as they do in literature.

A more important criticism, at least from our perspective in the humanities, is that I have been distressingly vague about this 'culture medium' in which literary and scientific ideas move and recombine. Documenting instances of exchange, particularly collisions resulting in the movement of ideas from literature to science, is still the greatest challenge we face in analysing these fields in parallel. I believe the best working model of how literary and scientific creators influence one another is still N Katherine Hayles's feedback loop, whereby both literary and scientific thinkers contribute new concepts and expressions to culture, and culture offers those concepts and expressions to each of them in turn.[5] Hayles's model makes an excellent start, leaving it to individual investigators to show case studies of the exchanges taking place. In an insightful review of *Networking*, Priscilla Wald has written that 'language mediates the relation between literature and science';[6] this is probably true, but whose language, when, and how?

Recently I have received some very valuable, educational criticism of *Membranes* from Duncan Bell, a graduate student in history at Cambridge University.[7] In his reading of nineteenth century British political texts, he has not encountered many metaphors involving the penetration of membranes by pathological organisms. He accepted that I saw them in the work of scientists and literary writers, but he could not accept my claim that politicians also used them, since they seemed to be absent from the arguments of any British imperial writer except Arthur Conan Doyle. Just how widespread were these metaphors of infection that I was calling cultural? Who thought that people, minds and nations were defined by permeable borders? Workers? Laboratory scientists? National leaders? Novelists? At what point can one claim that a metaphor is a cultural phenomenon?

Shawn Rosenheim, too, has pointed out that I never got beyond general statements about culture and language shaping individual writers' notions of identity, and it would be refreshing to see a specific case worked through in detail.[8] I have greatly admired Carlo Ginzburg's analysis of such a case in *The Cheese and the Worms*,[9] a study of exactly where a sixteenth century Italian heretic got his ideas. In the project in which I am currently engaged, I am trying to do the same kind of microhistory.

On the basis of these recent responses to my work, I would like to offer some ideas about how the study of nineteenth century literature and science may best develop as a field.

First, one can read science as literature, applying techniques of literary analysis to scientific texts and showing how cultural assumptions have been incorporated into scientific writing. The danger of this approach is the possibility of underestimating scientists' own conscious, active engagement with language and culture. For example, Rosenheim wrote that the real surprise of *Networking* was 'the semiotic sophistication of nineteenth century scientists'.[10] This should not have been a surprise. Scientists are aware that they are writing texts, and in exploring literature and science conjointly, it is crucial not to be patronizing and imply that literary scholars need to teach scientists ways of thinking with which they are unfamiliar. Scientists think actively about the language they use, and the assumption that they do not has caused a great deal of anger and miscommunication between the cultures of the humanities and science. When they have to invent new terms for phenomena they have observed that do not yet have names, scientists think as creatively as any poet. For example, when the physiologist Johannes Müller was seeking a name for the beautiful microorganisms he was fishing out of the Mediterranean Sea waves, he consulted the philologist Jakob Grimm. Together they devised the name 'pelagischer Auftrieb', or 'ocean-surface upwelling'.[11] Today these organisms are known as plankton.

More specifically, what does it mean to apply literary techniques to scientific writing? Must one be trained to do this? What does it involve? So far, the most common approach has been to reveal patterns in the rhetorical figures of scientific texts, especially their metaphors. Evelyn Fox Keller did this impressively in *Gender and Science*, now nearly two decades ago, showing how, from the seventeenth century onwards, many scientists have represented themselves as men who rip the veils off a resistant female nature.[12] Keller's analysis of classic scientific essays has been enormously valuable, but there is a danger when one examines literary texts in the same way. Jonathan Culler has called it Little Jack Hornerism, or proving one's intelligence by sticking in one's thumb and pulling out a metaphor.[13] Any patterns of rhetorical figures extracted need to form part of a reading that makes sense of the work as a whole.

In association with these searches for metaphorical patterns, then, come narrative analyses. There are rules about how science must be told, in oral presentations, articles, and histories of science. Both research reports and histories of science are narratives that can be analysed in terms of the writer's motivation for telling a story in a particular way.

Scientists write their own histories in many senses, and a second way to unite literature and science is to analyse fiction written by scientists. In my teaching, one of the stereotypes I have always tried hardest to combat is the one of 'literature types' and 'science types'. Insecurity about our identity drives us to classify each other, and it is a grievous mistake to presume that people who write literature cannot 'do' science, or that people who do science cannot write literature. Like Gillian Beer, I believe that a central aspect of both novel-writing and laboratory science is the visual imagination, the ability to envision a model system, manipulate it, and explain it to other people.[14] In *Membranes* I analysed Santiago Ramón y Cajal's *Vacation Stories*, five short stories written between 1885 and 1886 and published in 1905.[15] Cajal is well-known to neuroscientists, since his drawings of neurons are so superb that they still appear in most introductory neurobiology textbooks. Cajal shared the Nobel prize for medicine with Camillo Golgi (who invented the tissue stain he used) in 1906 for proving that neurons are independent cells. In his short stories, he showed to perfection how creativity can develop in parallel in literature and in the lab.

In Cajal's tale 'The Corrected Pessimist', a depressed young scientist who has failed to obtain a faculty position is about to commit suicide when the spirit of science suddenly appears to him and tells him that for a year, he must live with a new kind of vision: his eyes will be given the resolving power of a strong microscope. The disoriented scientist then begins to walk around Madrid, seeing the world as Cajal saw it through his microscope lenses. Cajal's descriptions in this story are truly ingenious. In one scene, the protagonist goes to the Prado and looks at the paintings as though he were seeing them through a microscope:

> If only he hadn't done it! What a terrible disillusionment! The magic spell of colour and outline had been completely dissolved. In its place, the loathsome mosaic revealed itself in all of its terrible nudity, the same image that had been following him like an hallucinatory obsession. First, he saw furrows, hills, and valleys formed by irregular deposits of amber varnish, all broken by cracks like the ones the summer sun makes in dried-out mud. Every contour of this angry, congealed sea emitted lively reflections like myriads of stars, disrupting the colour atrociously. Through the turbid varnish, he glimpsed ravines and sandy riverbeds and polychromatic pebbles, all scrambled and heaped together in the most nauseating confusion. These were the impressions received by Juan's astonished eyes when he regarded the sweet, pasty flesh of Murillo's virgins or the strong, honest, precise brush-strokes of Velázquez's paintings.[16]

I suspect that Cajal called these tales 'Vacation Stories' because they provided a much-needed opportunity to play, but fiction-writing also offered him something more valuable. For many scientists, literary creation provides a way to explore ideas emerging from ongoing experiments that cannot be published in journals because they lack evidence and/or violate an accepted scientific paradigm.

A third way of analysing literary and scientific texts in parallel is to select works that address related issues (whether mental faculties are located in particular parts of the brain, for instance), lay them out side by side, and let readers explore the relationships for themselves. Recently, I have done this in an anthology for Oxford University Press,[17] and I encourage everyone to do the same for particular subject areas, such as nineteenth century literature and technology. Anthologies offer undergraduates – especially science students – an excellent opportunity to explore the relations between literature and science.

Finally, a fourth way to combine literary and scientific studies is to write the history of science *as* literature. About five years ago, I realized that many of the scientists I have been studying – embryologist Ernst Haeckel, histologist Theodor Schwann, pathologist Rudolf Virchow, and physiologists Hermann Helmholtz and Emil Du Bois-Reymond – all studied with the Berlin physiologist Johannes Müller. Müller taught anatomy and physiology in Berlin from 1833–1858, and his favourite research subject was not experimental physiology but comparative anatomy, particularly the creation of museum collections. How could Haeckel, Schwann, Virchow, Du Bois-Reymond and Helmholtz have started with the same adviser and taken the ideas they once shared with him in such different directions?

The project, currently entitled *Müller's Lab*, has grown into a way to explore several questions at once: (1) How are personal life and work related, and how do personal relationships affect scientists' selection of research projects? (2) What motivates scientists to do their work on a day-to-day basis? (3) How do individual narratives of laboratory experiences evolve into an official history of science?

I have found that each of Müller's students has his own account of his adviser, and many of them contradict each other. Most were written long after the collaboration with Müller – sometimes as much as fifty years. Until recently, the official story of Müller in the history of science was that he was The Man (in Germany, at least) who turned physiology from a kind of philosophy into a rigorous experimental science subject to the laws of physics and chemistry. Strikingly, his students claim that they did this in spite of him, not because of him. The case of Müller and his students offers rich opportunities for exploring the relationships between scientific research, personality, and everyday life. Over the course of his career, Müller experienced at least five incapacitating depressions lasting six to eight months. At other times, he worked continuously, fuelled only by strong coffee. Müller also suffered from severe insomnia, and he may have committed suicide with an opium overdose in 1858. He served as Rector of Berlin University during the uprisings of 1848, and had to negotiate between radical students and the Prussian king. Through all of this, he continued performing research, making crucial contributions to neuroscience, endocrinology and zoology.

In examining the forces acting on Müller, his students and their science, I have tried to rewrite the history of science as I think William Faulkner might have composed it, comparing the students' contrasting perspectives. In his memorial address for Müller at the Prussian Academy of Sciences, Emil Du Bois-Reymond claimed that Müller understood nothing about the aesthetics of experimentation, and was held back by his belief in a life force unique to living organisms.[18] Ernst Haeckel wrote that Müller had committed suicide because he could not solve the riddle of how all living things were related – something that Haeckel himself claimed to have done by adopting Darwin's evolutionary theory.[19] Many historians of science have quoted these students' accounts of Müller uncritically, whereas all of them are written with the students' own interests in mind.[20] In the *Müller's Lab* project, I have intentionally juxtaposed these students' stories to show how different scientific history can sound depending on who is writing it. I have called this strategy 'writing the history of science *as* literature', because when I described it to my colleague Hans-Jörg Rheinberger at the Max Planck Institute for the History of Science, he said: 'This is a novel.'

In German, literary scholars are known as *Literaturwissenschaftler* (literary scientists), a word that in English is an oxymoron. In my native language, one can be a literary scholar *or* a scientist, but not both. To someone from England or America, 'literary scientist' is nonsensical in an extremely funny way. Like 'sanitary engineer', it seems like an overly prestigious title for someone who deals not with order but with mess. Of course, the German word *Wissenschaftler* could be translated as 'scholar', but that would make scientists 'nature scholars', and the usual German word for 'scholar' is *Gelehrte*. The fact that Germans consider both scientists and literary scholars to be *Wissenschaftler* reflects their confidence that both are building knowledge. In English-speaking cultures, scientists do their best to construct knowledge, aware that their findings may be refined or rejected by the next generation. But what do literary scholars do? Do we *know* more about *Middlemarch* than we did in 1872? Many non-academics regard literary scholars as wine connoisseurs, experts in good taste because of their experienced palates. This may be a consequence of English's conflation of *connaître* and *savoir*, of *kennen* and *wissen*, in the verb 'to know', but this does not explain why German literary scholars are *Wissenschaftler*, while those in America are non-scientists. As teachers, we convey biographical and historical information, and we foster critical thinking and logical argumentation. But do we build knowledge? Certainly not in the sense that scientists do.

By examining metaphors and other rhetorical figures, scholars of literature and science are exploring essential elements of knowledge, for metaphors provide the connecting links in many epistemological systems. Knowledge is always a temporary structure that evolves with time, and if it is a structure – a metaphor that may not be useful and must itself be examined – metaphors allow workers to build in new directions.

In creating the field of literature and science, the people for whom literary scholars most need to write are scientists. We should write not to educate or to convert the heathen, but to show our common interests. Literature and science will not survive as a field unless scholars can justify its value to people outside it. We must be able to explain to a biochemist, a stockbroker, a doctor, or a hard-working student what we do and what its value is. I would say that its value is eliminating unnecessary, wasteful conflicts about the relative worth of different fields, and promoting mutual respect by showing that literary scholars and scientists are both trying to understand people's role in the universe.

CONTAGIOUS SYMPATHIES: GEORGE ELIOT AND RUDOLF VIRCHOW

Kirstie Blair

In 1871, John Blackwood wrote to George Eliot, while reading her manuscript of *Middlemarch*: 'I have met old Brooke and curiously contagious creatures they are, if you found yourself talking with an amiable specimen of the sort I believe that at the end of the conversation you would feel as if you had equalled him.'[1] His comment is interesting because it picks up on Eliot's repeated use of the imagery of contagion in her novel, and on her use of scientific language (hence the reference to Brooke as a 'specimen'). Contagion in this comment acts as a form of sympathy: Blackwood notes that people can infect one another in social interactions, taking on each other's characteristics. He also points towards a common model for reading in the nineteenth century, that of contagion between text and reader based upon the sympathy induced by the reading process. In 1871, however, 'contagion' also had a particular frame of reference with regard to new theories about the transmission of disease. Blackwood's reference, showing that he uses 'contagion' in the most familiar sense of person-to-person transmission, might serve as an indication that 'contagionism' was back in fashion.

The 1870s were the decade in which germ theory, which gave new credibility to the notion of transmission between humans, started to emerge as the accepted cause of disease. As an editorial in the *Lancet* from October 1870 comments, new microscopic investigations into germs or 'microzymes' had started to 'remove much of the mystery which envelops the subject of contagion ... light is thereby being thrown from several quarters on the intimate character of contagia'.[2] Pasteur's work was known in Britain by this time, and after 1876,

Koch's investigations into anthrax seemed to definitely have proved the existence of 'germs' or 'microbes'. While there were still disagreements about precisely how germs operated, and about whether they were living organisms entering the body from outside or generated within it, by the late 1870s, as one medical writer notes, germ theory had been largely accepted by the profession, and with it the notion that most (if not all) diseases were contagious.[3] This represented a significant shift in thought. From the 1820s to the 1860s, anticontagionism, which emphasized environmental factors in the cause of disease – particularly atmospheric influences, or contamination from dirt and waste – had largely prevailed. Anticontagionism was a political as well as a medical issue, because support for public health measures – sanitation, education in hygiene, new systems of sewage and water distribution – was perceived as dependent on proof that disease was not contagious.[4] For British campaigners for sanitary reform and public health, such as Edwin Chadwick, T Southwood Smith or Henry Acland, anticontagionism was therefore vital.

When Eliot wrote in her *Middlemarch* notebook: 'Contagion – actual state of the question. Books concerning?', then, she was doubtless considering both debates over contagion and anticontagionist writing in the 1830s, and the shifts in thought occurring in the decade in which she was writing.[5] As in all its scientific knowledge, *Middlemarch* is doubly reflective here – immersed in the debates of its setting, while subtly ironizing these through references to later knowledge. This chapter argues that Eliot thinks through nineteenth century ideas about contagion in two ways. First, she plays with the language and imagery of atmospheric or miasmatic influence as part of a general consideration of the social and environmental aspects of disease, and its moral implications; and second she considers diseases, again both literally and metaphorically, as localized disturbances which spread from individual to individual, gradually corrupting a society. Rather than being something external which must be fought and defeated, disease tends to be seen as a distortion of that society, or of the individual himself. Anticontagionist rhetoric in *Middlemarch* subtly shifts into considerations of the effect of one person on another, and contagion itself comes to act as power does: in Eliot's description of Bulstrode's effect on his society, it 'propagates itself, spreading out of all proportion to its external means'.[6]

In exploring how Eliot exploits the rhetoric of contagion, and uses it to encompass the ways in which ideas and feelings might spread through society, I will focus on how her perspective may be influenced by the work of Rudolf Virchow, one of the greatest German scientists of the nineteenth century, and specifically by his writings on cellular pathology and on epidemic diseases. The potential for sympathetic contagion between Eliot's and Virchow's writings brings out the sense of *Middlemarch* as a novel which is itself explicitly infected by various discourses of science and medicine, and by continental as well as British theories. Virchow has received little attention in critical work on Eliot's influences, although it has long been recognized that Eliot uses cell theory, developed in the 1860s by Virchow and others, as a fruitful source of metaphor in *Middlemarch*, and that in his search for the 'primitive tissue' Lydgate narrowly misses finding the cell.[7] As I have argued elsewhere, cellular pathology was not a unified field, and in the various debates over the implications of this new theory in the 1860s, Eliot and Lewes were more or less decisively in Virchow's camp, echoing his most famous phrases and arguments.[8] Although Eliot's investigation into contagion encompassed the most advanced English thought on the subject, as well as research into German and French writers, I want to suggest that Virchow's powerful and influential arguments about the social conditions of disease, his pioneering combination of public health reform, politics and medical research, and his model of how contagion spread within a community of cells in the body, offer a valuable comparison to *Middlemarch*, and a model for what Eliot's Lydgate tries but fails to achieve.

Eliot's traditional provincial doctors in *Middlemarch* envisage disease as an alien intrusion or irruption into comfortable and healthy life: 'Disease in general was called by some bad name, and treated accordingly without shilly-shally – as if, for example, it were to be called insurrection, which must not be fired on with blank-cartridge, but have its blood drawn at once.'[9] The association of disease with 'insurrection' points to the political (as well as medical) conservatism of the established profession. Of the two local doctors, Dr Sprague 'had weight, and might be expected to grapple with a disease and to throw it; while Dr Minchin might be better able to detect it lurking and to circumvent it'.[10] Again, disease is personified as a criminal threat which can be isolated and defeated. Yet the imagery of the novel continually counteracts this claim. *Middlemarch* is a novel of miasmas, of influences and atmospheres, and as such it provides a subtle reflection upon the anticontagionist stance of its setting. Fred Vincy's typhoid fever, for example, which creates an important turning point in the plot in that it allows Lydgate to demonstrate his superior medical expertise, furthers the romance between him and Rosamond, and causes Fred himself to reflect on the dangerous consequences of his careless behaviour, is in part 'caught' from his unwise venture into 'a backstreet where you might as easily have been poisoned without expense of drugs as in any grim street in that unsanitary period'.[11] The type of disease Fred catches is also significant in demonstrating Eliot's double vision: Anne Hardy notes that typhoid was much discussed between 1826 and 1830, meaning that Lydgate, as a pioneering young doctor, would be up-to-date with the latest research, but also observes that in 1871 the typhoid fever of the Prince of Wales, blamed on the sanitation in the country house he was visiting, created a panic about sanitary arrangements.[12]

The source of Fred's fever seems clear, yet on another level this horse-buying expedition already signifies a moral infection: Fred's extravagance and bad judgement. Furthermore, these unsanitary backstreets recall the image of Lydgate, in Chapter 21, hunting for disease in the 'invisible thoroughfares which are the first lurking-places of anguish, mania and crime'.[13] An image drawn from anticontagionist rhetoric, the poisonous backstreets, is shifted from the literal to the metaphorical and relocated within the human body. Disease still 'lurks', but on the inside, in the pathways of nerves and brain, rather than in the external world.

The same occurs with miasmatic imagery. T Southwood Smith – a leading campaigner for public health in the first half of the century, whose work on fevers and epidemics Eliot cites in her notebooks – was one of many experts to write extensively on the dangers of marsh fog, mists and other pollutions of the air.[14] When Eliot describes Casaubon's desires, then, as clinging 'low and mist-like in very shady places', her language immediately implies a creepy unhealthiness, as does Celia's vivid imagining of his learning as 'a kind of damp which might saturate a neighbouring body' – it is as though he carries around his own infectious atmosphere.[15] As Virchow noted in 1868, the catch-all term 'typhus fever' 'literally means a fog or vapour, a clouding of the mind'.[16] The decay of Rosamond and Lydgate's marriage, likewise, is shown by the shift from a 'divine clearance of haze' as they first meet each other's eyes, to the 'chill fog which had gathered between them' by the time of Raffles's death. In Chapter 58, when Lydgate recognizes Rosamond's obstinate refusal to accede to his interests, the narrator comments: 'Lydgate was much worried, and conscious of new elements in his life as noxious to him as an inlet of mud to a creature that has been used to breathe and bathe and dart after its illuminated prey in the clearest of waters.'[17] 'Noxious' is a term strongly linked to atmospheric contagion, and this points towards a quotation from Stahl found in Eliot's notebooks: 'Disease, effort of the soul to throw off noxious influences' – it could be said that Lydgate spends much of the novel attempting (and failing) to do this.[18] As the imagery of muddied waters suggests, his marriage is beginning to seem like a form of pollution, a concept both etymologically and metaphorically linked to infection.

Elsewhere in the novel, contagious diseases are a model for alienation from society; so Will Ladislaw describes his poverty as 'leprosy', because it separates him from Dorothea, and Lydgate sees himself as a leper due to his association with Bulstrode. Bulstrode's downfall, indeed, is perhaps the key example of contagion, contaminating both Lydgate and Will, and creating a ripple effect within the community as a whole. When Bulstrode contemplates lending Lydgate money, the narrator comments: 'He did not measure the quantity of diseased motive which had made him wish for Lydgate's goodwill, but the quantity was none the less actively there, like an irritating agent in his blood.'[19] This is an image drawn from contagionist rather than anticontagionist rhetoric, implying that disease might be generated from within, from a 'morbid condition of the blood'.[20] Eliot plays on the irony of Bulstrode's public health aims – he is the primary mover behind the new Fever Hospital – by figuring his premonitions of disgrace as 'distinct and inmost as the shiver and the ache of oncoming fever'. There is a further irony in his pious declaration: 'I should have no interest in hospitals if I believed that nothing more was concerned therein than the cure of mortal diseases',[21] for 'mortal diseases', in Eliot, may consist of moral pathology as well as literal sickness. Bulstrode is right to see that health does not depend simply on curing a physical ailment, but he fails to apply this to his own case. The isolation he suffers after news of his past life spreads through the town is effectively a form of moral quarantine, seeking to contain his corrupting influence.

Charles Daubeny, a medical writer and early investigator into germs, wrote in an article owned by Lewes:

> Whilst … we are compelled to admit the existence of a specific principle capable of diffusion through various channels, either by the touch, by the breath, by the water of the infected localities, or, lastly, by the atmosphere itself, we must also assume that every living being possesses, inherent in itself, a certain power of resistance; so that it is quite conceivable that a weaker degree of the poison, may circulate innocuously through the community, and … may attack only those whose system is already in a state of greater or less disorder.[22]

Daubeny's account of infection recalls Suzanne Graver's comment, in her work on Eliot and community, that 'whenever consensus consists of hostility not sympathy, poison is in the air'.[23] But if the atmosphere of Middlemarch is always infected, it is only those who are already tainted, like Lydgate, who will be susceptible to attack. It is in Eliot's depictions of the way in which disease gradually undermines individual character, seizing on those 'whose system is already in a state of greater or less disorder', and from there moves outwards into society, that her views come into contact with Virchow's cell theory and his writings on pathology. Virchow had not discovered the cell, or been the first to argue for its importance, but his work on cellular pathology was vital, because he presented the most forceful argument and evidence that every cell developed from another cell ('omnis cellula e cellula') and, crucially, that disease functioned as an altered condition of cells: pathology was not something separate and unique, but simply a different set of conditions.[24] The focus on cells additionally implied, he argued, that disease should always be studied as something local – not as a nebulous condition affecting the entire system, but as a specific formation linked to a particular organ.[25] Medical historian Michael Worboys describes this localized pathology as the 'key conceptual revolution of the first half of the nineteenth century'.[26] It was potentially a concept with strong appeal for Eliot, who cites Southwood Smith's early account of local versus general origins of fever in her notebooks.[27] On one level, indeed, *Middlemarch* itself can be seen as an instance of investigating wider corruption – disease in the state as a whole – through a thorough small-scale study of local pathological conditions.

Cellular pathology effectively located contagion within the body, passing from cell to cell, but Virchow, as a campaigner for public health and a leading sanitary reformer, was wary of contagionist arguments that disease might propagate between as well as within individuals. For political reasons, and due to his personal investment in the concept of cells, then, Virchow did not initially welcome the germ theory, and his writings of the 1860s, those with which Eliot was most likely to be familiar, are cautiously anticontagionist in approach.[28] In an 1867 essay entitled 'On the New Advances in Pathology', published as part of the collection *Vier Reden über Leben und Kranksein*, a set of four essays owned by the Leweses, Virchow argued that pathology had finally relinquished the 'concept that disease has to some extent a being of its own, a form of existence, which has invaded the body as something foreign and simultaneously independent and is perceived as something separate from the parts of the body.'[29] Instead, as he wrote in an earlier statement on cellular pathology, doctors needed to realize that 'All pathological formations are either degenerations, transformations, or repetitions of typical physiological structures.'[30] In other words, disease is a development or an extension of what already exists. This theory had clear implications for Virchow's social ideas. His medical research was strongly framed by his liberal views on reform – Virchow had been a revolutionary for a short time in the heady days of 1848, and he never abandoned his belief in self-government, his distrust of centralized authority and his emphasis on individual self-improvement. As many medical historians and biographers have commented, these views shaped the direction of his medical research in that he saw cellular society as a model of social interaction, in which every individual had responsibility for himself, but could also affect those around him.[31] When he writes: 'I have myself attempted to solve the riddle of disease in terms of altered conditions of the cells'; and 'all diseases are in the last analysis reducible to disturbances, either active or passive, of large or small groups of living units', he is therefore thinking of a 'unit' as equivalent to a citizen in a cell-state.[32] As I note elsewhere, this quotation, and similar comments on cells, may be echoed by Lewes in *Problems of Life and Mind*, as well as by Eliot in her description of Lydgate as a 'unit who would make a certain amount of difference towards ... spreading change', but who effectively ends up spreading disease.[33] Virchow expands upon these ideas in the brilliant essay 'Atoms and Individuals', also owned by the Leweses:

> As in the lives of nations, so in the lives of individuals the state of health of the whole is determined by the well-being and close interrelation of the individual parts; disease appears when individual members begin to sink into a state of inactivity disadvantageous to the commonwealth, or to lead parasitic existences at the expense of the whole.[34]

If we read this in relation to *Middlemarch*, we could see, for instance, Bulstrode and Raffles as examples of parasitic individuals in different ways, and we could also note how disturbances caused by Casaubon's will or Featherstone's will, to take only two obvious examples, can spread outwards to affect a wide circle of individuals. Eliot is also, of course, interested in how passivity, or a 'state of inactivity', might function as almost more dangerous than activity; hence it is Lydgate's failure to make a conscious decision that leads to his marriage and his debts, and Bulstrode's complex negotiation between passivity and action in Raffles's death, where it is questionable whether his failure to prevent his housekeeper giving Raffles alcohol also constitutes an active disobedience to Lydgate's orders.

Rudolf Virchow was only one of the many writers Eliot and Lewes encountered, and in arguing for his influence I do not intend to limit the potential influence of other eminent British and German authorities. As Virchow himself acknowledged, Britain led the field in the early nineteenth century in terms of investigations into the social conditions of disease, agitation for public health reform, and sanitary campaigns. But there is reason to suggest that Virchow may have been more significant to Eliot and Lewes than has been recognized. They owned at least seven of his published works, plus a number of articles from the journal he edited, *Virchows Archiv*. Lewes, clearly very up-to-date in his knowledge of German science, owned *Cellular Pathology* in German (he cites it in *The Physiology of Common Life*), and was presented in 1859 with an English edition with Virchow's compliments, which he carefully read and annotated throughout. While medical historians have underplayed Virchow's influence in Britain in the 1860s, there is evidence that his reputation underwent a remarkable change and growth during this decade. In 1863, for instance, the *Lancet* prints some negative and xenophobic comments on *Cellular Pathology* in which the author claims that Virchow stole his ideas from prior English works; yet by 1868 the journal carried a highly favourable review of Virchow's lecture on 'Hunger-Typhus', and, in the next two years, continued to report on the ideas and actions of this 'celebrated Berlin investigator'.[35]

The *British Medical Journal*, in a more striking reversal, prints one hostile review of *Cellular Pathology* before 1870, when suddenly a short editorial piece describes Virchow as 'perhaps the most illustrious of living physicians', the 'eloquent and fearless opponent of all arbitrary exercise of power, and unflinching advocate of popular institutions', equally admirable as a pathologist and a patriot.[36] Further articles throughout 1871 describe his work, including an adulatory piece by a student who attended his lectures. In 1872, the *British Medical Journal* excitedly reported a rumour that he might be planning to settle in England permanently.[37] This sudden interest was as much political as medical: Virchow had been drawn to public attention in Britain as the leading opponent of Bismarck, and in the widely reported episode when he refused Bismarck's challenge to a duel, he was represented as forward-looking and democratic, as opposed to Bismarck's violent and antiquated outlook.[38] If Eliot were reading medical journals around 1870 in preparation for writing *Middlemarch*, her attention might well have been drawn to this pioneering campaigner for social and medical justice.

Moreover, in the medical world, Virchow's theories were gradually gaining acceptance. Both Lionel Beale and James Paget, for example, revised their editions of works on physiology and pathology to incorporate references to Virchow's theories, so in Paget's *Lectures on Surgical Pathology* in 1853 there were eight references to Virchow, and in the 1863 edition there were seventeen. Paget, an intimate friend of Lewes and Eliot, quickly became one of Virchow's closest friends, and frequently entertained him during his trips to London. Beale, whose work on tissues was also known by the Leweses, shifted from scornful references to the 'so-called cell' in the 1860s to a detailed description of the operation of cells in his 1872 book *Bioplasm*. While there is no proof that Virchow ever met Lewes, the circles in which they moved overlapped to an extent that makes their failure to meet each other surprising. As Lewes wrote on receiving his complimentary copy of *Cellular Pathology*: 'the greatest of German physiologists (whom I *don't* know) has just sent me a book of his'.[39] To stress the fact that he does not personally know Virchow, in this letter, seems to imply that he would have been expected to do so.

Lewes and Eliot therefore had first-hand knowledge of Virchow's writings, and it is entirely plausible that when Eliot wrote her note on contagion and contemplated her depiction of an ambitious young doctor, determined to find the ultimate structure of life and hence explain the source of disease, she might have turned to Virchow. Virchow is not, however, so much a model for Lydgate as a reproach. In 1832, Lydgate is fired with the ambition to run a provincial hospital to investigate Fevers which will become a centre for medical research – rather like the Pathological Institute Virchow set up in Berlin several decades later. But in his approach towards disease, Lydgate is a failure because he focuses solely on medical issues, to the neglect of social and political implications. This is very clearly shown in his conversation with Will Ladislaw about the Reform Bill in Chapter 46, in which he does not perceive the connection between 'the low state of pathology' and the low state of the country in general. '[Lydgate] was no radical in relation to anything but medical reform', the narrator notes dryly.[40] For a doctor supposedly committed to public health, this is fatal. As Virchow repeatedly and famously declared, medicine 'is a social science in its very bone and marrow', and the expression 'public health' in itself 'shows to those who have believed, and still believe, that medicine has nothing to do with politics the magnitude of their error'.[41] While he was a young man, even younger than Eliot's Lydgate, Virchow was sent to investigate an outbreak of typhus fever in Upper Silesia, and his report into conditions there presented one of the nineteenth century's strongest indictments of the failure of the government in matters of public health. He argued that long-term political reform, encompassing better education, a sense of civic and national pride, and decentralized government, was vital to prevent future epidemics. The translators of this report in the 1980s comment that 'even now it continues to set a standard for any attempt to understand and change the social conditions that produce illness'.[42] The experience of Upper Silesia not only spurred Virchow into politics, it convinced him that any medical man or scientist who saw himself as outside or above politics could not hope to effect lasting change. When he writes: 'During the times of the political movement one would only too often learn to one's regret what happens when men of science stand outside the movement or, as they much too readily suppose, above it',[43] he seems almost to be predicting Lydgate's fate.

We can readily see that Eliot, whether she knew of Virchow's writings on Upper Silesia or not, sympathizes with this view in *Middlemarch*. Lydgate's downfall is intimately linked to the way in which he compartmentalizes his life, and to his slightly arrogant disregard for the opinions of Middlemarch society, particularly of those who make up the majority of his patients. Although he discusses philanthropic schemes with Dorothea, it is never suggested that he is particularly interested in changing the environment in which the poor live; he considers only those social elements which bear directly on his cases, rather than perceiving that social elements underlie every case he sees. Gossip, rumour and superstition are contemptuously dismissed by him, but it is in this persistent unfolding of speculation about his behaviour and motives – seen in the conversations in the public house in Chapters 45 and 71, for instance – that the seeds of his moral downfall are sown. He cannot escape infection from this environment. As the narrator notes of ambitious men, in a discussion of Lydgate's scientific aims and the potential for their failure: 'Nothing in the world more subtle than the process of their general change! In the beginning they inhaled it unknowingly; you and I may have sent some of our breath towards infecting them, when we uttered our conforming falsities or drew our silly conclusions.'[44] While Lydgate ignores the trivial small talk of society, like Mr Brookes's inanities, it can be dangerously infectious.

When Lydgate asks the wrong questions about his detailed medical research into structure, thus missing what should be the focus of his investigations, the cell, he also hinders himself from appreciating the processes of contagion and infection, and the ways in which they proliferate both inside and outside the body. While he concentrates on the anticontagionist, external staples of 'ventilation and diet – that sort of thing',[45] he ignores the spread of diseased thought, feeling and morality within himself and other individuals, and between those individuals. Readers of Eliot who were familiar with theories about contagion would have noted how these interact within the novel. In addition, by considering the sympathies between fictional and medical description, English literature and German science, Rudolf Virchow and George Eliot, we can see how Eliot deliberately drew attention to the ways in which literature and medicine infect each other. In Virchow's passionate, quasi-philosophical meditations on health and disease, which frequently cite poetry and deliberately exploit religious rhetoric, she could have found another model of this fruitful contagion. While Eliot's other fictions are equally involved with different discourses, and aware of the work of scientists and doctors, no other novel deploys the rhetoric of disease and contagion to such effect.[46] Virchow once argued that epidemic disease might be eliminated, and society benefited more generally, by training physicians to produce 'long, detailed studies of local conditions'.[47] Eliot, in her field, does exactly this in Middlemarch.

FROM PARASITOLOGY TO PARAPSYCHOLOGY: PARASITES IN NINETEENTH CENTURY SCIENCE AND LITERATURE

Anne-Julia Zwierlein

Ruskin's Parasites: 'the Instinct for the Horrible'

Devising an educational course in natural history for his child-acquaintance, little Agnes, in letter 51 of *Fors Clavigera* (March 1875), John Ruskin dwells at some length on the kind of books he does *not* want Agnes to consult: 'most modern books on natural history only cease to be tiresome by becoming loathsome'.[1] While the odd book emphasizing 'mutual assistance' in the animal world meets with his approval, the rest come in for quite a bit of criticism. Louis Figuier's *The Insect World* (revised edition 1872), he exclaims, 'has made me sick with disgust by its descriptions, at every other leaf I opened, of all that is horrible in insect life'.[2] Most scorn is poured on the Reverend W Houghton's *Country Walks* (1869) and *Seaside Walks of a Naturalist with his Children* (1870), which strike Ruskin by their utter lack of any 'education ... in *gentleness*'. Several extracts from Houghton illustrate his point: in a mad scramble for peewits' eggs, special delight is taken by clergyman and children in the obvious anxiety and excitement of the female bird; and in a wild hunt by dogs and boys for salmon in a pool, they register, with joy: 'How immensely rapid is the motion of a frightened salmon!' These involuntarily funny and badly written passages conclude with the clergyman deciding to 'look for parasites' – the culmination of the general distastefulness, in Ruskin's opinion: 'But wait a little; some of the fish lie on the sand. I will look for parasites. Here, on this salmon, is a curious parasite, with a body an inch long, and with two long tail-like projections three times the length of the creature itself. It is a crustacean, and related to the *Argulus foliaceus*.'[3]

Ruskin ends by deploring what he diagnoses as 'this extraordinary instinct for the horrible, developing itself at present in the English mind ... so that sensation *must* be got out of death, or darkness, or frightfulness'.[4] Ruskin's – albeit ambivalent – rejection of the materialist science of his age, and especially the theory of evolution, is well known; one of his correspondents good-humouredly reproaches Ruskin with an attitude towards 'Darwin and Huxley, worthy only of a Psalmist or pretty economist of fifteen'.[5] In letter 53 (May 1875), Ruskin's idea of the craze for parasites as a specifically modern disease recurs as part of his interpretation of the Eighth Psalm. Far from fulfilling their God-ordained role as caring masters 'over all the works of [God's] hands', humans have destroyed creation.[6] Their interest is aroused not by what is good and wholesome, but by perverted and diseased aspects of nature; thus, for instance, his contemporaries are currently devouring 'journal accounts of new insect-plague on the vine'. He compares this kind of sensationalism with Old-Testament idolatry, quoting the words of Solomon: 'Yea, they worshipped those beasts also that are most hateful ...' (*Wisdom* 15), further expanding on this analogy in a footnote:

> n.: The instinct for the study of parasites, modes of disease, the lower forms of undeveloped creatures, and the instinctive processes of digestion and generation, rather than the varied and noble habit of life, – which shows itself so grotesquely in modern science, is the precise counterpart of the forms of idolatry (as of beetle and serpent, rather than of clean or innocent creatures), which were in great part the cause of final corruption in ancient mythology and morals.[7]

The study of parasites, for Ruskin, epitomizes what is wrong with modern society: the disturbance of traditional hierarchies, the misplaced emphasis on the marginal. His lifelong struggle for a holistic and spiritual experience of nature, for the values of hierarchy and place in defiance of a destabilized world, is a main strand also of *Fors Clavigera*. The spoiling of the countryside, and the waste and rubbish of industrialized society, are leitmotifs. Physical and mental pollution are, to Ruskin, inextricably linked, and England has degenerated into a 'mere heap of agonizing human maggots' without 'social structure'.[8] Robert Casillo has established a connection between Ruskin's discourse on parasites and his advocacy of the death penalty, taking his cue from Ruskin's repeated designation of criminals as 'partly men, partly vermin; what is human in them you must punish – what is vermicular, abolish'.[9] While this sounds as if a clear separation between centre and margin, wholesome nature and noxious parasite, were possible, elsewhere Ruskin is more ambiguous. Holding up nature as the expression of divine wisdom and organic growth, and as the model for human society, he also acknowledges a 'demonic aspect' in nature herself, 'creeping, and crawling, and rampant', resistant to control.[10] Mankind itself, he acknowledges, is 'still half-serpent, not extricated yet from its clay; a lacertine breed of bitterness'.[11] Ruskin is aware of social parasitism and capitalist exploitation, contrasting labourers with capitalist 'idlers' living in leisure and luxury. Yet, as Casillo remarks, he 'draws back from the revolutionary implications of his criticism. ... Far from challenging existing social hierarchy, he wants it purified morally and strengthened'.[12]

Thus, while Ruskin's writing evinces his desire to isolate, marginalize and expel the parasite from the natural and social system, he implicitly admits that parasites may be an inevitable part of that system. He is shying away, however, from arguments like those of Michel Serres, for whom, in a post-Romantic and postmodern culture parasitism has become 'the system itself' of human relationships.[13] In this chapter, I will examine the developing nineteenth century field of parasitology, looking at a representative choice of works by Charles Darwin, T Spencer Cobbold and other British and continental scientists, and at the reflection of this biological theme in literature from Charles Dickens and George Eliot to Bram Stoker and Arthur Conan Doyle. While there is a wealth of criticism on the literary figure of the parasite from Antiquity onwards, and in the field of nineteenth century studies especially on the novels of Zola and Balzac,[14] these studies argue exclusively on the grounds of literary history or poststructuralist musings in the style of Serres. Surprisingly, there are no sustained attempts to link nineteenth century literature with contemporary parasitological studies. The present chapter will advance a few steps towards remedying this situation. Taking my cue from Ruskin, the guiding questions will be how far parasites in these nineteenth century scientific and literary texts are seen in the light of the 'horrible' and marginal, how far they are accepted as inevitable, and how far a purpose and function within the natural system is ascribed to them. I will close by demonstrating how the biological phenomenon of the parasite is increasingly psychologized and interiorized in late-nineteenth century literature (if not in science): the parasite is always-already *within* ourselves – and even more: we are, as Doyle warns us, parasites *on* ourselves.

Nineteenth Century Parasitology: From Darwin to Cobbold

As the *Oxford English Dictionary* tells us, the ancient meaning of the term 'parasite' as derived from Greek comedy, a sponger, was common currency in the English language after the mid-sixteenth century. The biological sense of the term developed only in the early eighteenth century; the science of 'parasitology', however, is a late-nineteenth century acquisition, as is the verb 'parasitize', meaning 'to infest as a parasite'. The exchange between science and literature could not be closer in this case. While on the one hand an ancient literary topos gives a name to a newly emerging subfield of biological inquiries, on the other hand the literary stock figure of the sponger-parasite, fuelled by contemporary research, attains very concrete biological overtones in nineteenth century literature, as we will see below.[15] Parasitology as an institutionalized science was first mentioned in an 1893 *Times* article; in France, the first parasitological journal – the *Archives de parasitologie* – was launched in 1898; in 1908, the British journal *Parasitology* followed, founded by G H Nuttall, former assistant to Ray Lankester; only in 1920 was Nuttall officially appointed to a chair of parasitology at Cambridge.[16] When the *Encyclopaedia Britannica* (9th edition 1885) summarizes the state of the art in parasitological (or 'helminthological') studies, it becomes evident how international this research was – work by Küchenmeister, Cobbold, Davaine, Leuckart, and many others is cited; German, English and French research is taken into account.[17] In 1901, the German scientist Dr F Doflein provides a summary of existing research and classifications, such as the distinction between ectozoa and entozoa (parasites living on the outside of or inside their host), and the differentiation between varying degrees of mutualism in parasitical living arrangements: first, there is symbiosis, a mutual-aid arrangement between host and 'parasite', defined by de Bary in 1879; second, there is commensalism, the recycling by the parasite of nutrition discarded by the host; and third, there are the 'real parasites', which deprive their host organism of nutritional substance, thus weakening the host, in some cases triggering disease.[18] A closer look at some representative parasitological studies will now prepare us for a historically and scientifically grounded analysis of the parasite theme in nineteenth century literature.

Charles Darwin's interest in parasites, which he defined as '[a]n animal or plant living upon or in, and at the expense of, another organism',[19] is botanical and zoological, and only very occasionally (in *The Descent of Man*) medical. In *The Descent* (1871) parasites function primarily as important witnesses to the kinship of man and animal: Darwin emphasizes 'how closely man agrees in constitution with the higher mammals' by pointing to 'our liability to the same diseases, and to the attacks of allied parasites'.[20] On the whole, and throughout his scientific career, Darwin acknowledged parasites as well-adapted creatures, often citing them as examples of special beauty. In his *Journal of Researches into the Geology and Natural History of the various Countries visited by H.M.S. Beagle* (1839), he describes how 'the novelty of the parasitical plants' 'filled [him] with admiration'. In his notes on Rio de Janeiro, he enthuses about the 'wonderful and beautiful, flowering parasites ..., among which the beauty and delicious fragrance of some of the orchideae were most to be admired'. He finds most striking the evidence that coadaptation between organisms functions on the same principles all over the world: 'How singular is this relationship between parasitical fungi and the trees on which they grow, in distant parts of the world!'[21] Parasites are cited in the 'Introduction' to the Origin of Species (1859) as prime examples of successful 'co-adaptations of organic beings to each other and to their physical conditions of life', and again in his third chapter, on the 'Struggle for Existence', Darwin emphasizes: 'We see these beautiful co-adaptations ... in the humblest parasite which clings to the hairs of a quadruped or feathers of a bird; ... we see beautiful adaptations everywhere and in every part of the organic world.'[22]

Darwin is aware of the low esteem for parasites generally, and sometimes cannot help sharing it, as when he is repelled by the 'extraordinary and odious ... instinct' of slave-making ants, or of the ichneumonidae, wasps feeding and laying their eggs within the living bodies of caterpillars,[23] but he also often displays a gleeful iconoclasm:

> The following list completes, I believe, the terrestrial fauna [of the Cape Verde Islands]: a species of Feronia [a fly] and an acarus [a tick], which must have come here as parasites on the birds; a small brown moth, belonging to a genus that feeds on feathers; a staphylinus (Quedius) [a beetle] and a woodlouse from beneath the dung; and lastly, numerous spiders, which I suppose prey on these small attendants on, and scavengers of the waterfowl. The often-repeated description of the first colonists of the coral islets in the South Sea, is not, probably, quite correct: I fear it destroys the poetry of the story to find, that these little vile insects should thus take possession before the cocoa-nut tree and other noble plants have appeared.[24]

Here, in the Voyage of the Beagle, as in the Origin of Species, he enjoys destroying superficial, 'poetical' notions of nature, lifting the veil to point at the parasite or the struggle for existence behind birdsong and flower: 'We behold the face of nature bright with gladness ...; we do not see, or we forget that the birds which are idly singing round us mostly live on insects or seeds, and are thus constantly destroying life; or we forget how largely these songsters, or their eggs, or their nestlings, are destroyed by birds and beasts of prey ...'.[25] Through their participation in the universal struggle for life, however, parasites can fulfil useful functions in the natural system as a whole – for instance, by regulating the numbers of individuals in certain animal species which would otherwise multiply beyond control.[26]

Likewise, Otto Gruendler's 1850 medical dissertation, written in Latin, emphasizes that parasites are no aberrations of nature, but have their rightful place in the natural system: 'Parasitorum species diversae non fortuito aut naturae lusu nascuntur, sed arctissime cohaerent cum vi ac virtute naturae et certa ejus lege existunt.' They fulfil a purpose, and do not exist just for themselves: 'nihil modo sua causa esse creatum'.[27] Maximilian Perty, in his 1869 lecture *Ueber den Parasitismus in der organischen Natur (On Parasitism in Organic Nature)*, by contrast, tries but fails to leave moral considerations and anthropomorphizations out of the discussion. On the one hand, he emphasizes that whereas in human society individuals living at the expense of others are often less gifted than their fellow beings, this criterion cannot be applied to parasites in nature. On the other, when discussing the phenomenon of 'regressive metamorphosis' he explicitly proposes that it may be their deficient organization which forces parasites into their peculiar lifestyle[28] – and that some parasites may simply be of no benefit at all to the system. The exterior of these 'total parasites', he claims, immediately gives away their weakness and deficiency: they are of a 'strange, ugly, sometimes repulsive' appearance, often 'small, colourless or discoloured'.[29]

There is only one thing which this type of parasite, this 'proletarian' ['*Proletarier*'] can do well: produce offspring – some parasites even shedding all organs apart from the reproductive ones. Perty's term '*Proletarier*' transports class bias on a learned level: in Ancient Rome, 'proletarius' was Servius Tullius's designation for the poorer classes who could not serve the state with financial resources but only with their offspring, 'proles'.[30] Perty ends on a moralistic note, comparing the noble, 'open violence' of the beast of prey with the 'perfidious and clandestine' ways of the parasite, which kills slowly, after a prolonged period of sickness. While emphasizing that creative powers predominate over destructive ones both in nature and in society, he insists that the struggle for life is so ubiquitous that lower organisms may sometimes destroy higher ones,[31] and parasites may even infest other parasites – a phenomenon that 'P. GE.' in the *Encyclopaedia Britannica* calls 'hyperparasitism', and Serres calls the 'cascade'.[32] While humans are endowed with intelligence as a weapon, there is never any guarantee against the attack of parasites, which will continue to resist human powers.[33]

T Spencer Cobbold's treatise on *Parasites* (1879) equals Darwin in iconoclastic fervour, replying to Ruskin and other despisers of parasites that '[t]he study of the structure and economy of a humble parasite brings to the investigator no slight insight into the workings of nature. If these workings cannot at all times be pronounced to be "good and beautiful", they must at least be characterised as "true".'[34] Insisting that we consider entozoa (internal parasites) as 'a peculiar fauna, destined to occupy an equally peculiar territory' and manifesting a special form of coadaptation, Cobbold betrays an increasing predilection for such military metaphors: 'What our native country is to ourselves, the bodies of animals are to them. To attack, to invade, to infest, is their legitimate prerogative.' This seemingly generous attitude is often contradicted within the same volume – not least in the preface, where Cobbold expresses his hope that he 'should like to see a small army of helminthologists rise up and lay siege to the fortresses at present securely held by thousands of death-dealing parasites'.[35] The military rhetoric of invasion and repulsion, expertly described by Laura Otis in *Membranes* with respect to nineteenth century cell theory and bacteriology, sometimes carries away even this advocate of a neutral, scientific perspective.[36]

On the other hand, Cobbold energetically combats the still-prevailing prejudice that 'the internal parasites or entozoa [are] creatures either directly resulting from certain diseased conditions of their *hosts* or ... organisms which would not have existed if their *bearers* had been perfectly healthy', and the concomitant time-honoured superstition that parasites 'betoken evidence of Divine disfavour'.[37] How necessary such refutations still were becomes evident when we return to Gruendler's medical dissertation for a moment; here, some thirty years before Cobbold, the thesis was brought forward that often 'parasites' might just be, in fact, degenerated parts of the body itself: 'Quin etiam accuratior disquisitio interdum suspicionem et dubitationem nobis infert, utrum omnino de parasito, an de parte corporis degenerata instituenda sit.' Of course, here Gruendler is concerned in general with the danger of misinterpreting medical evidence; elsewhere, however, he does reveal uncertainty about how exactly parasites gain entry into their host's interior: 'nemo est, cui mirum videatur, rationem, qua in corpus humanum veniant, haud notam nobis esse'.[38] He seems, however, to be somewhat behind his time here, as the fact of generational change, the life-cycle of parasites from the larval to the adult stage through various host and 'interim host' organisms, was already partly known.[39] Doflein, in his résumé of nineteenth century parasitological research, differentiates between temporary and stationary parasitism, according to the varying lengths of parasitical sojourns within the host in the course of the parasite's life-cycle.[40] The question of whether parasites are extraneous to or originate in the affected organism itself had been decisively answered in connection with the refutation of 'spontaneous creation' – as T H Huxley summarizes in 1887, even 'in regard to parasites, every case which seemed to make for their generation from the substance of the animal, or plant, which they infest has been proved to have a totally different significance'.[41]

However, the question of whether parasites are intruders or indigenous to the host organism did continue to challenge scientists throughout the nineteenth century. J Hillis Miller notes that the term 'parasite' evokes at the same time 'proximity and distance, similarity and difference, interiority and exteriority';[42] and although this postmodern impressionism is to be regarded with some caution, it is true that, starting with Ruskin and considering other nineteenth century parasitologists and literary writers, the position accorded to the parasite always reveals the writer's attitude to the natural or social system as a whole. Literary texts in particular pose, with some urgency, the question of to what extent the host shares the parasite's nature, to what extent humans are 'still half-serpent', in Ruskin's words, or are hiding, more or less successfully, the 'savage within', as Dr Jekyll hides within his own nature the parasitical Mr Hyde, by whom he is finally vanquished. Related to this is the question of whether our biological and metaphorical 'membranes' are boundaries protecting our insides against parasites and bacteria – or whether they are permeable, and our organisms not clearly delimited entities at all.

Biological Parasitism in Nineteenth Century Literature

Many nineteenth century writers were fascinated by the position of parasites in nature: Robert Browning, in his poetry, frequently describes 'marginal' natural events such as 'the sudden appearance of mushrooms on moss, ... the horrible spread of a parasitical growth on the human body, ... the creeping growth of a seaplant which will ultimately overwhelm great rocks with its remorseless proliferation',[43] showing how 'central' they really are, and that divinity inheres even in these lowest forms of life. Thomas Hardy is likewise famous for his depictions of the smallest aspects of nature, such as 'tall blooming weeds emitting offensive smells – weeds whose red and yellow and purple hues formed a polychrome as dazzling as that of cultivated flowers'; the 'cuckoo-spittle', 'thistle-milk' and 'slug-slime' staining Tess's skin,[44] or the drying-out of ponds in the summer 'to a vaporous mud amid which the maggoty shapes of innumerable obscure creatures could be indistinctly seen, heaving and wallowing with enjoyment'.[45] In much bleaker terms, H G Wells's *The Time Machine* presents the future of mankind as a parasitical arrangement between two distinct species that have evolved from the human race: the Morlocks prey on the helpless Eloi, their 'fattened cattle', in what is, indeed, not symbiosis but fully-fledged parasitism. Similarly, in *The War of the Worlds* the Martians, injecting human blood into their 'degenerated' bodies through cannulas, are parasitical vampires; they are finally killed themselves by another species of parasite – by bacteria.

Indeed, the designation of bacteria as parasites was common towards the end of the nineteenth century, which saw the simultaneous rise of bacteriology and parasitology. Rudolf Virchow, for instance, described bacteria as 'parasites' in his 1885 essay 'Der Kampf der Zellen und der Bakterien' ('The Battle between

Cells and Bacteria').[46] As Otis reports, Santiago Ramón y Cajal, cell-biologist and winner of the 1906 Nobel prize, had actually written a novel, now lost, describing the 'epic struggles between leukocytes and parasites', that is, the white blood cells fending off bacteria intruding into the organism. Cajal repeatedly insisted on the egalitarian nature of infection, pointing out in vivid depictions that bacteria penetrate social boundaries with perfect ease.[47] This aspect held a certain fascination for the class-ridden Victorians: 'C. C.' in the *Encyclopaedia Britannica* section on 'Parasitism in Medicine' (9th edition 1885) describes several parasitic diseases in foreign countries, caused by poor living conditions and defective hygiene – emphasizing that they may easily spread to the white races and higher social classes as well: 'The disease ['*mal de los pintos*', a skin disease caused by a parasitical fungus], ... would appear to be one of the many forms of *morbus miseriae*; but it is contagious, and is sometimes seen in the well-to-do.'; '*Dracontiasis* or *Guinea-worm.* – ... common on the Guinea coast, and in many other tropical and subtropical regions. ... The black races are most liable, but Europeans of almost any social rank and of either sex are not altogether exempt.'[48]

Dickens: Parasitism and Retrogression

Charles Dickens points out, in *Bleak House* (1853) and numerous other novels, that miasmatic contagion (his explanation for infection, at a time before the discovery of bacteria) overcomes social barriers with ease, the infectious matter from the blood-stream of a destitute street boy taking 'revenge' for social inequality by condemning the idle rich to their deathbed. The danger of parasites is likewise ubiquitous. While we can detect in Dickens a tendency to reproach aristocrats and exploitative capitalists with parasitical existences, the phenomenon is by no means restricted to them – in fact, parasitism is shown to be so ubiquitous that one has to be constantly on the alert against it. In Victorian accounts of biological parasitism, we almost always find explicit parallels between parasitic stagnation in the animal world and the 'contented life of material enjoyment accompanied by ignorance and superstition' that human beings had to shun at all costs.[49] Parasites are disturbers of the organic social system, taking without giving, purely egotistical – as described by Virchow when he tried to demonstrate that the origin of disease is a combination of bacterial infection and cellular degeneration:

> What is an organism? A society of living cells, a tiny well-ordered state. ...
> As in the lives of nations, so in the lives of individuals the state of
> health of the whole is determined by the well-being and close
> interrelation of the individual parts; disease appears when individual

members begin to sink into a state of inactivity disadvantageous
to the commonwealth, or to lead parasitic existences at the expense
of the whole.[50]

The question remains: how do you recognize a parasite? First, the biologists'
attempts at explanation: Darwin asserts that '[t]he dependency of one organic
being on another, as of a parasite on its prey, lies generally between beings
remote in the scale of nature'. As he himself acknowledges, however, it is
rather difficult 'to define clearly what is meant by the organisation being higher
or lower'.[51] In the sixth edition of *Origin*, he adduced von Baer's tenets about
differentiation and specialization of the organism – that is to say he opted for
complexity as the clue to a 'higher' position on the scale of beings. But Darwin
was decidedly open-minded about this; for instance, when he describes the
life-cycle of the parasitical cirripede – which, upon finding a host, becomes
'fixed for life' as a parasite, losing its legs and antennae – he still insists that
'[i]n this last and complete state, cirripedes may be considered as either more
highly or more lowly organised than they were in the larval condition'. But in
the case of the males of the species, he is certain that 'the development has
assuredly been retrograde; for the male is a mere sack, which lives for a short
time, and is destitute of mouth, stomach, or other organ of importance,
excepting for reproduction'.[52] Similarly, Andrew Wilson, in 'Degeneration'
(1881), commented on the retrogression of the male rotifer, 'which in adulthood
lose[s] [its] limbs to become little more than [a] digestive tract' – even
metaphorically linking these observations with general warnings about the
'decay of civilizations'.[53] Another example, cited by Henry Drummond in *The
Natural Law in the Spiritual World* (1883), is the sacculina, a parasite on the
hermit crab. While in its youth 'it leads an active and independent life', it
then degenerates upon encountering a hermit crab: 'Whereupon the whole of
the swimming feet drop off, – they will not be needed again, and the animal
settles down for the rest of its life as a parasite.' As Drummond explicitly states,
this reprehensible behaviour is both a 'disregard of evolution' and an 'evasion
of the great law of work'.[54] Victorian ideas of the ethos of self-help versus the
dangers of social parasitism were clearly in the background.

The same moralizing work ethic can be detected in literary treatments of
the theme: Dickens's novels evince a fascination with members of the social
organism who refuse to contribute their own share of work and energy,
parasitically benefiting from other people's labour. Parasites in Dickens have
the advantage of being easily recognizable – at least for privileged focalizers
like Esther Summerson in *Bleak House*, or, through their grotesque physicality,
for the reader. Thus the parasitical capitalist Mr Smallweed, living off the
sweat of others, is described as a shapeless bundle of clothes, the embodiment

of a lack of energy, who has to be repeatedly shaken into some semblance of
form by his granddaughter. Similarly, the sponger Mr Turveydrop, who spends
his time as a 'model of Deportment', is 'pinched in, and swelled out, and got
up, and strapped down, as much as he could possibly bear' – and as J Hillis
Miller has observed, one suspects that 'the reality underneath is only a kind of
soft pulp or clay which would collapse into a formless mass if the rigid outer
crust were removed'.[55] By withdrawing from the cycles of production, the
parasite 'saves' his own energy and conserves his youth intact, like the parasite
Harold Skimpole in Bleak House, who refuses to subject himself to the laws of
time, work and wear, thereby remaining at least partly a child, '[with] more
the appearance ... of a damaged young man, than a well-preserved elderly
one'.[56] The parasite's lack of energy is classified as regressive by Dickens, as it
is by Wilson or Drummond.

Just as Skimpole can lord it over Mr Jarndyce as his willing host, the vampire-
like lawyer Mr Vholes is able to draw Richard Carstone completely into his
power, even though Esther recognizes the hypocritical role-playing and
dangerousness in each case: 'So slow, so eager, so bloodless and gaunt, I felt as
if Richard were wasting away beneath the eyes of this adviser, and there were
something of the Vampire in him.' Indeed, all the lawyers in Bleak House evoke
the image of 'maggots in nuts'.[57] They do not produce, they merely consume,
constipating the legal and social system (Mr Vholes's digestion problems are
highly symbolic).[58] Moreover, the parasite in Dickens, although ubiquitous, is
also always classified as marginal. Thus the lawyer Mr Tulkinghorn is 'smoke-
dried and faded, dwelling among mankind but not consorting with them, aged
without experience of genial youth'.[59] Like Skimpole, he is exempt from the
human life-cycle, and like the vampire in John Polidori's The Vampyre (1819),
Ur-text of the vampire genre, he is 'among mankind' but remains a distanced
observer, 'as if he could not participate [in their lives]' – regarding humans
not as fellow creatures, but as prey.[60]

Eliot: Parasitical Egotism and the Sense of Community

While in Dickens the parasite stands clearly outside the system, and has to be
extirpated from it – deposited in a scavenger's cart, as the parasite Mr Wegg is
at the end of Our Mutual Friend (1865)[61] – George Eliot's novels demonstrate
how difficult it often is to distinguish between parasites and productive beings,
between egotistical exploiters and selfless benefactors. Post-Romantic theories
of organicism, especially Herbert Spencer's theory of the 'Social Organism',
enabled nineteenth century scientists and creative writers to see the 'social
body' as an interdependent, complex mechanism. Eliot perfected the image of
the sensitive 'web of connections', especially in Middlemarch (1871–2), where

seemingly detached elements of the social body are shown latently to influence
the course of all other elements – in fact multiplying the system's complexity,
in the way parasites, according to Serres, generally do.[62] In *The Mill on the
Floss* (1860), however, Eliot had already insisted that parasites are a normal
part of every system, like Darwin admiring beautiful coadaptations in nature:
'Nature herself', the narrator observes, 'occasionally quarters an inconvenient
parasite on an animal towards whom she has otherwise no ill-will. What then?
We admire her care for the parasite.'[63] Indeed, with the same matter-of-factness
do 'human' parasites appear in *Middlemarch* – their manifestations are registered
without excitement by various characters throughout the novel. Thus Will
Ladislaw's first impulse on being approached by a stranger is to classify him as
'one of those political parasitic insects of the bloated kind' with whom he has
become so well acquainted recently; or Mrs Abel immediately classifies a new
face in her master's household as a parasite looking for his share of the goods:
'where there was property left, the buzzing presence of such large blue-bottles
seemed natural enough.'[64] While in Eliot nearly everyone can potentially
manifest parasitical tendencies at some time or another, the moral question
the novel explores in the languages of biology and parasitology is the relation
between egotism and community, 'whether we regard the earth as a putrefying
nidus for a saved remnant, including ourselves [and excluding others]', or
whether we learn to see, like Dorothea, that we are part of the 'palpitating life'
of the universe, and cannot draw boundaries between ourselves and others.[65]

Concerned as the novel is throughout with the ambiguous interplay between
free will and determinism, demonstration of unconscious motivation and
emphasis on duty and responsibility, Eliot's biological metaphors repeatedly
place her characters in such in-between positions. A famous example is the
look through the microscope at Mrs Cadwallader, comparing her behaviour to
that of a tiny animalcule in a water-drop: while her pandering activities are
first compared to the 'active voracity' of an animalcule devouring 'smaller
creatures', it turns out, under a stronger lens, that there are

> certain tiniest hairlets [= cilia, already detected by Leeuwenhoek and
> further investigated by G H Lewes and others[66]] which make vortices
> for these victims while the swallower waits passively at his receipt of
> custom. In this way, metaphorically speaking, a strong lens applied to
> Mrs Cadwallader's match-making will show a play of minute causes
> producing what may be called thought and speech vortices to bring her
> the sort of food she needed.[67]

By comparing the actions of this bourgeois pander to the feeding process of an
animalcule, the narrator reveals her behaviour to be entirely subconscious
and passive, reminiscent of the living habits of the parasitical ascidian described

by H G Wells in his – albeit partly facetious – essay 'Zoological Retrogression' (1891). This animal, having once arrived at the 'degenerated' stage of its life-cycle, spends 'the rest of [its] existence [in] a passive receptivity to what chance and the water bring along'.[68] At the time when Eliot was writing *Middlemarch*, her partner G H Lewes was busy with his five-volume *opus magnum*, *Problems of Life and Mind* (1874–9), and had already written *The Physiology of Common Life* (1859–60) as well as *Studies in Animal Life* (1862), where human organisms were shown to function like animal organisms, and any metaphysical speculation or Cartesian mind–body divide was strictly rejected.[69] Karen B Mann has insisted that 'George Eliot did indeed conceive of humanity as a species of animal', pointing to the prominence assigned to 'the two animal urges for food and reproduction of the species' in her revision of Lewes's *Problems of Life and Mind*.[70] The metaphorical language of her novels abundantly comments on humans as 'strange animals' and 'Christian Carnivora', exemplified in Mrs Cadwallader's voracity but also in the frequent images of human vampirism and parasitism.[71]

Whereas Rosamond sees her husband's medical pursuits as those of a 'morbid vampire', Lydgate, in return, sees his wife as a parasite: 'He once called her his basil plant; and when she asked for an explanation, said that basil was a plant which had flourished wonderfully on a murdered man's brains.'[72] Their marriage is a continual power-struggle which Rosamond wins, numbing him metaphorically through her 'torpedo-contact', inducing a 'creeping paralysis' in him. Even thoughts become, in the universe of this novel, 'mental food';[73] and, as Sally Shuttleworth has stated, 'the dinners required to feed gossip ... suggest a decidedly cannibalistic interpretation of the social organism'.[74] In the same cannibalistic vein, the inhabitants of Middlemarch, on Lydgate's first arrival in town, are said to be counting 'on swallowing ... and assimilating him very comfortably'. The phenomenon of capitalist exploitation, discussed by Ruskin and Dickens, also surfaces in Eliot's *Middlemarch*. The red-faced, jolly and uxorious businessman Mr Vincy, for instance, is revealed to be a 'vampire', 'one of those who suck the life out of the wretched handloom weavers in Tipton and Freshitt. That is how his family look so fair and sleek.'[75] As Carol Senf has noted, a resemblance can be detected between Eliot's metaphors and those of both Marx and Engels, 'who also used the vampire motif to condemn the irresponsible behavior of the capitalist class'.[76]

Eliot ultimately believes in the Spencerian idea of progress,[77] using its metaphors to depict a fundamentally human version of industrialization, of organic interdependences, demonstrating mankind's capability for 'social sympathy' and the victory of a sense of community and responsibility over parasitical egotism in Dorothea's awakening to the 'involuntary, palpitating life' around her.[78] In contradistinction to Polidori's distant and exploitative vampire, the morally superior being as depicted by Eliot recognizes and accepts his or her connection with the social organism as a whole. However, there are some uncanny moments of a distanced perspective *vis-a-vis* the social organism even in Eliot's own letters and diaries: Lewes occasionally designated humans as parasites on the universe, 'a parasitic animal living on a grander creature – an epizoon nestling in the skin of his planetary organism, which rolls through space like a ciliated ovum rolling through a drop of water'.[79] In almost identical words, Eliot emphasized in her diary the parasitical aspect of a coastal village at clinging to the rock at Ilfracombe: 'one cannot help thinking of man as a parasitic animal – an epizoon making his abode on the skin of the planetary organism'.[80] In fact, Serres does not come up with more than that when he insists that parasitism is one of the most basic survival strategies adopted across the living world, present whenever humans use animals for food and clothing. Considering human relations to be 'chaînes parasitaires', and human beings to be 'parasites universels' using plants, animals, and ultimately the planet as hosts,[81] Serres merely reiterates what nineteenth century scientists and writers, in their more materialist moments, had already fully expressed.

Stoker: Parasites and Proletarians

A similarly dark vision is presented in Bram Stoker's *Dracula* (1897). Jonathan Harker describes the Count as a parasite: lying in his coffin after one of his nightly excursions, the vampire appears 'bloated', 'like a filthy leech', 'gorged with blood'. The American vampire hunter, Quincey Morris, pronounces the word 'vampire' for the first time in the novel, introducing a reference point from contemporary biological inquiries when he compares Lucy's condition to that of a mare on the Pampas after '[o]ne of those big bats that they call vampires had got at her in the night'. Van Helsing takes up this suggestion later, referring not only to vampirical bats sucking dry cattle and horses at night, but also to another – mythological – species which allegedly drains the blood out of sailors during their sleep: 'and then in the morning are found dead men, white as even Miss Lucy was'.[82] In fact, Darwin himself, in the *Voyage of the Beagle*, reports seeing a 'Vampire bat' with his own eyes, doing his best to convince the sceptics back home in England.[83]

Apart from these zoological analogies, there is, however, another important theme that predominates throughout *Dracula*: the 'proneness' of the victim. Polidori had already established this theme – the vampire Lord Ruthven had attacked by preference the 'wanton wife' and the 'adulteress', females who seemed to feel a special attraction to him.[84] In Stoker's *Dracula* likewise, it is no coincidence that the flirtatious Lucy is the first victim to succumb to the vampire after his arrival in England. As Mary Douglas states in *Purity and Danger*, the female in mythic thinking routinely stands for the 'open' body without boundaries, symbolizing the danger of invasion. In other words, part of the vampire is always-already inside the victim – in this case, the gentlemanly vampire hunters have to defend Britain by defending their women who are, due to their own dangerous sexuality, especially liable to attack; a common enough displacement mechanism. On the sociological level, the danger is also always partly inside, as Doris Feldmann has pointed out when emphasizing that 'Dracula's houses in London look and smell like slum dwellings';[85] in other words, the danger of the vampire symbolizes the anxiety of the middle and upper classes about the increasing problems of poverty, urban slums and the physically and morally 'degenerated' lower classes. Dracula's invasion restages the internal struggle between proletariat and bourgeoisie which threatened the nation from within. And indeed, an especially striking feature of the parasite – or *Proletarier*, as Perty dubbed it – was its capacity to reproduce: Stoker's Dracula is superior to his pursuers in terms of longevity and reproductive energy, and Harker has anxious visions of a future London ridden with the monstrous descendants of the Count, a mob of parasites: 'This was the being I was helping to transfer to London, where, perhaps, for centuries to come he might, amongst its teeming millions, satiate his lust for blood, and create a new and ever-widening circle of semi-demons to batten on the helpless.'[86] Indeed, one of Van Helsing's most prominent concerns is that the boxes which Dracula uses for his sleep during the day be 'sterilized' – that his enormous reproductive energy, akin to that of parasites and bacteria, be cancelled.[87] The threat of the Count is closely linked with his fecundity; thus the gentlemen's pursuit of the vampire in *Dracula* is at the same time a battle against their own fears of sexual excess, threatening the social system from within.

Conan Doyle: Parasitology and Parapsychology

My last example, Arthur Conan Doyle's *The Parasite* (1894), will emphasize even more clearly that the literary figure of the 'parasite' had, by the end of the nineteenth century, been transferred on to an interiorized, pre-Freudian psychological (or rather, in this case, parapsychological) plane, the parasite symbolizing the protagonists' own deepest anxieties. This narrative was actually reissued by Doyle as a companion volume to Bram Stoker's tale *The Watter's Mou* in January 1895; considering that Stoker had made the first notes for *Dracula* in March 1890, but that the novel finally came out only in 1897, it is possible to argue for a direct influence of Doyle's depiction of sexual anxiety in *The Parasite* on Stoker's vampire novel. Doyle's text is concerned, as Charles

Higham has stated, with parapsychology as a vehicle for 'a strikingly personal revelation of neurotic sexual obsession'.[88] The narrative was later disowned by Doyle, and has never received a great deal of critical attention.

Events are recounted by the protagonist Gilroy, a professor of medicine, in his diary entries. He describes himself as a professed materialist but, at the same time, 'a highly psychic man', having been 'a nervous, sensitive boy, a dreamer, a somnambulist, full of impressions and intuitions. My black hair, my dark eyes, my thin, olive face, my tapering fingers, are all characteristic of my real temperament.' That his is a case of severe (pre-Freudian) repression becomes clear when he somewhat too emphatically contrasts his pursuit of exact science with his distaste for nebulous things like 'feelings, impressions, suggestions'.[89] The story traces the development of an obsessive fixation; as Serres stated about the parasite's host, he 'donne toujours, jusqu'à l'épuisement, parfois jusqu'à la mort, drogué d'une sorte de fascination'.[90] Witnessing West-Indian Miss Penelosa mesmerize his fiancée Agatha at a soirée, the narrator subsequently falls under her spell himself, until he confesses: 'I was her slave, body and soul'. When he repels her sexual advances during a lucid spell, Miss Penelosa swears revenge, inducing him to commit ever more outrageous trespasses, making him lose his position at the university as well as his health and sanity – he becomes 'the pitiable wreck of a man'.[91]

It is stressed from the outset that Miss Penelosa is not foreign-looking, no 'exotic other': 'Anyone less like my idea of a West Indian could not be imagined.' An entirely insignificant presence under normal circumstances, when exerting her mesmeric power she has an 'expression with which a Roman empress might have looked at her kneeling slave'. The story reveals on several levels that what is thought to be outside ourselves may really be inside; first, the protagonist is afraid that his strong response to the mesmerizing power might disclose 'the sudden upcropping of some lower stratum in my nature – a brutal primitive instinct suddenly asserting itself'.[92] This, then, would be a case of Hyde overpowering Jekyll. Later, however, Gilroy decides that 'those odious impulses for which I have blamed myself do not really come from me at all. They are all transferred from her ... I feel cleaner and lighter for the thought.' Thus dissociating himself entirely from any evil impulses of his own, he also for the first time introduces the term 'parasite':

> This woman, by her own explanation, can dominate my nervous organism. She can project herself into my body and take command of it. She has a parasite soul; yes, she is a parasite, a monstrous parasite. She creeps into my frame as the hermit crab does into the whelk's shell. I am powerless. What can I do? I am dealing with forces of which I know nothing.[93]

In fact, however, Gilroy's own opening description of the spring, of budding and fruitful nature, with its emphasis on 'the work of reproduction', had already established the sexual subtext. The protagonist-narrator, at this early point, had clearly felt inspired by the natural forces without to such an extent that internal and external worlds became one: 'I can see it without, and I can feel it within. We also have our spring when the little arterioles dilate, the lymph flows in a brisker stream, the glands work harder, winnowing and straining.'[94] Sexuality throughout is a homologue for everything that is dangerous, foreign and evil. Thus when Anne Cranny-Francis interprets the opening passage as producing 'an environment of health, vigour and beauty – into which Miss Penelosa comes as a kind of blight, a kind of alien evil', she merely reiterates a distinction the protagonist himself would like to make by locating the 'evil' entirely outside himself. Generally, however, Cranny-Francis analyses convincingly the mechanisms of repression and obsession in the text, finding in Gilroy's projection of his own guilt 'on to the woman involved in the act' a parallel to Victorian moral and sexual double standards, and the role that prostitutes played in this – as she argues – patriarchal and highly restrictive society.[95] But it is important that already at the beginning, even before the encounter with Miss Penelosa, the text clearly shows the protagonist to be hiding from himself the fact that the – sexually connoted – 'evil' forces are lurking within himself as well. His approach to nature is substantially transformed by his experiences: 'How sweet and gentle and soothing is Nature! Who would think that there lurked in her also such vile forces, such odious possibilities!'[96] While Darwin, as we saw above, had quite enjoyed his iconoclastic 'unmasking' of nature, pointing to the struggle for existence as the 'truth' behind birdsong, Doyle's protagonist accepts his epiphany much more hesitatingly.

Following the 'parasito-logic' that Serres has formulated – a parasite-infested society has only the choice between incorporating or expelling the unwanted element – Gilroy decides to kill 'this loathsome parasite'.[97] However, he is not allowed to carry out his plan: Miss Penelosa dies before he can reach her. There is no resolution, therefore, in the text. The question remains whether he would ever have been able to free himself of this parasite, and the illusion of his autonomy has been lastingly deconstructed. In Doyle's story, the figure of the parasite is revealed to be a psychological displacement mechanism, which brings to the fore what is already there: '[le parasite fait] affleurer le déjà présent'.[98] Postmodern theorists have thus not advanced beyond the diagnosis of nineteenth century literary texts. In science as in literature, pace Ruskin, the nineteenth century increasingly came to accept the parasite as an inevitable part of the natural and social system. It is true that this was no protection against later ideas about the 'Jewish parasite', nor against the twentieth century discourses of eugenics and racial hygiene – but that is a different story.

We should note, however, that in other respects the discourse about the parasite is an instance where science and literature can be seen to diverge more and more as they approach the *fin de siècle*. While nineteenth century parasitology, as we saw above in the writings of Cobbold, had been labouring successfully to demonstrate that parasites are neither divine punishments nor parts of our own organism revealing a 'deficiency' in ourselves, literary texts increasingly used the figure of parasitism to depict not only exploitative mechanisms in society, but also the 'darker' aspects of the human psyche. While science increasingly dissociated the victim's predisposition from the fact of his or her infection, in literature the language of parasitology (like the language of social anthropology, with its figure of the 'savage within') offered a way, before the advent of Freud, of describing psychological self-division, and the struggle between conscious and subconscious impulses.

13

SURGICAL ENGINEERING IN THE NINETEENTH CENTURY: *FRANKENSTEIN, THE ISLAND OF Dr MOREAU, FLATLAND*

Jürgen Meyer

The discursive overlap between nineteenth century literature and surgery is nothing new. Since the Renaissance,[1] surgery and fiction have often been eyed suspiciously, because in both fields, religious as well as ethical problems have played a significant role in public perception. Even today, with plastic surgery as an everyday clinical practice, surgery as art continues to be a provocative moral and political issue, as Gunter von Hagen's exhibition 'Körperwelten' has shown. Thus, although the nineteenth century interest in surgery may not be singular as such, in its employment of *fictional* surgery it is. Its 'anatomy literature' – comprising works by such authors as, among others, Mary Shelley, Charles Dickens and Elizabeth Gaskell – mirrors the social impact of the 1832 Anatomy Act, which extended the scope of legal dissection from 'unclaimed bodies' of criminals and paupers.[2] Initially featuring surgeons as executioners and murderers rather than as healers, fictional surgery represents both the largely disrespected non-scientific craft of a solitary quack and one of the leading research fields within the medical sciences, including a socio-medical dimension. Both aspects will be demonstrated here in Mary Shelley's *Frankenstein* (1818/31), Edwin A Abbott's *Flatland* (1884) and H G Wells's *Island of Dr Moreau* (1896), highlighting significant facets of a rather hostile nineteenth century literary image of the surgeon.

Since the late Middle Ages, the surgeon had been functionally separated, and educationally excluded, from the academic training of physicians and apothecaries; the job was considered a craft.[3] According to a German traveller in 1825, systematic training in general pathology was largely unknown in the syllabus of English universities.[4] The surgeon had, at best, to shave his customers and, more dramatically, carry out blood-letting operations, to cut away boils or, at worst, amputate wounded body-parts. Due to a high risk of death from (post-)operative infection diseases, surgery was the last option following other attempts at curing the patient. Apart from the risk of septic infection, the biggest problem was the pain inflicted by operations carried out without any anaesthesia. Opiates and morphine were commonly used to suppress pain, but these often led to addiction. Reliable means of easing pain during an operation did not exist, as we learn from Fanny Burney (1752–1840), who relates how, in her breast-cancer operation in September 1810, she was given no anaesthetic apart from a 'cambric handkerchief on [her] face':

> Yet – when the dreadful steel was plunged into the breast – cutting through veins – arteries – flesh – nerves – I needed no injunctions not to restrain my cries. ... When the wound was made, & the instrument was withdrawn, the pain seemed undiminished, for the air that suddenly rushed into those delicate parts felt like a mass of minute sharp & forked poniards, that were tearing the edges of the wound, – but when I again felt the instrument – describing a curve – cutting against the grain, if I may say so, while the flesh resisted in a manner so forcible as to oppose & tire the hand of the operator, who was forced to change from the right to the left – then, indeed, I thought I must have expired, I attempted no more to open my eyes.[5]

Both diagnosis and excision of a breast tumour were very delicate and strictly taboo procedures, as Burney's biographers indicate. Harman points out that in the time before the actual operation, the doctor neither saw his patient's diseased breast, nor did he examine it by touch.[6] Doody says that the operation was in fact such a sensitive issue that the patient arranged for it to take place 'in her own home; she did not inform her husband at the time, and cheated him into going out'.[7] Against the background of such socio-religious taboos on the one hand, and of the limited institutional facilities on the other, it is no wonder that British surgery in the first third of the nineteenth century profited only very slowly from the clinical progress on the Continent.

The demand for human corpses for purposes of training and research in a country without systematic surgical training was excessive. The 'Romantic image of the scientist as cold, inhuman and unable to relate to others',[8] driven by criminal energy, converged in the public stereotype of the surgeon, and '[t]he events in Edinburgh in 1828 were to clarify the fact that the dead body business had always been – in all but name – the medicine of murder'.[9] When Wordsworth was writing the famous line 'We murder to dissect', there were indeed people who profited from the lack of institutional research facilities, developing a trade whose horror exceeded every Gothic novel and murder mystery. This is shown in the 1828 Edinburgh scandal referred to by Marshall: after a lodger's natural death in a boarding-house run by William Hare and his companion, William Burke, the two owners had suffocated sixteen other guests. Eventually it turned out in court that the corpses had been sold to a respected anatomist, Robert Knox, for £7 each.[10] While other groups of body-snatchers, 'resurrectionists' and grave-robbers did not kill, they disinterred and sold the freshly buried. We are reminded of this practice by Victor Frankenstein when he points out that not only did he procure material from the slaughterhouse, but he also robbed the 'charnel-houses' near his lodgings, 'disturb[ing], with profane fingers, the tremendous secrets of the human frame' in order to gather parts of human carcasses for his enterprise.[11] Until the mid-nineteenth century, many Anglo-American students had received their medical training in German laboratories or in French hospitals, because institutional training facilities were much better on the Continent than in Britain – quite apart from the fact that corpses on the Continent were up to thirty times cheaper than they were in England.[12] Frankenstein, too, spends his academic training in Ingolstadt, this town then still hosting the first state-run Bavarian research centre for experimental anatomy which had survived the closure of the university in 1800. But he has no genuine institutional facilities to hand, and converts a 'solitary chamber' into his 'workshop of filthy creation',[13] as he calls it in retrospect. A real student-surgeon would have been invited personally to a professor's 'cabinet' for the development of his skills there, rather than in the 'confusion' of a classroom with up to 150 students.[14] This is what happens to Frankenstein when he is invited to Waldman's to be instructed privately, and is promised the use of Waldman's own laboratory equipment 'when I [i.e. Victor Frankenstein] should have advanced far enough in the science'.[15] Institutional laboratories were established in Germany after the Humboldt university reforms in the first third of the nineteenth century, and they were introduced much later in England.[16] Frankenstein's syllabus apparently includes the fields of physiology, anatomy and aetiology, or 'the minutiae of causation'.[17] He develops his knowledge in the field of 'morbid anatomy', an important part of surgical training in the first decades of the nineteenth century which traced surface symptoms back to organic defects. Not until

> ... 1840, a prospective student of medicine, whatever his country, could
> expect to be schooled in anatomy, including dissection, physiology,
> morbid anatomy, medical chemistry, materia medica or pharmacy, and

the theory and practice of medicine, and also to be introduced to the
actual practice of medicine, surgery, and midwifery in a hospital or under
the tutelage of a preceptor.[18]

The efforts to institutionalize surgery in Europe and America eventually had
their effects on the British health system. Anaesthetics, such as ether and
chloroform, were systematically introduced into the clinic in the 1840s, and
the chance discovery of the antiseptic effects of chlorine and carbolic by Ignaz
Semmelweis (1818–65) in Austria and by Joseph Lister (1827–1912) in
Scotland during the 1860s considerably reduced the death rate.[19] In the last
three decades of the nineteenth century, Anglo-American surgery, with its
new hygienic standards, made a big leap forward and, in the 1890s, took the
lead. The new clinical facilities raised the public reputation of surgery. They
opened the door to experimental surgery, but soon faced a strong
antivivisectionist movement in Britain. The former surgeon George Hoggan
considered 'anaesthetics as the greatest curse to vivisectable animals' in a public
letter to the *Morning Post* of February 2, 1875.[20] Surgery was considered both
destructive and creative; and the surgeon was caught in the discursive knots
connecting medicine, evolution, ethics and the law.

Frankenstein perverts the stereotypical activity of the surgeon by
compounding parts of dead corpses instead of removing diseased organs from
the living. Critics have analysed Frankenstein's – by the standards of the late
eighteenth century – rather bookish training, taking recourse to medieval and
early modern sources[21] as well as to recent biochemical experiments in natural
philosophy.[22] In the novel, Frankenstein himself refers to Albertus Magnus,
Cornelius Agrippa and Paracelsus, authorities whose theories Krempe ridicules
as 'nonsense'.[23] His competitor Waldman alludes to modern pioneers such as
Harvey, who discovered blood circulation, and Priestley's and Lavoisier's still
more recent discovery of 'the nature of the air we breathe',[24] but he reveres
the old authorities as the founders of modern knowledge. In her 1831 preface,
Shelley mentions Erasmus Darwin, and implicitly refers to the famous electricity
experiments carried out by the Italian chemist Galvani. However, she depicts
the surgical discourse as underdeveloped, and the novel generally lacks clinical
idiom. One of the most 'advanced' elements in the unspecific description of
surgery is Frankenstein's consideration of the difficulties posed by putting
together all the mechanical 'intricacies of fibres, muscles, and veins'[25] before
this compound can be animated by chemical means.[26] For his operations
Frankenstein uses tools which he refers to generically as 'instruments of life',[27]
but their precise nature remains unspecified.[28] The precautions a surgeon in
later decades would have taken before carrying out a vital operation, such as
the use of anaesthetics and antiseptics, are not available to him. He is ignorant
both of the exactitude required for vascular surgery and of the notion of the

animal cell, introduced into the clinical idiom by Rudolf Virchow (1821–1902) only in the mid-nineteenth century: Frankenstein refers to 'fibres' as the smallest units of human bodies. He is unaware of the emerging field of histology, sketched by the French surgeon Xavier Bichat (1771–1802) in his *Anatomie générale* (1801–2), listing twenty-one different kinds of tissue as the 'basic building blocks'[29] of the body, and concluding that any physical organ was an intricate combination of these tissues.[30] Needless to say, secondary effects, such as 'pigmentary disturbances, modifications of the passions, [and] alterations in the secretion of fatty tissue',[31] which Dr Moreau overcomes remain unmentioned as well.

Thus the most renowned literary representation of modern surgery in the early nineteenth century turns out to be a discursive blank: Frankenstein could never have become a well-trained surgeon according to later clinical standards. The deep systematic generation gap between a Romantic anatomist and a late-Victorian *vivisecteur* becomes visible in H G Wells's *The Island of Dr Moreau*. Wells allows the doctor to 'reel off [a] physiological lecture'[32] to the visitor-captive Edward Prendick. Initially, Prendick perceives the Beast Folk population of the island as a degenerate, crippled species of humans; later, however, he has to listen to Moreau singing the ambivalent praises of his own futile 'triumphs of vivisection,'[33] based on earlier success at developing expert skills in blood transfusion and the treatment of cancer, or 'morbid growths'.[34] On his desert island he has virtually exploded the fields of practical anatomy and physiology in dealing with 'question[s] armed with antiseptic surgery', and by 'transplanting tissue from one part of an animal to another, or from one animal to another, to alter its chemical reactions and methods of growth'.[35] While Frankenstein still sees the body largely as a mechanical composite of animal matter, Moreau can be seen as a member of a mid-century microscope-trained 'generation of researchers ... developing a new system, sometimes called bio-physics, that would seek the key to all the body's functions in the chemical-physical interaction of its most minimal elements'.[36] If Frankenstein composes an 'android' singularity from an assortment of body-parts collected in slaughterhouse and cemetery, Moreau creates a sub-human class from diverse animal species.

Both surgeons work in total isolation, but the reasons for their seclusion differ: Frankenstein intentionally avoids any cooperation, and works in secrecy, because he knows he is exceeding the limits of ethical as well as natural laws; while Moreau used to be a member of the scientific community, and was expelled from London only after his 'wantonly cruel'[37] experiments – his isolation is not based on voluntary retreat. The scandal of the 'Moreau horrors'[38] opens a significant cultural intertext for the novel which seems to have been underestimated.[39] Wells (1866–1946) was a Bachelor of Science with a degree in biology, a highly decorated Fellow of the Zoological Society and a Fellow of the College of Preceptors. He knew that experimental surgeons had a very bad reputation, fostered by the controversy over vivisection in the last decades of the nineteenth century. The controversy began after the French psychiatrist Valentin Magnan (1835–1916) had been invited to Norwich in August 1874 by the British Medical Association, and allowed to induce epilepsy in two dogs by an intravenous injection of absinthe.[40] This experiment ended in a riot, and was hotly debated in public; an agitation arose which, in 1875, culminated in the foundation of the National Anti-Vivisectionist Society (NAVS) by Francis Power Cobbe (1822–1904). Paris-trained surgeon Hoggan had written in his letter to the *Morning Post* that 'experimental physiologists … seldom show much pity; on the contrary, in practice they frequently show the reverse'.[41] The debate finally led to the Cruelty to Animals Act of 1876, even though the antivivisectionists who favoured total abolition were not happy with it. In a pamphlet against the euphemistic discourse of experimental surgery entitled 'Vivisection and Its Two-Faced Advocates' (1882), Cobbe blames the excessive consumption of animals:

> Again, as to the number of animals dissected alive, the Treatises make us suppose it to be enormous. … Flourens told Blatin that Magendie had sacrificed 4,000 dogs to prove Bell's theory of the nerves, and 4,000 to disprove the same; and that he, Flourens, had proved Bell was right by sacrificing some thousand more. … Turn we now to the popular Articles; and we find mention only of the very smallest numbers. Sir William Gull minimizes Bernard's stove-baked dogs to six and Professor Yeo brings down those of Professor Rutherford's victims to twelve, every reference to numbers being apparently, like those of the Fuegians, limited to the digits of physiologists.[42]

Wells may have been inspired to give his fictional doctor a Francophone name[43] by the fact that France was a centre of advanced surgical education in the mid-nineteenth century, and by such people as Magnan and Claude Bernard (1813–78). In 1865, Bernard had published in his *Introduction à l'étude de la médicine expérimentale* a defence of vivisection legitimizing the necessity of experiments, in which he outlines a surgical tradition through the ages, and reasons about the ethics of surgery. Here, he points out that 'no anatomist feels himself in a horrible slaughter-house; under the influence of a scientific idea, he delightedly follows a nervous filament through stinking living flesh, which to any other man would be an object of disgust and horror'.[44] Bernard elevates surgery on the social scale, and vindicates it against the antivivisectionists' reproaches of cold-blooded utilitarianism. The surgeon, he claims, patiently carries the burden of the diseased flesh, perfecting human society and animal world alike.[45]

Moreau does not only, like Bernard, construe a genealogy of experimental surgery from the Middle Ages to the late eighteenth century;[46] he also refers to the pain inflicted on the animals as a surface problem irrelevant to the surgeon, and thus turns out to be a pitiless vivisectionist of the French school. In the physiological lecture, he explains pain away as 'a little thing', weighed against the cosmic dimension of his idea.[47] An embodiment of Bernard's ideal *vivisecteur*, Moreau 'no longer hears the cry of animals, he no longer sees the blood that flows, he sees only his idea',[48] and points at a distinction between himself and the 'others' in the same way as Bernard, whose surgeon is 'absorbed by the scientific idea which he pursues', and therefore less a 'man of fashion' obeying short-sighted materialistic principles than 'a man of science'.[49] Moreau's biography includes details such as the exclusion from an English scientific community and the subsequent expulsion from the country – possible reminders of the 1874 British Medical Association scandal.

Wells also raises the question of what happens to the newly shaped, physically restructured creatures. On the one hand, they bear distinct animal traits; on the other, they can be educated, because '[t]he mental structure is even less determinate than the bodily'.[50] The regression or 'reversion' of the Beast Folk after Moreau's death indicates that nature, 'the hereditary factor', governs the 'acquired factor' – to use the dichotomy discussed since Lamarck's ideas about evolution. Charles Darwin's cousin Francis Galton (1822–1911) had then initiated the nature/nurture debate which Stover wrongly assigned to Wells himself.[51] Galton relaunched the old philosophical debate on the basis of 'scientific' data in the early 1880s, when he analysed the correlation of inherited and acquired characteristics in his studies entitled *Hereditary Genius* (1869) and *English Men of Science* (1874), in which he pointed out that inherited, 'natural' characteristics dominated acquired features developed individually by way of education ('nurture'). Thus, he was a modern proponent of state-directed eugenics, a concept first benevolently considered but later dismissed by Wells as a 'sham science'.[52] In his study *Finger Prints* (1892), Galton describes his Anthropometric Laboratory, opened in 1884,[53] and draws on Alphonse Bertillon's register of Paris criminals, established in 1883.[54] According to Galton and other theorists of the time, the physical form of the skull and the individual's character were correlated, as were origin and intellect. He samples data such as skull size, foot span, length of the middle finger, body height, and eye colour.[55] Galton's objective was to record and index unchanging physical qualities (e.g. fingerprints) for a variety of uses beyond the forensic, ranging from 'descriptive purposes' to 'investigations into race and heredity' and 'questions of symmetry and correlation'.[56] In fact, he insisted on administrative schemes involving a biographical index and eugenic certificates.

Galton's ideas and practices had immediately drawn the sharp criticism of Edwin A Abbott (1838–1926), headmaster of London City School, a trained theologian and scholar who published, among other things, a Shakespearian Grammar and a biography of Francis Bacon. The Anthropometric Laboratory in South Kensington was opened in 1884, and Abbott's *Flatland*, published in the same year, can be regarded as a direct satirical response. *Flatland* is set in a plane world which must be considered as part of an ensemble of parallel worlds, including imaginary Pointland, one-dimensional Lineland and three-dimensional Sphereland.[57] The population of Flatland consists of geometrical shapes, ranging from simple lines (representing women) via triangles (lower class, proletarians), squares (middle class), and polygons of sorts (upper class) to circles (priests). These shapes represent social strata as well as living forms. It turns out that the sons are privileged over their ancestors: 'It is a Law of Nature with us that a male child shall have one more side than his father, so that each generation shall rise (as a rule) one step in the scale of development and nobility.'[58]

In the case of its growing an additional side, the infant is taken away from its natural parents and delivered to step-parents in the respective higher social class, so that the infant does not inherit, by regression, the more primitive class-consciousness of his ancestors: Here, nurture dominates nature – figuratively expressed in the direct correspondence of laterality, sex, class and intellect. Not only sides, but also angles are relevant in this correlation, and they are dynamic entities. Thus, by mischievous or careless misconduct, angles may be reduced. The first-person narrator (ambiguously referred to as 'A Square' in the subtitle of the novel) reports a case in his own family, when one of his triangular forefathers degenerated from 59°30' to 58°,[59] a loss in status restored only five generations later. Irregularities are heavily stigmatized in this society and often associated with low intellect and criminal disposition, for which reason the authorities of the Flatland 'Sanitary and Social Board' advocate the idea of a certificate documenting not only the origin of a shape, but also its innocence and purity. Thus, anticipating questions from a three-dimensional reader, Square comments on the need for such a certificate in a footnote: 'no Lady of any position will marry an uncertified Triangle'.[60] This idea of a certificate is highly reminiscent of the one projected by Galton.

In his dystopia, Abbott carries such ideas much further, and projects them into a millennial future in which socio-medical surgery, as propagated by Wells in his *Modern Utopia* twenty years later, has already become a matter of fact. Since 'the art of healing … has achieved some of its most glorious triumphs in the compressions, extensions, trepannings, colligations, and other surgical and diaetetic operations',[61] Square mentions that

[o]ur physicians have discovered that the smaller and tender sides of an infant Polygon of the higher class can be fractured, and his whole frame reset, with such exactness that a Polygon of two or three hundred sides sometimes ... overleaps two or three hundred generations, and as it were doubles at a stroke, the number of his progenitors and the nobility of his decent.[62]

The high degree of ethical callousness in this society now becomes fully visible, for, as Square wryly comments, this surgical engineering is carried out at the expense of many infants' lives: 'Many a promising child is sacrificed in this way. Scarcely one out of ten survives', and the remains of lethal frame-settings are buried in the 'Neo-Therapeutic Cemetery'.[63] Little wonder that this society is not only eugenic, but also one which authoritatively advocates euthanasia:

Not that I should be disposed to recommend (at present) the extreme measures adopted in some States, where an infant whose angles deviate by half a degree from the correct angularity is summarily destroyed at birth. ... Advocating ... a *Via Media*, I would lay down no fixed or absolute line of demarcation; but at the period when the frame is just beginning to set, and when the Medical Board has reported that recovery is improbable, I would suggest that the Irregular offspring be painlessly and mercifully consumed.[64]

Although this analysis of the literary texts in the light of selected clinical developments in nineteenth century Europe has shown that surgery was always perceived as an ambivalent art, creating fears and hopes alike, we can notice a change in the nature of this image. Developing from the stereotype of the surgeon as quack at the beginning of the nineteenth century into that of the mid-century 'executioner–surgeon',[65] the late-Victorian *vivisecteur* conveys large-scale socio-biological ideas. Frankenstein's primitive body-snatching business is gradually charged with sensitive ideological issues, such as class and race. This creates the heavy dependence on 'the' (Natural) Law in Victorian society, challenged and broken only by those who set up their own legal system based on unlawful ideologies, as displayed in the case of Dr Moreau.[66] The same holds true for Abbott's Flatlanders. Owing to his serial production of hybrid creatures by which he outdoes his ancestor, Moreau seems to be, at first glance, a close relative of Frankenstein.[67] The two, however, differ significantly in their objectives. Unlike Frankenstein's, Moreau's idea is not the individual desire to test the limits of an individual's creative power but, by finding out 'the extreme limit of plasticity in a living shape', to 'outburn all the animal'[68] and to generate a subset of society, designed in his own image. Frankenstein and Moreau both escape 'technical' complications such as the matching of correct blood groups or graft rejection (problems solved only in the twentieth century), but Abbott's Flatlanders are more advanced in terms of social surgery, showing that surgery can be used for the artificial advancement of the privileged at the expense of individual lives.

Each of the texts discussed features an image of surgery as a science taking vengeance on the individuals who use it; if Frankenstein and Moreau are physically destroyed, in *Flatland* the ethical callousness of the 'social surgeons' in state administration lashes back on its populace. By the time of Abbott's dystopian reflection on the craft, possibly a response to Galton's ideas, the term 'surgery' has acquired a collective dimension, augmenting the traditional meaning of a medical operation. Finally, in a much more prophetic vein than Shelley or even Wells, Abbott raises questions which – reformulated in the idioms of genetic engineering and (aesthetic) plastic surgery – have not yet been answered.

14

'SERIOUS' SCIENCE VERSUS 'LIGHT' ENTERTAINMENT? FEMININITY CONCEPTS IN NINETEENTH CENTURY BRITISH MEDICAL DISCOURSE AND POPULAR FICTION

Merle Tönnies

Hegemonic versus Popular Discourse

The two discourses analysed here were diametrically opposed to each other in the nineteenth century. On the one hand, medicine was becoming ever more securely institutionalized as a 'scientific' discipline; on the other, popular fiction was deliberately 'non-serious' – a genre that might be avidly read, but at the same time was always considered to lack 'respectability'. This was particularly true of the sensation novels of the 1860s, on which the present discussion will focus. Countless reviews reviled them for appealing to their readers' baser instincts, and thereby producing effects verging on the 'illegitimate'. Indeed, in ideological terms medicine can be considered a classic example of a 'dominant' discourse which expresses and supports the opinions of the ruling circles of society. Medical writers invest these beliefs with the authority inherent in the doctor–patient relationship, and (in the terminology of Louis Althusser, Antonio Gramsci and Roland Barthes) 'naturalize' them by grounding them in the biological basis of human existence. Sensation fiction, by contrast, can be considered part of 'popular' culture in the Cultural Studies understanding of this term, developed especially by John Fiske and Stuart Hall. While preserving an (often threadbare) veil of conformity, sensation novels contain representations that challenge the dominant ideology on a number of levels, and thereby offer subversive pleasures to those excluded or suppressed by the social power structure.

The two discourses can thus be seen as engaged in a constant ideological contest. This is particularly graphic in one of the key conflict zones of the age, the definition of 'acceptable' femininity. Doctors explicitly described the perpetuation of existing gender relations as 'essential to the well-being of our social system'.[1] They were, moreover, very much aware of sensation novels as a potential threat to male hegemony. George Black's *Young Wife's Advice Book* (1888), for instance, cautioned mothers that the 'undue mental excitement … caused by the reading of sensation novels' had 'a tendency to accelerate the occurrence of menstruation'.[2] As detailed in many medical textbooks, the precocious development of the sexual organs endangered a girl's health, and thereby menaced a key social value, the 'pre-eminence of English women' in their 'vigour of constitution, soundness of judgment, and … rectitude of moral principle'.[3] As if they were contagious, these fictional representations impressed themselves on the bodies of their female readers and infected them with their rebellious contents. The unconventionality and potential subversiveness of the sensation novels' female portraits have already been examined by Lyn Pykett (1992), Ann Cvetkovich (1992), Nicholas Rance (1991) and others. This chapter, by contrast, will analyse how far these 'popular' works – which, after all, did feature doctors and asylum settings – actively took part in the ideological controversy about femininity in which the medical writers thought themselves involved.

Two Views of Women's (Dis)abilities

From the point of view of the twentieth and twenty-first centuries, the established nineteenth century concept of womanhood is usually summed up in the form of Coventry Patmore's 'angel in the house' and John Ruskin's equal but separate 'spheres' for men and women.[4] Dating from the 1850s and 1860s, these two texts restated the ruling ideology in the 'sensation' period, but in practice the Victorian gender hegemony had already been in place well before the queen ascended the throne. In order to defend it against real and imaginary attacks, doctors naturalized 'proper' femininity, stressing that – much more than with man – woman's reproductive organs and the 'functions' associated with them 'influenced the whole life of the individual'.[5] Due to the 'reflex relationship of the uterus with the sensory, motor and mental functions of the brain',[6] her special 'feminine' characteristics first and foremost took the form of typical (dis)abilities: it was 'a physiological fact' that intellectually, women were 'weighed unfairly' for competition with man,[7] far too emotional and timid to carry out any great projects or stand up against misfortune. With little self-reliance and determination, they clung to their homes and were 'easily quelled by any opposing forces'.[8] If they did act with 'vigour and determination', this was only an instinctive response to an emergency,[9] which was often 'punished' by a bout of hysteria immediately afterwards.[10] Indeed, this disease was said to attack strong and fearless women especially frequently[11] – as if their bodies revenged themselves for being taxed beyond the 'proper' feminine limits.

The sensation-novel heroines evince a very wide range of such apparently 'masculine' capabilities. Lydia Gwilt in Wilkie Collins's *Armandale* (1864–6), for instance, shows a high degree of independence, readily venturing into new spheres in pursuit of revenge and ambition – not of a classic 'feminine' aim like charity.[12] She plans at least two moves ahead and is always ready to exploit her sexual attraction to make weak men like Mr Bashwood do her bidding. One of her male opponents accordingly exclaims: 'What a lawyer she would have made, ... if she had only been a man!'[13] For her, the established view of feminine capabilities is simply an occasion for ironic sideswipes at her accomplice, Mother Oldershaw: 'Some brute of a man says in some book which I once read, that no woman can keep two separate trains of ideas in her mind at the same time. I declare you have almost satisfied me that the man is right.'[14] Miss Gwilt even manages to turn the medical opinion against the extremely negative representative of the profession in the novel, the quack sanatorium director: 'You, who know women so well,' she silences his unwanted questions, 'ought to know that they act on impulse.' The doctors' image of emotional, unstable women is cited more seriously when the heroine's resolution seems temporarily under threat. She repeatedly depends on laudanum, the chief helper of nineteenth century women with nervous complaints, to get some sleep, and even explicitly finds her 'nerves ... all unstrung'.[15] Contrary to medical expectations, however, these moments of frailty never impair her actions. When it is really necessary, she always responds with self-control and courage – right down to poisoning the man she takes to be Armandale with the instruments provided by the doctor.

A woman like Lydia Gwilt is clearly representative of the type of sensation-novel heroine that the standard critical opinion has linked with Mary Elizabeth Braddon's 'female' strand of the genre (and especially with her classic *Lady Audley's Secret* [1862]) much more than with Collins[16] – a distinction that this chapter shows to be much overrated. After all, Collins takes special care to ensure that the reader is allowed to follow Miss Gwilt's thoughts in letters and diary entries without the intervention of the (apparently male) omniscient narrator. In addition, key elements of her story are intensified in a later novel

and thus seem to have been of lasting interest to Collins. Madame Fontaine in
Jezbel's Daughter (1880) is an even more accomplished poisoner, but
nevertheless remains almost as close to the reader as her predecessor. She is in
a position to avail herself of her late husband's – a doctor's – lethal legacy
unencumbered by the interferences to which Miss Gwilt is subjected by 'her'
doctor. Madame Fontaine manipulates her surroundings with great cunning
and foresight, defying the efforts of more than one doctor to expose her
machinations. She both exploits her sexual attractiveness, 'bewitch[ing]' a
harmless old man and discarding him as soon as he is no longer useful, and
ingratiates herself as a 'guardian angel' (in her own words) with the (rich)
family into which she wants her daughter to marry.[17] Appearing gentle, modest,
'sweet and patient', 'the very ideal of the nurse with fine feelings and tender
hands', she displays perfectly all the traits of the 'true woman' content with
the domestic circle whom the medical establishment idealized with such
poetical enthusiasm.[18] She is more successful in this respect than Lydia Gwilt,
whose red hair – 'the one unpardonably remarkable shade of colour which the
prejudice of the Northern nations never entirely forgives' – and wayward temper
are serious obstacles, though she, too, has her moments.[19]

Medicine's 'moral insanity' and Sensational Crime

This element of the two heroines' strategy can be read as a direct reference to
medical literature's anxieties about women's potential for 'artifice' and
'dissimulation'. Most frequently, such worrying behaviour was excluded from
women's 'normal' character by ascribing it to disease. Hysteria, *the* inherently
feminine illness of nineteenth century Britain, was invoked particularly often.
According to Thomas Laycock's seminal theory, 'hysterical cunning' was
considered to derive from the excessive development of feminine qualities
under the influence of the ovaries. While patients possessed '*utmost modesty of
deportment, and grace of figure and movement*', their typical feminine astuteness
'degenerate[d] into mere artfulness of monomaniacal cunning'.[20] As the last
term indicates, this symptom was often thought to take the hysterical woman
into the realm of 'insanity' itself.[21] Her unacceptable actions were thereby
branded with the strongest possible label of deviancy,[22] while the remaining
feminine characteristics were saved from any doubt; they were part of her
'natural' state, from which she diverged only under the sway of disease. In this
understanding, hysterical 'cunning' could be widened to include aberrant
actions of the gravest possible import: 'Physicians have recorded numerous
instances of strange and motiveless deceptions, thefts, and crimes practised by
young women, even by ladies of unexceptionable morals, excellent education,
and high rank.'[23]

Hysteria could thus verge on a rather contested form of mental illness, the 'moral insanity' first postulated by James Cowles Prichard. He defined the disease as the 'perversion of the natural feelings, affections, inclinations, temper, habits, moral dispositions and natural impulses, without any remarkable disorder or defect of the intellect'.[24] 'Deviant' actions that seemed out of character in a person could therefore constitute the only evidence of moral insanity. As Prichard himself recognized, this meant that the distinction between 'insanity and acts of a criminal nature' could be difficult.[25] Doctors (as well as lawyers) continued to fret that this diagnosis might be used to protect genuine vice from its just punishment.[26] Nevertheless, moral insanity featured as a standard category in medical textbooks throughout the century.[27] Although it was less inherently 'feminine' than hysteria, women were still considered the more likely sufferers.[28]

It is noteworthy that murder by 'sly poisoning' featured prominently among the crimes committed by hysterical and morally insane patients.[29] Not only the dissembling, but even the (attempted) homicides of Lydia Gwilt and Madame Fontaine might thus be understood as signs of illness rather than vice. Miss Gwilt's intermittent nervous symptoms have already been pointed out, and her counterpart in *Jezbel's Daughter* is even more extreme. Towards the end of the novel, when her criminal activities intensify, her nervousness does as well, so that she suffers from paroxysms and faints repeatedly.[30] While the majority of writers on moral insanity stipulated that the deed committed should have no apparent motive,[31] some doctors allowed the label to be applied even to perfectly plausible actions motivated, for instance, by revenge.[32] These two sensation novels can thus be taken to flirt with the diagnosis that the medical establishment would most probably have attached to their heroines, especially as both of them have at least one feminine trait which could thereby have been salvaged as an expression of their 'true' nature: Madame Fontaine is intensely devoted to her daughter, and Lydia Gwilt feels genuine love for Midwinter, which intermittently interferes with her evil purposes. Ironically, she refers to these womanly feelings as 'madness',[33] thereby highlighting the fact that the novels pointedly refuse to dismiss their heroines' evil disposition as insanity, and thus end up mixing 'deviant' and classically 'feminine' traits. Madame Fontaine herself decisively rejects a medical explanation with regard to another poisoner: 'I can understand the murderess becoming morally intoxicated with the sense of her own tremendous power.'[34] This exultation then comes over her as well: 'The power that I have dreamed of all my life is mine at last! Alone among mortal creatures, I have Life and Death for my servants.' Accordingly, the narrator pronounces that she too possesses a 'wicked nature', just as Collins himself describes his heroine as 'cruel, false, and degraded' in the novel's dedication.[35] Fittingly, none of the doctors involved in her case even considers possible insanity. Similarly, Miss Gwilt knows that despite her occasional nervousness, she is 'a fiend in human shape' rather than a victim of illness. In this text, the desire to explain away 'badness' as 'madness' is at the same time openly ridiculed: The respectable female visitors to the asylum see 'something in [Lydia Gwilt's] face, utterly unintelligible to them', which they instinctively classify as 'madness'.[36] The narrator and more perceptive characters, by contrast, invoke animal metaphors (e.g. 'cat', 'tigress'),[37] thereby stressing – just as the character's own description does – that the danger inherent in her cannot be contained by medical intervention. Instead of becoming passive objects of the physicians' art, both heroines remain in control of their own destinies.

Rebellious Patients and Angry Heroines

Against this background, medical discourse can even be read as realizing to some extent that the diagnosis of insanity was connected with the assertion of male power over recalcitrant women. Doctors emphasized with regard to their 'insane' female patients that a strict so-called 'moral treatment' or 'control' was necessary, by which they were reintegrated into the established system of social relations:

> If the patient should be of a temper to make attempts at *resistance*, and to refuse compliance with the reasonable wishes of her medical attendant, a firm *determination* on the part of her husband, or other most influential friend or friends to see those wishes complied with, must be exerted in such a way as not to fail to impress her mind with a conviction of the absolute expediency of *submission*.[38]

'Peevishness' and 'irritability' (especially towards the husband) were even routinely cited as the first signs of so-called 'puerperal insanity'.[39] In a similar way, the petulancy of pubescent girls was regarded as a 'state of miniature insanity', with Edward John Tilt explicitly linking this mood with the patients' discontent that 'woman was made dependent, tied to hearth and home by a long chain of never-ending infirmities'.[40] Such insurrection obviously had to be 'treated' by medical authority. *Armandale* graphically mocks this procedure by making a more advanced kind of 'moral treatment' (for cases of impending madness) the key innovation in the evil doctor's asylum.[41] On the whole, the novels can be taken to oppose the medical establishment's efforts to rein in women by representations of unrestrained female anger and rebelliousness. In this way, they also predispose their readers to believe the explanation that Miss Gwilt gives for her wickedness: it is no inherent character trait, but a result of the hard life she has led.[42] Likewise, the narrator of *Jezbel's Daughter* cautions potentially censorious readers with regard to the evil woman: 'thank God that you were not tempted as she was'.[43] If society does not offer its women better opportunities, it is no wonder they start availing themselves of illegal means – which doctors then have to cover up with the redeeming veil of 'insanity'.

Sensational Extremes of Self-Confessed Madness and Wrongful Confinement

References to the prevalent medical discourse are still intensified in Braddon's *Lady Audley's Secret*.[44] This protagonist's characteristics and actions could have been taken straight from a case study like Thomas Smith Clouston's of 'a very gentle-looking lady, with a pale, pretty face, light hair, and blue eyes, a singularly kind, pleasant, winning manner, and a soft quiet voice', who nevertheless suffered from 'sudden and unaccountable outbreaks of dangerous violence'.[45] As with Lady Audley, the designation of the aggressive acts as 'insanity' was especially helpful here, as it validated the correspondence between outward beauty and moral perfection in which the doctors firmly believed;[46] the apparent exception to the 'rule' was simply due to illness. Clouston's case had strong features of 'impulsive insanity', which medical discourse considered to be closely linked with 'moral insanity', since it could also occur without any impairment of the intellectual faculties.[47] Fittingly, Lady Audley, too, is more impulsive than the other heroines. Although she acts rationally enough (and by no means lapses into the passive emotionality that medical writers considered 'natural' for women), she herself thinks she 'can't plot horrible things': 'My worst wickednesses have been the result of wild impulses.'[48]

The parallels with 'moral insanity' are even more striking. Setting fire to houses, as Lady Audley does in order to kill Robert, her male opponent, is explicitly quoted as a symptom,[49] and just as John Charles Bucknill and Daniel Hack Tuke pointed out for moral insanity, '[a]ll benevolent and kindly affections, all prudent regard for the feelings of others' have disappeared with her.[50] Moreover, medical writers stressed the hereditary element in moral insanity, which was considered to assert itself especially forcefully in the mother-daughter line.[51] The protagonist's mother (who had inherited this predisposition from her own parent) indeed went insane at the birth of her daughter – a clear case of 'puerperal insanity', which was said to account for 10 per cent of all new occurrences of female madness.[52] It became chronic (as in the novel) if it was not treated within two days,[53] and doctors expressly named poverty, which Lady Audley sees as having severely affected her mother's life, as a predisposing cause towards this affliction.[54] The protagonist herself escapes the 'critical period' of childbirth,[55] but her life then follows Prichard's theory that moral insanity often breaks out at 'some reverse of fortune' or 'the loss of some beloved relative'.[56] When her husband leaves her in poverty to make his fortune in Australia, she becomes 'subject to fits of violence and despair', which 'resolve ... themselves into [the] desperate purpose' of running away and changing her identity; unprotected by the early training advocated by Maudsley to prevent the outbreak of hereditary madness,[57] she has turned morally insane.

Lady Audley's Secret not only invokes the doctors' views in much greater detail than Collins's novels, but the heroine herself explicitly claims 'insanity' in the strict medical sense. In this way, Braddon's novel becomes much more ambiguous. In contrast to Collins' characters, Lady Audley unreservedly surrenders her mind to medical authority. Thereby she abandons her assertive independence, but is at the same time absolved from all responsibility for her life after her husband's departure. This allows her to affirm, apparently sincerely: 'I was not wicked when I was young, ... I was only thoughtless. I never did any harm – at least, never wilfully.'[58] If she is ill, then the early life of the woman who – in contrast to the other heroines – seems to be completely devoid of genuine redeeming traits is reclaimed for conventional womanhood. After all, physicians consistently affirmed that with moral insanity there was a profound 'change in the moral character of the individual'.[59]

Lady Audley herself really seems to believe in her own madness (which, of course, at the same time makes her views inherently dubious). In the novel as a whole, however, the instinctive distrust of a faithful dog[60] and the metaphors applied to her (taken from the field of sorcery rather than from the animal realm),[61] serve as almost clichéd markers of wickedness, contradicting the insanity explanation. Indeed, the heroine herself is at least unconsciously aware of the ideological import of the discourse to which she submits. Threatening Robert, she explains that 'such fancies [his investigations] have sometimes conducted people, as apparently sane as yourself, to the life-long imprisonment of a private lunatic asylum' – madness is a construction used to banish those who engage in socially undesirable pursuits. It is thus rather appropriate that while accepting the dominant medical opinion on her case, Lady Audley refuses to see her confinement in an asylum as a suitable treatment, accusing Robert of having 'used [his] power basely and cruelly'.[62]

Most importantly, the medical expert called in by Robert curiously refuses to follow the reasoning of his own profession. Before learning about the protagonist's murderous actions, he is convinced that she is not mad, '[b]ecause there is no evidence of madness in anything that she has done'.[63] This assessment completely leaves out the above-cited established view that 'moral' and 'impulsive' insanity can coexist perfectly well with unimpaired intelligence. Once he has met the offending woman, the physician complies with Robert's wish to have her certified, but still does not even consider the medical categories into which her case fits so perfectly. He concedes only that '[t]here is latent insanity': 'The lady is not mad; but she has the hereditary taint in her blood. She has the cunning of madness, with the prudence of intelligence. ... She is dangerous!' The representative of the dominant discourse in the novel thus reveals that the textbook diagnosis of Lady Audley's case would be nothing but a method of containing 'danger'. Ironically, this is, of course, exactly what he then proceeds to do, shutting the deviant woman away where she will not be able to do any more harm.[64]

Compared with Collins's two works, Braddon's ideological stance is thus subversive rather than openly confrontational here. Interestingly, she had already contributed to the struggle about 'proper' femininity in a slightly earlier, rather obscure novel, which works much more along Collins's lines. The Black Band, which was published as a book only in 1877, in a heavily abridged form, was serialized for fifty-two weeks in 1861–2 in The Halfpenny Journals; A Magazine for All Who Can Read. Written at the very inception of the sensation genre, it was thereby addressed to an exclusively working-class audience, whereas – to the horror of the critical establishment – Lady Audley's Secret and Collins's novels found favour in middle-class circles as well. In The Black Band Lady Edith Vandeleur – in contrast to Lady Audley, of truly aristocratic origin and a dark, mysterious beauty – is consummately wicked and ambitious. She cold-bloodedly attempts to murder the husband she has married for money, then commits bigamy with equal determination. Later, she unscrupulously and cunningly betrays her second husband to his enemies. The standard medical opinion on such female behaviour is again cited in the novel, but in contrast to Lady Audley's Secret, there is no ambiguity. The two representatives of male authority, Lady Edith's first husband and her father, simply use this discourse (embodied by shadowy doctor figures without a voice of their own)[65] to exclude her from society, even though they are well aware that – as the foiled poisoner protests – 'I am not mad; I am a vile and wicked wretch – but I am not mad'.[66] Indeed, Lady Edith is not even troubled by the nervousness which intermittently assails Collins's two characters. This direct and fundamental attack on the ideological work performed by medicine may be connected with the intended readership of the text, who will have been less constrained by the femininity stereotype than middle-class audiences, and will generally have been more interested in clear-cut descriptions than in equivocal subtleties. Tellingly, Lady Edith lacks the redeeming features of Collins's wicked women, and does not suffer any remorse,[67] which would have made her character more (or too) complex.

Sensational Nonconformity and Commercial Success

It should be noted, however, that the overall success of both The Black Band and Collins's Armandale and Jezbel's Daughter came nowhere near that of the more guarded *Lady Audley's Secret*. Open ideological struggles may thus have been too disquieting for some sections of the reading public. Braddon's best-known novel, by contrast, embodies 'popular' literature to perfection, allowing readers both to protest against the dominant ideology and to rest assured in their own ultimate conformity; as Lady Audley herself pleads 'madness', the reader can believe in the established femininity concept together with her.

On the whole, both male and female sensation novelists were thus very much aware of the dominant medical discourse, and opposed it in many of their works with equal radicalism. These novels' deeply 'serious' statements on female power and anger sometimes seem to have gone a little too far for potential readers, who looked for 'lighter' entertainment. Another key example, Charles Reade's *Hard Cash* (1863), indeed predicts such a reaction. The appropriately named wicked Edith Archbold burns with assertive sexual desire, but is not only clearly *compos mentis*, but even the matron of the depicted lunatic asylum. When she turns into 'one of the best wives and mothers in England' without any medical intervention, the narrator scoffs that such an outcome 'will offend my female readers and their unchristian prejudices'.[68] Ironically, most 'literary' nineteenth century novels were 'lighter' in this respect. Their female characters did not take on the medical establishment as an opponent, and therefore remained more harmless in ideological terms. The 'madwoman' was generally relegated to the 'attic' here, whereas the sensation novels put all the standard 'symptoms' of deviancy centre-stage – and presented the character as 'sane' at the same time.

15

NIGHT TERRORS: MEDICAL AND LITERARY REPRESENTATIONS OF CHILDHOOD FEAR

Sally Shuttleworth

In his 1905 essay on 'Infantile Sexuality', Freud observes:

> It is noticeable that writers who concern themselves with explaining the characteristics and reactions of the adult have devoted much more attention to the primaeval period which is comprised in the life of the individual's ancestors – have, that is, ascribed much more influence to heredity – than to the other primaeval period, which falls within the lifetime of the individual himself – that is, to childhood.[1]

Freud's insight, with its location of the secrets of identity not solely in the racial history explored by anthropologists and evolutionary biologists, but also in that other sphere of dauntingly unknowable prehistory – childhood – has often been taken as an originary moment. In this chapter, I would like to explore the prehistory of that moment itself, focusing specifically on the domain of childhood terrors.

Dreams and nightmares were, of course, central to the Romantic imagination, and to the psychoanalytic project initiated by Freud. My interest lies, however, in the space between these bounds: in the interchange between the literary and medical domains which takes place in the mid-nineteenth century, when child night terrors first enter medical textbooks. In current childhood manuals, and sites on the web, there is still much debate as to why a normal, apparently happy child should be precipitated into a state of seemingly inexplicable terror. This question also fuelled mid-Victorian attempts to explore, and rework, understandings of the child mind. My analysis starts with a cluster of texts published between 1847 and 1854 which all explored the phenomenon of childhood fear: Charles West's *Lectures on the Diseases of Infancy and Childhood* (1848, 3rd rev. edn. 1854), Charlotte Brontë's *Jane Eyre* (1847), Harriet Martineau's *Household Education* (1849) and Anna Jameson's *Commonplace Book* (1854).

In her essay 'A Revelation of Childhood', published in her *Commonplace Book*, Anna Jameson demands: 'how much do we know of that which lies in the minds of children? We know only what we put there.'[2] Her question forms part of the mid-Victorian literary interest in the workings of the child mind which was stimulated so forcefully by Dickens (who had recently published *David Copperfield*) and Brontë. Jameson attacks educators who regard childhood as 'so much material placed in our hands to be fashioned to a certain form according to our will or our prejudices' and as merely a preparatory state to be left behind. Instead she wishes to explore 'that inward, busy, perpetual activity of the growing faculties and feelings' of which, paradoxically, a child can give no account:

> To lead children by questionings to think about their own identity, or observe their own feelings, is to teach them to be artificial. To waken self-consciousness before you awaken conscience is the beginning of incalculable mischief. Introspection is always, as a habit, unhealthy; introspection in childhood, fatally so.[3]

In a sense, Jameson is here following the very practice of which she complains: putting on to childhood her own preconceptions – childhood is defined as a state of unselfconsciousness. To reflect on experience or one's own identity is to forfeit the state of childhood, to become instead 'artificial'. (One is reminded here of Mrs Reed's paradoxical injunction to Jane Eyre to be 'more natural' and to acquire a 'more childlike disposition').[4]

Jameson challenges ideas of the child as merely an empty vessel waiting to be filled, but subscribes instead to a model of childhood innocence which differentiates the world of the child from that of the adult. This is not, however, the blithe innocence, and superior wisdom, of Wordsworth's child in 'We are Seven'. The image of childhood Jameson proceeds to unveil is one dominated by fear: 'fear of darkness and supernatural influences. As long as I can remember anything, I remember those horrors of my infancy. How they had been awakened I do not know.'[5] These horrors are both inexplicable and lifelong, enduring in the memory as the defining modality of childhood. Originally vague in form, these 'haunting, thrilling, stifling terrors' start to take shape under the impact of literary illustrations on her young imagination. She is tormented by the figure of Apollyon looming over Christian from an edition of *Pilgrim's Progress*, and by a spectre summoned by an engraving of the ghost in *Hamlet*: 'O that spectre! for three years it followed me up and down the dark staircase, or stood by my bed: only the blessed light had power to exorcise it.' This, then, is not a static form, but one that moves, its 'supernatural light' filling the dark spaces that surround her. It is less threatening, however, than other less identifiable spirits, and here she turns to the Bible to create a language of articulation:

> But worse, perhaps, were certain phantasms without shape, – things like the vision in Job – 'A *spirit passed before my face; it stood still, but I could not discern the form thereof*': – and if not intelligible voices, there were strange unaccountable sounds filling the air around with a sort of mysterious life.[6]

It is not clear whether the Book of Job gave form to her fears in childhood, or whether as an adult she is invoking the Bible both to explain and to give cultural and historical authority to these troubling, largely inexplicable, fears.

Jameson is at pains to point out that she was not, as the above might suggest, a timid, unadventurous child: 'In daylight I was not only fearless, but audacious'. Light and dark produce two different creatures. Drawing on her Romantic heritage, she defines her terrors as 'visionary sufferings', thus elevating them to signs of Romantic sensibility. They 'pursued' her, she notes, until the age of twelve, and could easily have affected her mental stability for life: 'If I had not possessed a strong constitution and strong understanding, which rejected and contemned my own fears, even while they shook me, I had been destroyed.'[7] Here a Victorian commitment to self-control is brought to bear on the workings of the unconscious mind. Jameson's verdict shares the spirit of the discussion of Hartley Coleridge's childhood in the *Edinburgh Review* (1851), which traced the 'unhealthy' way in which his childhood visions had been allowed to dominate his mental development: 'It is not a predominance of intellect, but a deficiency of will, which banishes us from the world of reality, and converts into a gilded prison the palace-halls of the imagination.'[8] Great artists like Shakespeare or Dante, the reviewer argues, 'ever continue lords over themselves, and ... the Spirits whom they summon go and come alike at their command'.[9] This emphasis on the power of will, and the ability to control one's visions, forms part of the early-Victorian response to mental illness, as epitomized in John Barlow's text *Man's Power over Himself to Prevent or Control Insanity* (1843).[10] Barlow himself was not a physician, but he drew heavily on the works of John Conolly and other medical theorists, taking up their arguments that we are all subject to visions and delusions, but only those of weak mind succumb, and enter a state of insanity:

> He who has given a proper direction to the intellectual force, and thus obtained an early command over the bodily organ by habituating it to processes of calm reasoning, remains sane amid all the vagaries of sense; while he who has been the slave, rather than the master of his animal nature, listens to its dictates without question even when distorted by disease – and is mad. A fearful result of an uncultivated childhood![11]

Jameson clearly subscribes to similar theories on the importance of cultivating strength of mind in childhood. Her argument shifts abruptly to a book she has read on the treatment of the insane – unfortunately not identified – which urges absolute veracity as a curative principle: 'Now, it is a good sanitary principle, that what is curative is preventive; and that an unhealthy state of mind, leading to madness, may, in some organisations, be induced by that sort of uncertainty and perplexity which grows up where the mind has not been accustomed to truth in its external relations.'[12] How exact attention to truth could have cured or prevented Jameson's fears as described here is unclear. What is clear, however, is that she is directly placing her experiences within the context of childhood breakdown and madness: a lesser mind would have succumbed to madness. Drawing on contemporary discourses of insanity, she makes the logical leap herself, to place her childhood experiences within the frame of incipient insanity.

Jameson's account of her childhood sufferings has strong parallels in two texts published a few years before. Reading Jameson, it is difficult not to make an immediate link to Brontë's *Jane Eyre* (1847), where Jane, locked in the Red Room, experiences terror that her Uncle Reed might arise from the dead, a terror that climaxes with the sight of a light gleaming on the wall:

> I can now conjecture readily that this streak of light was, in all likelihood, a gleam from a lantern, carried by some one across the lawn; but then, prepared as my mind was for horror, shaken as my nerves were by agitation, I thought the swift-darting beam was a herald of some coming vision from another world. My heart beat thick, my head grew hot; a sound filled my ears, which I deemed the rushing of wings: something seemed near me; I was oppressed, suffocated: endurance broke down – I uttered a wild, involuntary cry.[13]

This episode is set within the frame of an adult, objective explanation – the lantern being carried across the lawn – but the emotional force overrides such rationalism, establishing for generations of future readers an image of Victorian childhood as one defined by terror. Yet the seemingly irrational outbursts of emotion are seen, nonetheless, as a fitting response to an unjust social and familial order, where the voice of the child holds no sway. Where Jameson sets her childhood terror solely in terms of her own responses to texts, illustrations, and the play of light and dark, Brontë shows how susceptibility has been created by adult injustice.

The eruption of *Jane Eyre* into the Victorian cultural consciousness was matched, in tenor if not effect, by Harriet Martineau's *Household Education*, a form of manual for child-rearing, based on Martineau's own childhood recollections. Brontë, on reading it, was reported to have said that it was like meeting her own 'fetch', or ghost, although it is unclear whether she read the articles serialized prior to *Jane Eyre* in the *People's Journal*, or the book published afterwards in 1849.[14] Martineau, like Jameson, insists that parents know little of the sufferings that pass within a child's mind: 'No creature is so intensely reserved as a proud and timid child: and the cases are few in which the parents know anything of the agonies of its little heart, the spasms of its nerves, the soul-sickness of its days, the horrors of its nights.'[15]

She speaks of her own sufferings, of which she never told her family: 'I had a dream at four years old which terrified me to such an excess that I cannot now recal [sic] it without a beating of the heart.'[16] Some of her worst fears were of lights and shadows – the magic lantern, or the shadows from the lamplighter's torch: 'Many an infant is terrified at the shadow of a perforated night-lamp, with its round spaces of light. Many a child lives in perpetual terror of the eyes of portraits on the walls, – or of some grotesque shape in the pattern of the paper-hangings.'[17] Paradoxically, the night-lamp which was designed to comfort the child only increases her terror. As in the Jameson and Brontë examples, flickering half-light, and the uncertain domain between light and dark, evoke states of imaginative fear.

The cumulative effect of these texts is to create an image of Victorian childhood dominated by terror. If one turns to nineteenth century medical texts, however, one finds virtual silence, until this period, on the subject of night terrors. The Victorians were deluged by domestic medicine and child-rearing manuals, but as far as I have been able to trace, none before 1848 devoted space to child night terrors or nervous disorders, although an awareness of childhood delusions is implicit in many of the psychiatric discussions of adult insanity. Manuals on child-rearing and diseases covered the practicalities of nursing, feeding and physical illnesses, while general texts on domestic medicine had entries on nightmare or incubus, without reference to children.[18] One partial exception was Robert Macnish's popular 1830 text, *The Philosophy of Sleep*. Although this work does not have a section on child dreams, it notes at one point that children are more apt to have dreams of terror than adults,

many of them leaving an indelible impression.[19] Although children can have
visions of joy, childhood 'is also tortured by scenes more painful and
overwhelming than almost ever fall to the share of after-life.'[20] The dream
state itself is also characterized as one where judgement is weak, as in children.
Macnish thus establishes an important continuum between childhood and
the dream state. He also, influentially, breaks down the barriers between
dreaming and waking, exploring the categories of daymare, waking dreams
and reverie, all of which he sees as closely allied.[21] Nightmares, he argues, can
occur when one is awake, and he himself had undergone 'the greatest tortures,
being haunted by spectres, hags, and every sort of phantom' while in full
possession of his faculties.[22] Macnish's account of dreams and waking
nightmares was highly influential in the Victorian period. Dickens owned a
copy, and quoted him in his 1851 letter on dreams; while the Reverend Brontë
notes approvingly against the entry on nightmare in the family copy of Graham's
Modern Domestic Medicine: 'Dr McNish ... has justly described the sensations
of Night mare, under some modifications – as being amongst the most horrible
that oppress human nature – an inability to move, during the paroxysm –
dreadful visions of ghosts etc.'[23]

Despite the strong interest, from the Romantic period onwards, in the
phenomena of dreams and apparitions, the first time child night terror figures
as a category in a nineteenth century medical manual is in Charles West's
Lectures on the Diseases of Infancy and Childhood (1848).[24] At this time, West
was Senior Physician to the Royal Infirmary for Children, and also a lecturer
at the Middlesex Hospital. He was already campaigning for the establishment
of a hospital for sick children, which was to open in Great Ormond Street in
1852, with strong support from Dickens.[25] The lecture on Night Terrors starts
abruptly with a graphic depiction of a child who awakes in terror: 'The child
will be found sitting up in its bed, crying out as if in an agony of fear, "oh dear!
oh dear! take it away! father! mother!" while terror is depicted on its
countenance, and it does not recognise its parents.'[26] West cites various case
histories, including those where terrors can occur nightly over a period of months,
but he is nonetheless firm that the cause is physiological – intestinal disorders.
In this he is following a long-established tradition which sought to explain
nightmares according to a purely physiological function.[27] From this point on,
night terrors became a standard entry in domestic medical journals and works
on child-rearing, usually citing West.[28] Interestingly, despite the close
correlations with adult nightmare, it is a diagnosis applied specifically to
children. Rather than trace the development of the concept of night terrors in
the work of others, however, I am particularly concerned with West's own
reworkings of his arguments.

In 1854 he published a third, revised edition of his text, including an additional section on 'Disorders of the Mind in Childhood, and Idiocy'. He retains the original explanation for night terrors as caused by digestive problems, but then moves straight into considering 'some other forms of *disorder of the highest functions of the brain in early life*'.[29] Without acknowledgement, his form of diagnosis has shifted, and night terrors has become one of a new category of child mental disorders. His aim is now to convince his readers that 'perversion of the intellect or of the moral faculties, as distinguished from mere feebleness of mind, is met with in childhood as well as in adult age, and deserves to be regarded and to be treated as insanity no less in the one case than in the other.'[30]

West has taken the first step towards the medicalization of the child mind, offering one of the first explicit treatments in English of childhood mental disorder. The dream state as defined by Macnish and others, where intellectual control is in abeyance, has become a defining characteristic of the child mind and, by extension, of a state of insanity. In childhood, West notes:

> ... the intellectual powers are imperfectly developed, the feelings and the impulses are stronger, or, at least, less under control, than they become with advancing years ... Mental disorders, then, show themselves in the exaggeration of those feelings, the uncontrollable character of those impulses; in the ability or the indisposition to listen to that advice or be swayed by those motives which govern other children.[31]

Mental disorder, the loss of intellectual or emotional control, is thus just a heightened state of childhood. This shift in perceptions of the child mind marks a crucial turning point. Whereas before, childhood had been excluded from discussions of insanity on the grounds that it was a disorder which could attack only fully developed minds, it is now possible to see in the child's very freedom from adult mental constraint the groundings of insanity. The name of this disorder, West suggests, is moral insanity, a term developed earlier in the century by James Prichard to define a form of insanity where 'a morbid perversion of the natural feelings' exists without any 'remarkable disorder' of the 'intellect or knowing and reasoning faculties'.[32] Moral insanity is clearly a diagnosis Mrs Reed would have been very happy to apply to that 'unnatural' child, Jane Eyre.[33]

What made West change his mind about the aetiology of night terrors? In part it might have been the establishment of the Great Ormond Street Hospital, which permitted him to observe children for longer stretches, and overnight, but did those passionate literary texts published over this period also have an effect? In the case of Martineau and Jameson, the suggestion is openly made that the activities of an overactive imagination in childhood can lead to insanity.

Both celebrate the imagination, but also, – almost self-punishingly, given their interest in fictional form, – insist on the pernicious effects of falsehood: Thus Jameson, in the essay on 'Pestilence of Falsehood' in her *Commonplace Book*, notes: 'I am for fumigating the atmosphere when I suspect that falsehood, like pestilence, breathes around me'; while Martineau observes that lying is 'a moral disease', and if a child is not truthful, he should have the same help 'as if he were suffering under some disgusting bodily disorder'.[34] Although both writers paint graphic pictures of the sufferings of childhood, when terror can create delusions and hallucinations that dominate perception, they both nonetheless subscribe to the Victorian doctrines of 'truth' and abhorrence of the 'lie'.[35]

Jameson's own confusions are not replicated in James Crichton Browne's seminal essay 'The Psychical Diseases of Early Life' (*Asylum Journal of Mental Science*, 1860), where he draws on Jameson's autobiographical recollections of 'the shaping spirit of imagination' which 'haunted' her inner life in childhood, and accounts of Hartley Coleridge's invention of an imaginary land as a child, as well as West's work on night terrors, to argue that the delusions of childhood lead to mental derangement in maturity. Indeed it is possible for children themselves to suffer from a variety of forms of insanity. Supplementing West's account of night terrors with details from his own practice, he argues that '[m]any cases of infantile insanity owe their origin to fear'.[36] Night terrors and daydreams are now firmly placed on a continuum which leads directly to mental derangement, setting the agenda for the development of child psychiatry in the later decades of the century.

Before turning to examine the subsequent history of ideas of night terrors in the nineteenth century, I would like to take a step back to consider the earlier history of the idea, and to investigate Romantic explorations of childhood fear, which fed into these mid-century examples. Romantic writers were, of course, deeply preoccupied with the world of dreams, and, as Alan Richardson and Jennifer Ford have shown, were also intensely engaged with theories of the mind which might account for such phenomena.[37] Part of these explorations encompassed child terrors. In the opening pages of Maria Edgeworth's *Harrington* (1817), we are presented with the trauma of the six-year-old Harrington's encounter with Simon the Jew, an old clothes collector, whose face is caught in the flare of a torch.[38] Harrington consequently suffers terrors day and night. As the candle retreats at night he feels 'an indescribable agony of terror', and sees 'faces around me grinning, glaring, receding, advancing, all turning at last into one and the same face of the Jew with the long beard, and the terrible eyes, and that bag in which I fancied were mangled limbs of children'.[39] As in Martineau's account, the inner life of the child is dominated by fears, but in Edgeworth's narrative these terrifying visions are assigned to an exterior cause. The hard-hearted maid, Fowler, has aroused Harrington's fears by claiming that the Jew would carry him away in his bag if he did not come to bed. A form of Hartleyan associative psychology is grafted on to a discourse of the nervous body – as outlined, for example, by Thomas Trotter in *A View of the Nervous Temperament* (1807).[40] Once the associative links are understood and confronted, Harrington can be cured.

The associative logic is made quite plain – the fears are caused not by the mysterious play of light, or the emergence of a strange figure, but, rather, entirely by lower-class foolishness. This explanatory move is found throughout nineteenth century texts (and of course earlier): a lower-class member of the household is made responsible for the otherwise inexplicable disturbance of middle-class domestic order.[41] Thus Martineau denounces mothers who allow ignorant nurses to frighten children 'with goblin stories, or threats of the old black man. ... The instances are not few of idiotcy [sic] or death from terror so caused.'[42] Martineau's suggestion that death can be caused by nurse's tales, takes to an extreme the distrust and scapegoating focused on the disruptive figure of the working-class nurse who held sway in the middle-class nursery.[43] Jane Eyre, of course, was terrified by Bessie's tales of the 'Gytrash', which remain with her in adulthood, but a far more virulent attack on the irresponsibility of nurses in the telling of tales comes, rather surprisingly, from that great defender of the fairy tale, Charles Dickens, in his 1860 piece 'Nurse's Stories'. Dickens finds that the people and places he knew in childhood were as nothing compared with those he had been introduced to by his nurse before he was six years old,

> ... and used to be forced to go back to at night without at all wanting to go. If we all knew our own minds (in a more enlarged sense than the popular acceptation of that phrase), I suspect we should find our nurses responsible for most of the dark corners we are forced to go back to, against our wills.[44]

The nurse is portrayed as harbouring a 'fiendish enjoyment of my terrors'; her account of the shipwright who sold his soul to the devil, and became overrun with rats, occasioned in the young Dickens sensations of rats cascading over his body, so that '[a]t intervals ever since, I have been morbidly afraid of my own pocket, lest my exploring hand should find a specimen or two of those vermin in it.'[45] The account is clearly tailor-made for Freudian analysis, but for Dickens, whose fascination with the formation of the child mind extended throughout his work, the analysis is here abruptly cut short by resorting to that customary object of blame: the nurse. Despite Dickens's own zest in retelling the tale, the 'dark corners' of his mind are attributed to the lack of control, and indeed sadistic impulses, of his working-class carer.

The other Romantic text I want to look at briefly is Charles Lamb's 'Witches, and other Night-fears' (1821), which offers a rather different structure of explanation for childhood distress. The account of his childhood terror is very

similar to that of Jameson; only the text this time is Thomas Stackhouse's
History of the Bible, and the engraving is that of the Witch of Endor summoning
the spirit of Samuel. Lamb observes that he never lay down between the ages
of four and eight without seeing that spectre. Yet, he continues,

> Be old Stackhouse then acquitted in part, if I say, that to his picture of
> the Witch raising up Samuel – (O that old man covered with a mantle!)
> I owe – not my midnight terrors, the hell of my infancy – but the shape
> and manner of their visitation. ... It is not book, or picture, or the
> stories of foolish servants, which create these terrors in children. They
> can at most but give them a direction.[46]

Neither books nor servants bear the blame, but, rather, inherited structures of
the brain. Lamb reinforces his argument by drawing on the example of 'little
T. H.' (Thornton Hunt, Leigh Hunt's eldest child), who had been brought up
'with the most scrupulous exclusion of every taint of superstition' and heard
no tales of goblins, apparitions, or bad men; and yet 'from his little midnight
pillow, this nurse-child of optimism will start at shapes, unborrowed of tradition,
in sweats to which the reveries of the cell-damned murderer are tranquillity.'[47]
Like Edgeworth, Jameson and Martineau, Lamb is disturbed by a child's capacity
to experience such seemingly unwarranted terror, but turns for an answer to a
notion of ancestral forms. Thus, gorgons and hydras, he argues, 'may reproduce
themselves in the brain of superstition – but they were there before. They are
transcripts, types – the archetypes are in us, and eternal'. The fact that these
terrors predominate in the period of sinless infancy is thus explained, and we
are afforded, he suggests, 'a peep at least into the shadow-land of pre-
existence'.[48] Where Wordsworth envisages a child trailing clouds of glory from
its previous existence, Lamb seems to conjure up a Dantesque *Inferno*. The
effect is rapidly undercut, however, as the rest of the essay is spent comically
lamenting how prosaic his dreams have become.

Edgeworth and Lamb, writing at roughly the same time, offer two very
different explanatory models for night terrors, but models that continue to
echo down the century. For Edgeworth, the source of night terrors is external
to the child; hence the problem can be solved by careful vetting of one's nurses.
Although later nineteenth century texts are less mechanistic in their analysis,
and show terror evoked independently of nurses' foolish tales, there is
nevertheless a strong investment in both the Jameson and Martineau texts in
the belief that fears can be controlled by rationality. Nurses are once again
scapegoated. Behind many of these texts one can trace the bafflement of
parents: why should their child wake up screaming every night? It is noteworthy
that all the medical and literary texts I have looked at insist that it is sheer
cruelty to a child to leave it either alone, or without a light, at night. Thus

Robert Carter, for example, argues in 1855 that '[t]error at night, depending either upon simple dread of solitude or darkness, or upon distressing dreams, or upon the tricks and falsehoods of nurses and attendants, is a source of disease that should be guarded against most completely'.[49] He advises that 'a young child, whether ailing or not, should never be left in the dark, and never alone, when it is possible to avoid doing so; while one who is naturally excitable, or easily terrified, should always, upon waking, find a familiar face at hand'.[50] Clearly these instructions are for middle-class parents with nurses at their disposal. What is interesting here is the assumption that it is not unusual for a child to be scared of the dark or solitude, and that it is the duty of parents to guard their children against these conditions. The very solution to the problem, however, was the much-maligned nurse, seen elsewhere as the actual begetter of the original terrors. Like Edgeworth and Martineau, Carter speaks of the untold evils created by threatening children with 'bugbears' which have 'destroyed the health or intellect of many'.[51]

Lamb's explanation eschews attributing blame to the nurse, suggesting instead that fears are latent in us all. In a form of almost Jungian argument, he argues that there are archetypes which haunt our dreams. In the Romantic period, however, there was no system of causal explanation to carry forward such a model. Yet later in the century, Darwinism, rather surprisingly, was to offer a materialist framework which could accommodate such idealist notions. In his 'Biographical Sketch of an Infant' (1877), Darwin pondered on the fear his son expressed at the zoological gardens on seeing the 'beasts in houses': '... and we could in no manner account for this fear. May we not suspect that the vague but very real fears of children, which are quite independent of experience, are the inherited effects of real dangers and abject superstitions during ancient savage times?'[52] Contrary to the usual assumptions, evolutionary biology, with its vista of animalistic descent, was not always an alarming prospect for the Victorians. In this case, Darwin finds it deeply reassuring to be able to account for his son's disturbance in terms of patterns of inherited memories. His account makes literal Freud's analogy of childhood and prehistoric times.

Writing in mid-century, Martineau and Jameson sought explanations for child terror in external sources: the nurse's tale, or inadequate forms of child-rearing. Post-Darwin, new forms of explanation became available, bringing with them a whole new disciplinary framework. From the 1880s onwards, childhood study, largely based on loosely framed evolutionary assumptions, developed rapidly in both Europe and the USA. In Britain such studies were led by George Eliot and Lewes's friend, James Sully, whose 1895 *Studies of Childhood* marks the institution in England of this area as a disciplinary field. Sully, and other theorists, developed the study of childhood fear, with Sully moving gradually to accept a model grounded in evolutionary theory. In

Illusions: A Psychological Study (1881), he speculated as to whether a child might have 'a sort of reminiscence of prenatal, that is, ancestral experience', concluding that the idea was a 'fascinating one, worthy to be a new scientific support for the beautiful thought of Plato and Wordsworth', but that in 'our present state of knowledge' any such reasoning would probably appear 'too fanciful'.[53] In *Studies of Childhood* he returns to precisely this area, exploring in depth the foundation of child fears, satisfied now that he was not dwelling too much in the domain of the fanciful. While drawing on evolutionary explanations, he rejects Darwin's suggestion that children feel instinctive fear of animals and also dismisses explanations based on servants' stories.[54] Instead he develops a theory of childhood imagination, celebrating children's creativity (while nonetheless also paralleling their terrors to those of animals and 'savages').[55] His evolutionary vision of childhood is a far more benign one than the terror-struck model of the mid-century. Its positive tone finds echoes in the literature of the period, where one can trace a similar preoccupation with childhood dreams and patterns of evolutionary explanation. The horrors of Robert Louis Stevenson's *The Strange Case of Dr Jekyll and Mr Hyde* (1886) are countered, for example, by Sarah Grand's *The Beth Book* (1897), which celebrates Beth's 'further faculty' and her dreams which place her in touch with her ancestors: here human evolution and inheritance gives rise not to nightmares, but to the capacity for enhanced imaginative play.[56] Although Sully sought to throw off the legacy of earlier explanations and to create a more positive image of childhood itself, and the power of inheritance, he nonetheless ends his chapter on childhood fear with a discussion of the brutality of those who have charge of children, and delight in playing on their terrors. Such is the enormity of this behaviour that he resorts to the 'old dogma' that the devil can enter men and women to explain it: 'For here we seem to have to do with a form of cruelty so exquisite, so contrary to the oldest of instincts, that it is dishonouring to the savage and to the lower animals to attempt to refer it to heredity.'[57] Where reversion to inherited instincts had been for Darwin a way of explaining away childhood terror, Sully here inverts the evolutionary form of explanation to suggest that the behaviour of child-carers who construct tales to terrify children is a form of refined cruelty that only the most perverted forms of civilization can produce.

In his essay on 'Infantile Sexuality', Freud dismisses the idea that nurses' stories are the cause of childhood fear; rather fear of the dark is caused by a child's fear of losing the person they love. However, the idea that nurses and fairy tales were responsible for childhood fear continued to remain current (and, indeed, has more recently been transmuted in debates on computer games and videos, etc., where the dreaded electronic companion fulfils the role of the corrupting nurse). In *Handicaps of Childhood*, published in 1917, Bruce

Addington reinforced the traditional warnings about nurses' stories, with a graphic image of psychological damage: 'Every ugly thing told to the child, every shock, every fright given him, will remain like minute splinters in the flesh to torture him all his life long.' Like a parent baffled by the sufferings of his child, Addington seeks an explanation for the barbarism of the First World War, and finds it 'in the fact that the offending nation is one among whom the myth, the legend and fairy tale have pre-eminently flourished'.[58] The night terrors of the whole of Europe are to be blamed on nurses' tales.

For the Victorians, as indeed for ourselves, states of child terror were threateningly inexplicable, undercutting ideas of childhood as a state of happy innocence, or models of associationist psychology which suggested that children, with their limited levels of experience, would be incapable of entering into the states of terror that could afflict adults. Although Romantic explorations of dreams and nightmares produced various studies of child terror, it was not until the mid-nineteenth century, with that decisive clustering of literary and medical texts, that the concept of night terror, as a specific childhood affliction, entered the medical lexicon. West here quickly adjusted his diagnosis from physiological (digestive processes) to psychological (incipient mental disorder) in keeping with the emerging forms of explanation in both literary and psychiatric discourse. As the preoccupation with nurses' stories suggests, this was a subject that crossed constantly between disciplines, as writers and medics sought to penetrate these 'dark corners' of the child mind. What united all the forms of explanation was an attempt to find an external cause, whether this was the corruption introduced into the middle-class nursery by the working-class nurse and her terrifying tales, or the evolutionary influence of inherited memories, which finds a source for child terror not in the workings of its own mind, but in the dim reaches of prehistory. Although they were utterly different in form, both modes of explanation operated to preserve the boundaries of childhood purity. The force of the literary texts tended to cut across such reassuring distinctions, however, to suggest, whatever explanations were invoked, that terror was indeed intrinsic to the childhood state.

16

SENSUOUS KNOWLEDGE

Kate Flint

Knowledge is a sensuous business. Let us consider, for example, how we may come to know a whale. The cetology chapters of *Moby-Dick* are famed, or notorious, for their obsessive cataloguing of whale information and whale lore. Taxonomies of whales are laid out for us; engravings and illustrations of the huge beast are described. But, Ishmael tells us, while both giving us this information and laying out its deficiencies, these accounts are far from reliable. To know – if not to understand – the whale fully, one must encounter the creature at first hand. The hand, indeed, is indispensable. Squeezing away at the tubs of cooled, crystallized and solidifying sperm, Ishmael engages in the most sensuous of activities: 'I bathed my hands among those soft, gentle globules of infiltrated tissues ...; as they richly broke to my fingers, and discharged all their opulence, like fully ripe grapes their wine; ... I snuffed up that uncontaminated aroma, – literally and truly, like the smell of spring violets.'[1] Other occasions demand the use of other senses. A desperate, injured whale makes 'sharp, cracking, agonized respirations' through the spasmodic dilation and contraction of his spout-hole.[2] Chapters 64 and 65 suggest the different ways in which whale may be savoured: broiled as steaks or the scraps fried brown and crisp; fins pickled; fluke-ends soused. And sight is essential to watchers on board a whaling boat, waiting for the 'straight perpendicular twin-jets of the Right Whale,' or the Sperm Whale's single forward-slanting spout, which 'presents a thick slanted bush of white mist':[3] the visual markers of whale identity and potential profitability. Brought out of the element which conceals it, the up-close visual knowledge we are given of the whale itself ranges from the architectural vaulting of its rib cage to the rich aesthetic appeal of those portions of a whale's flesh which adhere to its blanket of blubber, 'of an exceedingly rich, mottled tint, with a bestreaked snowy and golden ground, dotted with spots of the deepest crimson and purple. It is plums of rubies, in pictures of citron.'[4]

Published in 1850, *Moby-Dick* appeared in the middle of a century fascinated by the power and proliferation of visible evidence, and by the developments in technology which enhanced the scope and availability of visual information.[5] This fact was increasingly commented upon on both sides of the Atlantic. As 'J. B. C.', writing in *Macmillan's Magazine* in 1893, proclaimed:

> The supremacy of one sense over all the others is now so completely established that the world of our waking moments is a world of sights, even as the world of our dreams is a world of visions. We are always looking, and but rarely listening; always attending to the shapes and colours before our eyes, seldom noticing the sounds which reach our ears. The visible has become the real, while the audible and the tangible appear but as casual properties of the visible.[6]

Yet despite the Victorians' well-documented captivation with the faculty of sight, the writer of this piece may have been somewhat premature in assuming the relegation of the other senses, the premise on which he went on to develop his own focus on the importance of sound. For what Melville comprehensively acknowledges in *Moby-Dick* – and in this he does no more than replicate, in sustained fashion, what novelists on both sides of the Atlantic were simultaneously exploring and representing – is the necessary engagement of the whole human body in the act of knowing the material world. Even if acts of looking preoccupied the Victorians – a recapitulation, after all, of the role which the faculty of sight has traditionally occupied in the Western hierarchy of the senses – developments in a range of epistemologies during the period ensured that the other senses also formed the subject of a range of investigations in physiology, psychology and anthropology. If we are to gain as full a picture as possible of how the Victorians experienced and interpreted their social and material world, we need to pay attention to the way they figured the whole range of sensory perception.

We are currently witnessing a boom of interest in Victorian material culture: in the circulation and display of commodities, fetishized or otherwise; in the hidden life of domestic objects, the material and associative properties of 'things' potentially go way beyond their specular existence, or their placement and presence within space. To know a thing is to be aware not just of its appearance, but of its substance: its feel, its odour, even its taste, and possibly its sound – certainly the soundscape which surrounds it. Recognizing the properties of things is to acknowledge that their social life (to borrow and extend Arjun Appadurai's phrase) – their interaction with those who own, or exchange, or sell, or admire, or recoil from them – is dependent on far more than mere ocular observation of their actuality. As Victor Burgin has succinctly put it, 'subjectivity "takes place" in corporeal space':[7] space determined by the distance between the observer and the matter perceived, to be sure, but also complicated by the different ways in which sound, smell and taste all penetrate the body's boundaries, rendering it porous; and space obliterated by the meeting of surface and surface that constitutes touch.

This endeavour certainly has a good deal in common with the notion of cultural phenomenology that Steven Connor proposed in 2000, in a number of *Critical Quarterly* co-edited by himself and David Trotter. 'Cultural phenomenology', he writes, 'would enlarge, diversify and particularise the study of culture. Instead of readings of abstract social and psychological structures, functions and dynamics, cultural phenomenology would home in on substances, habits, organs, rituals, obsessions, pathologies, processes and patterns of feeling.'[8]

In its appropriation from the phenomenological tradition of a desire to articulate the 'in-the-worldness of all existence', cultural phenomenology would reintroduce a somatic dimension to cultural experience that Connor sees as being absent from cultural studies and cultural materialism, and open up the possibility of recognizing intersubjectivity as a factor of consciousness, thus going beyond Husserl, Heidegger and Levinas's reluctance to consider collective or impersonal life.[9] While Connor does not elaborate on the historical dimensions of the operations of both the individual consciousness and the potential for intersubjectivity that the sensory world offers us, Trotter's piece on 'The New Historicism and the Psychopathology of Everyday Modern Life' engages specifically with the nineteenth century sensorium.[10] He offers a reading of reactions to certain unpleasant smells, such as Esther Lyons's fastidious aversion to the odour of tallow candles in *Felix Holt*; and the foetid interiors encountered by sanitary inspectors and by social reformers. In exploring the ways in which we experience, conceptualize and remember smells, Trotter builds on the fascination with the noxious and the abject that he analyses from a more visual angle in *Cooking with Mud* (2000); in dwelling on the odoriferously unpleasant, his ideas also relate to such work as Alain Corbin's *The Foul and the Fragrant* (1986), sections of Peter Stallybrass and Allon White's *The Politics and Poetics of Transgression* (1986), and the visceral nausea investigated by William Miller in *The Anatomy of Disgust* (1997). He uses the anthropologist Dan Sperber's work on smell to remind us that despite the hundreds of thousands of smells which we are capable of distinguishing, none of the world's languages seems to contain anything like the linguistic capacity to provide an olfactory taxonomy comparable, say, to that available for the classification of colours. Moreover, as Sperber also points out, while we may

recognize smells easily, they are hard to recall, at least without our memory
invoking a visual stimulus first. As Trotter usefully explains, smell has much in
common with sound: unless we can pinpoint where it is coming from, it has
the capacity to disrupt our sense of location in the world.

In addition, both smell and hearing are experienced as forms of physical
invasion, a blurring of the distinction between our body and what lies outside
it. Part of the problems (both epistemological and environmental) with both
smell and sound lie in the very fact of their inescapability. In an important
article on 'Civilisation and Noise' (1878), the psychologist James Sully notes
that while one can 'at will shut off completely, or nearly so, the avenues of the
eye ... nature has, in the case of man, left the ear without any power of self-
protective movement'.[11] As the philosophical writer Edmund Gurney explained
in 1880: '[w]e carry about an habitual instinct of having around us a certain
amount of space in which we are alone, and any sudden violence to this instinct
is very unnerving'.[12] Particularly disorientating is sudden noise, or noise which
comes from a direction that one cannot determine (and which hence severs
the interpretative relationship between ear and eye). These are variables which
underline the perceiver's vulnerability. The assault on personal space is the
more pronounced when one considers that noise quite literally invades the
body. As Bruce Smith has recently eloquently put it, writing in the context of
the soundscape of early modern England: 'About hearing you have no choice:
you can shut off vision by closing your eyes, but from birth to death, in waking
and sleep, the coils of flesh, the tiny bones, the hair cells, the nerve fibers are
always at the ready.'[13] While vision, as he goes on to explain, fixes objects out
there, away from the perceiving self, the sounds that one hears reverberate
inside one. Such an apprehension of noise as a physiological presence within
our own bodies was alluded to by John Tyndall when, in his influential book
Sound (1867; revised and enlarged 1875), he wrote how '[n]oise affects us as
an irregular succession of shocks. We are conscious while listening to it of a
jolting and jarring of the auditory nerve.'[14] Moreover, one might note that
while many people may simultaneously be present within a noisy environment,
the sensation of having one's own body invaded is something which makes
one acutely conscious of one's individuation, one's isolation even. The
pioneering sociologist Georg Simmel, in an extraordinarily perspicacious article
of 1907 which deals with the 'sociology of the senses' in relation to modernity,
writes of how the senses are indispensable to our apprehension of the social
and of community: 'they lead us into the human subject as its mood and emotion
[we observe a face, hear a voice] and out to the object as knowledge of it.'[15]
Yet, as he also writes:

> The modern person is shocked by innumerable things, and innumerable
> things appear intolerable to their senses which less differentiated, more

robust modes of feeling would tolerate without any such reaction. The individualizing tendency of modern human beings and the greater personalization and freedom of choice of a person's commitments must be connected to this. With his or her sometimes directly sensual and sometimes aesthetic mode of reacting, the person cannot immediately enter into traditional unions or close commitments in which no one enquires into their personal taste or their personal sensibility. And this inevitably brings with it a greater isolation and a sharper circumscribing of the personal sphere.[16]

It is precisely the uncontrollable, penetrative, disruptive potential of scents that make them such a powerful stimulus to memory. Rather than dwelling on nauseous recollection, as Trotter does, we might think of the rose-and-lilac-scented night breeze of stanza XCV of *In Memoriam*, which allows Hallam to 'touch' Tennyson from the past; or the 'odour of heliotrope' that has the power to stir Lord Henry in that most smell-aware of novels, *The Picture of Dorian Gray*, or the way in which the smell of a blackcurrant bush would always act synecdochally for Pip, recalling 'that evening in the little garden by the side of the lane' when he talked to Biddy about his expectations, the embarrassed memory of his blind snobbishness lingering unspoken in the moral air.[17] It may well be true that, as Diane Ackerman has argued in her provocative and evocative (if Eurocentric) *A Natural History of the Senses* (1990), '[o]ur senses connect us intimately to the past, connect us in ways that most of our cherished ideas never could'– although we may interpret the senses differently from our forebears, the information sent to our senses, and sent by them, is the same.[18] Indeed, sensual knowledge can provide us with the illusion that we are in some kind of direct, visceral contact with earlier times: Paula Power, in Thomas Hardy's *A Laodicean* (1881), walks down a street in Lisieux where '[s]mells direct from the sixteenth century hung in the air in all their original integrity and without a modern taint'.[19] But a full *historical* phenomenology must take into consideration the historical dimensions not just of *what* is perceived by the senses, but of *how* that perception was theorized and understood, giving it an intellectual as well as a corporeal dimension. 'Sensory orders', as Constance Classen has reminded us, 'are not static entities, they change over time just as cultures do.'[20] What I am calling for is an understanding not only of how the Victorians interpreted the knowledge given them by their senses, but of how they interpreted the senses themselves. In other words, how were their hypotheses about sensual perception inflected by, and how did they inform, social assumptions of various kinds?

These questions are increasingly being posed, and addressed, by Victorian scholars. Recently, two books have appeared that concentrate on the work performed by particular senses: John Picker's *Victorian Soundscapes*, and Janice

Carlisle's *Common Scents: Comparative Encounters in High-Victorian Fiction*.[21]
Picker's study of Victorian interest in the 'subjective nature of sensation' means
that he, rightly, does not attempt to reconstruct a singular Victorian soundscape –
although he is fully alert, sequentially, to such phenomena as the street noises
which drive Thomas Carlyle to soundproof his study, or the phonograph's ability
to capture the voice. His emphasis, rather, is on 'an analysis of the experiences
of particular individuals listening under special cultural influences and with
discernable motivations ... for hearing as they did'.[22] Janice Carlisle, too,
concentrates upon the cultural values enacted through and by the senses,
particularly the sense of smell, and shows that these were often regarded as
'second nature', taken for granted. Both these critics are interested in how the
senses register modernity: whether the ear accommodates, or is jarred by, the
impact of technology and commerce; whether the nose registers the proximity
of the poor or the odor that belongs to the habits of another – and often
threateningly socially ascendant – class.

Yet the mid-Victorian fascination with the senses was one which went far
beyond acknowledging their importance in establishing a literal and figurative
sense of place, and – as Carlisle outlines most usefully in her introduction –
was central to the dominant strand of investigation in the natural sciences
which sought to link the physiological with the psychological: in other words,
the experimental psychology of George Henry Lewes and Alexander Bain.
This may well be gauged by the fiction of Wilkie Collins, where he foregrounds
a number of individuals who are challenged in their relationship to the material
world: notably the deaf-mute Madonna Blyth (*Hide and Seek*, 1854), the blind
Leonard Frankland (*The Dead Secret*, 1857), the blind Lucilla in *Poor Miss
Finch* (1872), the angrily dwarfish Miserrimus Dexter in *The Law and the Lady*
(1874) and the deaf Lodger in 'The Guilty River' (1886). Collins's interest in
obstacles to full physical functioning – in those who, as Alexander Bain would
put it, lack one or more of their 'intellectual' senses, the senses that provide
what he thought of as objective information – may well stem in part from his
own problems with his eyesight, but it must be placed within a broader Victorian
concern with the operation of the senses – not just, to be sure, in scientific
works exploring developments in physiology and psychology, but in more
popular texts, often with a theological bias which sought to stress the spiritual
consolation that could come from physical deprivation, like John Kitto's
The Lost Senses (1845). But while many of Collins's figures might seem
sensationally different from the assumed norm, he employs them not just to
add unusual elements to his plots but to make his readers reflect on the
broad operations of phenomenological knowledge, and the simultaneous
reliability and instability of what, in *The Moonstone*, Collins terms 'the
evidence of [the] senses'.[23]

To pay close attention to the knowledge provided through the senses in fact brings us sharply up against the limitations of such knowledge. My final sustained literary example, George Meredith's anguished commemoration of marital unhappiness, Modern Love (1862), makes this abundantly clear. This is a poem framed by the anxieties of what it means to 'know': it demands evidence. Is the speaker's wife being physically unfaithful to him? Is the love between them dead? Why does she kill herself? 'By this he knew she wept with waking eyes', the poem opens – but what is actually conveyed by this factual observation of the sobbing emotional distress that shakes their marital bed?[24] 'He knew all',[25] the penultimate stanza concludes – but what is this 'all'? That she really did love him? That she believed he loved her, but could not bear to put this realization to the test of continued life? That she knew he no longer loved her, and committed suicide as an act of vengeance upon him? How far is the speaker, in any case, convincing himself that he knows what he wants to believe? 'Ah, what a dusty answer gets the soul / When hot for certainties in this our life!'[26] This anguished acknowledgement of the impossibility of full and confident understanding has been prepared for by the repeated failure of the senses, throughout the poem, to offer any stable grounds for knowledge. Sight, for one, is obscure and threatening. One cannot see quite what it is, at the poem's end, that 'moves dark as yonder midnight ocean's force'.[27] Nor does sensory response anchor a protagonist to the here and now. The touch of a cheek salt with tears against the man's kiss, the sound of the 'sharp scale of sobs'[28] lifting his wife's breast, have the power to haunt him and complicate his thoughts. While the smell of the 'sweet wild rose' has the power to 'revive' the time when in his mistress's eyes 'I stood alive',[29] this further emphasizes memory's ability to ambush both one's emotions and also the temporal framework of one's thoughts. The cheating and cheated-on wife, her world disrupted, 'has desires of touch, as if to feel / That all the household things are things she knew',[30] but the material histories and connotations provided by 'thing theory' are going to be of little avail when emotional dynamics are unsure, insecure and illegible.

What Meredith puts before us in this poem are two different types of imperfect knowledge: the challenge of registering material signs, but lack of the information necessary to interpret them fully; and the phenomenon which I am more interested in here: the fact that one picks up on a mood, an atmosphere, an emotion, registers affect – but one cannot quite put one's finger on what has set off one's very marked response or, indeed, quite find the words to describe one's own sensations. To return momentarily to Collins, this is the kind of moment registered by Walter Hartright when he first sets eyes on Laura Fairlie: 'Sympathies that lie too deep for words, too deep almost for thoughts, are touched, at such times, by other charms than those which the senses feel

and which the resources of expression can realise.'[31] The only word Hartright
has at his disposal to describe this is 'mystery', but this is a secular catch-all
phrase for him to hide behind. One potential way into understanding this type
of knowledge is explored by Teresa Brennan in her posthumously published
The Transmission of Affect. Brennan's work is part of a wider current tendency
to see the workings of the mind as intimately tied in with the workings of the
body: neuroscience has returned psychoanalytic study, at least in some quarters,
to the same physiological basis that preoccupied its mid-nineteenth century
forerunners. Brennan is especially concerned with understanding that process
which she describes as 'social in origin but biological and physical in affect':[32]
how we pick up on the atmosphere of a room or the mood of another person,
and how what is happening outside us registers itself on our own bodies; how,
as she puts it, 'we are not self-contained in terms of our energies. There is no
secure distinction between the "individual" and the "environment"';[33] nor –
and this is what I want to stress – 'between the biological and the social'.[34] For
the process by which 'one person's or group's nervous and hormonal systems
may be brought into alignment with another's'[35] – the process that neurologists
call 'entrainment' – involves above all smell: not *conscious* smell, like Pip
smelling a blackcurrant bush, but 'unconscious olfaction'. Brennan uses the
example of pheromones – molecules which can be airborne, and communicate
chemical information: which signal aggression, or sexual attraction, or
depression, and allow states of feeling to be transmitted, even when no verbal
conversation takes place. 'There is', Brennan reminds us, 'no field of human
action that does not involve hormonal messages.'[36]

Brennan's particular fascination lies not just with the transmission of these
messages, but with why we may resist as well as absorb them, and what this
process may have to say about the boundaries of identity. But to conclude, I
want to return to the mid-nineteenth century, and to remind us that, well
before the discovery of pheromones, the concept which George Henry Lewes
termed 'unconscious sensibility' was under investigation, and that the terms
of this investigation were firmly rooted in biology. Lewes, in Chapter VIII of
The Physiology of Common Life (1859), entitled 'Feeling and Thinking', tells us
that '[w]e shall do well to hold fast by the maxim that to *have a sensation*, and
to be *conscious* of it, are two different things.'[37] For we continually live in what
Lewes – anticipating the more influential terminology of William James – called
'a vast and powerful stream of sensation'.[38] He illustrates this by referring to
his immediate circumstances:

> While I am writing these lines the trees are rustling in the summer
> wind, the birds are twittering among the leaves, and the muffled sounds
> of carriages rolling over the Dresden streets reach my ear; but because
> the mind is occupied with trains of thought these sounds are not

perceived, until one of them becomes importunate, or my relaxed attention turns towards them. Nevertheless, when unperceived, the sounds reached my ear; and excited sensory impressions: if these sensory impressions are not to be called sensations, because they were not perceived, they must have *some* name given to them, and a name which will indicate that they are affections of the sensitive organism.[39]

In other words, the reader's daily experience is continually composed of sensations, and his or her states of mind proceed from this fact. Lewes demands not just that we should be alert to the information which reaches us through the operation of particular senses, but that we should acknowledge that we are receiving information from the outside world all the time, and that the quality of what we received – even though we may not be conscious at all of our environment, unless we pay particular attention to it – will, nonetheless, affect our mood, and our very sense of being. Affect is constantly in process.

The ebullient energy which one day exalts life, and the mournful depression which the next day renders life a burden almost intolerable, are feelings not referable to any of the particular sensations; but arise from the massive yet obscure sensibilities of the viscera, which form so important a part of the general stream of Sensation.[40]

It was this condition to which Lewes gave the title 'Unconscious Sensibility'.

Whether we are picking up on the information transmitted silently by other individuals, or in a more diffuse way still by our general environment, we come to see, therefore, that it is precisely *because* of the difficulties of providing any kind of taxonomy of sensory knowledge, because we cannot by any means safely separate out the sources of our impressions, that the senses demand our careful attention. The ways in which their operations are interpreted as well as experienced point us, on the one hand, to the shared circumstances of living in the world, to culture as constituted by interaction. At the same time, however, the operations of association and memory on which the processing of sensory perceptions depends, both consciously and unconsciously, will remain inescapably individualized. 'The phenomena of sensation', wrote James Sully in *Sensation and Intuition* (1874), 'constitute in a peculiar manner the borderland of physiology and psychology.'[41] And current work on the connections between biology and mood, body and mind, is increasingly bringing out the ways in which Victorian studies of the senses anticipated the investigations of today in their interest not just in the operations of sight, smell, touch and hearing, but in the ways in which we respond to the continual and complex stimuli reaching us from the material world.

Notes

Introduction Unmapped Countries: Biology, Literature and Culture in the Nineteenth Century

1   Waugh 2004, p. 63.
2   Beer [1983] 2000; Levine 1988.
3   Carroll 2004.
4   See, for instance, Bowler 1988 and Paradis 1997.
5   Ground-breaking studies in this area are Shuttleworth 1984; Otis 1994, 1999, 2001; Armstrong 2003.
6   Spencer 1999 [1857], p. 297.
7   Darwin 1996 [1859], pp. 61, 395.
8   See the *Oxford English Dictionary* s.v. 'Biology': '... E19 – The science of life, dealing with the morphology, physiology, anatomy, behaviour, origin and distribution of living organisms; occas. = physiology. Also, life processes and phenomena collectively.'
9   Coleman 1977 [1971], p. 14.
10   ibid., p. 3.
11   ibid., p. 11.
12   ibid., p. 161.
13   See ibid., p. 165.
14   See Shuttleworth 1984.
15   Eliot 1996 [1871–2], pp. 784–5.
16   Quoted in Coleman 1977 [1971], p. 111.
17   See Morton 1984, p. 46.
18   See Otis 1999, 2001.
19   See Cordle 1999, p. 7.
20   See Beer 2000 [1983], p. 96.
21   Cantor and Shuttleworth (eds.) 2004, p. 4.
22   See Huxley 1893 [1880]; Arnold 1974 [1882], Snow 1959; Leavis 1962.
23   Levine (ed.) 1987, pp. 3–4.
24   See Foucault 1966 on the concept of the 'episteme'.
25   See Bachelard 1934, 1938; Fleck 1935, 1989 [1927–60].
26   See White 1973, p. 63.
27   See Gross 1990, p. 7.

28   See Seel 2004.
29   Snow 1963, p. 70.
30   See Pethes 2003, p. 199.
31   See Kuhn 1962.
32   See Shapin 1994.
33   Barthes 1967.
34   See, for example, Hayles (ed.) 1991; Freese 1997; Sokal and Bricmont 1998.
35   Kuhn 1969, p. 407.
36   See Lepenies 1983, *passim*, especially p. 52.
37   See Schönert 1997, p. 44.
38   Eliot 1998 [1876], p. 235.
39   See Shapin 1994; Schaffer and Shapin 1985; Shapin and Barnes 1979.
40   See the readings in Beer 1983 [2000]; Levine 1988.
41   See Peckham 1959.
42   Virchow 1959, p. 80.

Chapter 1   'This Questionable Little Book': Narrative Ambiguity in Nineteenth Century Literature of Science

1   Michael Whitworth (Whitworth 2001) has also advanced a promising method of combining the use of textual content and context through an emphasis on literary form, which he has applied to the early twentieth century. Doing this, he argues, permits generalization about texts as well as acknowledging the modernists' conscious consideration of form in both literature and physics (in the sense of formal description rather than mechanistic explanation). See also Shires 2001.
2   See Genette 1980.
3   See Aczel 1998.
4   See Fludernik 2001.
5   See, for example, Banfield 1982.
6   Stanzel 1984.
7   Historically informed studies of travel literature have formed a notable and encouraging exception to this rule. See, for example, Pratt 1992; Ryan 1996; Hulme and Youngs (eds) 2002.
8   Watt 1964.
9   See, for example, Frasca-Spada and Jardine (eds) 2000. On Victorian fiction in general, see Flint 1993, 2001; Eliot 2001.
10 Shapin 1994, p. xxvi.
11 McKeon's argument is summarized in McKeon 1988, pp. 20–2. On Bakhtin's dialectic, see Bakhtin 1981.
12 Bentham 1962a, 1962b. Though the publication date for the *Introductory View ... for Non-Lawyers* (1962a) appears earlier (c.1810), it was actually written after the *Rationale ... Applied to English Practice*, which appeared first as a series of manuscripts and was later collated into a single volume in 1827 by J S Mill.
13 Bentham 1962b, vol. 7, pp. 427–32.
14 Bowring in Bentham 1962b, vol. 6, p. 205.

15 'The aim [in this account of evidence] has all along been to give to the branch of legislation here in question the form of *an art*, and in respect of comprehensiveness as well as precision, the form (but if possible without the repulsiveness) of a science.' (Bentham 1962a, Chapter I, § 2.)

16 ibid., § 1.

17 Bentham 1962b, vol. 6, p. 208; original emphasis.

18 See Morrell and Thackray 1981; Morrell 1997.

19 Shelley, 'Author's Introduction to the Standard Novels Edition', in Shelley 1994 [1818], p. 195.

20 Marilyn Butler summarizes the story thus: 'When Columbus was told by a courtier that anyone might have discovered the Indies, he allegedly challenged all present to stand an egg on end. After everyone failed, he did it himself by crushing the end.' (ibid., p. 260)

21 See Butler 1994; Sleigh 1998; Morus (ed.) 2002.

22 *Sartor Resartus* first appeared in serial form in Scotland; its earliest publication in book form (apart from a limited run in 1834) was in America in 1836.

23 The first British edition, reprinted from *Fraser's Magazine* (1834), and the second American edition (1837) are among those attributed only to 'Sartor'.

24 See particularly Carlyle 2002 [1833–4], Book 1, Chapters 2 and 11; Book 2, Chapter 10; and Book 3, Chapters 9 and 12.

25 See Gray 2002.

26 See ibid., p. xxi.

27 Eco and Sebeok (eds) 1983; see especially Harrowitz 1983.

28 For contemporary responses to Poe's hoaxes see, for example, Thompson (ed.) 1984, pp. 1430–3; Clarke (ed.) 1991, vol. 2, pp. 135–6.

29 See Wheeler 1985, p. 91.

30 See Yeo 1993; Richards 1996.

31 John Herschel's A *Preliminary Discourse of the Study of Natural Philosophy* (Herschel 1851 [1830]) was another post-Benthamite attempt to justify a purely inductive scientific methodology.

32 Whewell 2000 [1847], p. 186.

33 Though Darwin referred explicitly to Bacon, the connection was clear to his readers. See also Huxley 1893, vol. 1, pp. 57–8.

34 See Desmond 1989.

35 See Morus 1992.

36 Page (ed.) 1974, pp. 123–4.

37 See Pykett 1994, p. 5.

38 Many readers, however, take away the impression that the egotistical and distinctly partial Count Fosco has the last word. See Conclusion for a brief discussion about the docility or otherwise of readers.

39 In his works for adults, Kingsley emphasizes the empirical, yet weighs it through the moral. Kingsley 1880, *passim*.

40 See Kingsley 1880, pp. 201–60.

41 Kingsley 1994 [1863], p. 51.

42 Wells 1995 [1895], p. 78.

43 McKeon (1988) addresses this question in the early modern context.

44 See Flint 1993 as an example of this approach.

Chapter 2 Vestiges of English Literature: Robert Chambers

1 Beer 2000.

2 See Glass, Temkin and Straus (eds) 1959.

3 Secord 2000.

4 ibid., p. 97.

5 Sichert 2003, pp. 201–2.

6 See Stierstorfer 2001, esp. pp. 101–11.

7 Jeffrey 1811, p. 275.

8 See Stierstorfer 2001, p. 178, n. 172.

9 See Chambers 1836, p. 104.

10 ibid., p. 82.

11 ibid., p. 104.

12 Chambers 1836, p. 57.

13 Jeffrey 1811, p. 283.

14 Chambers 1836, p. 268.

15 See Ireland 1884, p. xviii.

16 Chambers 1822, pp. 123–7.

17 Chambers 1844, p. 57.

18 ibid., p. 105.

19 ibid., pp. 144–5.

20 ibid., pp. 223–4.

21 Blumenberg 2000, p. 11.

22 ibid., pp. 17–19.

23 Quoted in Secord 2000, p. 9.

24 ibid., p. 90.

25 Chambers 1822, p. 203.

26 Secord 2000, p. 9.

27 Chambers 1844, pp. 351–2.

28 ibid., pp. 350–1.

29 ibid., p. 212.

30 'If there is any thing more than another impressed on our minds by the course of the geological history, it is, that the same laws and conditions of nature now apparent to us have existed throughout the whole time, though the operation of some of these laws may now be less conspicuous than in the early ages, from some of the conditions having come to a settlement and a close' (ibid., p. 146). Here Chambers has turned George Lyell's scientific method of construing the past exclusively on laws observable in the present into an ontological statement about cosmologic principles. (Compare Secord 1997, pp. xix–xx.)

31 Chambers 1844, p. 148.

32   Darwin 1996 [1859], pp. 171–2.
33   Beer 2000, p. 57.

Chapter 3   Aestheticism, Immorality and the Reception of Darwinism in Victorian Britain

1   Darwin, F (ed.) 1887, vol. 3, p. 95.
2   Desmond and Moore 1991, p. 581.
3   See, for instance, Levine (ed.) 1987.
4   Beer 1996, p. 210.
5   J Murray to C Darwin, July 1, 1870, DAR 171, Darwin Manuscript Collection, Cambridge University Library. Quoted with the permission of the Syndics of Cambridge University Library.
6   Murray to Darwin, September 28, [1870], DAR 171.
7   Murray to Darwin, October 10, [1870], DAR 171.
8   Darwin 1871, vol. 2, p. 345.
9   ibid., p. 345n.; the translation is provided in Darwin 2004 [1871], p. 645n.
10   Darwin 1994, letter 7312, p. 321.
11   Smith to Darwin, March 26, 1867, DAR 85.
12   Waitz 1863, pp. 105–6.
13   [Hedley] 1871, p. 3.
14   [Dallas] 1872, p. 398.
15   Yeazell 1991, p. 219.
16   [Leifchild] 1871, p. 276; Darwin 1871, vol. 1, pp. 207–8.
17   See Secord 2000, p. 164.
18   [Dawkins] 1871, p. 195.
19   ibid., pp. 234–5.
20   [Morley] 1866, p. 147.
21   [Baynes] 1871, pp. 75, 71.
22   Swinburne 1871, p. 82.
23   [Baynes] 1871, p. 77.
24   Laughton 1898, vol. 1, p. 370.
25   See [Reeve] 1874,.pp. 2–3.
26   [Baynes] 1871, pp. 71–2; 1873, p. 494.
27   [Baynes] 1871, p. 75; 1873, p. 492.
28   See Dawson 2003.
29   [Baynes] 1873, p. 496; 1871, pp. 71, 98.
30   [Baynes] 1871, p. 72; 1873, pp. 502–3.
31   [Baynes] 1873, p. 503.
32   Rooksby 1997, p. 135.
33   [Morley] 1866, pp. 145, 147; [Baynes] 1871, p. 72.
34   Swinburne 1866, p. 30.
35   Darwin 1871, vol. 1, p. 339; Swinburne 1866, pp. 178, 182.
36   Tennyson 1859, pp. 244–5.

37   ibid., p. 250; Darwin 1871, vol. 1, p. 101.
38   [Tennyson] 1850, p. 183; [Chapman] 1861, p. 187.
39   Huxley 1894, p. 52.
40   Darwin 1983–, vol. 11, p. 655.
41   ibid., vol. 13, p. 5.
42   Darwin, F (ed.) 1887, vol. 1, pp. 100–1.
43   Small 1994, p. 47.
44   Swinburne 1888, pp. 127–9.
45   Darwin, F (ed.) 1887, vol. 3, pp. 135–6.
46   Mivart 1873, p. 608.
47   [Mivart] 1874, p. 70.
48   Browne 2002, pp. 355–6.

Chapter 4   Constructing Darwinism in Literary Culture

1   See Manuel and Manuel 1979; Bloomfield 1932; Davis 1981; Knapp 1994.
2   Specifically discussed by Rosen 1946; Schwartz 1998; Porter 2001.
3   From many excellent accounts on the impact of Darwinism on creative literature, see especially Morton 1984; Beer 1983, 1996; Christie and Shuttleworth (eds) 1989. For science fiction, see Dick 1982; Mendelsohn and Nowotny (eds) 1984; Crowe 1986; Margolis 2000.
4   For general accounts of the relations between biology and Victorian culture see Burrow 1966; Oldroyd and Langham (eds) 1983; Jardine, Secord and Spary (eds) 1996; Lightman (ed.) 1997. For the transformation of society by biology, see particularly Jones 1980; Young 1985.
5   See Darwin 1964 [1854]. Authoritative résumés of historical research into Darwin and Darwinism are given by Kohn (ed.) 1985; Amigoni and Wallace (eds) 1995; Hodge and Radick (eds) 2003. The history of evolutionary theory is discussed by Bowler 2003. Current biographies are by Browne 1995, 2002; Desmond and Moore 1991. Ruse 1999 is a vigorous exposition of the central tenets of Darwinism; while Mayr 1991 gives a distinguished modern biologist's view. Bowler 1988 gives a salutary reevaluation of Darwin's place in the Victorian transformation of thought. Background texts relating to the Victorian idea of progress are Bury 1920; Passmore 1970; Bowler 1989.
6   The religious implications are brought out by Turner 1974, 1993; Moore 1979; Lindberg and Numbers (eds) 1986; Corsi 1988; Ellegard 1990; Brooke 1991; Brooke and Cantor 1998. For an accessible overview of the Victorian religious crisis see Wilson 1999.
7   Chamberlin and Gilman (eds) 1985; Pick 1989; Jay and Neve (eds) 1999. See also Webster (ed.) 1981; Bowler 1983.
8   For example, Greenslade 1994; Kelly 1981; Navarette 1998; Childs 2001.
9   See Desmond 1994, 1997.
10 See McCook 1996.
11 Snigurowicz 1999. Pastrana is discussed in Bondeson 1997; Gylseth and Toverud 2003; Browne and Messenger 2003. See also Altick 1978.
12 See Janson 1952; Tompkins 1994; Zuckerman 1998.

13 Browne 2001.

14 Darwin 1981 [1871]. Sexual selection in culture is analysed by Yeazell (ed.) 1986; Jann 1994; Bender 1996; Parrinder 1997. Gender issues are further explored by Schiebinger 1993; Moscucci 1990; Richardson and Willis (eds) 2000; Kaye 2002. See also Richardson 1999.

15 White 1871, p. 5.

16 Carleton is discussed in Dzwonkosi (ed.) 1986, Part 1, pp. 84–5.

17 Potterkin 1876. See p. 29, where a Mr Browne is cited as author. It has not been possible to identify either William Alfred Browne or the publisher, Ryder of Uttoxeter, Staffordshire.

18 Bierbower 1894. Austin Bierbower also published the *Socialism of Christ, or, Attitude of Early Christians towards Modern Problems*, Chicago, 1890.

19 See Bierbower 1894, p. 223.

20 See Hexter 1952.

21 Authoritative studies in the social history of geography are Driver 1999; Livingstone 2003.

22 See Shapin 1994.

23 See Campbell 1999.

24 See Mangum 1998; Budd 1997.

25 See Kevles 1995. The linkage between Darwinian theory, hereditarianism and human society is explored by Searle 1976; Bowler 1986; Peel (ed.) 1998.

26 Zola 2000, p. 196. First published in Paris 1893. For a useful critical account, see Pollard (ed.) 1995.

27 Medical issues relating to degeneration theory in France are discussed in Nye 1984; Dowbiggin 1991. See also Frey 1978; Darbouze 1997.

28 See Kemp 1982; Huntington 1982.

29 See Holtsmark 1981.

30 Discussed in Dutton 1995; Bedermann 1995; Hall (ed.) 1994; Budd 1997.

Chapter 5 Close Encounters with a New Species: Darwin's Clash with the Feminists at the End of the Nineteenth Century

1 Revised in 1916 as *The Sexes in Science and History*.

2 Watterson 1895, p. 796.

3 Michie 1999, p. 409.

4 See Erskine 1995.

5 Translated into English in 1864.

6 Huxley 1865, p. 72.

7 Some feminist authors, such as Evelleen Richards (1983, 1989, 1997) and Rosemary Jann (1994, 1997), have suggested that the main aim of Huxley and the other new Darwinian theorists was to justify the *status quo*. Whereas ideological assumptions undeniably pervaded evolutionary thought, these authors probably underestimate the deep drive for knowledge and the genuine concern for their fellow beings underpinning the thoughts and actions of at least some of the male scientists in question, Darwin above all.

8   Darwin 1998 [1874], p. 584.

9   We agree here with George Levine (2003), who criticizes 'the all too common assumption [by cultural critics] that Darwin's implication in the values and ideals of his own culture somehow closed off the possibility that his work extends beyond the limits of that culture to make genuine discoveries' (p. 38). As Levine rightly says, having read Darwin's work, his letters and his notebooks, one can only concede that 'his highest priority was not to enforce his sexist assumptions or his preferred economic theories but to get it right' (p. 43).

10 See Cronin 1994 [1991].

11 Mivart 1871, p. 71.

12 [Leifchild] 1871, p. 277. Reviewer identified in the online *Athenaeum* index.

13 See, for example, Geary 1999 [1998]; Mealey 2000; see Cronin 1994 [1991]; Vandermassen 2004 for an overview.

14 See Russett 1989, p. 45.

15 Romanes 1887, p. 666.

16 Mosedale (1978) provides a detailed discussion of the work of Spencer, Romanes, and Geddes and Thomson.

17 See Helsinger, Sheets and Veeder 1983.

18 See Erskine 1995.

19 See Wedgwood 1889. Wedgwood adhered to the (mistaken) idea that some mental qualities were transmitted only in the male line, and others only in the female line.

20 See McSweeney 1991.

21 See de Bont 2002; Ioteyko 1906.

22 See Browne 2002.

23 From her paper 'Sur la natalité', a communication read before the Société d'Anthropologie de Paris in 1874. Cited in translation in Harvey 1997, p. 146.

24 See Pardo Bazán 1996.

25 Corelli 1905, pp. 147–8, original emphasis.

26 ibid., p. 172.

27 All were Americans except Schreiner, who was South African.

28 See Wallace 1890. Although Wallace had always opposed Darwin's theory of sexual selection, in this article he espouses the idea for the first time, but only with regard to humans. The idea of female choice as a driving force of evolution settles a difficult problem for him: how to advance the human race without objectionable eugenic measures. A first precondition is socialism. Only then, he argues, will women become truly economically independent, and able to exercise free sexual choice. As Wallace feels confident that they will choose only high-quality men, the future of the race is thereby ensured (see Fichman 1997).

29 *Women and Economics* was reprinted seven times in the United States and Britain in the twenty-five years following its publication. It was translated into seven languages. *Woman and Labour* had two English editions by 1914; it was translated into Dutch in 1911, and into German in 1914 (see Love 1983).

30 Gilman 1998 [1898], pp. 19–20.

31 Gilman 2002 [1903], p. 85.

32 For a good introduction to the social philosophy of Gilman, as well as to its intellectual roots, see Egan 1989; see also Doskow 1997.

33 Schreiner 1978 [1911], p. 78.
34 ibid., p. 185. See ibid., note 15 for further references. Today, however, the term 'instinct' is hardly used any more in evolutionary biology, as we now know that it takes environmental input for almost any inclination to manifest itself, whatever the species. Note, too, that these differences between the sexes are just average differences, that there is a great deal of overlap, and that their expression is culturally mediated, which means that we may expect a great – but not endless – amount of cultural and historical variety.
35 Blackwell 1875, p. 111.
36 See Richards 1997.
37 According to Jann (1997), the reviewers' estimation of the book's scientific merits seem to be directly related to their degree of sympathy with Gamble's conclusions.
38 See Richards 1983, 1989, 1997.
39 See, for example, Ridley 2003.
40 See Russett 1989, p. 102.
41 See Browne 2002.
42 Wilson 2002, p. 185.

Chapter 6 Mutual Aid, a Factor of Peter Kropotkin's Literary Criticism

1 Sellers 1896, p. 537.
2 Miller 1976, p. 3; Morland 1977, pp. 125–72.
3 Ford 1931, p. 133.
4 Woodcock and Avakumovic 1950, p. 227.
5 Miller 1976, p. 173.
6 Huxley 1888, p. 163.
7 ibid., p. 165.
8 Kropotkin 1907a [1902], p. 4.
9 Kropotkin 1906 [1899], p. 464.
10 Kropotkin 1907a [1902], pp. 59–60.
11 ibid., pp. 11–12.
12 ibid., p. 2.
13 Kropotkin devotes entire chapters to each of these subjects.
14 Kropotkin 1907a [1902], p. 275.
15 ibid., pp. 226–36.
16 ibid., p. xv.
17 ibid., p. 228.
18 ibid., p. xvii.
19 ibid., p. 229.
20 Huxley 1888, p. 171.
21 The connection between Kropotkin's theory and anarchism was immediately pounced upon, for example by an unsympathetic reviewer in an article entitled 'Anarchy in Science'; see Anon. 1902.
22 Woodcock and Avakumovic 1950, p. 263. Several of Kropotkin's later articles in Nineteenth Century evince a thoroughgoing Neo-Lamarckism. These include 'The

Direct Action of Environment on Plants' (1910) and 'The Inheritance of Acquired Characteristics' (1912).

23   Kropotkin 1907a [1902], pp. 299–300.
24   ibid., p. 14.
25   ibid., pp. 211–12.
26   ibid., pp. 163–4.
27   Kropotkin 1907b [1892], p. 139.
28   Kropotkin 1907a [1902], p. 211.
29   ibid., p. 215.
30   Kropotkin 1905, p. 10.
31   Kropotkin 1907a [1902], p. 212.
32   Kropotkin 1907b [1892], p. 138.
33   ibid., p. 140.
34   ibid., p. 139.
35   Kropotkin 1907a [1902], pp. 116–17.
36   ibid., p. 278.
37   Kropotkin 1907b [1892], p. 131.
38   ibid., pp. 141, 142.
39   Kropotkin 1992 [1880], p. 58.
40   ibid., p. 67.
41   Kropotkin 1905, p. 222.
42   ibid., pp. 244–5.
43   ibid., p. 245.
44   ibid., p. 226.
45   ibid., pp. 237–9.
46   ibid., p. 125.
47   ibid., p. 250.
48   ibid., p. 253.
49   ibid., p. 86.
50   Kropotkin 1992 [1880], pp. 53–4.
51   Kropotkin 1923 [1901], p. 41; original emphasis.
52   Kropotkin 1905, p. 85.
53   ibid., p. 299.

Chapter 7   The Savage Within: Evolutionary Theory, Anthropology and the Unconscious in *Fin-de-siècle* Literature

1   Whyte 1959, p. 63. See also Ellenberger 1970.
2   Whyte 1959, p.21.
3   See especially Mighail 1999.
4   See, for instance, Beer 1983; Morton 1984; Street 1975.
5   See Botting 1999, p. 19.
6   Quoted ibid., pp. 18–19.
7   Stocking 1987, p. 150. See also Kuklik 1991.

8   Quoted from Stocking 1987, p. 156.
9   Tylor 1903 [1871], vol. 1, p. 16.
10 ibid., p. 234.
11 Stocking 1987, p. 185.
12 ibid.
13 For a contemporary critique, see Boas 1896.
14 Wells 1975, p. 211.
15 See also Taylor 1997.
16 Quoted from Schlaeger 1995, p. 139.
17 Quoted from Whyte 1959, p. 133.
18 Guerard 1958, p. 39.
19 See Goetsch 1984.
20 Stevenson 1962 [1886], p. 21.
21 ibid., p. 48.
22 Darwin 1989 [1871], Part II, p. 644.
23 Quoted from Persak 1994, p. 13.
24 Stevenson 1962 [1886], pp. 19, 60, 61, 37, 38, 53.
25 ibid., pp. 13, 55, 5.
26 ibid., p. 53.
27 Quoted from Stocking 1987, p. 153.
28 Quoted ibid., p. 225.
29 See Persak 1994, p. 15. See also Block 1981-2.
30 Stevenson 1962 [1886], p. 50.
31 See Arata 1996; Mighail 1999, pp. 145-53; Rosner 1998.
32 Stevenson 1962 [1886], p. 56.
33 Darwin 1998 [1872], p. 241.
34 Garrett 1988, p. 61.
35 Stevenson 1962 [1886], p. 58.
36 See the contribution by Garrett to Veeder and Hirsch 1988; Brennan 1997;
    Heath 1986.
37 Stevenson 1962 [1886], p. 48.
38 Freud 1991, p. 43.
39 Stevenson 1962 [1886], p. 50.
40 Freud 1991, pp. 285, 327.
41 Stevenson 1962 [1886], p. 53.
42 Thomas 1990, p. 239.
43 See Griffith 1995, p. 6.
44 Conrad 1960 [1899], pp. 92-3.
45 Julia Briggs, quoted from Clemens 1990, p. 4.
46 For Hardy, see especially Goetsch 1993; Gose 1963; Radford 2003.
47 Berthoud 1978, p. 54.
48 See Fleishman 1967, pp. 89-90; Griffith 1995, pp. 83-7.
49 Conrad 1960 [1899], pp. 134, 155.
50 See Krasner 1992, p. 135.

51   Conrad 1960 [1899], p. 144.

52   Patrick Brantlinger wrongly believes that for Conrad evil is an inherently African quality. See Brantlinger 1988, pp. 255–70.

53   See Conrad 1960 [1899], p. 142.

54   See Brantlinger 1988; Griffith 1995; Johnson 1997; Saveson 1972; Shaffer 1993.

55   See the surveys in Murfin (ed.) 1989; Treddell (ed.) 1998.

56   Moser 1957, p. 47.

57   See Brantlinger 1988; Johnson 1997.

58   See Goetsch 1985; Wasserman 1974.

59   Conrad 1960 [1899], pp. 96, 119, 97.

60   Wasserman 1974, p. 329.

61   Conrad 1960 [1899], p. 149. See Miller 1966, p. 36.

62   Conrad 1960 [1899], p. 114. See Griffith 1995, esp. pp. 93–4.

63   Freud 1991, p. 356.

64   ibid., p. 357.

65   Freud 1965, p. 57.

Chapter 8   Homer on the Evolutionary Scale: Interrelations between Biology and Literature in the Writings of William Gladstone and Grant Allen

1   See Alter 1999; Beer 1989.

2   Quoted in Aarsleff 1967, p. 209. On Richard Garnett's review of Richardson's (1835), Webster's (1828), and Johnson's (1818 in Todd's revision) dictionaries published in the *Quarterly Review* 56, September 1835, 295–330, see Aarsleff 1967, p. 209. Similarly, C F Keary pointed at the significance of comparative philology for the study of the history of ideas: 'In whatever way speech began, there can be no doubt that the successive changes of sounds leave on record the best history we can ever obtain of the early development of ideas, and that this history has been opened to the world, in recent days only, by the growth of Comparative Philology.' (Keary 1881, pp. 471–2)

3   Author's translation. Goethe 1998 [1810], p. 28: '… es hatte von jeher etwas Gefährliches, von der Farbe zu handeln, dergestalt, daß einer unserer Vorgänger gelegentlich gar zu äußern wagt: Hält man dem Stier ein rotes Tuch vor, so wird er wütend; aber der Philosoph, wenn man nur überhaupt von Farbe spricht, fängt an zu rasen'.

4   As early as 1802, Thomas Young published his theory that 'the sensitive filament of the nerve may consist of three portions, one for each principal colour' (quoted in Jahn [ed.] 1998, p. 493). Young's publication 'On the Theory of Light and Colours' had great influence on Helmholtz (Von Helmholtz 2003 [1883], pp. 6–7), whose theory of trichromacy (1866) recognizes three types of cones in the retina, with pigments varying in the wavelength of light to which they respond (Jahn [ed.] 1998, p. 493). Pigments were discovered in 1842 by August David Krohn. This was followed by vigorous research into pigments, with Willibald Kühne and his school at Heidelberg at the forefront (ibid.).

5   See Allen 1878a, p. 32. Like children, the 'native uncivilised races' were taken to represent an early stage in the development of mankind. James Sully, for instance,

puts 'uncivilised man' on a par with children when he states that the 'uncivilised man and the child find no difficulty in conceiving their familiar quadrupeds talking, behaving and acting quite in a human fashion' (Sully 1879, p. 605). Similarly, Grant Allen argues that the beauty of flowers is appreciated neither by 'savages' nor by children (Allen 1880a, p. 452). See further Jann 1994, p. 290; Bowler 1989, p. 120.

6   Author's translation. Geiger 1878 [1871], p. 46: 'Wir können von dem Knochengerüste und vielleicht der ganzen äußeren Erscheinung einer untergegangenen Thierspecies durch geologische Funde eine Anschauung gewinnen; wir können aus Schädelresten auf ein unvollkommenes Menschengeschlecht der Urzeit allgemeine Schlüsse ziehen: doch über die Art, wie der Kopf gedacht haben mag, dessen Trümmer sich in dem Neanderthale als ein Problem für die Gegenwart aufbewahrten, möchte es schwer sein, sich aus seinem Anblick irgend eine Vorstellung zu bilden. Glücklicherweise hat auch die Geschichte des Geistes ihre urweltlichen Reste, ihre Ablagerungen und Versteinerungen anderer Art: sie bieten lehrreichere Aufschlüsse, als man zu glauben geneigt sein sollte; sie führen, sorgfältig verfolgt, zu vielleicht unerwarteten, allein, wie ich glaube, darum nicht weniger sicheren Ergebnissen'. Geiger examined Greek literature, the Rigveda hymns, the Zend-Advesta and other writings. Geiger's lecture was published posthumously by his brother Alfred in the collection *Entwickelungsgeschichte der Menschheit*. It appeared in English translation in 1880 as *Contributions to the History of the Development of the Human Race* (Geiger 1880). Lazarus Geiger (1829–70), who, from 1861 until his death, was professor in the Jewish high school at Frankfurt am Main, is best known for his work *Ursprung und Entwickelung der menschlichen Sprache und Vernunft* (Stuttgart, 1868), in which he intended to show that the evolution of human reason is closely bound up with that of language. For Geiger, see Rosenthal 1883; Peschier 1871. Darwin's cousin and friend Hensleigh Wedgwood emphasized in 1833 that it is much more difficult to trace the 'original form' from linguistic remnants than from fossil remains, which 'have for the most part been preserved by the protecting soil in which they were embedded'. The 'relics of the immaterial world', however, 'have been worn, until, like pebbles on the beach, they have lost every corner and distinctive mark, and hardly a vestige remains to indicate the original form' (quoted in Beer 1989, p. 159).

7   Magnus 1877a; Magnus's publications were reviewed in *Mind* 3, 1878, 151.

8   See Magnus 1877a, p. 33.

9   ibid., pp. 11, 5–6.

10   See ibid., pp. 12–14 n. 3. Among the publications Magnus refers to are Friedrich Vischer's *Aesthetik* (1851–57) and Hermann Steinthal's *Der Ursprung der Sprache* (1877).

11   See ibid., pp. 19, 22.

12   *Studies on Homer and the Homeric Age* (1858), *Juventus Mundi* (1869), *Homeric Synchronism* (1876). For Gladstone as a critic of Homer, see Myers 1958, pp. 94–122.

13   See Myers 1958, p. 6. This idea had been challenged by the German classicist Friedrich August Wolf in *Prolegomena ad Homerum* (1795), where he argues that the *Iliad* and the *Odyssey* are the works of many singers, a view shared by Lazarus Geiger (Geiger 1878 [1871], p. 6).

14   Gladstone 1858, p. 483. Homer's 'reputed blindness' is based on the portrayal of the blind bard in the eighth book of the *Odyssey*. Gladstone 'rejected the supposition that this [his lack of colour terms] was due to any defect in his

individual organisation' (Gladstone 1877, p. 366). To him, Homer's blindness is a 'mere tradition', and not based on any proof (Gladstone 1858, p. 484).

15 See Gladstone 1877, p. 368.

16 Gladstone 1858, p. 457.

17 See Gladstone 1877, p. 381.

18 See ibid., p. 386.

19 See ibid., p. 380–1.

20 See ibid., pp. 374, 380–1, 386.

21 Gladstone 1858, p. 488.

22 Gladstone 1877, p. 367.

23 John Lubbock's experiments had, for instance, shown that bees can distinguish between colours (Lubbock 1882; see also Allen 1884, p. 456). In the course of the booming research into social insects, mental and psychic qualities that had been perceived to be unique to humankind (such as social organization, colour sense, psychic qualities, memory, language, intelligence and feelings) were ascribed to social insects. This contributed to the blurring of boundaries between humans and animals, and thus supported Darwin's conviction, expressed most explicitly in his *Descent of Man*, that 'man possesses the same senses as the lower animals' (Darwin 1952 [1871], p. 287), and that animals are 'excited by the same emotions as ourselves' (ibid., pp. 289–90). Moreover, Darwin contested the view that language was a uniquely human possession (ibid., pp. 297–301; see Beer 1986, p. 219; Beer 1989, pp. 154–6). As Gillian Beer points out, although in the *Origin* Darwin avoids the topic of man, his readers would have realized the implications of his arguments for man's place in nature (Beer 1986, p. 213). In the introduction to his *Descent of Man*, Darwin explains: 'During many years I collected notes on the origin or descent of man, without any intention of publishing on the subject, but rather with the determination not to publish, as I thought that I should thus only add to the prejudices against my views. It seemed to me sufficient to indicate, in the first edition of my *Origin of Species*, that by this work "light would be thrown on the origin of man and his history"; and this implies that man must be included with other organic beings in any general conclusion respecting his manner of appearance on this earth.' (Darwin 1952 [1871], p. 253) The anthropomorphization of animals, popularized by illustrations and animal stories, rendered Darwin's arguments compelling and popularized them (Durant 1985, pp. 291–2; Voss 2001, p. 102).

24 See Royle 1980, p. 171. The freethinkers used Darwinism to attack the concept of the mind as a unique characteristic of man. Annie Besant translated Ludwig Büchner's essay 'Mind in Animals' (1880) immediately after its publication. Büchner was president of the German Freethought Society [*Freidenkerbund*], established in Frankfurt in 1881 (Royle 1980, p. 78).

25 Clodd 1900, pp. 71–2.

26 Geiger assumed a gradual susceptibility for colour perception. He thought that in the early stage of human development only a vague recognition of undifferentiated colour existed, and that man had become aware of colours in the order they appear in the spectrum (Geiger 1878 [1871], pp. 48, 58).

27 See Darwin 1996 [1859], pp. 67–107.

28 See Magnus 1877a, pp. 44–6.

29 In substantiation of his theory, Magnus cites a German work on colour in relation to the arts and crafts (Magnus 1877a, p. 50). According to the author, one B von Bezold, the interest among young girls in pretty clothing may be conducive to the training of their colour sense. This, he suggests, might explain that the colour sense is more developed in women than in men.

30 See Magnus 1877a, p. 9.

31 See ibid., pp. 11–12.

32 See Gladstone 1877, p. 369.

33 ibid., p. 371.

34 Darwin, in a letter to Gladstone (dated October 2, 1877), calls his attention to an essay that criticizes Magnus's theory (de Beer 1958, pp. 88–9; Morley 1908, p. 108).

35 Wallace 1878, p. 246.

36 Peter Morton writes that Allen 'gave complete satisfaction to the inner Darwinian circle for the rest of his productive life. ... He was such an excellent propagandist that this alone might account for his high regard among the Darwinists. Huxley, at least, was astute enough to realize that Allen could command the ear of a wide, profoundly non-intellectual, fickle, middle-class audience: that stratum of English society which was, and remains, most impermeable to abstract theories ... spoon-feeding was Allen's forte. Even Darwin recognized it in his pleasantly enthusiastic way; in an undated letter he told Allen: "who can tell how many young persons your chapters may bring up to be good working evolutionists!"' (Morton 1984, p. 139). In a letter to Allen (dated May 2, 1882), T H Huxley praises Allen's *Vignettes of Nature* (1881): 'I find much to admire in the way you conjoin precision with popularity – a very difficult art' (quoted in Clodd 1900, p. 112). For Allen's contributions to popular scientific journalism, see Amigoni 2004. The bibliography of Allen's work, compiled by Peter Morton, is indicative of the scope of Allen's writings and his literary productivity; see www.ehlt.flinders.edu.au/english/GA/GAHome.htm (last viewed June 8, 2004).

37 Allen 1878b.

38 In 2003, two scholars at the University of Hong Kong argued that trichromacy did not help our frugivorous ancestors to distinguish between fruit and leaves, but instead helped primates to find tender red leaves bursting with nutritional value (Travis 2003).

39 Allen was appointed Professor of Mental and Moral Philosophy in a black college in Spanish Town in 1873. He returned to England in 1876.

40 Allen 1878a, p. 32. *Tropical Nature*, pp. 189–192, 223–4. See 'The Colour Sense', on his forthcoming book, in *Nature*, November 14, 1878, p. 32.

41 See Allen 1878b, p. 129. In his essay 'Queen Dido's Realm', Allen calls attention to the coloration in wasps, which, since wasps are carnivorous and mainly neuters, cannot be accounted for by sexual selection but by repulsion (Allen 1894, p. 530).

42 Allen 1878b, pp. 130–1. If primitive tribes have a colour sense, – thus Allen's reasoning – the semi-civilized Homeric Akhaians must have been able to distinguish between colour, too (Allen 1878b, pp. 130–1).

43 Allen 1879a, p. 505.

44 Allen 1879b, p. 302.

45   See Allen 1878b, p. 129.

46   Allen 1879a, p. 94.

47   Allen 1878b, p. 131. '[T]he need for colour-terms was not yet felt among a race of non-manufacturing warriors, and because the gleam of bronze, the light of day, the bright or lowering sky, the indefinite hues of man and horse and cattle, were far more relatively important than the pure tints of flowers and insects, or the almost unknown art-products of Egypt, Phoenicia and Assyria'.

48   Smith 1877, p. 100. By way of an example from Athenaeus Delpnos, Smith illustrates that the Greeks themselves were aware of the insufficiency of the poetic vocabulary of colour, a fact which, Smith emphasizes, one has to keep in mind in any attempt to measure the development of the colour sense among the Greeks (ibid.).

49   Wallace 1878, p. 247.

50   In order to find out whether and to what extent a correlation between colour perception and linguistic expression exists, Magnus had sent a questionnaire to missionaries and traders with a set of colours to be distinguished and named by 'uncivilized people' (Magnus 1880, p. 2). His findings demonstrated that colour perception is as developed in 'primitive tribes' as among Europeans and proved the discrepancy between colour vision and colour vocabulary (ibid., pp. 6, 34–5). See also Berlin and Kay 1969, pp. 139–45, who refer to Magnus's work as 'the most comprehensive and conclusive of his time' (p. 145). Virchow supported the independence of colour vocabulary and colour perception: The Nubians he had examined were able to discriminate between colours in all parts of the spectrum, yet lacked the colour terms for them (Segall et al. 1966, p. 39). Rivers reopened the issue at the turn of the century, when he claimed that he had discovered several groups which 'showed different stages in the evolution deduced by Geiger from ancient writings' (Rivers 1901a, p. 46). Rivers believed that his work showed that the scarcity of colour terms 'had some definite cause, probably of a physiological nature' (ibid., p. 46), and that 'they [the natives] have a certain degree of insensitiveness to this colour, as compared with a European. We have, in fact, a case in which deficiency in colour language is associated with a corresponding defect in colour sense' (ibid., p. 52). Thus, his findings, Rivers claims, lend 'some support to the view of Gladstone and Geiger' (Rivers 1901b, p. 49). Berlin and Kay suspect that 'what Rivers took to be informants' confusion in perception of blue was in fact the result of his inability to effectively communicate, through interpreters, the distinction between the perceptual and naming tasks' (Berlin and Kay 1969, p. 148). See also Woodworth 1910.

51   In their 1969 publication Basic Color Terms, Brent Berlin and Paul Kay suggest that the number of basic colour terms tends to increase with the complexity of the civilization. This is how they explain the relative poverty of colour terminology among the ancients which was noted in numerous nineteenth century publications (see, for example, Prantl 1978 [1849]; Müller 1887, p. 299).

52   Wallace, for instance, argues that '[c]olour-names, being abstractions, must always have been a late development in language' (Wallace 1878, p. 247).

53   See Allen 1880a, p. 446. In his essay 'Aesthetic Feeling in Birds', Allen argued that birds display a sense of taste, hearing, form and symmetry and thus 'aesthetic endowments of a very high order' (Allen 1880b, p. 659). Allen also found a love of music among certain reptiles; in Jamaica he observed the common house-lizard, for instance, listening 'with evident interest and attention to the playing of a piano'

(ibid., p. 653). Similarly, James Sully tried to 'vindicate the musical capabilities of animals' (Sully 1879, pp. 606–7), which he explained by sexual selection (ibid., p. 616). 'Man', Sully argued, 'can no longer boast of being the sole artist' (ibid., p. 605). In 'Our Debt to Insects', Allen suggested that 'it is probable that all insects possessing the colour sense, possess also a certain aesthetic taste for colour' (Allen 1884, p. 464), and in 'The Origin of the Sense of Symmetry' he found a sense of symmetry also in the 'web of the geometrical spider' and in 'the hexagonal cells of the honey-bees' (Allen 1879b, p. 303). Even the origin of the sublime, he argued in yet another essay, can be found 'lower down in the animal scale than in the limits of humanity itself. The desire to produce an *effect* is one which man shares with many of the higher vertebrates' (Allen 1878c, p. 324).

54 Allen 1880a, p. 447.

55 ibid., p. 450.

56 Earlier, in his *Physiological Aesthetics*, Allen had endeavoured to 'elucidate physiologically the nature of our Aesthetic Feelings' (Allen 1977 [1877], p. 1).

57 Allen 1880a, p. 447.

58 ibid., p. 464.

59 ibid., p. 451.

60 Allen emphasizes that 'we must never forget that the taste for scenery on a large scale is confined to comparatively few races, and comparatively few persons among them. Thus, ... [t]he Russians "run through Europe with their carriage windows shut."' (Allen 1880a, p. 461) Comfort, to Allen, is a prerequisite for the appreciation of nature: 'So long as communications are difficult and roads bad, this agricultural aspect of natural beauty will remain uppermost. It is difficult to appreciate scenery in the midst of practical discomforts.' Thus, '[e]ven in our own time and place, amongst our own race, one may see a similar aesthetic level with farmers and labourers' (ibid., p. 462).

61 Allen 1878d, p. 64. Allen distinguishes between literature 'which aims at imparting knowledge [works on the natural sciences], and that which aims at imparting pleasure [poetry, romance, and the mass of belles-lettres generally]' (Allen 1977 [1877], p. 243).

62 Allen 1880a, p. 446.

63 ibid., p. 461.

64 See ibid., p. 460.

65 ibid. See also Allen's *Physiological Aesthetics*: 'Plot-interest is of greatest importance in Romance, narrative Poetry, and historical Painting; ideal sensuous or emotional feeling predominates in descriptive or lyrical Poetry, landscape Painting, and Music.' The child and 'the savage' is pleased with the former (Allen 1977 [1877], p. 211).

66 Allen 1880a, p. 459.

67 See Allen 1878d, p. 73.

68 Ibid. In his *Physiological Aesthetics*, Allen illustrates this point with the lily of the valley: 'Thus the word *lily of the valley* excites in us not only an ideal consciousness of the flower so called, but also a very slight wave of that pleasurable feeling which an actual lily produces in us through the senses of sight and smell ... the faint emotional waves generated by language exercise in a minor degree the same nervous plexuses which would be exercised more fully by the original vivid waves of which they are copies' (Allen 1977 [1877], pp. 247–8).

69   Allen 1878d, p. 73.
70   Levine 1987, p. 9.
71   Darwin 1952 [1871], p. 287.

Chapter 9   'Naturfreund' or 'Naturfeind'? Darwinism in the Early Drawings of Alfred Kubin

1   For an overview of Kubin's visual *oeuvre* see Hoberg (ed.) 1990.
2   Kubin illustrated over 140 books. In all, including Otto Julius Bierbaum's *Samalio Pardulus*, Fyodor Dostoevsky's *Doppelgänger*, Edgar Allan Poe's *The Tell-Tale Heart*, Wilhelm Hauff's *Märchen*, E.T.A. Hoffmann's *Night Tales*, Gerard de Nerval's *Aurélia*, Oskar Panizza's *Council of Love*, and François Marie Arouet Voltaire's *Candide*. See also Kubin 1974, p. 67.
3   For an overview of the literary work, see Geyer 1995.
4   See ibid., pp. 28–9.
5   Paul Klee, quoted in Werkner 1986, p. 214 (author's translation).
6   Vassily Kandinsky, quoted ibid. (author's translation).
7   Geyer 1995, p. 27 (author's translation).
8   Kubin 1974, pp. 22–3: 'ein Dasein nach Murgens *Zigeunerleben*' (author's translation).
9   Franz Blei, *Erzählungen eines Lebens* (1930), quoted in Werkner 1986, p. 28: '... ein schmächtiger, immer schwarzgekleideter Jüngling mit dem blassen Knabengesicht, das sich zur Verdüsterung ein bißchen anstrengte und scheu tat wie ein junger Wolf, den man aus der Grube ans Licht gezogen hat' (author's translation).
10   See also Hoberg 1995, p. 23.
11   Kubin 1974, p. 102: 'in einen violetten Samtmantel gehüllt aus einem Mauseschädel Absinth trinken, um meine Phantasie zu beleben' (author's translation).
12   Hedwig 1967, p. 2: 'Grauen vor den Abgründen des Daseins; ein urwelthaftes Angstgefühl.' (author's translation)
13   Some scholars have already identified evolutionary themes in Kubin's literary *oeuvre*. Andreas Geyer's discussion of Kubin's texts points to the preponderance of simian symbolism (e.g. Giovanni the Barber in *Die andere Seite*, or *Die Wissenschaft*, 1901–2) which is often highly sexualized, particularly in drawings such as *Eine für Alle* and *Die Geilheit*. Geyer also cites an emphasis on the intellect and brain mass as a yardstick for biological superiority, and the animalization of mankind as an indication of evolutionary themes (see Geyer 1995, pp. 59–67).
14   See *Kämpfende Büffel* (1900); *Groteske* (1900–1).
15   See *Polyp* (1898–9); *Sturmvogel* (1903); *Die Wahrheit* (1902–3); *Der Frosch* (1904?); *Die Jagd* (1900–1); *Der Verfolgte* (1902–3).
16   See *Die Pest* (1903–4); *Syphillis* (1902); *Elefantiasis* (1900–1); *Cholera* (1898–9).
17   Bölsche 1976 [1887], p. 56 (author's translation).
18   Kubin 1995b [1904], in Geyer 1995, pp. 244–5 (author's translation).
19   Kubin 1995a [1902], reprinted in Geyer 1995, pp. 234–40. Geyer's remarks ibid., pp. 33, 128–30 (author's translation).

20   *Der Unhold* (c.1900), 31 x 20.5cm. Private Collection Switzerland. Reproduced in *Alfred Kubin*, Kunstmuseum Winterthur, 1986. Cat. No. 73.

21   c.1899. 27.4 x 21.8 cm. Oberösterreichisches Landesmuseum Linz. Inv. No. HA 7361.

22   See Rudwick 1992, p. 45.

23   *Das Gezüchte* (1903). Städtische Galerie im Lenbachhaus. Kub. No. 202. Reproduced in Hoberg 1990, catalogue No. 78.

24   See Kubin's *The Flame* (1900); also Geyer's discussion of the *Geschlechtstrieb* as a key factor in Kubin's understanding of evolution (Geyer 1995, *passim*).

25   For example *Fabeltier* (1903–4); *Die Promenade* (1904); *Die Katze* (1903); *Schatzwächter* (1903).

26   In Kubin 1995c, p. 261.

27   See Massey Czerkas and Glut 1982, p. 43. Other dinosaur illustrations by Knight were published in *The Century Illustrated Magazine*, Vol. LV, No.1, November 1897.

28   'Ein Zyklus von Wandgemälden Knights, die Tiere der Vorzeit in landschaftl. Umgebung darstellend (1896/1900) schmückt die Halle der fossilen Wirbeltiere des gen. Museums zu den naturhistor. Museen zu Paris, London u. München' (Thieme and Becker 1927, p. 591).

29   In Hoberg (ed.) 1990, p. 209.

30   Kubin 1974, p. 20: 'kopierte zum Zeitvertrieb Bilder aus der *Gartenlaube*' (author's translation).

31   See [Kubin] n.d.

32   They included Otto Julius Bierbaum, Franz Blei, Max Dauthendey, Max Halbe and Karl Wolfskehl.

33   Geyer argues that evolutionary themes in Kubin's writings were inspired by his readings of Nietzsche and Schopenhauer. While this may have been the case, it should not be confused with Kubin's engagement with Darwinism. See Geyer 1995, pp. 59–67.

34   Kubin 1974, p. 8: 'Dann aber ließ ich allein in aller Heimlichkeit den zurückgehaltenen grausamen Instinkten volle Freiheit; in irgendeinem Gartenwinkel versteckt auf der Erde liegend, veranstaltete ich Folterszenen an armen kleinen Tieren, die so unglücklich gewesen waren, meinen Machtbereich zu kreuzen, und ich muß gestehen, so scheußlich ich das auch heute finde und so oft ich es später bereut habe, ich empfand doch starke Lustgefühle dabei' (author's translation).

35   Kubin, 'Tip und Giovanni', in Kubin 1974, pp. 197–205.

36   ibid., p. 68: 'Ich war von jeher Naturfreund, sammelte seit meinen Knabentagen Käfer und Schmetterlinge, hielt mir Reptilien, Fische, Vögel, mit Leidenschaft ihrer Beobachtung hingegeben' (author's translation).

37   ibid., p. 9: 'Meine größten Freuden gaben mir jetzt Märchenbücher, auch beschäftigte ich mich viel mit Naturgeschichte und füllte meine Freizeit mit Vogel- und Fischfang aus' (author's translation).

38   ibid., p. 16: '[Außer all diesen überströmenden Empfindungen] genoß ich meine Freiheit mit vollen Zügen. Ich kaufte mir ein Fahrrad, hielt mir Schlangen und allerhand Gewürm in Käfigen ...' (author's translation).

39   ibid., p. 72: 'Wir besuchten den Maler R. [Reinhold] Koeppel in Waldhäuser, und das stundenlange Wandern in dem dunklen Grün, Baum an Baum, Wurzel an

Wurzel, erregte in uns einen seltsamen Rausch, der in diesem gewaltigen Pflanzenleben seinen geheimen Grund haben muß. Es ist das unbeschreiblich Urweltliche, das die Seele so elementar bedrängt' (author's translation).

40   ibid., pp. 92–3: 'Hier in Zwickledt hatten wir die schönsten Aquarien, afrikanische Frösche, einen Leguan, Eichhörnchen und Haselmäuse, auch die Jugendliebhaberei des Käfersammelns tauchte für ein paar Jahre wieder auf' (author's translation).

41   ibid., p. 40: 'Im nächsten Vierteljahr ... gab [ich] mich der Beobachtung meiner verschiedenen Tiere hin, darunter ein munterer Affe, ein zahmes Reh, Katzen, Aquarien und Käfersammlungen, und streifte stundenlang im Wald und Feld umher' (author's translation).

Chapter 10 Cells and Networks in Nineteenth Century Literature

1   Otis 1999, 2001.
2   Rothfield 1992.
3   Lenoir 1994.
4   Eliot 1865, p. 46.
5   Hayles 1990, p. xiv.
6   Wald 2003.
7   Personal communication, December 2003–January 2004. See also Bell 2004, Bell n.d.
8   Rosenheim 2003.
9   Ginzburg 1992 [1976].
10   Rosenheim 2003, p. 199.
11   Haberling 1924, pp. 289–90.
12   Keller 1985.
13   Culler used this expression in an introductory literary theory course at Cornell University in autumn 1986.
14   Beer discusses the role of the visual imagination in literature and science in Beer 1983.
15   For an English translation of these stories, see Ramón y Cajal 2001.
16   ibid., pp. 146–7.
17   Otis (ed.) 2002.
18   Du Bois-Reymond 1887.
19   Müller's biographer, Wilhelm Haberling, quotes a letter from Haeckel to his family shortly after Müller's death in which Haeckel speculated that Müller had died of a self-inflicted opium overdose. See Haberling 1924, pp. 450–1.
20   For a discussion of the way Müller's students' scientific interests shaped their memorial addresses to their teacher, see Jardine 1997.

Chapter 11 Contagious Sympathies: George Eliot and Rudolf Virchow

1   Blackwood to Eliot, June 2, 1871, in Eliot 1954–78, vol. 5, p. 148.
2   *Lancet* 1870, 1, p. 473.

3   See Drysdale 1878, pp. 8–9. On the rise of germ theory, see Worboys 2000. He suggests that the transitional period, in terms of theories of contagion, was between 1865 and 1880 (pp. 2–3).

4   For a clear account of anticontagionism, see Ackerknecht 1948, 1953.

5   In Pratt and Neufeldt 1979, p. 61.

6   Eliot 1985 [1871–2], p. 184.

7   See Dale 1989, pp. 78–9; Forrester 1990.

8   See Blair 2001, *passim*. This article examines the various uses made of the cell theory in British and German physiology and sociology, and argues that Lewes's conception of a cellular model in his scientific writings and Eliot's use of the cell in *Middlemarch* are most akin to Virchow's theories, and may directly allude to his work.

9   Eliot 1985 [1871–2], p. 171.

10   ibid., p. 212.

11   ibid., p. 271.

12   Hardy 1993, pp. 151–93.

13   Eliot 1985 [1871–2], p. 195.

14   Smith 1830, p. 354.

15   Eliot 1985 [1871–2], pp. 462, 311.

16   Virchow 1868, p. 4.

17   Eliot 1985 [1871–2], pp. 145, 814, 631.

18   Cited in Pratt and Neufeldt 1979, p. 23.

19   Eliot 1985 [1871–2], pp. 589, 796, 761.

20   Smith 1830, p. 19. Smith is discussing the views of several authorities that fever is generated from the blood, views which he then refutes.

21   Eliot 1985 [1871–2], pp. 570, 155.

22   Daubeny 1855, p. 88. Eliot and Lewes owned an offprint of this article (see Baker [ed.] 1977, p. 49).

23   Graver 1984, p. 220.

24   See Virchow 1860, pp. 458–9 on contagious cells; and 'Atoms and Individuals' (1859), in Virchow 1959 on pathological cell formations.

25   For information on Virchow's cellular pathology and on his medical writings in general, see Otis 1999; Ackerknecht 1953; Coleman 1977.

26   Worboys 2000, p. 28.

27   Pratt and Neufeldt 1979, p. 58, citing Smith 1830, pp. 26–7.

28   On Virchow and anticontagionism, see McNeely 2002; Otis 1999; Ackerknecht 1953.

29   'On the New Advances in Pathology' (1867), in Virchow 1959, p. 99.

30   'Cellular Pathology' (1855), in Virchow 1959, p. 80.

31   See especially Otis 1999; Ackerknecht 1953 on the implications of Virchow's cell theory for his politics. Boyd also discusses his medical work in terms of his theories of the state, and McNeely 2002 provides a useful account of Virchow's liberal ideologies.

32   ibid., p. 100.

33   Eliot 1985 [1871–2], p. 175. See Blair 2001, p. 9.

34 'Atoms and Individuals' (1859), in Virchow 1959, p. 139.

35 For an account of the lecture criticizing Virchow by Professor Gulliver, see *Lancet* 1863, 2, p. 30; for the review of his lecture on typhus, see *Lancet* 1868, 1, p. 561; for the favourable editorial see *Lancet* 1869, 1, p. 689.

36 Anon. 1870.

37 On Virchow's organization of 'sanitary trains' in Germany to help the wounded, see *British Medical Journal* 1871, 1, p. 101. On Virchow as teacher, see Swanzy 1871, pp. 637–8.

38 See *The Times*, 4 June 1865, p. 5 and 13 June 1865, p. 12 for accounts of Bismarck's challenge and Virchow's response.

39 Lewes to Blackwood, 26 November 1860, in Eliot 1954–78, vol. 8, p. 273.

40 Eliot 1985 [1871–2], pp. 504, 383.

41 'Public Health Services' (1848), in Virchow 1985, p. 14.

42 Taylor and Rieger 1984, p. 201.

43 Virchow 1854, 'Species-Makers and Specifics', from *Virchows Archiv* 6, cited in Rather 1990, p. 56.

44 Eliot 1985 [1871–2], p. 174.

45 ibid., p. 118.

46 Although Eliot frequently uses bodily illness in a metaphorical sense in her novels (hence Latimer's sensitivity in 'The Lifted Veil', or Captain Wybrow's 'syncope' in 'Mr Gilfil's Love Story'), I have found very little use of metaphors of contagion outside *Middlemarch*. The exception may be the essay 'Diseases of Small-Authorship' in *Impressions of Theophrastus Such*, in which Vorticella's writing is perceived as a tumour, a 'noxious and disfiguring' cell formation, which has a deleterious effect on those forced to read it. See Eliot 1913, p. 224.

47 Cited in McNeely 2002, p. 18.

Chapter 12 From Parasitology to Parapsychology: Parasites in Nineteenth Century Science and Literature

1 Ruskin 1907 [1872–84], vol. 28, letter 51: 'Humble Bees', March 1875, pp. 270–95, p. 278.

2 ibid., p. 279. Bingley's *Animal Biography* (1804), by contrast, is praised for its lively and imaginative descriptions of animal life, especially its illustrations of 'mutual assistance' (ibid., p. 278).

3 ibid., pp. 289–90.

4 ibid., p. 291.

5 ibid., vol. 28, correspondence appended to letter 53 (May 1875), p. 337.

6 ibid., pp. 316–34, 325.

7 ibid., p. 333, 333 n.

8 ibid., vol. 29, letter 85 (January 1878), p. 320 n.

9 ibid., vol. 27, letter 35 (November 1873), p. 649. See Casillo 1985, p. 541.

10 Ruskin 1907 [1872–84], vol. 27, letter 26 (February 1873), p. 483.

11 Ruskin 1905 [1869], p. 365.

12 Casillo 1985, p. 561. See also Ruskin 1907 [1872–84], vol. 29, pp. 172, 294; vol. 28, p. 103.

13   Paraphrased in Telotte 1999, p. 13.

14   See Baran 1993; Behrendt 1985; Kaminskas 1997, 2000; Paulson 1985; Pfeiffer 1997.

15   On the etymology and the Greek-comedy stock type, see Perty 1869, p. 3; Knorr 1875.

16   See Enzensberger 2001, p. 203. Katz, Despommier and Gwadz 1982, 'Contents', gives a survey of the historical research into parasites, enumerating the eighteenth- and nineteenth century discoveries by German, British and French scientists.

17   See 'GE., P.' and 'C., C.' 1885, and the entire section on 'Parasitism': ibid., pp. 258–71.

18   Doflein 1901, pp. 4, 9.

19   Darwin 1996 [1859], Appendix II: 'Glossary of Principal Scientific Terms' [added for the 5th edition in 1869], pp. 410–26, 421.

20   Darwin 1981 [1871], p. 191.

21   Darwin 1969 [1839], p. 11 (on 'Bahia, or San Salvador. Brazil'), pp. 22, 231.

22   Darwin 1996 [1859], pp. 5, 51.

23   See ibid., p. 179; also Enzensberger 2001, p. 165, on Darwin's 1860 letter to Asa Gray.

24   Darwin 1969 [1839], p. 10.

25   Darwin 1996 [1859], pp. 52–3.

26   See ibid., p. 190.

27   Gruendler 1850, p. 7.

28   See Perty 1869, p. 5, and ibid. on 'rückschreitende Metamorphose' (author's translation); this phenomenon is also described by Darwin, Wilson or Drummond, see below.

29   ibid., p. 6: 'Bei diesen entschiedensten Schmarotzern treten dann die Charaktere der Schwäche und Mangelhaftigkeit sehr augenfällig in der äußeren Erscheinung hervor, so wie sie häufig auch etwas Fremdartiges, Unschönes, manchmal Widerliches haben, oft klein, blaß, von abweichender Färbung sind' (author's translation).

30   ibid. See Enzensberger 2001, p. 160.

31   See Perty 1869, pp. 43, 40, 43.

32   See 'GE., P.' 1885, p. 261; and Serres 1980, pp. 9–24: 'La cascade'.

33   See Perty 1869, p. 44.

34   Cobbold 1879, p. vii.

35   ibid., pp. 2–3, viii.

36   See Otis 1999.

37   Cobbold 1879, p. 2; original emphasis.

38   Gruendler 1850, pp. 8–9, 33.

39   Johann Steenstrup's study *Ueber den Generationenwechsel, oder die Fortpflanzung und Entwickelung durch abwechselnde Generationen* (1842) had already been published; Gruendler could have known that parasites can enter the host organism at one stage and exit it at another stage of their own life-cycle. At least, Gruendler does note, on p. 34, that the oestrus enters the horse's maw after having been swallowed by the animal. See also Enzensberger 2001, p. 145.

40 Doflein 1901, p. 4. See also 'GE., P.' 1885, p. 261, on the 'migration from one host to another' of certain species of parasites.

41 Huxley 1968 [1887], pp. 116–7. See also 'GE., P.' 1885, p. 258, on the refutation of the theory of spontaneous generation.

42 Miller 1979, p. 219.

43 Miller 1975, pp. 83–4.

44 Hardy 1988 [1891], p. 127.

45 Hardy 1969 [1878], p. 216.

46 Virchow 1885, p. 9: 'Zuerst die Entdeckung des Parasiten, dann die Erforschung seiner Lebensweise, dann die Frage: wie erzeugt er die Krankheit?'; translation by Otis 1999, p. 24: 'First the discovery of the parasite, then the investigation of its etiology, then the question: how does it give rise to the disease?'

47 For the Cajal passage, see Otis 1999, p. 72; on Cajal's ideas on the 'open-hearted and essentially egalitarian nature of the microbe', see ibid., p. 119.

48 'C., C.' 1885, pp. 270, 271.

49 See Lankester 1880, p. 61.

50 Virchow 1959 [1859], p. 139.

51 Darwin 1996 [1859], pp. 63, 356.

52 ibid., p. 357. On Darwin's fascination with crustaceans, see also Stott 2002.

53 Morton 1984, p. 92, paraphrasing Wilson 1881.

54 Drummond 1883, pp. 343–4, quoted in Morton 1984, pp. 92–3.

55 Miller 1958, p. 185.

56 Dickens 1996 [1853], p. 81.

57 ibid., pp. 854 and 145.

58 On the themes of circulation and constipation, see also Trotter 1988, pp. 68–136.

59 Dickens 1996 [1853], p. 611.

60 See Telotte 1999, p. 12.

61 See Dickens 1989 [1865], p. 790.

62 '[Le parasite] multiplie la complexité ... il excite la production, il exalte, il accélère les échanges de ses hôtes.' (Serres 1980, p. 252)

63 Eliot 1996a [1860], p. 27. See also the discussion in Shuttleworth 1984, p. 61.

64 Eliot 1996b [1871–2], pp. 572, 656.

65 ibid., pp. 581–2, 741.

66 See Lewes 1862, pp. 11–12: in animalcules, cilia are 'the means of drawing in food – for which purpose they surround the mouth, and by their incessant action produce a small whirlpool into which the food is sucked'.

67 Eliot 1996b [1871–2], p. 55.

68 Wells 2000 [1891], p. 8.

69 Eliot 1966, Quarry One, no. 26.

70 Mann 1981, p. 196.

71 Eliot 1996b [1871–2], pp. 305, 310. See also Senf 1987.

72 Eliot 1996b [1871–2], pp. 622, 782.

73 ibid., pp. 621, 723, 656.

74 Shuttleworth 1984, p. 150.

75 Eliot 1996b [1871–2], pp. 144, 307.

76 Senf 1987, p. 90. See also ibid. on Engels's 'capitalist vampires' and 'vampire middle classes', and on Marx's designation of 'Capital' as 'vampire-like' 'dead labour'; also Shuttleworth 1984, p. 150.

77 See Spencer 1860.

78 Eliot 1996b [1871–2], p. 741.

79 Lewes 1858, pp. 30–1; quoted in Wormald 1996, n. 22.

80 Eliot 1954–8, vol. 2, pp. 241–2: 'Journal, Ilfracombe, 8 May–26 June 1856'.

81 See Serres 1980, p. 18, and quotations on pp. 252, 290.

82 Stoker 2003 [1993], pp. 59–60, 162, 205.

83 See Darwin 1969 [1839], p. 25: 'The Vampire bat is often the cause of much trouble, by biting the horses on their withers. The injury is generally not so much owing to the loss of blood, as to the inflammation which the pressure of the saddle afterwards produces. The whole circumstance has lately been doubted in England; I was therefore fortunate in being present when one was actually caught on a horse's back.'

84 Telotte 1999, p. 13.

85 Feldmann 1998, p. 370.

86 Stoker 2003 [1993], p. 60.

87 See Arata 1996, p. 117.

88 Higham 1976, p. 124.

89 Conan Doyle 1930, pp. 4, 5.

90 Serres 1980, p. 14.

91 Conan Doyle 1930, pp. 34, 52.

92 ibid., pp. 7, 9, 23.

93 ibid., pp. 26, 27.

94 ibid., p. 3.

95 Cranny-Francis 1988, pp. 98, 102.

96 Conan Doyle 1930, p. 31.

97 ibid., p. 40. On Serres, see Brown 2002, pp. 16–17.

98 Serres 1980, p. 281.

Chapter 13 Surgical Engineering in the Nineteenth Century: Frankenstein, The Island of Dr Moreau, Flatland

1 The fifteenth and sixteenth centuries gave rise to anatomically faithful representations of dissected human corpses (e.g., pregnant women opened, showing their foetuses). A double bind between anatomists and artists was established, and sometimes the artist *was* the better anatomist. The efforts to anatomize and dissect bodies could not have gained their ambivalent reputation between provocation and fascination without any artistic talent in the visualizations – and at the same time, artists could not have taken a glimpse at the secrets of divine creation without the surgical interest in mapping bodies (see Lyons and Petrucelli 2003, p. 410). If surgery was considered a necessary evil, it is no surprise that in the course of the debate about the legitimacy of literature, accusers *and* defenders of fiction referred to medical discourse: Most notably, in *The Schoole of Abuse* (1579) Stephen

Gosson pictures himself as an academically trained physician, handing the 'patient', poetry, over to the 'surgeon', or censor, who jumps to the rescue when scholarly, medical 'cunning' has failed (see Gosson 1868 [1579], p. 17). Surgery served as a metaphor for censorship, while 'anatomy' was a term used for the discursive charting of the globe and the cosmos, as well as the mapping of mental attitudes, such as that of Absurdity (Thomas Nashe), or Melancholy (Robert Burton).

2   Marshall 1995, p. 14.

3   Only in 1745 did the London Company of Surgeons separate from the barbers' guild, but there was no access for surgeons to the Royal Society. While the physician enjoyed his theoretical education at a medical faculty, surgical education was in the private hands of skilled anatomists, and practical training was received at the big London hospitals outside of universities, or on the battlefield (see Bonner 1995, p. 44). Academic training for surgeons was hardly available, the Medical Faculty of the University at Edinburgh, founded in 1736, being an exception to the rule (see Lyons and Petrucelli 2003, pp. 533–4).

4   See Bonner 1995, p. 148.

5   Quoted from Harman 2000, p. 306. Another authentic account of such an operation is given by Michael Cudmore Fuller in the context of describing operation practices before 1846. Fuller recalls a girl who, being a 'repulsive spectacular' since her severe burning of neck and shoulders in childhood, 'gladly consented to Mr. Skey's suggestion of operation': 'The patient was tied to the operating table as was customary in those days, but before many minutes of the operation had elapsed her cries and entreaties to be untied and allowed to remain as she was were the most frightful that can be imagined. As the operation, which was necessarily a lengthy one, proceeded, her cries became more terrible, first one and then another student fainted, and ultimately all but a determined few had left the theatre unable to stand the distressing scene' (quoted from Wallace 1982, p. 143).

6   See Harman 2000, p. 305.

7   Doody 1988, p. 314.

8   Haynes 1994, p. 91.

9   Marshall 1995, p. 23.

10   See Porter 1999, p. 317.

11   Shelley 1992 [1818], p. 53.

12   See Bonner 1995, p. 87.

13   Shelley 1992 [1818], p. 53.

14   See Bonner 1995, p. 240.

15   Shelley 1992 [1818], p. 48.

16   See Bonner 1995, p. 231 *passim*.

17   Shelley 1992 [1818], p. 51.

18   Bonner 1995, p. 145.

19   See Lyons and Petrucelli 2003, pp. 553–4.

20   Quoted in French 1975, p. 415.

21   See Smith 1994.

22   See Mellor 1995.

23   Shelley 1992 [1818], p. 45. Little wonder that Frankenstein should describe the result of his efforts less in medical terms than in literary ones, using (anti-)Petrarchist

images to refer to the creature's almost transparent skin. Besides, 'his hair was lustrous black, and flowing, his teeth of pearly whiteness', but his eyes are watery, and the monster is characterized by 'a shrivelled complexion and straight black lips' (Shelley 1992 [1818], p. 56).

24   ibid., p. 47.

25   ibid., p. 52.

26   Presumably Shelley knew the printed version of Davy's address to the Royal Institution of Surgeons, given in 1802. The actual animation of the monster happens against the background of Aldini's far-reaching experiments carried out with human corpses between 1802 and 1804, which restored, for a short time, natural respiration to such a degree that a corpse blew out a candle-light (see Mellor 1995, pp. 124–5).

27   Shelley 1992 [1818], p. 56.

28   Although the material 'instruments of life' needed for the operation proper remain shadowy, their metaphoric cutting edge is much more precise: After Frankenstein's escapist plunge from anatomy into the less daringly ambitious field of philology, he considers his former teachers' judgements of him a dissection by words, Waldman using verbal 'instruments which were to be afterwards used in putting [him] to a slow and cruel death', and Krempe's praise of Frankenstein having 'inflicted torture' on him (all quotes ibid., p. 66): Words take over the function of cutting tools – for Frankenstein, there is no division between words and objects.

29   Porter 1999, p. 307.

30   See Otis (ed.) 2002, p. 151.

31   Wells 1996 [1896], p. 132.

32   ibid.

33   ibid. Straub points out that Moreau's rhetoric betrays his actual failure: 'for all its conviction, Moreau's speech regularly stumbles, halts, breaks down, and falls into the coma of ellipses' (Straub 2002, p. xxiii). If the surgeon's discourse is a language which fails him, the victim has none. Pain can hardly be verbalized in discursive language, as has been pointed out (Scarry 1985, pp. 14–15,161–80). Prendick's rather sparse descriptions of the animal's cries support this observation, and the reader never gets the victim's own viewpoint.

34   Wells 1996 [1896], p. 89.

35   ibid., p. 135.

36   Gordon 2003, p. 57.

37   Wells 1996 [1896], p. 89.

38   ibid., p. 88.

39   Haynes (1994, p. 350 n. 22); Parrinder (1995, p. 56) refer to the antivivisectionist debate only in passing. That it was a very current issue is made clear by French, who quotes the following figures: 'In 1880, the London Anti-Vivisection Society was proud of holding twelve meetings in three months; by the end of the century, it had an "Anti-Vivisection Van" touring the country, while British Union lectures totalled more than 500 yearly' (French 1975, p. 254). So far, Moreau's 'physiological lecture' seems usually to have been read against the overpowering background of Wells's own early non-fictional essays and Thomas Henry Huxley's evolutionary ideas (see Haynes 1980; Stover 1990; Parrinder 1995; and Stover's introduction to his 1996 edition of the text, Wells 1996 [1896]).

40 See French 1975, pp. 55–6.

41 ibid., pp. 414–5.

42 Quoted from Otis (ed.) 2002, p. 217.

43 Other explanations of Moreau's name include 'water or death' (Haynes 1980, p. 33, and 1994, p. 351 n. 25), but it seems more convincing that Wells referred to Gustave Moreau, painter of half-human, half-animal hybridities such as the 1864 painting *Oedipus and the Sphinx* (see Stover in his 1996 introduction to the text, Wells 1996 [1896], pp. 36–8).

44 Quoted from Otis (ed.) 2002, p. 207.

45 Contrary to any expectations raised by reading *The Island of Dr Moreau*, Wells himself, in his essay 'The Province of Pain', refers pejoratively to 'the activity of the Society for the Prevention of Cruelty to Animals in our midst, and ... the zealous enemies of the British Institute of Preventive Medicine' (Wells 1996 [1896], p. 214, App. Ia).

46 See ibid., p. 133.

47 ibid., p. 138.

48 Otis (ed.) 2002, p. 207.

49 ibid.

50 Wells 1996 [1896], p. 136.

51 See ibid., pp. 2, 225.

52 Wells 1998, vol. 2, No. 1045.

53 See Galton 1892, pp. 35–8.

54 See ibid., p. 155.

55 See ibid., p. 162.

56 ibid., p. 131.

57 For a more detailed discussion of the socio-medical and mathematical aspects in *Flatland*, see Meyer 2003.

58 Abbott 2001 [1884], p. 44.

59 See ibid., p. 61.

60 ibid., p. 45 n.

61 ibid., p. 77.

62 ibid., p. 100.

63 ibid.

64 ibid., pp. 77–8.

65 Marshall 1995, p. 36.

66 See Reed 1990, pp. 139–41.

67 See Haynes 1994, pp. 155–6.

68 Abbott 2001 [1884], pp. 141, 146.

Chapter 14 'Serious' Science versus 'Light' Entertainment? Femininity Concepts in Nineteenth Century British Medical Discourse and Popular Fiction

1 Anon. 1861, p. 16.

2 Black 1888, p. 5.

3 Tilt 1852, pp. 181–2.

4 See Patmore n.d. [1854–6]; Ruskin 1905 [1864].

5 Clouston 1887, p. 529. See also Mercier 1890, p. 239.

6 Clouston 1887, p. 520. See also Maudsley 1874a, p. 469.

7 ibid., p. 468.

8 Campbell 1891, p. 55. See also Carpenter 1844, pp. 729–30; Walker 1840, pp. v, vii, ix, 28, 31, 34–5.

9 See Carpenter 1844, p. 729. See also Walker 1840, pp. 36–7.

10 See Carter 1853, p. 32.

11 See Skey 1867, p. 52.

12 See, for example, Tilt 1857, p. 130; Johnson 1850, p. 29.

13 Collins 1989 [1864–6], p. 436.

14 ibid., p. 257. See e.g. also her ironic invocation of the 'facts' that women do not know how to find their way out of desperate situations (p. 258), and that 'a lady has no passions' (p. 668).

15 ibid., pp. 763, 614, see also p. 531.

16 See, for example, Showalter 1977, p. 162; Cvetkovich 1992, pp. 73, 99.

17 See Collins 1995 [1880], pp. 44, 224.

18 ibid., p. 82; and Anon. 1851, p. 36.

19 Collins 1995 [1880], pp. 334, 460, 604. With Madame Fontaine, the narrator himself foregrounds her hypocrisy, ironically praising her 'art', which '[e]ven a French actress might have envied' (p. 147). Moreover, it comes to light in old letters that she has ample experience in dissembling, having 'feign[ed] respect and regard for a man whom [she] despise[d] with [her] whole heart' almost throughout her married life (p. 64).

20 Anon. 1851, pp. 31–3 (original emphasis). See also Laycock 1840, pp. 353–4.

21 Laycock accordingly also describes the symptoms as 'insane cunning' (ibid., p. 353). See also Donkin 1892, p. 621.

22 See Zedner 1991, p. 270; Showalter 1995, p. 124.

23 Anon. 1851, p. 33. See also Campbell 1891, p. 224.

24 Prichard 1835, p. 6.

25 ibid., p. 397.

26 Blandford, for instance, insists that mental delusions will be found in all genuine cases of moral insanity if they are only examined carefully (1871, pp. 315–17). See also Maudsley's doubts whether 'persons suffering from moral insanity should in every case be exempted from all responsibility for what they do wrong' (1874b, p. 181).

27 See, for example, Clouston 1887, pp. 347–9.

28 See Anon. 1851, p. 34.

29 ibid., p. 33. See also Campbell 1891, p. 224; Prichard 1835, p. 21.

30 Collins 1995 [1880], pp. 172, 192, 202, 208. Even before, she considers herself momentarily 'mad with [her] troubles' and 'a little hysterical' (pp. 125–6). She also fears that she is beginning to lose her 'best treasure', her 'steadiness of mind' (p. 127).

31 See, for example, Clouston 1887, p. 333; Prichard 1835, pp. 21–2.

32　See, for example, Bucknill and Tuke 1858, pp. 200, 214. Maudsley observed that the patient's mental resources may even seem greater than in sanity (1874b, p. 172).

33　Collins 1995 [1880], p. 531.

34　ibid., p. 67.

35　ibid., pp. 129, 224, xii.

36　ibid., p. 594; see also pp. 259, 770.

37　ibid., pp. 457, 438.

38　Davis 1836, vol. 2, p. 1203 (emphasis added). For the concept of 'moral treatment'/ 'control' see, for example, Prichard 1835, p. 279; Maudsley 1870, p. 80; Anon. 1851, p. 34. With regard to the nineteenth century American context, Rosenberg has indeed read hysteria as a power struggle between male doctors and female patients (1985, pp. 207–11).

39　See Maudsley 1895, p. 417; Davis 1836, vol. 2, p. 1201; Bucknill and Tuke 1858, p. 239.

40　Tilt 1857, p. 265; Tilt 1851, p. 70.

41　Collins 1989 [1864–6], p. 772.

42　ibid., pp. 536, 661.

43　Collins 1995 [1880], p. 224.

44　This novel is probably cited most frequently with regard to the representation of female madness in the nineteenth century. Not surprisingly, it plays an important role in Showalter's argument (1995, pp. 71–3).

45　Clouston 1887, pp. 325–6.

46　See Anon. 1851, p. 21.

47　See Maudsley 1874b, pp. 132, 143.

48　Braddon 1987 [1862], pp. 297–8.

49　Prichard 1835, p. 404. See also Campbell 1891, p. 224; Bucknill and Tuke 1858, p. 214.

50　Braddon 1987 [1862], pp. 347, 350, 356; see Bucknill and Tuke 1858, p. 329. See also Maudley 1874b, p. 171.

51　See, for example, Prichard 1835, p. 12, Clouston 1887, p. 349 on hereditary moral insanity, as well as Bucknill and Tuke 1858, pp. 243–4 on the mother–daughter line in the transmission of insanity.

52　Braddon 1987 [1862], p. 350. See Mercier 1890, p. 241.

53　See Davis 1836, vol. 2, p. 1203.

54　Braddon 1987 [1862], p. 351. See Clouston 1887, p. 496.

55　See the title of Tilt 1851.

56　Prichard 1835, pp. 12–13.

57　Braddon 1987 [1862], p. 353. See Maudsley 1895, p. 541.

58　Braddon 1987 [1862], p. 297.

59　Prichard 1835, p. 24. See also Bucknill and Tuke 1858, p. 329.

60　Braddon 1987 [1862], p. 78. In Jezbel's Daughter, this role is played by the simple-minded Jack, who possesses 'the dog's enviable faculty of distinguishing correctly between people who are, and the people who are not, their true friends' (p. 153).

61　See, for example, 'magic power of fascination' (p. 6), 'witchery' (p. 222), 'syren' (p. 283) and 'mermaid' (p. 321).

62 Braddon 1987 [1862], pp. 273, 391.

63 ibid., p. 377. The gist of this statement is continuously echoed by twentieth century researchers, who claim that 'Lady Audley's real secret is that she is *sane* and moreover, representative' (Showalter 1977, p. 167; original emphasis). See also Rance 1991, p. 121; Pykett 1992, p. 94; Cvetkovich 1992, p. 48.

64 Braddon 1987 [1862], pp. 379, 381.

65 Braddon 1998 [1861–2], p. 121.

66 ibid., p. 99.

67 For example, ibid., pp. 402, 426, 577.

68 Reade 1914 [1863], p. 610.

Chapter 15 Night Terrors: Medical and Literary Representations of Childhood Fear

1 Freud 1953, p. 173.

2 Jameson 2000, p. 77.

3 ibid.

4 Brontë 2000a [1847], p. 7.

5 Jameson 2000 [1854], p. 80.

6 ibid., p. 81.

7 ibid.

8 De Vere 1851, p. 71.

9 ibid.

10 Barlow 1843. The book, based on a lecture given by the Reverend Barlow to the Royal Institution, was then published in a cheap, accessible edition for general readers ('Small Books on Great Subjects').

11 ibid., p. 12. The classic case used in virtually all discussions of this subject was that of a bookseller, Nicolai of Berlin, who was subject to visitations from various apparitions, but realized they were delusions, and so kept his sanity. See Conolly 1964 [1830], p. 109.

12 Jameson 2000 [1854], p. 81.

13 Brontë 2000a [1847], p. 17.

14 See Martineau 1877, vol. 2, p. 324. For further details, see the Introduction to Brontë 2000a [1847], pp. x–xi. The essays which were to form *Household Education* were partially serialized in the *People's Journal*, 1846–7.

15 Martineau 1849, p. 90.

16 ibid.

17 ibid., p. 99.

18 See, for example, Graham 1826, which was owned, and frequently consulted, by the Brontë family.

19 See Macnish 1830, p. 55.

20 ibid.

21 Macnish's work formed part of extensive investigations into the phenomena of visions, dreams and apparitions in the early-Victorian period, from David Brewster's *Letters on Natural Magic* (1835) and John Abercrombie's *Inquiries Concerning the Intellectual Powers and Investigation of Truth* (1843) to the more down-market *The Night Side of Nature* (1848) by Catherine Crowe.

22 Macnish 1830, p. 136.

23 See Dickens 1988 [1850–2], pp. 276–7. Dickens owned the later 1838 edition of
    The Philosophy of Sleep. For a discussion of the Reverend Brontë's annotations in
    his copy of *Modern Domestic Medicine* see Shuttleworth 1996, ch. 2.

24 Discussions of bad dreams in childhood had figured periodically, however, from
    Hippocrates onwards. See Walk 1964, p. 754.

25 For an account of Charles Dickens's support of the hospital, see Kosky 1989.
    Dickens wrote a strong appeal on behalf of the hospital, 'Drooping Buds', which
    was published in *Household Words* on April 3, 1852, shortly after the hospital
    opened (ibid., ch. 8). He continued his involvement, with an impassioned speech
    at a fund-raising dinner in 1858 (ibid., ch. 10). Unfortunately, there are no surviving
    records of any discussions between Charles West and Dickens on the subject of
    childhood illnesses.

26 West 1848, p. 127.

27 Even Macnish, who had imbibed many more Romantic attitudes to dreaming,
    believing that 'Dreams are the media under which imagination unfolds the ample
    stores of its richly decorated empire' (1830, p. 96), also invoked the digestive
    processes as a form of explanation: 'Why are literary men, deep thinkers, and
    hypochondriacs peculiarly subject to night-mare? The cause is obvious. Such
    individuals have generally a bad digestion' (ibid., p. 143). Explanations of dreams
    based on digestive disorders can be traced back to classical times. See Ford 1998,
    pp. 10–17.

28 See, for example, Tanner 1858, pp. 276-9.

29 West 1854, p. 188. Emphasis in original.

30 ibid., p. 189.

31 ibid.

32 Prichard 1998 [1835], p. 252. Interestingly, although West arrived at this theory
    of childhood mental disorder through his analysis of night terrors, it is a form that
    Prichard defines as existing independently of any insane illusion or hallucination.

33 Brontë herself was, of course, aware of the category of moral insanity, writing in
    one of her letters that Bertha Mason was an example of 'moral madness': Brontë
    2000b [1848–51], p. 3: letter to W S Williams, January 4, 1848.

34 See Jameson 1854, p. 112: Martineau 1849, pp. 166, 172.

35 See Kucich 1994 for an exploration of the Victorian preoccupation with lying.

36 Browne 1860, pp. 304–5, 303–4, 313. It is not clear which edition of the West he
    used; his details on Hartley Coleridge were drawn from the *Edinburgh Review*
    article cited above.

37 See Ford 1988.

38 See Edgeworth 1999, pp. 167–8. Logan 1997, ch. 5, offers a very sophisticated
    reading of *Harrington*, linking it to Dugald Stewart's theories of the 'contagion of
    sympathetic imitation' (p. 120).

39 Edgeworth 1999, p. 169.

40 For a short discussion of associationism, its reworking in the Victorian period,
    and a selection of primary texts, see Taylor and Shuttleworth (eds) 1998, pp. 65–162.

41 John Locke, in *Some Thoughts Concerning Education*, had blamed childhood fears
    on wicked nurses and servants 'whose usual method is to awe children and keep
    them in subjection by telling them of Raw Head and Bloody Bones, and such
    other names as carry with them the idea of something terrible and hurtful, which

they have reason to be afraid of when alone, especially in the dark' (Locke 1989, sect. 138).

42 Martineau 1849, p. 98.

43 Mary Poovey has discussed the transgressive force of the figure of the governess who simultaneously entered the domain of paid employment but also took over the roles of the mother within the home; see Poovey 1989, ch. 5, 'The Anathematized Race: The Governess and *Jane Eyre*'. Similar arguments can be made with reference to the nurse who also, in the case of the wet-nurse, takes on the most intimate physical role of motherhood.

44 The essay, first published in *All the Year Round* in 1860, formed part of Charles Dickens's collection, *The Uncommercial Traveller*, published subsequently in that year: Dickens 1958 [1860], p. 150.

45 ibid., p. 156.

46 Lamb 1968 [1903], pp. 67–8. The book referred to was Thomas Stackhouse, *New History of the Holy Bible from the Beginning of the World to the Establishment of Christianity* (1737).

47 ibid., p. 68.

48 ibid., pp. 67–8, 68. Coleridge had similarly turned to a theory of dreams that relied on the notion of forms external to the individual mind, drawing on Andrew Baxter's *Enquiry into the Nature of the Human Soul* (1737), which suggested that beings or spirits enter the mind during sleep. See Ford 1998, pp. 18–22.

49 Carter 1855, p. 196.

50 ibid., p. 343.

51 ibid., p. 345.

52 Darwin 1877, p. 288. The notes for this article were originally written nearly forty years before, in 1839–42, in his notebook recording the development of his son, William. In the original note, written on April 2, 1842, Darwin noted his 'instinctive feeling of fear'. Although he does not explicitly assign it to an inherited instinct, he suggests '[t]his fear has certainly come without any experience of danger or hurt, & may be compared to young mice trembling at a cat the first time, they see one'. The original notebook is reprinted in Darwin 1988 [1847–50], pp. 410–33: 'Appendix III, Darwin's Observations on His Children'; here: p. 422.

53 Sully 1887 [1881], p. 281.

54 Sully 1993 [1895], pp. 208–9, 213–14.

55 ibid., pp. 220–1.

56 See Grand 1980 [1897], pp. 27–8.

57 Sully 1993 [1895], p. 226.

58 Addington 1917, pp. 243, 261.

Chapter 16 Sensuous Knowledge

1 Melville 1967 [1851], p. 348.

2 ibid., p. 245.

3 ibid., p. 320.

4 ibid., p. 349.

5 I have discussed this extensively in *The Victorians and the Visual Imagination* (Cambridge: Cambridge University Press, 2000), where I make the point of arguing,

however, that the Victorian fascination with the visible went hand in hand with a compelling concern about what one could *not* see. Melville, with his endless associative and metaphysical play around whales and whiteness – notoriously both 'the visible absence of color, and at the same time the concrete of all colors' (ch. 42) – could hardly have dissented. The extension of my concern in this book – the simultaneous recognition of the importance of the senses as a whole to the Victorians, and yet a recognition of the information they could not deliver – underpins my argument here.

6   [Carlill, J B] J. B. C. 1893, p. 438.
7   Burgin 1996, p. 129.
8   Connor 2000, p. 3.
9   See ibid.
10   Trotter 2000.
11   Sully 1878, p. 710.
12   Gurney 1880, p. 37.
13   Smith 1999, p. 6.
14   Tyndall 1875 [1867], p. 48.
15   Simmel 1997 [1907], p. 111.
16   ibid., pp. 118–19. I have elaborated on the effects of sound, and on changing attitudes to the auditory world in Flint 2003, from which I have drawn some of the materials in this paragraph.
17   Dickens 1999 [1861], p. 117.
18   Ackerman 1995 [1990], p. xvi.
19   Hardy 1912 [1881], p. 444. I am indebted to Megan Ward for this reference.
20   Classen 1993, p. 7.
21   Picker 2003; Carlisle 2004.
22   Picker 2003, p. 14.
23   Collins 1999 [1868], p. 351.
24   Meredith 1983 [1862], I.
25   ibid., XLIX.
26   ibid., L.
27   ibid.
28   ibid., XVI.
29   ibid., XLV.
30   ibid., XXII.
31   Collins 1996 [1859–60], p. 50.
32   Brennan 2004, p. 3.
33   ibid., p. 6.
34   ibid., p. 7.
35   ibid., p. 9.
36   ibid.
37   Lewes [1860], vol. 2, p. 38.
38   ibid., p. 49.
39   ibid., p. 40.
40   ibid., pp. 47–8.
41   Sully 1874, p. 37.

Bibliography

Introduction Unmapped Countries: Biology, Literature and Culture in the Nineteenth Century

Works Cited

Primary Literature

Arnold, M, 1974 [1882], 'Literature and Science', in *Matthew Arnold: The Complete Prose*, ed. H R Super, 11 vols, 1960–77, vol. 10, Ann Arbor, University of Michigan Press, pp. 51–73.

Darwin, C, 1996 [1859], *The Origin of Species*, ed. G Beer, Oxford, Oxford University Press.

Eliot, G, 1996 [1871–2], *Middlemarch*, ed. D Carroll, introd. F Bonaparte, Oxford, Oxford University Press.

Eliot, G, 1998 [1876], *Daniel Deronda*, ed. Graham Handley, Oxford, Oxford University Press.

Huxley, T H, 1893 [1880], 'Science and Culture', in *Science and Education: Essays*, London, Macmillan, pp. 134–59.

Spencer, H, 1999 [1857], 'Progress: Its Law and Cause', in *Victorian Prose. An Anthology*, ed. R J Mundhenk and L McCracken Fletcher, New York, Columbia University Press, pp. 295–303.

Virchow, R, 1959, *Disease, Life and Man*, ed. and trans. L J Rather, Stanford, CA, Stanford University Press.

Secondary Literature

Armstrong, C, 2003, *Romantic Organicism*, London, Palgrave.

Bachelard, G, 1934, *Le nouvel esprit scientifique*, Paris, Presses Universitaires de France.

Bachelard, G, 1938, *La formation de l'esprit scientifique*, Paris, Vrin.

Barthes, R, 1967, 'Science versus Literature', *The Times Literary Supplement*, September 28, 98.

Beer, G, 2000 [1983], *Darwin's Plots: Evolutionary Narrative in Darwin, George Eliot and Nineteenth Century Fiction*, Cambridge, Cambridge University Press.

Bowler, P J, 1988, *The Non-Darwinian Revolution: Reinterpreting a Historical Myth*, Baltimore, Johns Hopkins University Press.

Cantor, G, and Shuttleworth, S, eds, 2004, *Science Serialized: Representations of the Sciences in Nineteenth Century Periodicals*, Cambridge, MA, MIT Press.

Carroll, J, 2004, *Literary Darwinism: Evolution, Human Nature, and Literature*, New York, Routledge.

Coleman, W, 1977 [1971], *Biology in the Nineteenth Century: Problems of Form, Function, and Transformation*, Cambridge, Cambridge University Press.

Cordle, D, 1999, *Postmodern Postures: Literature, Science and the Two Cultures Debate*, Aldershot, Ashgate.

Fleck, L, 1935, *Entstehung und Entwicklung einer wissenschaftlichen Tatsache: Einführung in die Lehre vom Denkstil und Denkkollektiv*, Basel, B. Schwabe & Co.

Fleck, L, 1989 [1927–60], *Erfahrung und Tatsache: Gesammelte Aufsätze*, Frankfurt am Main, Suhrkamp.

Foucault, M, 1966, *Les mots et les choses: Archéologie des sciences humaines*, Paris, Gallimard.

Freese, P, 1997, *From Apocalypse to Entropy and Beyond: The Second Law of Thermodynamics in Post-War American Fiction*, Essen, Die Blaue Eule.

Gross, A, 1990, *The Rhetoric of Science*, Cambridge, MA, Harvard University Press.

Hayles, K, ed., 1991, *Chaos and Order: Complex Dynamics in Literature and Science*, Chicago, University of Chicago Press.

Kuhn, T S, 1962, *The Structure of Scientific Revolutions*, Chicago, University of Chicago Press.

Kuhn, T S, 1969, 'Comment', *Comparative Studies in Society and History* 11, 403–12.

Leavis, F R, 1962, 'Two Cultures? The Significance of C P Snow', *The Spectator* No. 6976, 9 March, 297–304.

Lepenies, W, 1983, 'Transformation and Storage of Scientific Traditions in Literature', in *Literature and History*, ed. L Schulze and W Wetzels, Lanham, MD, University Press of America, pp. 37–63.

Levine, G, ed., 1987, *One Culture: Essays in Science and Literature*, Madison, University of Wisconsin Press.

Levine, G, 1988, *Darwin and the Novelists*, Chicago, University of Chicago Press.

Morton, P, 1984, *The Vital Science: Biology and the Literary Imagination, 1860–1900*, London, George Allen & Unwin.

Otis, L, 1994, *Organic Memory: History and the Body in the Late Nineteenth and Early Twentieth Centuries*, Lincoln, University of Nebraska Press.

Otis, L, 1999, *Membranes: Metaphors of Invasion in Nineteenth Century Literature, Science, and Politics*, Baltimore, MD, Johns Hopkins University Press.

Otis, L, 2001, *Networking: Communicating with Bodies and Machines in the Nineteenth Century*, Ann Arbor, University of Michigan Press.

Paradis, J G, 1997, 'Satire and Science in Victorian Culture', in *Victorian Science in Context*, ed. B Lightman, Chicago, University of Chicago Press, pp. 143–75.

Peckham, M, 1959, 'Darwinism and Darwinisticism', *Victorian Studies* 3, 3–40.

Pethes, N, 2003, 'Literatur- und Wissenschaftsgeschichte: Ein Forschungsbericht', *Internationales Archiv für Sozialgeschichte der deutschen Literatur* 28.1, 181–231.

Schaffer, S, and Shapin, S, 1985, *Leviathan and the Air-Pump: Hobbes, Boyle and the Experimental Life*, Princeton, NJ, Princeton University Press.

Schönert, J, 1997, 'Neue Ordnungen im Verhältnis von "schöner Literatur" und Wissenschaft', in *Die Literatur und die Wissenschaften 1770–1930*, ed. K Richter, J Schönert and M Titzmann, Stuttgart, Metzler, pp. 39–48.

Seel, M, 2004, 'Weltverstrickt: Das Verstehen verstehen. Über den Sinn der Geisteswissenschaften', *Die Zeit*, April 22, 48.

Shapin, S, and Barnes, B, 1979, 'Darwin and Social Darwinism: Purity and History', in *Natural Order: Historical Studies of Scientific Culture*, ed. S Shapin and B Barnes, Beverly Hills, CA, Sage Publications, pp. 95–121.

Shapin, S, 1994, *A Social History of Truth: Civility and Science in Seventeenth Century England*, Chicago, University of Chicago Press.

Shuttleworth, S, 1984, *George Eliot and Nineteenth Century Science: The Make-Believe of a Beginning*, Cambridge, Cambridge University Press.

Snow, C P, 1959, *The Two Cultures and the Scientific Revolution*, Cambridge, MA, Harvard University Press.

Snow, C P, 1963, *The Two Cultures: A Second Look*, Cambridge, Cambridge University Press.

Sokal, A, and Bricmont, J, 1998, *Intellectual Impostures: Postmodern Philosophers' Abuse of Science*, London, Profile Books.

Waugh, P, 2004, 'Evolution as Redemption? Scientific Fundamentalism and the Crisis of Value in Literary Culture', *Anglistik: Mitteilungen des Deutschen Anglistenverbandes* 15.1, 63–72.

White, H, 1973, *Metahistory: The Historical Imagination in Nineteenth Century Europe*, Baltimore, MD, Johns Hopkins University Press.

Chapter 1 'This Questionable Little Book': Narrative Ambiguity in Nineteenth Century Literature of Science

Works Cited

Primary Literature

Bentham, J, 1962a [1810?], *An Introductory View of the Rationale of Evidence; For the Use of Non-Lawyers as well as Lawyers*, in *The Works of Jeremy Bentham*, ed. J Bowring, 1838–43, 11 vols, repr. New York, Russell & Russell, vol. 6.

Bentham, J, 1962b [1827], *Rationale of Judicial Evidence, Specially Applied to English Practice*, in *The Works of Jeremy Bentham*, ed. J Bowring, 1838–43, 11 vols, repr. New York, Russell & Russell, vols 6–7.

Buckley, A B, 1878, *The Fairy-Land of Science*, London, Stanford.

Carlyle, T, 2002 [1833–4], *Sartor Resartus: The Life and Opinions of Herr Teufelsdröckh*, ed. A Gray, Edinburgh, Canongate.

Herschel, J, 1851 [1830], *A Preliminary Discourse of the Study of Natural Philosophy*, 2nd ed., London, Longman, Brown, Green & Longmans.

Huxley, T H, 1893, *Collected Essays*, 9 vols, London, Macmillan.

Kingsley, C, 1880, *The Works of Charles Kingsley*, 1880–5, 28 vols, vol. 19: *Scientific Lectures and Essays*, London, Macmillan.

Kingsley, C, 1994 [1863], *The Water Babies: A Fairy Tale for a Landbaby*, Ware, Hertfordshire, Wordsworth.

Masson, D, 1859, *British Novelists and Their Styles: Being a Critical Sketch of the History of British Prose Fiction*, Cambridge, Macmillan.

Poe, E A, 1994, *Selected Tales by Edgar Allan Poe*, London, Penguin.

Shelley, M, 1994 [1818], *Frankenstein, or, the Modern Prometheus*, ed. M Butler, Oxford, Oxford University Press.

Weber, A S, ed., 2000, *Nineteenth Century Science: A Selection of Original Texts*, Peterborough, Ontario, Broadview.

Wells, H G, 1995 [1895], *The Time Machine*, London, Dent.

Whewell, W, 2000 [1847], *The Philosophy of the Inductive Sciences, Founded Upon Their History*, 2nd ed., 2 vols, in *Nineteenth Century Science: A Selection of Original Texts*, ed. A S Weber, Peterborough, Ontario, Broadview, pp. 174–89.

Secondary Literature

Aczel, R, 1998, 'Hearing Voices in Narrative Texts', *New Literary History* 29, 467–500.

Bakhtin, M, 1981, *The Dialogic Imagination: Four Essays by M. M. Bakhtin*, trans. C Emerson, ed. M Holquist, Austin, University of Texas Press.

Banfield, A, 1982, *Unspeakable Sentences: Narration and Representation in the Language of Fiction*, London, Routledge & Kegan Paul.

Butler, M, 1994, 'Introduction' and 'The *Quarterly Review* and Radical Science, 1819', in Shelley, M, *Frankenstein, or, the Modern Prometheus*, ed. M Butler, Oxford, Oxford University Press, pp. ix–li, 229–51.

Clarke, G, ed., 1991, *Edgar Allan Poe: Critical Assessments*, 4 vols, Sussex, Helm.

David, D, ed., 2001, *The Cambridge Companion to the Victorian Novel*, Cambridge, Cambridge University Press.

Desmond, A, 1989, *The Politics of Evolution*, Chicago, University of Chicago Press.

Eco, U, and Sebeok, T A, eds, 1983, *The Sign of Three: Dupin, Holmes, Peirce*, Bloomington, Indiana University Press.

Eliot, S, 2001, 'The Business of Victorian Publishing', in *The Cambridge Companion to the Victorian Novel*, ed. D David, Cambridge, Cambridge University Press, pp. 37–59.

Flint, K, 1993, *The Woman Reader, 1837–1914*, Oxford, Oxford University Press.

Flint, K, 2001, 'The Victorian Novel and Its Readers', in *The Cambridge Companion to the Victorian Novel*, ed. D David, Cambridge, Cambridge University Press, pp. 17–36.

Fludernik, M, 2001, 'New Wine in Old Bottles? Voice, Focalization, and New Writing', *New Literary History* 32, 619–38.

Frasca-Spada, M, and Jardine, N, eds, 2000, *Books and the Sciences in History*, Cambridge, Cambridge University Press.

Genette, G, 1980, *Narrative Discourse: An Essay in Method*, trans. J E Lewin, Ithaca, NY, Cornell University Press.

Gray, A, 2002, 'Introduction', in Carlyle, T, *Sartor Resartus: The Life and Opinions of Herr Teufelsdröckh*, ed. A Gray, Edinburgh, Canongate, pp. xxi–xxii.

Harrowitz, N, 1983, 'The Body of the Detective Model: Charles S. Peirce and Edgar Allan Poe', in *The Sign of Three: Dupin, Holmes, Peirce*, ed. U Eco and T A Sebeok, Bloomington, Indiana University Press, pp. 179–97.

Hulme, P, and Youngs, T, eds, 2002, *The Cambridge Companion to Travel Writing*, Cambridge, Cambridge University Press.

McKeon, M, 1988, *The Origins of the English Novel, 1600–1740*, London, Radius.

Morrell, J, and Thackray, A, 1981, *Gentlemen of Science: Early Years of the British Association for the Advancement of Science*, Oxford, Clarendon Press.

Morrell, J, 1997, *Science, Culture and Politics in Britain, 1750–1870*, Aldershot, Ashgate.

Morus, I, 1992, 'Different Experimental Lives: Michael Faraday and William Sturgeon', *History of Science* 30, 1–28.

Morus, I, ed., 2002, *Bodies/Machines*, Oxford, Berg.

Page, N, ed., 1974, *Wilkie Collins: The Critical Heritage*, London, Routledge & Kegan Paul.

Pratt, M L, 1992, *Imperial Eyes: Travel Writing and Transculturation*, London, Routledge.

Pykett, L, 1994, *The Sensation Novel: From* The Woman in White *to* The Moonstone, Plymouth, Northcote House.

Richards, J L, 1996, 'Observing Science in Early Victorian England: Recent Scholarship on William Whewell', *Perspectives on Science* 4, 231–47.

Ryan, S, 1996, *The Cartographic Eye: How Explorers Saw Australia*, Cambridge, Cambridge University Press.

Shapin, S, 1994, *A Social History of Truth: Civility and Science in Seventeenth Century England*, Chicago, University of Chicago Press.

Shires, L M, 2001, 'The Aesthetics of the Victorian Novel: Form, Subjectivity, Ideology', in *The Cambridge Companion to the Victorian Novel*, ed. D David, Cambridge, Cambridge University Press, pp. 61–76.

Sleigh, C, 1998, 'Life, Death and Galvanism', *Studies in History and Philosophy of Biological and Biomedical Sciences* 29C, 219–48.

Stanzel, F K, 1984, *A Theory of Narrative*, Cambridge, Cambridge University Press.

Thompson, G R, ed., 1984, *Edgar Allan Poe: Essays and Reviews*, New York, Library of America.

Watt, I, 1964, *The Rise of the Novel: Studies in Defoe, Richardson and Fielding*, 2nd ed., Berkeley, University of California Press.

Wheeler, M, 1985, *English Fiction of the Victorian Period, 1830–1890*, London, Longman.

Whitworth, M, 2001, *Einstein's Wake: Relativity, Metaphor, and Modernist Literature*, Oxford, Oxford University Press.

Yeo, R, 1993, *Defining Science: William Whewell, Natural Knowledge, and Public Debate in Early Victorian Britain*, Cambridge, Cambridge University Press.

Chapter 2   Vestiges of English Literature: Robert Chambers

Works Cited

Primary Literature

Chambers, R, 1822, 'Vindication of the World and of Providence', *The Kaleidoscope; or, Edinburgh Literary Amusement. A Periodical Miscellany, Chiefly Humorous* 8, 12 January, 123–7, repr. in R Chambers, 1994, *Vestiges of the Natural History of Creation and Other Evolutionary Writings*, ed. J A Secord, Chicago, University of Chicago Press, pp. 199–203.

Chambers, R, 1836, *History of English Language and Literature*, Edinburgh, William & Robert Chambers.

Chambers, R, 1844, *Vestiges of the Natural History of Creation*, London, John Churchill.

Darwin, C, 1996 [1859], *The Origin of Species*, ed. G Beer, Oxford, Oxford University Press.

Ireland, A, 1884, 'Introduction to the Twelfth Edition', in R Chambers, *Vestiges of the Natural History of Creation*, 12th ed., London, William & Robert Chambers, pp. vii–xxxi.

Jeffrey, F, 1811, 'Art. I. The Dramatic Works of John Ford ...', *Edinburgh Review* 18, 275–304.

Secondary Literature

Beer, G, 2000 [1983], *Darwin's Plots: Evolutionary Narrative in Darwin, George Eliot and Nineteenth Century Fiction*, Cambridge, Cambridge University Press.

Blumenberg, H, 2000, *Die Lesbarkeit der Welt*, 5th ed., Frankfurt am Main, Suhrkamp.

Glass, B, Temkin, O, and Straus, W, eds, 1959, *Forerunners of Darwin: 1745–1859*, Baltimore, MD, Johns Hopkins University Press.

Secord, J A, 1997, 'Introduction', in C Lyell, *Principles of Geology*, ed. J A Secord, London, Penguin, pp. ix–xliv.

Secord, J A, 2000, *Victorian Sensation: The Extraordinary Publication, Reception, and Secret Authorship of* Vestiges of the Natural History of Creation, Chicago, University of Chicago Press.

Sichert, M, 2003, 'Functionalizing Cultural Memory: Foundational British Literary History and the Construction of National Identity', *Modern Language Quarterly* 64.2, 199–217.

Stierstorfer, K, 2001, *Konstruktion literarischer Vergangenheit: Die englische Literaturgeschichte von Warton bis Courthope und Ward*, Heidelberg, Universitätsverlag C Winter.

Chapter 3   Aestheticism, Immorality and the Reception of Darwinism in Victorian Britain

Works Cited

Primary Literature

[Baynes, T S], 1871, 'Swinburne's *Poems*', *Edinburgh Review* 134, 71–99.

[Baynes, T S], 1873, 'Darwin on *Expression*', *Edinburgh Review* 137, 492–528.

[Chapman, J], 1861, 'Equatorial Africa, and Its Inhabitants', *Westminster Review* 20 n.s., 137–87.

[Dallas, W S], 1872, 'The Descent of Man', *Westminster Review* 42 n.s., 378–400.

Darwin, C, 1871, *The Descent of Man and Selection in Relation to Sex*, 2 vols, London, John Murray.

Darwin, C, 1983 –, *The Correspondence of Charles Darwin*, 13 vols to date, ed. F H Burkhardt *et al.*, Cambridge, Cambridge University Press.

Darwin, C, 1994, *A Calendar of the Correspondence of Charles Darwin, 1821–1882, with Supplement*, ed. F H Burkhardt and S Smith, Cambridge, Cambridge University Press.

Darwin, C, 2004 [1871], *The Descent of Man*, ed. J Moore and A Desmond, London, Penguin.

Darwin, F, ed., 1887, *The Life and Letters of Charles Darwin*, 3 vols, London, John Murray.

[Dawkins, W B], 1871, 'Darwin on the *Descent of Man*', *Edinburgh Review* 134, 195–235.

[Hedley, J C], 1871, 'Evolution and Faith', *Dublin Review* 17 n.s., 1–40.

Huxley, T H, 1894, *Evolution and Ethics*, London, Macmillan.

Laughton, J K, 1898, *Memoirs of the Life and Correspondence of Henry Reeve*, 2 vols, London, Longmans, Green.

[Leifchild, J R], 1871, '[Review of] *The Descent of Man and Selection in Relation to Sex* by Charles Darwin', *Athenaeum*, 275–7.

Mivart, St G J, 1873, 'Contemporary Evolution', *Contemporary Review* 22, 595–614.

[Mivart, St G J], 1874, 'Primitive Man: Tylor and Lubbock', *Quarterly Review* 137, 40–77.

[Morley, J], 1866, 'Mr. Swinburne's New Poems', *Saturday Review* 22, 145–7.

[Reeve, H], 1874, 'Mill's *Essays on Theism*', *Edinburgh Review* 141, 1–31.

Swinburne, A C, 1866, *Poems and Ballads*, London, Edward Moxon.

Swinburne, A C, 1871, *Songs Before Sunrise*, London, F S Ellis.

Swinburne, A C, 1888, 'Dethroning Tennyson: A Contribution to the Tennyson-Darwin Controversy', *Nineteenth Century* 23, 127–9.

[Tennyson, A], 1850, *In Memoriam*, London, Edward Moxon.

Tennyson, A, 1859, *Idylls of the King*, London, Edward Moxon.

Waitz, T, 1863, *Introduction to Anthropology*, trans. J F Collingwood, London, Longman.

Secondary Literature

Beer, G, 1996, *Open Fields: Science in Cultural Encounter*, Oxford, Clarendon Press.

Browne, J, 2002, *Charles Darwin: The Power of Place*, London, Jonathan Cape.

Dawson, G, 2003, 'Intrinsic Earthliness: Science, Materialism and the Fleshly School of Poetry', *Victorian Poetry* 41, 113–29.

Desmond, A, and Moore, J, 1991, *Darwin*, London, Michael Joseph.

Levine, G, ed., 1987, *One Culture: Essays in Science and Literature*, Madison, University of Wisconsin Press.

Rooksby, R, 1997, *A. C. Swinburne: A Poet's Life*, Aldershot, Scolar Press.

Secord, J A, 2000, *Victorian Sensation: The Extraordinary Publication, Reception, and Secret Authorship of* Vestiges of the Natural History of Creation, Chicago, University of Chicago Press.

Small, H, 1994, '"In the Guise of Science": Literature and the Rhetoric of Nineteenth Century English Psychiatry', *History of the Human Sciences* 7, 27–55.

Yeazell, R B, 1991, *Fictions of Modesty: Women and Courtship in the English Novel*, Chicago, University of Chicago Press.

Chapter 4   Constructing Darwinism in Literary Culture

Works Cited

Primary Literature

Bierbower, A, 1894, *From Monkey to Man; or, Society in the Tertiary Age. A Story of the Missing Link Showing the First Steps in Industry, etc*, Chicago, Dibble Publishing Co.

Darwin, C, 1964 [1859], *On the Origin of Species by Means of Natural Selection, or the Preservation of Favoured Races in the Struggle for Life*, facsimile edn., introd. E Mayr, Cambridge, MA, Harvard University Press.

Darwin, C, 1981 [1871], *The Descent of Man and Selection in Relation to Sex*, 2 vols, facsimile edn., introd. J T Bonner and R M May, Princeton, NY, Princeton University Press.

Potterkin, J [pseud], 1876, *Two 'Missing Links'; or, the Homokins and the Kamons. An Account of Some Wonderful Discoveries Recently Made in Central Africa, by Jonas Potterkin, Esq., Fellow of the Society for the Propagation of Impossible Theories. By W. A. B.*, Uttoxeter, Ryder.

White, R G, 1871, *The Fall of Man, or the Loves of the Gorillas, A Popular Scientific Lecture upon the Darwinian Theory of Development by Sexual Selection, by a Learned Gorilla*, New York, Carleton & Co., London, S Low & Co.

Zola, E, 2000 [1893], *Doctor Pascal, or Life and Heredity*, trans. E A Vizetelly, Stroud, Gloucestershire, Sutton Publishing Ltd.

Secondary Literature

Altick, R D, 1978, *The Shows of London*, Cambridge, MA, Harvard University Press.

Amigoni, D, and Wallace, J, eds, 1995, *Charles Darwin's* The Origin of Species: *New Interdisciplinary Essays*, Manchester, Manchester University Press.

Bederman, G, 1995, *Manliness and Civilization: A Cultural History of Gender and Race in the United States, 1880–1917*, Chicago, University of Chicago Press.

Beer, G, 1983, *Darwin's Plots: Evolutionary Narrative in Darwin, George Eliot and Nineteenth Century Fiction*, London and Boston, MA, Routledge & Kegan Paul.

Beer, G, 1996, *Open Fields: Science in Cultural Encounter*, Oxford, Clarendon Press.

Bender, B, 1996, *The Descent of Love: Darwin and the Theory of Sexual Selection in American Fiction, 1871–1926*, Philadelphia, University of Pennsylvania Press.

Bloomfield, P, 1932, *Imaginary Worlds, or, the Evolution of Utopia*, London, Hamish Hamilton.

Bondeson, J, 1997, *A Cabinet of Medical Curiosities*, Ithaca, NY, Cornell University Press.

Bowler, P J, 1983, *The Eclipse of Darwinism: Anti-Darwinian Evolution Theories in the Decades around 1900*, Baltimore, MD, Johns Hopkins University Press.

Bowler, P J, 1986, *Theories of Human Evolution: a Century of Debate, 1844–1944*, Baltimore, MD, Johns Hopkins University Press.

Bowler, P J, 1988, *The Non-Darwinian Revolution: Reinterpreting a Historical Myth*, Baltimore, MD, Johns Hopkins University Press.

Bowler, P J, 1989, *The Invention of Progress: The Victorians and the Past*, Oxford, Basil Blackwell.

Bowler, P J, 2003, *Evolution: The History of an Idea*, 3rd edn., completely rev. and expanded, Berkeley, University of California Press.

Brooke, J H, 1991, *Science and Religion: Some Historical Perspectives*, Cambridge, Cambridge University Press.

Brooke, J H, and Cantor, G N, 1998, *Reconstructing Nature: The Engagement of Science and Religion*, Edinburgh, T & T Clark.

Browne, J, 1995, *Charles Darwin: Voyaging*, New York, Knopf.

Browne, J, 2001, 'Darwin in Caricature: A Study in the Popularization and Dissemination of Evolution', *Proceedings of the American Philosophical Society* 145, 496–509.

Browne, J, 2002, *Charles Darwin: The Power of Place*, New York, Knopf.

Browne, J, and Messenger, S, 2003, 'Victorian Spectacle: Julia Pastrana, the Bearded and Hairy Female', *Endeavour* 27:4, 155–9.

Burrow, J, 1966, *Evolution and Society: A Study in Victorian Social Theory*, Cambridge, Cambridge University Press.

Budd, M A, 1997, *The Sculpture Machine: Physical Culture and Body Politics in the Age of Empire*, Basingstoke, Macmillan.

Bury, J B, 1920, *The Idea of Progress: An Inquiry into Its Origin and Growth*, London, Macmillan.

Campbell, M B, 1999, *Wonder and Science: Imagining Worlds in Early Modern Europe*, Ithaca, NY, Cornell University Press.

Chamberlin, J E, and Gilman, S L, eds, 1985, *Degeneration: The Dark Side of Progress*, New York, Columbia University Press.

Childs, D J, 2001, *Modernism and Eugenics: Woolf, Eliot, Yeats, and the Culture of Degeneration*, Cambridge, Cambridge University Press.

Christie, J, and Shuttleworth, S, eds, 1989, *Nature Transfigured: Science and Literature, 1700–1900*, Manchester, Manchester University Press.

Corsi, P, 1988, *Science and Religion: Baden-Powell and the Anglican Debate, 1800–1860*, Cambridge, Cambridge University Press.

Crowe, M J, 1986, *The Extraterrestrial Life Debate, 1750–1900: The Idea of a Plurality of Worlds from Kant to Lowell*, Cambridge, Cambridge University Press.

Darbouze, G, 1997, *Dégénérescence et régénérescence dans l'oeuvre d'Émile Zola et celle de Manuel Zeno Gandía: étude comparée*, New York, Peter Lang.

Davis, J C, 1981, *Utopia and the Ideal Society: A Study of English Utopian Writing 1516–1700*, Cambridge, Cambridge University Press.

Desmond, A J, 1994, *Huxley: The Devil's Disciple*, London, Michael Joseph.

Desmond, A J, 1997, *Huxley: Evolution's High Priest*, London, Michael Joseph.

Desmond, A J, and Moore, J R, 1991, *Darwin*, London, Michael Joseph.

Dick, S J, 1982, *Plurality of Worlds: The Origins of the Extraterrestrial Life Debate from Democritus to Kant*, Cambridge, Cambridge University Press.

Dowbiggin, I R, 1991, *Inheriting Madness: Professionalisation and Psychiatric Knowledge in Nineteenth Century France*, Berkeley, University of California Press.

Driver, F, 1999, *Geography Militant: Cultures of Exploration in the Age of Empire*, Oxford, Blackwell.

Dutton, K R, 1995, *The Perfectible Body: The Western Ideal of Physical Development*, London, Dutton.

Dzwonkosi, P, ed., 1986, *American Literary Publishing Houses, 1638–1899*, Michigan, Bruccoli Clark.

Ellegard, A, 1990, *Darwin and the General Reader: The Reception of Darwin's Theory of Evolution in the British Periodical Press, 1859–1872*, repr. ed. Chicago, University of Chicago Press.

Frey, J A, 1978, *The Aesthetics of the Rougon-Macquart*, Madrid, J Porrúa Turanzas.

Greenslade, W, 1994, *Degeneration, Culture and the Novel, 1880–1940*, Cambridge, Cambridge University Press.

Gylseth, C H, and Toverud, L O, 2003, *Julia Pastrana: The Tragic Story of the Victorian Ape Woman*, trans. D Tumasonis, Stroud, Sutton.

Hall, D E, ed., 1994, *Muscular Christianity: Embodying the Victorian Age*, Cambridge, Cambridge University Press.

Hexter, J H, 1952, *More's Utopia: The Biography of an Idea*, Princeton, NJ, Princeton University Press.

Hodge, J, and Radick, G, eds, 2003, *The Cambridge Companion to Darwin*, Cambridge, Cambridge University Press.

Holtsmark, E B, 1981, *Tarzan and Tradition: Classical Myth in Popular Literature*, Westport, CT, Greenwood Press.

Huntington, J, 1982, *The Logic of Fantasy: H G Wells and Science Fiction*, Guildford, NY, Columbia University Press.

Hurley, K, 1997, *The Gothic Body: Sexuality, Materialism, and Degeneration at the Fin de Siècle*, Cambridge, Cambridge University Press.

Jann, R, 1994, 'Darwin and the Anthropologists: Sexual Selection and Its Discontents', *Victorian Studies* 37, 287–306.

Janson, H W, 1952, *Apes and Ape Lore in the Middle Ages and the Renaissance*, London, Warburg Institute, University of London.

Jardine, N, Secord, J A, and Spary, E, eds, 1996, *Cultures of Natural History*, Cambridge, Cambridge University Press.

Jay, M, and Neve, M, eds, 1999, *1900: a Fin-de-Siècle Reader*, London, Penguin.

Jones, G, 1980, *Social Darwinism and English Thought: The Interaction between Biological and Social Theory*, Sussex, Harvester Press.

Kaye, R A, 2002, *The Flirt's Tragedy: Desire without End in Victorian and Edwardian Fiction*, Charlottesville, University Press of Virginia.

Kelly, A, 1981, *The Descent of Darwin: The Popularization of Darwinism in Germany, 1860–1914*, Chapel Hill, University of North Carolina Press.

Kemp, P, 1982, *H G Wells and the Culminating Ape: Biological Themes and Imaginative Obsessions*, London, Macmillan.

Kevles, D J, 1995, *In the Name of Eugenics: Genetics and the Uses of Human Heredity*, rev. edn., Cambridge, MA, Harvard University Press.

Knapp, J, 1994, *An Empire Nowhere: England, America, and Literature from* Utopia *to* The Tempest, Berkeley, University of California Press.

Kohn, D, ed., 1985, *The Darwinian Heritage*, Princeton, NJ, Princeton University Press in association with Nova Pacifica.

Lightman, B, ed., 1997, *Victorian Science in Context*, Chicago, University of Chicago Press.

Lindberg, D, and Numbers, R, eds, 1986, *God and Nature: Historical Essays on the Encounter between Christianity and Science*, Berkeley, University of California Press.

Livingstone, D N, 2003, *Putting Science in Its Place: Geographies of Scientific Knowledge*, Chicago, University of Chicago Press.

Mangum, T, 1998, *Married, Middle-Brow and Militant: Sarah Grand and the New Woman Novel*, Ann Arbor, University of Michigan Press.

Manuel, F E, and Manuel, F P, 1979, *Utopian Thought in the Western World*, Oxford, Basil Blackwell.

Margolis, J, 2000, *A Brief History of Tomorrow*, London, Bloomsbury.

Mayr, E, 1991, *One Long Argument: Charles Darwin and the Genesis of Modern Evolutionary Thought*, Cambridge, MA, Harvard University Press.

McCook, S, 1996, '"It may be truth, but it is not evidence": Paul Du Chaillu and the Legitimation of Evidence in the Field Sciences', *Osiris* 11, 177–97.

Mendelsohn, E, and Nowotny, H, eds, 1984, *Nineteen Eighty-Four: Science between Utopia and Dystopia*, Dordrecht, Reidel.

Moore, J R, 1979, *The Post-Darwinian Controversies*, Cambridge, Cambridge University Press.

Morton, P, 1984, *The Vital Science: Biology and the Literary Imagination, 1860–1900*, London, George Allen & Unwin.

Moscucci, O, 1990, *The Science of Women, Gynaecology and Gender in England, 1800–1929*, Cambridge, Cambridge University Press.

Navarette, S J, 1998, *The Shape of Fear: Horror and the Fin-de-Siècle Culture of Decadence*, Lexington, University Press of Kentucky.

Nye, R, 1984, *Crime, Madness and Politics in Modern France: The Medical Concept of National Decline*, Princeton, NJ, Princeton University Press.

Oldroyd, D, and Langham, I, eds, 1983, *The Wider Domain of Evolutionary Thought*, Dordrecht, Reidel.

Parrinder, P, 1997, 'Eugenics and Utopia: Sexual Selection from Galton to Morris', *Utopian Studies: Journal of the Society for Utopian Studies 8, 1–12.

Passmore, J, 1970, *The Perfectibility of Man*, London, Duckworth.

Peel, R A, ed., 1998, *Essays in the History of Eugenics*, London, The Galton Institute.

Pick, D, 1989, *Faces of Degeneration: A European Disorder, c.1848–c.1918*, Cambridge, Cambridge University Press.

Pollard, P, ed., 1995, *Émile Zola Centenary Colloquium 1893–1993: London, 23–25 September 1993*, London, Émile Zola Society.

Porter, R, 2001, 'The Wilkins Lecture 2000: Medical Futures', *Notes & Records of the Royal Society of London 55, 309–29.

Richardson, A, 1999, 'The Eugenisation of Love: Sarah Grand and the Morality of Genealogy', *Victorian Studies 42, 227–55.

Richardson, A, and Willis, C, eds, 2000, *The New Woman in Fiction and in Fact: Fin-de-Siècle Feminisms*, London, Macmillan.

Rosen, G, 1946, 'Medicine in Utopia, from the Eighteenth Century to the Present', *Ciba Symposium 7, 188–200.

Ruse, M, 1999, *The Darwinian Revolution: Science Red in Tooth and Claw*, 2nd edn., Chicago, University of Chicago Press.

Schiebinger, L, 1993, *Nature's Body: Sexual Politics and the Making of Modern Science*, London, Pandora.

Schwartz, W B, 1998, *Life without Disease: The Pursuit of Medical Utopia*, Berkeley, University of California Press.

Searle, G, 1976, *Eugenics and Politics in Britain, 1900–1914*, Leyden, Noordhoff.

Shapin, S, 1994, *A Social History of Truth: Gentility, Credibility and Scientific Knowledge in Seventeenth Century England*, Chicago, University of Chicago Press.

Snigurowicz, D, 1999, 'Sex, Simians, and Spectacle in Nineteenth Century France; or, How to Tell a "Man" from a Monkey', *Canadian Journal of History 34, 51–81.

Tompkins, P, 1994, *The Monkey in Art*, New York, Scala Books.

Turner, F M, 1974, *Between Science and Religion*, New Haven, CT, Yale University Press.

Turner, F M, 1993, *Contesting Cultural Authority: Essays in Victorian Cultural Life*, Cambridge, Cambridge University Press.

Webster, C, 1981, ed., *Biology, Medicine and Society, 1840–1940*, Cambridge, Cambridge University Press.

Wilson, A N, 1999, *God's Funeral*, London, John Murray.

Yeazell, R B, ed., 1986, *Sex, Politics, and Science in the Nineteenth Century Novel*, Baltimore, MD, Johns Hopkins University Press.

Young, R M, 1985, *Darwin's Metaphor: Nature's Place in Victorian Culture*, Cambridge, Cambridge University Press.

Zuckerman, S, 1998, *The Ape in Myth and Art*, London, Verdigris.

Chapter 5   Close Encounters with a New Species: Darwin's Clash with the Feminists at the End of the Nineteenth Century

Works Cited

Primary Literature

Corelli, M, 1905, *Free Opinions Freely Expressed*, London, Archibald Constable & Company.

Darwin, C, 1964 [1859], *On the Origin of Species by Means of Natural Selection, or the Preservation of Favoured Races in the Struggle for Life*, facsimile edn., introd. E Mayr, Cambridge, MA, Harvard University Press.

Darwin, C, 1998 [1874], *The Descent of Man and Selection in Relation to Sex*, 2nd edn., New York, Prometheus Books.

Eliot, G, 1956 [1871–2], *Middlemarch*, London, J M Dent & Sons Ltd.

Eliot, G, 1979 [1876], *Daniel Deronda*, New York, Signet.

Gamble, E Burt, 1894, *The Evolution of Woman: An Inquiry into the Dogma of her Inferiority to Man*, New York, G P Putnam's Sons.

Geddes, P, and Thomson, J A, 1889, *The Evolution of Sex*, London, Walter Scott.

Gilman, C Perkins, 1998 [1898], *Women and Economics*, New York, Dover Publications.

Gilman, C Perkins, 2002 [1903], *The Home: Its Work and Influence*, Lanham, MD, Altamira Press.

Haggard, H Rider, 1886, *She*, London, MacDonald & Company.

Huxley, T H, 1899 [1865], 'Emancipation – Black and White', in *Science and Education: Essays*, London, Macmillan, pp. 66–75.

Ioteyko, I, 1906, 'Bibliothèque biologique et sociologique de la femme', *La revue psychologique* 2, 382–415.

[Leifchild, J R], 1871, 'The Descent of Man, and Selection in Relation to Sex', *The Athenaeum*, March 4, 275–7.

Mivart, St G, 1871, 'Darwin's *Descent of Man*', *The Living Age*, October 14, 67–90.

Pardo Bazán, E, 1996, *'Torn Lace' and Other Stories*, trans. M C Urruela, New York, The Modern Language Association of America.

Romanes, G J, 1887, 'Mental Differences Between Men and Women', *The Nineteenth Century* 21, 654–72.

Schreiner, O, 1978 [1911], *Woman and Labour*, London, Virago.

Wallace, A R, 1890, 'Human Selection', *Fortnightly Review* 48, 325–37.

Watterson, H, 1895, 'The Woman Question Once More', *The Century* 49.5, 796.

Wedgwood, J, 1889, '"Male and Female Created He Them"', *Contemporary Review* 56, 120–33.

Secondary Literature

Blackwell, A, 1875, *The Sexes Throughout Nature*, New York, G.P Patnam's Sons.

Browne, J, 2002, *Charles Darwin: The Power of Place*, Princeton, Princeton University Press.

Cronin, H, 1994 [1991], *The Ant and the Peacock: Altruism and Sexual Selection from Darwin to Today*, New York, Cambridge University Press.

Davenport-Hines, R, 1991 [1990], *Sex, Death and Punishment: Attitudes to Sex and Sexuality in Britain since the Renaissance*, London, Fontana.

de Bont, R, 2002, '"Onbeschaamde geleerden hebben zijn naaktheid betast": Het vertoog over genialiteit, waanzin en degeneratie in België omstreeks 1900', *Bijdragen en Mededelingen betreffende de Geschiedenis der Nederlanden* 117, 46–76.

Doskow, M, 1997, 'Charlotte Perkins Gilman: The Female Face of Social Darwinism', *Weber Studies* 14.3, 9–22.

Egan, M, 1989, 'Evolutionary Theory in the Social Philosophy of Charlotte Perkins Gilman', *Hypatia* 4.1, 102–19.

Erskine, F, 1995, '*The Origin of Species* and the Science of Female Inferiority', in *Charles Darwin's* The Origin of Species: *New Interdisciplinary Essays*, ed. D Amigoni and J Wallace, Manchester, Manchester University Press, pp. 95–121.

Fichman, M, 1997, 'Biology and Politics: Defining the Boundaries', in *Victorian Science in Context*, ed. B Lightman, Chicago, University of Chicago Press, pp. 94–118.

Geary, D, 1999 [1998], *Male, Female: The Evolution of Human Sex Differences*, Washington, DC, American Psychological Association.

Gilmour, R, ed., 1993, *The Victorian Period: The Intellectual and Cultural Context of English Literature, 1830–1890*, Harlow, Longman.

Harvey, J, 1997, 'Strangers to Each Other: Male and Female Relationships in the Life and Work of Clémence Royer', in *Uneasy Careers and Intimate Lives: Women in Science, 1789–1979*, ed. P G Abir-Am and D Outram, New Brunswick, NJ, Rutgers University Press, pp. 147–71.

Helsinger, E, Lauterbach Sheets, R, and Veeder, W, 1983, *The Woman Question: Social Issues, 1837–1883*, Manchester, Manchester University Press.

Jann, R, 1994, 'Darwin and the Anthropologists: Sexual Selection and Its Discontents', *Victorian Studies* 37, 287–306.

Jann, R, 1997, 'Revising the Descent of Woman: Eliza Burt Gamble', in *Natural Eloquence: Women Reinscribe Science*, ed. B Gates and A Shteir, Madison/London, The University of Wisconsin Press, pp. 147–63.

Leatherdale, W, 1983, 'The Influence of Darwinism on English Literature and Literary Ideas', in *The Wider Domain of Evolutionary Thought*, ed. D Oldroyd and I Langham, Dordrecht, Reidel, pp. 1–26.

Levine, G, 2003, '"And If It Be a Pretty Woman All the Better" – Darwin and Sexual Selection', in *Literature, Science, Psychoanalysis, 1830–1970: Essays in Honour of Gillian Beer*, ed. H Small and T Tate, Oxford, Oxford University Press, pp. 37–51.

Love, R, 1983, 'Darwinism and Feminism: The "Woman Question" in the Life and Work of Olive Schreiner and Charlotte Perkins Gilman', in *The Wider Domain of Evolutionary Thought*, ed. D Oldroyd and I Langham, Dordrecht, Reidel, pp. 113–31.

McSweeney, K, 1991, *George Eliot (Marian Evans): A Literary Life*, London, Macmillan.

Mealey, L, 2000, *Sex Differences: Developmental and Evolutionary Strategies*, San Diego, CA, Academic Press.

Michie, H, 1999, 'Under Victorian Skins: The Bodies Beneath', in *A Companion to Victorian Literature and Culture*, ed. H Tucker, Malden/Oxford, Blackwell, pp. 407–24.

Mosedale, S, 1978, 'Science Corrupted: Victorian Biologists Consider "The Woman Question"', *Journal of the History of Biology* 11.1, 1–55.

Richards, E, 1983, 'Darwin and the Descent of Women', in *The Wider Domain of Evolutionary Thought*, ed. D Oldroyd and I Langham, Dordrecht, Reidel, pp. 57–111.

Richards, E, 1989, 'Huxley and Woman's Place in Science: The "Woman Question" and the Control of Victorian Anthropology', in: *History, Humanity and Evolution: Essays for John C. Greene*, ed. J Moore, New York, Cambridge University Press, pp. 253–84.

Richards, E, 1997, 'Redrawing the Boundaries: Darwinian Science and Victorian Women Intellectuals', in: *Victorian Science in Context*, ed. B Lightman, Chicago, University of Chicago Press, pp. 119–42.

Ridley, M, 2003, *Nature Via Nurture: Genes, Experience and What Makes Us Human*, London, Fourth Estate.

Russett, C Eagle, 1989, *Sexual Science: The Victorian Construction of Womanhood*, Cambridge, MA, Harvard University Press.

Vandermassen, G, 2004, 'Sexual Selection: A Tale of Male Bias and Feminist Denial', *European Journal of Women's Studies* 11.1, 9–26.

Wilson, E, 2002, 'Biologically Inspired Feminism: Response to Helen Keane and Martha Rosengarten, "On the Biology of Sexed Subjects"', *Australian Feminist Studies* 17.39, 283–5.

Chapter 6   Mutual Aid, a Factor of Peter Kropotkin's Literary Criticism

Works Cited

Primary Literature

Anon., 1902, 'Anarchy in Science', *The Outlook in Life, Politics, Finance, Letters, and the Arts* 10.247, October 25, 350–1.

Huxley, T, 1888, 'The Struggle for Existence: A Programme', *Nineteenth Century* 23.132, February, 161–80.

Kropotkin, P, 1905, *Ideals and Realities in Russian Literature*, London, Duckworth & Co.

Kropotkin, P, 1906 [1899], *Memoirs of a Revolutionist*, London, Swan Sonnenschein & Co.

Kropotkin, P, 1907a [1902], *Mutual Aid, a Factor of Evolution*, rev. edn., London, William Heinemann.

Kropotkin, P, 1907b [1892], *The Conquest of Bread*, London, The Knickerbocker Press.

Kropotkin, P, 1923 [1901], *Modern Science and Anarchism*, 2nd edn., London, Freedom Press.

Kropotkin, P, 1992 [1880], 'To the Young', in *Words of a Rebel*, trans. G Woodcock, Montreal, Black Rose Books, pp. 44–64.

Sellers, E, 1896, 'Our Most Distinguished Refugee', *The Contemporary Review* 66, October, 537–49.

Secondary Literature

Ford, F M, 1931, *Reminiscences 1894–1914: Return to Yesterday*, London, Victor Gollancz.

Miller, M, 1976, *Kropotkin*, Chicago, University of Chicago Press.

Moreland, D, 1997, *Demanding the Impossible? Human Nature and Politics in Nineteenth Century Social Anarchism*, London, Cassell.

Reszler, A, 1972, 'Peter Kropotkin and His Vision of Anarchist Aesthetics', *Diogenes* 78, 52–63.

Woodcock, G, and Avakumovic, I, 1950, *The Anarchist Prince: A Biographical Study of Peter Kropotkin*, London, T.V. Boardman & Co.

Chapter 7 The Savage Within: Evolutionary Theory, Anthropology and the Unconscious in *Fin-de-siècle* Literature

Works Cited

Primary Literature

Conrad, J, 1960 [1899], *Heart of Darkness*, in *Youth. Heart of Darkness. The End of the Tether*, London, Dent.

Darwin, C, 1989 [1871], *The Descent of Man and Selection in Relation to Sex*, in *The Works of Charles Darwin*, ed. P H Barrett and R B Freeman, 29 vols, 1986–9, New York, New York University Press, vol. 22.

Darwin, C, 1998 [1872], *The Expression of the Emotions in Man and Animals*, ed. P Ekman, Oxford, Oxford University Press.

Freud, S, 1965, *New Introductory Lectures on Psycho-Analysis*, in *Standard Edition of the Complete Psychological Works*, ed. J Strachey, 24 vols, 1953–74, London, Hogarth Press.

Freud, S, 1991, *Civilization, Society and Religion*, ed. A Dickson, London, Penguin.

Stevenson, R L, 1962 [1886], *Dr Jekyll & Mr Hyde. The Merry Men and Other Tales*, London, Dent.

Tylor, E B, 1903 [1871], *Primitive Culture*, 4th edn., 2 vols, London, John Murray.

Wells, H G, 1975, 'Human Evolution: An Artifical Process', in: *H G Wells: Early Writings in Science and Science Fiction*, ed. R M Philmus and D Y Hughes, Berkeley, University of California Press, pp. 211–19.

Secondary Literature

Arata, S, 1996, *Fictions of Loss in the Victorian Fin de Siècle*, Cambridge, Cambridge University Press.

Beer, G, 1983, *Darwin's Plots: Evolutionary Narrative in Darwin, George Eliot, and Nineteenth Century Fiction*, London, Routledge & Kegan Paul.

Berthoud, J, 1978, *Joseph Conrad: The Major Phase*, Cambridge, Cambridge University Press.

Block, E, 1981–2, 'James Sully, Evolutionist Psychology, and Late Victorian Gothic Fiction', *Victorian Studies* 25, 443–67.

Boas, F, 1896, 'The Limitations of a Comparative Method of Anthropology', *Science* 4.103, 901–8.

Botting, F, 1999, 'The Gothic Production of the Unconscious', in *Spectral Readings: Towards a Gothic Geography*, ed. G Byron and D Punter, Basingstoke, Macmillan, pp. 11–36.

Brantlinger, P, 1988, *Rule of Darkness: British Literature and Imperialism, 1830–1914*, Ithaca, NY, Cornell University Press.

Brennan, M C, 1997, *The Gothic Psyche: Disintegration and Growth in Nineteenth Century English Literature*, Columbia, Camden.

Clemens, V, 1990, *The Return of the Repressed: Gothic Horror from* The Castle of Otranto *to* Alien, Albany, NY, SUNY Press.

Ellenberger, H F, 1970, *The Discovery of the Unconscious*, New York, Basic Books.

Fleishman, A, 1967, *Conrad's Politics*, Baltimore, MD, Johns Hopkins University Press.

Garrett, P, 1988, 'Cries and Voices: Reading *Jekyll and Hyde*', in: *Dr Jekyll and Mr Hyde After One Hundred Years*, ed. W Veeder and G Hirsch, Chicago, University of Chicago Press, pp. 59–72.

Goetsch, P, 1984, '*Oliver Twist* als Stadtroman', in *Wirklichkeit und Dichtung*, ed. U Halfmann, K Müller and K Weiss, Berlin, Duncker, pp. 91–113.

Goetsch, P, 1985, 'Funktionen der Sprachkritik und-skepsis in der modernen englischen Literatur', *Literaturwissenschaftliches Jahrbuch der Görres-Gesellschaft* 26, 227–51.

Goetsch, P, 1993, *Hardys Wessex-Romane: Mündlichkeit, Schriftlichkeit, kultureller Wandel*, Tübingen, Narr.

Gose, E B, 1963, 'Psychic Evolution: Darwinism and Initiation in *Tess of the d'Urbervilles*', *Nineteenth Century Fiction* 18, 261–72.

Griffith, J W, 1995, *Joseph Conrad and the Anthropological Dilemma*, Oxford, Oxford University Press.

Guerard, A, 1958, *Conrad the Novelist*, Oxford, Oxford University Press.

Heath, S, 1986, 'Psychopathia sexualis: Stevenson's *Strange Case*', *Critical Quarterly* 28, 93–108.

Johnson, A J M, 1997, 'Victorian Anthropology, Racism, and *Heart of Darkness*', *Ariel* 28.4, 111–31.

Krasner, J, 1992, *The Entangled Eye: Visual Perception and the Representation of Nature in Post-Darwinian Narrative*, New York, Oxford University Press.

Kuklik, H, 1991, *The Savage Within: The Social History of British Anthropology, 1885–1945*, Cambridge, Cambridge University Press.

Mighail, R, 1999, *A Geography of Victorian Fiction: Mapping History's Nightmares*, Oxford, Oxford University Press.

Miller, J H, 1966, *Poets of Reality: Six Twentieth Century Writers*, Cambridge, MA, Harvard University Press.

Morton, P, 1984, *The Vital Science: Biology and the Literary Imagination, 1860–1900*, London, George Allen & Unwin.

Moser, T, 1957, *Joseph Conrad: Achievement and Decline*, Cambridge, MA, Harvard University Press.

Murfin, R C, ed., 1989, *Joseph Conrad: Heart of Darkness. A Case Study in Contemporary Criticism*, New York, St. Martin's Press.

Persak, C, 1994, 'Spencer's Doctrines and Mr. Hyde: Moral Evolution in Stevenson's *Strange Case*', *Victorian Newsletter* 86, 13–18.

Radford, A, 2003, *Thomas Hardy and the Survivals of Time*, Aldershot, Ashgate.

Rosner, M, 1998, '"A Total Subversion of Character": Dr. Jekyll's Moral Insanity', *Victorian Newsletter* 93, 27–31.

Saveson, J E, 1972, *Joseph Conrad: The Making of a Moralist*, Amsterdam, Rodopi.

Schlaeger, J, 1995, 'Der Diskurs der Exploration und die Reise nach Innen', in: *Weltbildwandel: Selbstdeutung und Fremderfahrung im Epochenübergang vom Spätmittelalter zur frühen Neuzeit*, ed. H J Buchorski and W Röcke, Trier, WVT, pp. 135–45.

Shaffer, B, 1993, '"Rebarbarizing Civilization": Conrad's African Fiction and Spencerian Sociology', *Publications of the Modern Language Association of America* 108, 45–58.

Stocking, G W, 1987, *Victorian Anthropology*, London, Collier Macmillan.

Street, B V, 1975, *The Savage in Literature: Representations of 'Primitive' Society in English Fiction, 1858–1920*, London, Routledge.

Taylor, J B, 1997, 'Obscure Recesses: Locating the Victorian Unconscious', in: *Writing and Victorianism*, ed. J B Bullen, London, Longman, pp. 137–77.

Thomas, R R, 1990, *Dreams of Authority: Freud and the Fictions of the Unconscious*, Ithaca, NY, Cornell University Press.

Treddell, N, ed., 1998, *Joseph Conrad: Heart of Darkness*, Duxford, Icon Books.

Veeder, W and Hirsch, G, eds, 1988, *Dr Jekyll and Mr Hyde After One Hundred Years*, Chicago, University of Chicago Press.

Wasserman, J, 1974, 'Narrative Presence: The Illusion of Language in *Heart of Darkness*', *Studies in the Novel* 6, 327–38.

Whyte, L L, 1959, *The Unconscious Before Freud*, London, Tavistock.

Chapter 8   Homer on the Evolutionary Scale: Interrelations between Biology and Literature in the Writings of William Gladstone and Grant Allen

Works Cited

Primary Literature

Allen, G, 1878a, 'Colour Sense', *Nature* 14, November 1878, 32.

Allen, G, 1878b, 'Development of the Sense of Colour', *Mind* 3, 129–32.

Allen, G, 1878c, 'The Origin of the Sublime', *Mind* 3, 324–39.

Allen, G, 1878d, 'Dissecting a Daisy', *The Cornhill Magazine* 37, 61–75.

Allen, G, 1879a, *The Colour Sense: Its Origin and Development; an Essay in Comparative Psychology*, London, Trübner.

Allen, G, 1879b, 'The Origin of the Sense of Symmetry', *Mind* 4, 301–16.

Allen, G, 1880a, 'Aesthetic Evolution in Man', *Mind* 5, 445–64.

Allen, G, 1880b, 'Aesthetic Feeling in Birds', *The Popular Science Monthly* 17, 650–63.

Allen, G, 1884, 'Our Debt to Insects', *The Gentleman's Magazine* 256, 452–69.

Allen, G, 1894, 'Queen Dido's Realm', *Longman's Magazine* 23, 521–31.

Allen, G, 1977 [1877], *Physiological Aesthetics*, facsimile, New York, Garland.

Clodd, E, 1900, *Grant Allen: A Memoir*, London, Grant Richards.

Darwin, C, 1952 [1871], *The Descent of Man*, in *The Origin of Species by Means of Natural Selection; The Descent of Man and Selection in Relation to Sex*, Encyclopaedia Britannica, Great Books of the Western World, 49, Chicago et al., pp. 254–600.

Darwin, C, 1996 [1859], *The Origin of Species*, ed. G Beer, Oxford, Oxford University Press.

Geiger, L, 1878 [1871], 'Ueber den Farbensinn der Urzeit und seine Entwickelung', in *Zur Entwickelungsgeschichte der Menschheit: Vorträge*, 2nd edn., Stuttgart, J G Cotta'sche Verlagsbuchhandlung, pp. 45–60.

Geiger, L, 1880, *Contributions to the History of the Development of the Human Race*, trans. D Asher, London, Trubner & Co.

Gladstone, W E, 1858, *Studies on Homer and the Homeric Age*, 3 vols, Oxford, Oxford University Press, vol. 3.

Gladstone, W E, 1869, *Juventus Mundi*, London, Macmillan.

Gladstone, W E, 1876, *Homeric Synchronism*, London, Macmillan.

Gladstone, W E, 1877, 'The Colour Sense', *The Nineteenth Century and After* 2, 366-88.

Goethe, J W, 1998 [1810], *Schriften zur Farbenlehre*, I, in *Johann Wolfgang Goethe: Gesamtausgabe der Werke und Schriften*, ed. R Habel, 22 vols, Essen, Phaidon, vol 21.

Keary, C F, 1881, 'The Homeric Words for "Soul"', *Mind* 6, 471–83.

Lubbock, J, 1882, *Ants, Bees and Wasps*, New York, Kegan Paul.

Magnus, H, 1877a, *Die geschichtliche Entwickelung des Farbensinnes*, Leipzig, Veit.

Magnus, H, 1877b, *Die Entwickelung des Farbensinnes*, Jena, Dufft.

Magnus, H, 1880, *Untersuchungen über den Farbensinn der Naturvölker*, Jena, Fraher.

Müller, M, 1887, *The Science of Thought*, New York, Charles Scribner's Sons, 2 vols, vol. 1.

Peschier, E, 1871, *Lazarus Geiger: sein Leben und Denken*, Frankfurt am Main, Auffarth.

Prantl, K, 1978 [1849], *Aristoteles. Über die Farben. Erläutert durch eine Übersicht der Farbenlehre der Alten*, repr. Aalen, Scientia.

Rivers, W H R, 1901a, 'Primitive Colour Vision', *Popular Science Monthly* 59, 44–58.

Rivers, W H R, 1901b, *Reports of the Cambridge Anthropological Expedition to Torres Straits*, 6 vols, 1901–35, Cambridge, Cambridge University Press, vol. 2.

Rosenthal, L A, 1883, *Lazarus Geiger: seine Lehre vom Ursprung der Sprache und Vernunft und sein Leben*, Stuttgart, Scheible.

Smith, W R, 1877, 'The Colour Sense of the Greeks', Letter to the Editor of *Nature*, *Nature* 6, December 1877, 100.

Sully, J, 1879, 'Animal Music', *Cornhill Magazine* 40, 605–21.

von Helmholtz, H, 2003 [1883], *Wissenschaftliche Abhandlungen*, 3 vols, Hildesheim, Georg Olms, vol. 2.

Wallace, A R, 1878, 'The Colours of Plants and the Origin of the Colour Sense', in *Tropical Nature and Other Essays*, London, Macmillan, pp. 220–48.

Woodworth, R S, 1910, 'The Puzzle of Color Vocabularies', *The Psychological Bulletin* 7, 325–34.

Secondary Literature

Aarsleff, H, 1967, *The Study of Language in England, 1780–1860*, Princeton, NJ, Princeton University Press.

Alter, S G, 1999, *Darwinism and the Linguistic Image: Language, Race, and Natural Theology in the Nineteenth Century*, Baltimore, MD, Johns Hopkins University Press.

Amigoni, D, 2004, 'Carving Coconuts, the Philosophy of Drawing Rooms, and the Politics of Dates: Grant Allen, Popular Scientific Journalism, Evolution, and Culture in the *Cornhill Magazine*', in *Culture and Science in the Nineteenth Century Media*, ed. L Henson *et al.*, Aldershot, Ashgate, pp. 251–61.

Beer, G, 1986, '"The Face of Nature": Anthropomorphic Elements in the Language of *The Origin of Species*', in *Languages of Nature: Critical Essays on Science and Literature*, ed. L J Jordanova, New Brunswick, Rutgers University Press, pp. 212–43.

Beer, G, 1989, 'Darwin and the Growth of Language Theory', in *Nature Transfigured: Science and Literature, 1700–1900*, ed. J Christie and S Shuttleworth, Manchester, Manchester University Press, pp. 152–70.

Berlin, B, and Kay, P, 1969, *Basic Color Terms: Their Universality and Evolution*, Berkeley, University of California Press.

Bowler, P J, 1989, *The Invention of Progress: The Victorians and the Past*, Oxford, Basil Blackwell.

de Beer, Sir G, 1958, 'Further Unpublished Letters of Charles Darwin', *Annals of Science* 14, 83–115.

Durant, J, 1985, 'The Ascent of Nature in Darwin's *Descent*', in *The Darwinian Heritage*, ed. D Krohn, Princeton, NJ, Princeton University Press, pp. 283–306.

Jahn, I, ed., 1998, *Geschichte der Biologie*, 3rd rev. edn., Jena, Fischer.

Jann, R, 1994, 'Darwin and the Anthropologists: Sexual Selection and Its Discontents', *Victorian Studies* 37, 287–306.

Levine, G, 1987, 'One Culture: Science and Literature', in *One Culture: Essays in Science and Literature*, ed. G Levine, Madison, University of Wisconsin Press, pp. 3–32.

Morley, J, 1908, *The Life of William Ewart Gladstone*, 2 vols, London, Edward Lloyd Ltd, vol. 2.

Morton, P, 1984, *The Vital Science: Biology and the Literary Imagination, 1860-1900*, London, George Allen & Unwin.

Myers, J L, 1958, *Homer and His Critics*, ed. D Gray, London, Routledge.

Royle, E, 1980, *Radicals, Secularists and Republicans: Popular Free Thought in Britain, 1866–1915*, Manchester, Manchester University Press.

Segall, M H, Campbell, D T, and Herskovits, M J, 1966, *The Influence of Culture on Visual Perception*, Indianapolis, W Bobbs-Merrill.

Travis, J, 2003, 'Visionary Research: Scientists Delve into the Evolution of Colour Vision in Primates', *Science News*, 11 October.

Voss, J, 2001, '"Sklaverei im Ameisenstaat": Die darwinistische Tiergeschichte als gattungstheoretischer, Problemfall in *Das Ausland*', *Berliner Hefte zur Geschichte des literarischen Lebens* 4, 101–16.

Wolf, F A, 1985, *Prolegomena to Homer*, trans. and introd. A Grafton, G W Most and J E G Zettel, Princeton, NJ, Princeton University Press.

Chapter 9   'Naturfreund' or 'Naturfeind'? Darwinism in the Early Drawings of Alfred Kubin

Works Cited

Primary Literature

Bölsche, W, 1976 [1887], 'Darwin in der Poesie', in *Die naturwissenschaftlichen Grundlagen der Poesie: Prolegomena einer realistischen Ästhetik*, Tübingen, Max Niemeyer, pp. 75–87.

Kubin, A, 1974, *Aus meinem Leben: Gesammelte Prosa mit 73 Abbildungen*, ed. U Riemerschmidt, Munich, Spangenberg.

Kubin, A, 1995a [1902], 'Einige Worte über das Schaffen und den Menschen Alfred Kubin', in *Träumer auf Lebenszeit: Alfred Kubin als Literat*, ed. A Geyer, Vienna, Böhlau, pp. 234–40.

Kubin, A, 1995b [1904], 'Selbstmordbrief', in *Träumer auf Lebenszeit: Alfred Kubin als Literat*, ed. A Geyer, Vienna, Böhlau, pp. 244–5.

Kubin, A, 1995c, *Alfred Kubin 1877–1959*, ed. P Assmann, Wien, Residenz Verlag.

[Kubin, A], n.d., *Inventar der Bibliothek Alfred Kubins im Kubin-Haus des Landes Oberösterreich in Zwickledt/Wernstein, bearbeitet von Dr. Alfred Marks*, 3 vols, Oberösterreichisches Landesmuseum Linz.

Secondary Literature

Geyer, A, 1995, *Träumer auf Lebenszeit: Alfred Kubin als Literat*, Vienna, Böhlau.

Hedwig, A, 1967, *Phantastische Wirklichkeit: Interpretationsstudie zu Alfred Kubins Roman Die andere Seite*, Munich, Wilhelm Fink.

Hoberg, A, ed., 1990, *Alfred Kubin 1877–1959*, Munich, Spangenberg.

Hoberg, A, 1995, 'Alfred Kubin – Die Inszenierungen eines Künstlers im München der Jahrhundertwende', in *Die andere Seite der Wirklichkeit: Ein Symposium zu Aspekten des Unheimlichen, Phantastischen und Fiktionalen*, ed. P Assmann and P Kraml, Linz, Kubin-Projekt, pp. 11–28.

Massey Czerkas, S, and Glut, D F, 1982, *Dinosaurs, Mammoths and Cavemen: The Art of Charles R. Knight*, New York, E P Dutton Inc.

Rudwick, M, 1992, *Scenes from Deep Time: Early Pictorial Representations of the Prehistoric World*, Chicago, University of Chicago Press.

Thieme, U, and Becker, F, 1927, *Thieme-Becker Künstlerlexikon: Allgemeines Lexikon der bildenden Künstler*, ed. H Vollmer, 37 vols, Leipzig, Engelmann, vol. 20.

Werkner, P, 1986, *Austrian Expressionism: The Formative Years*, Palo Alto, CA, The Society for the Promotion of Science and Scholarship.

Chapter 10 Cells and Networks in Nineteenth Century Literature

Works Cited

Primary Literature

Du Bois-Reymond, E, 1887, 'Gedächtnisrede auf Johannes Müller', in *Reden*, 2 vols, Leipzig, Veit, vol. 2, pp. 143–334.

Eliot, G, 1865, 'The Influence of Rationalism', *Fortnightly Review* 1, 46.

Haberling, W, 1924, *Johannes Müller: Das Leben des Rheinischen Naturforschers*, Leipzig, Akademische Verlagsgesellschaft.

Otis, L, ed., 2002, *Literature and Science in the Nineteenth Century: An Anthology*, Oxford, Oxford University Press.

Ramón y Cajal, S, 2001, *Vacation Stories: Five Science Fiction Tales*, trans. L Otis, Urbana, Chicago, University of Illinois Press.

Secondary Literature

Beer, G, 1983, *Darwin's Plots: Evolutionary Narrative in Darwin, George Eliot and Nineteenth Century Fiction*, London, Routledge & Kegan Paul.

Bell, D, 2004, 'Dissolving Distance: Technology, Space, and Empire in British Political Thought, c.1770–1900', submitted to *The Journal of Modern History*.

Bell, D, n.d., 'Building Greater Britain: Empire and Federation in Victorian Political Thought, c.1870–1900', first chapter of doctoral dissertation, Cambridge.

Ginzburg, C, 1992 [1976], *The Cheese and the Worms: The Cosmos of a Sixteenth-Century Miller*, trans. J Tedeschi and A Tedeschi, Baltimore, MD, Johns Hopkins University Press.

Hayles, N K, 1990, *Chaos Bound: Orderly Disorder in Contemporary Literature and Science*, Ithaca, NY, Cornell University Press.

Jardine, J, 1997, 'The Mantle of Müller and the Ghost of Goethe: Interactions between the Sciences and Their Histories', *History and the Disciplines: The Reclassification of Knowledge in Early Modern Europe*, ed. D R Kelley, Rochester, NY, The University of Rochester Press, pp. 297–317.

Keller, E F, 1985, *Reflections on Gender and Science*, New Haven, CT, Yale University Press.

Lenoir, T, 1994, 'Helmholtz and the Materialities of Communication', *Osiris* 9, 185–207.

Otis, L, 1999, *Membranes: Metaphors of Invasion in Nineteenth Century Literature, Science, and Politics*, Baltimore, MD, Johns Hopkins University Press.

Otis, L, 2001, *Networking: Communicating with Bodies and Machines in the Nineteenth Century*, Ann Arbor, University of Michigan Press.

Rosenheim, S, 2003, 'Review of *Networking: Communicating with Bodies and Machines in the Nineteenth Century*', *Modernism/Modernity* 10.1, 199–200.

Rothfield, L, 1992, *Vital Signs: Medical Realism in Nineteenth Century Fiction*, Princeton, NJ, Princeton University Press.

Wald, P, 2003, 'Review of *Networking: Communicating with Bodies and Machines in the Nineteenth Century*', *Perspectives in Biology and Medicine* 46.3, 453.

Chapter 11 Contagious Sympathies: George Eliot and Rudolf Virchow

Works Cited

Primary Literature

Anon., 1870, 'A Medical Statesman', *British Medical Journal* 2, 149.

Beale, L, 1861, *On the Structure of the Simple Tissues of the Human Body*, London, John Churchill.

Beale, L, 1872, *Bioplasm*, London, John Churchill.

Daubeny, C, 1855, 'On the Influence of the Lower Vegetable Organisms in Production of Epidemic Disease', *Edinburgh New Philosophical Journal* 2, 88–112.

Drysdale, J, 1878, *The Germ Theory of Infectious Diseases*, London, Baillire, Tindall and Cox.

Eliot, G, 1913, *Impressions of Theophrastus Such*, Edinburgh, William Blackwood.

Eliot, G, 1954–78, *The George Eliot Letters*, 9 vols, ed. G S Haight, New Haven, CT, Yale University Press.

Eliot, G, 1985 [1871–2], *Middlemarch*, ed. W H Harvey, Harmondsworth, Penguin.

Paget, J, 1863, *Lectures on Surgical Pathology*, rev. edn., London, Longman *et al.*

Pidduck, I, 1847, 'The Cause, Prevention and Treatment of Typhus Fever', *Lancet* 2, 176.

Pratt, J, and Neufeldt, V, eds, 1979, *George Eliot's Middlemarch Notebooks*, Berkeley, University of California Press.

Smith, T S, 1830, *A Treatise on Fever*, London, Longman, Rees, Orme, Brown & Green.

Swanzy, H, 1871, 'Recollections of the Medical School of Berlin', *British Medical Journal* 1, 637–8.

Virchow, R, 1860, *Cellular Pathology*, trans. F Chance, London, John Churchill.

Virchow, R, 1862, *Vier Reden über Leben und Kranksein*, Berlin, n.p.

Virchow, R, 1868, *On Famine Fever and Some of the Other Cognate Forms of Typhus*, London, Williams & Norgate.

Virchow, R, 1959, *Disease, Life and Man*, ed. and trans. L J Rather, Stanford, CA, Stanford University Press.

Virchow, R, 1985, *Collected Essays on Public Health and Epidemiology*, 2 vols, ed. and trans. L J Rather, Canton, MA, Watson.

Secondary Literature

Ackerknecht, E, 1948, 'Anticontagionism between 1821 and 1867', *Bulletin of the History of Medicine* 22, 562–93.

Ackerknecht, E, 1953, *Rudolf Virchow: Doctor, Statesman, Anthropologist*, Madison, University of Wisconsin Press.

Baker, W, ed., 1977, *The George Eliot–George Henry Lewes Library: An Annotated Catalogue*, New York, Garland.

Blair, K, 2001, 'A Change in the Units: Middlemarch, G. H. Lewes and Rudolf Virchow', *George Eliot–George Henry Lewes Studies* 40–1, 9–24.

Boyd, B, 1991, *Rudolf Virchow: The Scientist as Citizen*, New York, Garland.

Coleman, W, 1977, *Biology in the Nineteenth Century: Problems of Form, Function and Transformation*, Cambridge, Cambridge University Press.

Dale, P A, 1989, *In Pursuit of a Scientific Culture*, Madison, University of Wisconsin Press.

Forrester, J, 1990, 'Lydgate's Research Project in Middlemarch', *George Eliot–George Henry Lewes Studies* 16–17, 2–7.

Graver, S, 1984, *George Eliot and Community: A Study in Social Theory and Fictional Form*, Berkeley, University of California Press.

Hardy, A, 1993, *The Epidemic Streets: Infectious Disease and the Rise of Preventive Medicine, 1856–1900*, Oxford, Clarendon Press.

McNeely, I, 2002, *'Medicine on a Grand Scale': Rudolf Virchow, Liberalism and the Public Health*, London, Wellcome.

Otis, L, 1999, *Membranes: Metaphors of Invasion in Nineteenth Century Literature, Science, and Politics*, Baltimore, MD, Johns Hopkins University Press.

Rather, L J, 1990, *A Commentary on the Medical Writings of Rudolf Virchow*, San Francisco, Norman.

Taylor, R, and Rieger, A, 1984, 'Rudolf Virchow on the Typhus Epidemic in Upper Silesia: An Introduction and Translation', *Sociology of Health and Illness* 6, 201–17.

Worboys, M, 2000, *Spreading Germs: Disease Theories and Medical Practice in Britain, 1865–1900*, Cambridge, Cambridge University Press.

Chapter 12 From Parasitology to Parapsychology: Parasites in Nineteenth Century Science and Literature

Works Cited

Primary Literature

'C., C.', 1885, 'Parasitism in Medicine', in *The Encyclopaedia Britannica: A Dictionary of Arts, Sciences and General Literature*, 9th edn., Edinburgh, Adam and Charles Black, pp. 269–71.

Cobbold, T S, 1879, *Parasites: A Treatise on the Entozoa of Man and Animals, including Some Account of the Ectozoa*, London, J. & A. Churchill.

Conan Doyle, A, 1930, The Parasite – *The Captain of the 'Pole Star'* – Other Tales, in *The Crowborough Edition of the Works of Sir Arthur Conan Doyle*, Garden City, NY, Doubleday, pp. 3–53.

Darwin, C, 1969 [1839], *Journal of Researches into the Geology and Natural History of the Various Countries Visited by H.M.S. Beagle, under the Command of Captain Fitzroy, R.N. from 1832 to 1836*, London, Henry Colburn, 1839, facsimile repr. Brussels, Impression Anastaltique Culture et Civilisation.

Darwin, C, 1981 [1871], *The Descent of Man and Selection in Relation to Sex*, 2 vols, facsimile edn., introd. J T Bonner and R M May, Princeton, NJ, Princeton University Press.

Darwin, C, 1996 [1859], *The Origin of Species*, ed. G Beer, Oxford, Oxford University Press.

Dickens, C, 1989 [1865], *Our Mutual Friend*, ed. M Cotsell, Oxford, Oxford University Press.

Doflein, F, 1901, *Die Protozoen als Parasiten und Krankheitserreger, nach biologischen Gesichtspunkten dargestellt*, Jena, Gustav Fischer.

Drummond, H, 1883, *The Natural Law in the Spiritual World*, London, Hodder & Stoughton.

Eliot, G, 1954–78, *The George Eliot Letters*, ed. G S Haight, 9 vols, New Haven, CT, Yale University Press.

Eliot, G, 1966, *Quarry for Middlemarch*, ed. A T Kitchel, *Nineteenth Century Fiction* 4 (1949–50), supplement, repr. New York, AMS Press.

Eliot, G, 1996a [1860], *The Mill on the Floss*, ed. G S Haight, introd. D Birch, Oxford, Oxford University Press.

Eliot, G, 1996b [1871–2], *Middlemarch*, ed. D Carroll, introd. F Bonaparte, Oxford, Oxford University Press.

'GE., P.', 1885, 'Animal Parasitism', in *The Encyclopaedia Britannica: A Dictionary of Arts, Sciences and General Literature*, 9th edn., Edinburgh, Adam and Charles Black, pp. 258–64.

Gruendler, O, 1850, *De parasitis hominis, Dissertatio inauguralis medica*, Berlin, B. Schlesinger.

Hardy, T, 1969 [1878], *The Return of the Native*, ed. J Gindin, New York, Norton.

Hardy, T, 1988 [1891], *Tess of the d'Urbervilles*, ed. J Grindle and S Gatrell, Oxford, Oxford University Press.

Huxley, T H, 1968 [1887], 'The Progress of Science', in *Collected Essays*, 9 vols, vol.1: *Method and Results*, repr. New York, Greenwood Press, pp. 42–129.

Knorr, Dr, 1875, 'Die Parasiten bei den Griechen. Die Parasitennamen bei Alciphron', in *Programm des städtischen Gymnasiums zu Belgard 1874/75*, Belgard, Albert Kelemp.

Lankester, R, 1880, *Degeneration: A Chapter in Darwinism*, London, Macmillan.

Lewes, G H, 1858, *Sea-Side Studies at Ilfracombe, Tenby, the Scilly Isles, and Jersey*, Edinburgh, W. Blackwood and Sons.

Lewes, G H, 1862, *Studies in Animal Life*, London, Smith, Elder & Co.

Perty, M, 1869, *Ueber den Parasitismus in der organischen Natur. Populär-wissenschaftlicher Vortrag, gehalten 1869 zu Bern*, in *Sammlung gemeinverständlicher wissenschaftlicher Vorträge*, ed. R Virchow and F von Holtzendorff, 4th series, issue 73–96, Berlin, S.G. Lüderitz'sche Verlagsbuchhandlung, 1869 and 1870.

Ruskin, J, 1905 [1869], *The Queen of the Air*, in *The Works of John Ruskin*, ed. E T Cook and A Wedderburn, London, George Allen, 39 vols, 1903–12, vol. 19, pp. 283–423.

Ruskin, J, 1907 [1872–84], *Fors Clavigera: Letters to the Workmen and Labourers of Great Britain*, in *The Works of John Ruskin*, ed. E T Cook and A Wedderburn, London, George Allen, 39 vols, 1903–12, vols 27–29.

Spencer, H, 1860, 'The Social Organism', *Westminster Review*, n.s. 17, 90–121.

Stoker, B, 2003 [1993], *Dracula*, ed. M Hindle, London, Penguin.

Virchow, R, 1885, 'Der Kampf der Zellen und der Bakterien', *Archiv für pathologische Anatomie und Physiologie und für klinische Medizin* 101, 1–13.

Virchow, R, 1959 [1859], 'Atoms and Individuals', in *Disease, Life and Man*, ed. and trans. L J Rather, Stanford, CA, Stanford University Press.

Wells, H G, 1977 [1895], *The Time Machine*, ed. F D MacConnell, New York, Oxford University Press.

Wells, H G, 1995 [1898], *The War of the Worlds*, ed. D Y Hughes and B W Aldiss, New York, Oxford University Press.

Wells, H G, 2000 [1891], 'Zoological Retrogression', in *The Fin de Siècle: A Reader in Cultural History, c.1880–1900*, ed. S Ledger and R Luckhurst, Oxford, Oxford University Press, pp. 5–12.

Wilson, A, 1881, 'Degeneration', *Gentleman's Magazine* 250, 485–98.

Secondary Literature

Arata, S, 1996, *Fictions of Loss in the Victorian Fin de Siècle*, Cambridge, Cambridge University Press.

Baran, J J, 1993, 'Predators and Parasites in *Le Père Goriot*', *Symposium: A Quarterly Journal in Modern Foreign Literatures* 47.1, 3–15.

Beer, G, 2000 [1983], *Darwin's Plots: Evolutionary Narrative in Darwin, George Eliot and Nineteenth Century Fiction*, Cambridge, Cambridge University Press.

Behrendt, P F, 1985, 'Dangerous Wounds: Vampirism as a Social Metaphor in Zola's *Thérèse Raquin*', *The European Studies Journal* 2.2., 32–40.

Brown, S D, 2002, 'Michel Serres: Science, Translation and the Logic of the Parasite', *Theory, Culture and Society* 19.3, 1–27.

Casillo, R, 1985, 'Parasitism and Capital Punishment in Ruskin's *Fors Clavigera*', *Victorian Studies* 29.1, 537–67.

Cranny-Francis, A, 1988, 'Arthur Conan Doyle's *The Parasite*: The Case of the Anguished Author', in *Nineteenth Century Suspense: From Poe to Conan Doyle*, ed. C Bloom *et al.*, Houndmills, Macmillan, pp. 93–106.

Enzensberger, U, 2001, *Parasiten: Ein Sachbuch*, Frankfurt, Eichborn Verlag.

Feldmann, D, 1998, 'Stoker's/Coppola's Dracula: Victorian Culture Then and Now', in *Anglistentag 1997 Giessen: Proceedings*, ed. R Borgmeier, H Grabes and A H Jucker, Trier, Wissenschaftlicher Verlag Trier, pp. 369–78.

Higham, C, 1976, *The Adventures of Conan Doyle: The Life of the Creator of Sherlock Holmes*, London, Hamish Hamilton.

Kaminskas, J, 1997, '*La Fortune des Rougon*: des origines et des parasites', *Excavation: Émile Zola and Naturalism* 10, 172–82.

Kaminskas, J, 2000, 'Structures parasitaires dans la trilogie de Plassans', *Les cahiers naturalistes* 74, 33–42.

Katz, M, Despommier, D D, and Gwadz, R W, 1982, *Parasitic Diseases*, New York, Springer-Verlag.

Mann, K B, 1981, 'George Eliot's Language of Nature: Production and Consumption', *English Literary History* 48, 190–216.

Miller, J H, 1958, *Charles Dickens: The World of his Novels*, Cambridge, MA, Harvard University Press.

Miller, J H, 1975, *The Disappearance of God: Five Nineteenth Century Writers*, Cambridge, MA, Harvard University Press.

Miller, J H, 1979, 'The Critic as Host', in *Deconstruction and Criticism*, ed. H Bloom *et al.*, New York, Seabury Press, pp. 217–53.

Morton, P, 1984, *The Vital Science: Biology and the Literary Imagination, 1860–1900*, London, George Allen & Unwin.

Otis, L, 1999, *Membranes: Metaphors of Invasion in Nineteenth Century Literature, Science, and Politics*, Baltimore, MD, Johns Hopkins University Press.

Paulson, W, 1985, 'Le cousin parasite: Balzac, Serres et le demon de Maxwell', *Stanford French Review* 9, 397–415.

Pfeiffer, H, 1997, 'Balzacs Parasiten: Grenzen der Repräsentation in den *Parents Pauvres*', in *Konkurrierende Diskurse: Studien zur französischen Literatur des 19. Jahrhunderts*, ed. B Wehinger, Stuttgart, Franz Steiner, pp. 239–56.

Senf, C A, 1987, 'The Vampire in *Middlemarch* and George Eliot's Quest for Historical Reality', *The New Orleans Review* 14.1, 87–97.

Serres, M, 1980, *Le parasite*, Paris, Bernard Grasset.

Shuttleworth, S, 1984, *George Eliot and Nineteenth Century Science: The Make-Believe of a Beginning*, Cambridge, Cambridge University Press.

Stott, R, 2002, 'Darwin's Barnacles: Mid-Century Victorian Natural History and the Marine Grotesque', in *Transactions and Encounters: Science and Culture in the Nineteenth Century*, ed. R Luckhurst and J McDonagh, Manchester, Manchester University Press, pp. 151–81.

Telotte, J P, 1999, 'A Parasitic Perspective: Romantic Participation and Polidori's *The Vampyre*', in *The Blood is the Life: Vampires in Literature*, ed. L G Heldreth and M Pharr, Bowling Green, KY, Bowling Green State University Popular Press, pp. 9–18.

Trotter, D, 1988, *Circulation: Defoe, Dickens, and the Economies of the Novel*, London, Macmillan.

Wormald, M, 1996, 'Microscopy and Semiotic in *Middlemarch*', *Nineteenth Century Literature* 50, 501–24.

Chapter 13 Surgical Engineering in the Nineteenth Century: Frankenstein, The Island of Dr Moreau, Flatland

Works Cited

Primary Literature

Abbott, E A, 2001 [1884], *Flatland: A Romance of Many Dimensions, Told by A Square*, ed. I Stewart, Cambridge, Perseus Publications.

Galton, F, 1892, *Finger Prints*, London, Macmillan.

Gosson, S, 1868 [1579], *The Schoole of Abuse*, ed. E Arber, London, Alex Murray & Son.

Shelley, M, 1992 [1818], *Frankenstein, or: The Modern Prometheus*, ed. M Hindle, Harmondsworth, Penguin.

Wells, H G, 1996 [1896], *The Island of Dr Moreau: A Critical Text of the 1896 London First Edition, with an Introduction and Appendices*, ed. L Stover, Jefferson, NC, McFarland.

Wells, H G, 1998, *The Correspondence of H G Wells*, 4 vols, ed. D C Smith, London, Pickering & Chatto.

Secondary Literature

Bonner, T N, 1995, *Becoming a Physician: Medical Education in Britain, France, Germany, and the United States, 1750–1945*, New York, Oxford University Press.

Doody, M A, 1988, *Frances Burney: The Life and Works*, New Brunswick, Rutgers University Press.

French, R D, 1975, *Antivivisection and Medical Science in Victorian Society*, Princeton, NJ, Princeton University Press.

Gordon, J, 2003, *Physiology and the Literary Imagination: Romantic to Modern*, Gainesville, University of Florida Press.

Harman, C, 2000, *Fanny Burney: A Biography*, London, HarperCollins.

Haynes, R, 1980, *H G Wells: Discoverer of the Future. The Influence of Science on His Thought*, New York, New York University Press.

Haynes, R, 1994, *From Faust to Strangelove: Representations of the Scientist in Western Literature*, Baltimore, MD, Johns Hopkins University Press.

Levine, G, 1979, 'The Ambiguous Heritage of *Frankenstein*', in *The Endurance of Frankenstein: Essays on Mary Shelley's Novel*, ed. G Levine and U C Knoepflmacher, Berkeley, University of California Press, pp. 3–30.

Lyons, A S, and Petrucelli II, R J, 2003, *Die Geschichte der Medizin im Spiegel der Kunst*, 2nd edn., Cologne, Dumont.

Marshall, T, 1995, *Murdering to Dissect: Grave-Robbing, Frankenstein and the Anatomy Literature*, Manchester, Manchester University Press.

Mellor, A K, 1995, 'A Feminist Critique of Science', in *Mary Shelley: Frankenstein*, ed. F Botting, Houndmills, Macmillan, pp. 107–39.

Meyer, J, 2003, 'Nur ein viktorianisches Dilemma? *Flatland* zwischen zwei Wissenschaftskulturen', in *In the Footsteps of Queen Victoria: Wege zum viktorianischen Zeitalter*, ed. C Jansohn, Münster, LIT, pp. 153–76.

Otis, L, ed., 2002, *Literature and Science in the Nineteenth Century: An Anthology*, Oxford, Oxford University Press.

Parrinder, P, 1995, *Shadows of the Future: H G Wells, Science Fiction and Prophecy*, Liverpool, Liverpool University Press.

Porter, R, 1999, *The Greatest Benefit to Mankind: A Medical History of Humanity*, New York, Norton.

Reed, J R, 1990, 'The Vanity of Law in *The Island of Dr Moreau*', in *H G Wells under Revision: Proceedings of the International H G Wells Symposium London, July 1986*, ed. P Parrinder and C Rolfe, Selingsgrove, Susquehanna University Press, pp. 134–44.

Scarry, E, 1985, *The Body in Pain*, New York, Oxford University Press.

Schenkel, E, 2001, *H G Wells: Der Prophet im Labyrinth. Eine essayistische Erkundung*, Vienna, Zsolnay.

Smith, C, 1994, '*Frankenstein* and Natural Magic', in *Frankenstein, Creation and Monstrosity*, ed. S Bann, London, Reaktion Books, pp. 33–54.

Stover, L, 1990, 'Applied Natural History: Wells vs. Huxley', in *H G Wells under Revision: Proceedings of the International H G Wells Symposium London, July 1986*, ed. P Parrinder and C Rolfe, Selingsgrove, Susquehanna University Press, pp. 125–33.

Straub, P, 2002, 'Foreword', in *H G Wells: The Island of Dr Moreau*, ed. P Straub, New York: Random House, pp. xi–xxxi.

Wallace, A F, 1982, *The Progress of Plastic Surgery: An Introductory History*, Oxford, Willem A Meeuws.

Chapter 14 'Serious' Science versus 'Light' Entertainment? Femininity Concepts in Nineteenth Century British Medical Discourse and Popular Fiction

Works Cited

Primary Literature

1. Sensation Novels

Braddon, M E, 1987 [1862], *Lady Audley's Secret*, ed. D Skilton, Oxford, Oxford University Press.

Braddon, M E, 1998 [1861–2], *The Black Band; or, The Mysteries of Midnight*, ed. J Carnell, Hastings, The Sensation Press.

Collins, W, 1989 [1864–6], *Armandale*, ed. C Peters, Oxford, Oxford University Press.

Collins, W, 1995 [1880], *Jezbel's Daughter*, Stroude, Alan Sutton.

Reade, C, 1914 [1863], *Hard Cash. A Matter-of-Fact Romance*, London, Chatto & Windus.

2. Medical Texts

Anon., 1851, 'Woman in her Psychological Relations', *The Journal of Psychological Medicine and Mental Pathology* 4, 18–50.

Anon., 1861, 'A Lady amongst the Students', *Lancet* 2, 6 July, 16.

Black, G, 1888, *The Young Wife's Advice Book. A Guide for Mothers on Health and Self-Management*, 6th ed., London, Warwick House.

Blandford, G F, 1871, *Insanity and Its Treatment. Lectures on the Treatment, Medical and Legal, of Insane Patients*, Edinburgh, Oliver & Boyd.

Bucknill, J C, and Tuke, D H, 1858, A Manual of Psychological Medicine. Containing the History, Nosology, Description, Statistics, Diagnosis, Pathology, and Treatment of Insanity, London, Churchill.

Campbell, H, 1891, Differences in the Nervous Organisation of Man and Woman. Physiological and Pathological, London, Lewis.

Carpenter, W B, 1844, Principles of Human Physiology, with their Chief Application to Pathology, Hygiene, and Forensic Medicine, 2nd edn., London, Churchill.

Carter, R B, 1853, On the Pathology and Treatment of Hysteria, London, Churchill.

Clouston, T S, 1887, Clinical Lectures on Mental Diseases, 2nd edn., London, Churchill.

Davis, D D, 1836, The Principles and Practice of Obstetric Medicine in a Series of Systematic Dissertations on Midwifery, and on the Diseases of Women and Children, London, Taylor & Walton, 2 vols.

Donkin, H B, 1892, 'Hysteria', in A Dictionary of Psychological Medicine, Giving the Definition, Etymology and Symptoms of the Terms Used in Medical Psychology. With the Symptoms, Treatment and Pathology of Insanity and the Law of Lunacy in Great Britain and Ireland, ed. D H Tuke, London, Churchill, vol. 1, pp. 618–27.

Johnson, W, 1850, The Morbid Emotions of Women. Their Origin, Tendencies, and Treatment, London, Simpkin, Marshall & Co.

Laycock, T, 1840, A Treatise on the Nervous Diseases of Women; Comprising an Inquiry into the Nature, Causes, and Treatment of Spinal and Hysterical Disorders, London, Longman, Orme, Brown, Greene, & Longmans.

Maudsley, H, 1870, Body and Mind. An Inquiry into their Connection and Mutual Influence, Specially in Reference to Mental Disorders, London, Macmillan.

Maudsley, H, 1874a, 'Sex in Mind and Education', The Fortnightly Review, n.s. 15, 466–83.

Maudsley, H, 1874b, Responsibility in Mental Disease, London, King.

Maudsley, H, 1895, The Pathology of Mind. A Study of Its Distempers, Deformities and Disorders, 2nd edn., London, Macmillan.

Mercier, C A, 1890, Sanity and Insanity, London, Scott.

Patmore, C, n.d. [1854–6], The Angel in the House together with The Victories of Love, London, George Routledge.

Prichard, J C, 1835, A Treatise on Insanity and other Disorders Affecting the Mind, London, Sherwood, Gilbert & Piper.

Ruskin, J, 1905 [1864], 'Of Queen's Gardens', in J Ruskin, The Works of John Ruskin, ed. E T Cook and A Wedderburn, London, George Allen, 39 vols, 1903–12, vol. 18, pp. 109–44.

Skey, F C, 1867, Hysteria. Six Lectures, London, Longmans, Green, Reader & Dyer.

Tilt, E J, 1851, On the Preservation of the Health of Women at the Critical Periods of Life, London, Churchill.

Tilt, E J, 1852, Elements of Health and Principles of Female Hygiene, London, Bohn.

Tilt, E J, 1857, The Change of Life in Health and Disease. A Practical Treatise on the Nervous and Other Affections Incidental to Women at the Decline of Life, 2nd edn., London, Churchill.

Walker, A, 1840, Woman Physiologically Considered as to Mind, Morals, Marriage, Matrimonial Slavery, Infidelity and Divorce, 2nd edn., London, Baily.

Secondary Literature

Cvetkovich, A, 1992, *Mixed Feelings: Feminism, Mass Culture, and Victorian Sensationalism*, New Brunswick, Rutgers University Press.

Pykett, L, 1992, *The 'Improper' Feminine: The Women's Sensation Novel and the New Woman Writing*, London, Routledge.

Rance, N, 1991, *Wilkie Collins and Other Sensation Novelists: Walking the Moral Hospital*, Basingstoke, Macmillan.

Rosenberg, C S, 1985, *Disorderly Conduct: Visions of Gender in Victorian America*, New York, Knopf.

Showalter, E, 1977, *A Literature of Their Own: British Women Novelists from Brontë to Lessing*, Princeton, NJ, Princeton University Press.

Showalter, E, 1995, *The Female Malady: Women, Madness, and English Culture, 1830–1980*, repr. London, Virago.

Zedner, L, 1991, *Women, Crime and Custody in Victorian England*, Oxford, Clarendon Press.

Chapter 15 Night Terrors: Medical and Literary Representations of Childhood Fear

Works Cited

Primary Literature

Addington, B H, 1917, *Handicaps of Childhood*, London, Kegan, Paul, Trench, Trubner & Co.

Barlow, J, 1843, *On Man's Power over Himself to Prevent or Control Insanity*, London, William Pickering.

Brontë, C, 2000a [1847], *Jane Eyre*, ed. M Smith, introd. S Shuttleworth, Oxford, Oxford University Press.

Brontë, C, 2000b [1848–51], *The Letters of Charlotte Brontë, with a Selection of Letters by Family and Friends*, vol. 2: *1848–51*, ed. M Smith, Oxford, Clarendon Press.

Browne, J C, 1860, 'Psychical Diseases of Early Life', *Asylum Journal of Mental Science* 6, 284–320.

Carter, R B, 1855, *On the Influence of Education and Training in Preventing Diseases of the Nervous System*, London, John Churchill.

Conolly, J, 1964 [1830], *An Inquiry Concerning the Indications of Insanity, with suggestions for the better protection and care of the insane*, repr. and introd. R Hunter and I Macalpine, London, Dawsons.

Darwin, C, 1877, 'A Biographical Sketch of an Infant', *Mind* 7, 283–94.

Darwin, C, 1988 [1847–50], *The Correspondence of Charles Darwin*, 13 vols to date, 1983 –, ed. F H Burkhardt *et al.*, vol. 4: *1847–1850*, Cambridge, Cambridge University Press.

De Vere, 1851, 'Review of *Poems by Hartley Coleridge. With a Memoir of His Life. By His Brother. And Essays and Marginalia* by Hartley Coleridge', *Edinburgh Review* 94, 64–97.

Dickens, C, 1958 [1860], *The Uncommercial Traveller and Reprinted Pieces*, London, Oxford University Press.

Dickens, C, 1988 [1850–2], *The Letters of Charles Dickens*, vol. 6: *1850–52*, ed. G Storey, K Tillotson and N Burgis, Oxford, Clarendon Press.

Edgeworth, M, 1999, *The Novels and Selected Works of Maria Edgeworth*, vol. 3: *Leonora: Harrington*, ed. M Butler and S Manly, London, Pickering & Chatto.

Freud, S, 1953, *The Standard Edition of the Complete Psychological Works*, ed. J Strachey, vol. 7: *A Case of Hysteria, Three Essays on Sexuality; and Other Works*, London, Hogarth Press.

Graham, T J, 1826, *Modern Domestic Medicine*, London, Simpkin Marshall *et al.*

Grand, S, 1980 [1897], *The Beth Book: Being a Study of the Life of Elizabeth Caldwell Maclure, A Woman of Genius*, introd. E Showalter, New York, Dial Press.

Jameson, A, 1854, *A Commonplace Book of Thoughts, Memories, and Fancies, Original and Selected*, London, Longman, Brown, Green and Longmans.

Jameson, A, 2000 [1854], 'A Revelation of Childhood', in *A Commonplace Book of Thoughts, Memories, and Fancies, Original and Selected*, repr. in *Records of Girlhood: An Anthology of Nineteenth Century Women's Childhoods*, ed. V Sanders, Aldershot, Ashgate, pp. 76–88.

Lamb, C, 1968 [1903], 'Witches, and other Night-fears', in *The Works of Charles and Mary Lamb*, vol. 2: *Elia and The Last Essays of Elia*, ed. E V Lucas, London, Methuen & Co, repr. New York, AMS Press, pp. 67–8.

Locke, J, 1989, *Some Thoughts Concerning Education*, ed. J W Yolton and J S Yolton, Oxford, Clarendon Press.

Macnish, R, 1830, *The Philosophy of Sleep*, Glasgow, W. R. McPhun.

Martineau, H, 1849, *Household Education*, London, Smith, Elder & Co.

Martineau, H, 1877, *Harriet Martineau's Autobiography, with Memorials by Maria Weston Chapman*, 3 vols, London, Smith, Elder & Co.

Prichard, J C, 1998 [1835], *A Treatise on Insanity and Other Disorders Affecting the Mind*, in *Embodied Selves: An Anthology of Psychological Texts, 1830–1890*, ed. J B Taylor and S Shuttleworth, Oxford, Clarendon Press, pp. 251–6.

Stackhouse, T, 1737, *New History of the Holy Bible from the Beginning of the World to the Establishment of Christianity*, London.

Sully, J, 1887 [1881], *Illusions: A Psychological Study*, 3rd edn., London, Kegan, Paul, Trench & Co.

Sully, J, 1993 [1895], *Studies of Childhood*, repr. London, Routledge/Thoemmes Press.

Tanner, T H, 1858, *A Practical Treatise on the Diseases of Infancy and Childhood*, London, Henry Renshaw.

West, C, 1848, *Lectures on the Diseases of Infancy and Childhood*, London, Longman, Brown, Green and Longmans.

West, C, 1854, *Lectures on the Diseases of Infancy and Childhood*, 3rd rev. edn., London, Longman, Brown, Green and Longmans.

Secondary Literature

Ford, J, 1998, *Coleridge on Dreaming: Romanticism, Dreams and the Medical Imagination*, Cambridge, Cambridge University Press.

Kosky, J, 1989, *Mutual Friends: Charles Dickens and Great Ormond Street Hospital*, London, George Weidenfeld Nicolson.

Kucich, J, 1994, *The Power of Lies: Transgression in Victorian Fiction*, Ithaca, NY, Cornell University Press.

Logan, P, 1997, *Nerves and Narratives: A Cultural History of Hysteria in Nineteenth Century British Prose*, Berkeley, University of California Press.

Poovey, M, 1989, *Uneven Developments: The Ideological Work of Gender in Mid-Victorian England*, London, Virago.

Richardson, A, 1988, *British Romanticism and the Science of Mind*, Cambridge, Cambridge University Press.

Shuttleworth, S, 1996, *Charlotte Brontë and Victorian Psychology*, Cambridge, Cambridge University Press.

Taylor, J B, and Shuttleworth, S, eds, 1998, *Embodied Selves: An Anthology of Psychological Texts, 1830–1890*, Oxford, Clarendon Press.

Walk, A, 1964, 'The Pre-History of Child Psychiatry', *British Journal of Psychiatry* 110, 754–67.

Chapter 16 Sensuous Knowledge

Works Cited

Primary Literature

[Carlill, J B], J. B. C., 1893, 'In the Realm of Sound', *Macmillan's Magazine* 67, 438–43.

Collins, W, 1996 [1859–60], *The Woman in White*, ed. J Sutherland, Oxford, Oxford University Press.

Collins, W, 1999 [1868], *The Moonstone*, ed. J Sutherland, Oxford, Oxford University Press.

Dickens, C, 1999 [1861], *Great Expectations*, ed. E Rosenberg, New York, Norton.

Gurney, E, 1880, *The Power of Sound*, London, Smith, Elder & Co.

Hardy, T, 1912 [1881], *A Laodicean*, London, Macmillan & Co.

Lewes, H G, 1860 [1859], *The Physiology of Common Life*, 2 vols, 2nd edn., Leipzig, Bernhard Tauchnitz.

Melville, H, 1967 [1851], *Moby-Dick*, ed. H Hayford and H Parker, New York, Norton.

Meredith, G, 1983 [1862], *Selected Poems*, ed. K Hanley, Manchester, Carcanet.

Spencer, H R, 1877 [1855], *The Principles of Psychology*, New York, D. Appleton & Co.

Sully, J, 1874, *Sensation and Intuition: Studies in Psychology and Aesthetics*, London, Henry S. King & Co.

Sully, J, 1878, 'Civilisation and Noise', *Fortnightly Review* 30, 704–20.

Tyndall, J, 1875 [1867], *Sound*, rev. and enlarged edn., London, Longmans, Green & Co.

Secondary Literature

Ackerman, D, 1995 [1990], *A Natural History of the Senses*, New York, Vintage Books.

Appadurai, A, 1986, 'Introduction: Commodities and the Politics of Value', in *The Social Life of Things: Commodities in Cultural Perspective*, ed. A Appadurai, Cambridge, Cambridge University Press, pp. 3–63.

Brennan, T, 2004, *The Transmission of Affect*, Ithaca, NY, Cornell University Press.

Brown, B, 2001, 'Thing Theory', *Critical Inquiry* 28, 1–16.

Burgin, V, 1996, In/Different Spaces: Place and Memory in Visual Culture, Berkeley, University of California Press.

Carlisle, J, 2004, Common Scents: Comparative Encounters in High-Victorian Fiction, New York, Oxford University Press.

Classen, C, 1993, Worlds of Sense: Exploring the Senses in History and Across Cultures, London, Routledge.

Connor, S, 2000, 'Making an Issue of Cultural Phenomenology', Critical Quarterly 42, 2–6.

Corbin, A, 1994 [1986], The Foul and the Fragrant: Odour and the Social Imagination, trans. M Koshan, London, Picador.

Crary, J, 2000, Suspensions of Perception: Attention, Spectacle, and Modern Culture, Cambridge, MA, MIT Press.

Flint, K, 2000, The Victorians and the Visual Imagination, Cambridge, Cambridge University Press.

Flint, K, 2003, 'Sounds of the City: Virginia Woolf and Modern Noise', in Literature, Science, Psychoanalysis, 1830–1970: Essays in Honour of Gillian Beer, ed. H Small and T Tate, Oxford, Oxford University Press, pp. 181–94.

Miller, W I, 1997, The Anatomy of Disgust, Cambridge, MA, Harvard University Press.

Picker, J M, 2003, Victorian Soundscapes, New York, Oxford University Press.

Rindisbacher, H J, 1992, The Smell of Books: A Cultural-Historical Study of Olfactory Perception in Literature, Ann Arbor, University of Michigan Press.

Simmel, G, 1997 [1907], 'Sociology of the Senses' ['Soziologie der Sinne'], trans. M Ritter and D Frisby, in Simmel on Culture, ed. D Frisby and M Featherstone, London, Sage, pp. 109–20.

Smith, B R, 1999, The Acoustic World of Early Modern England: Attending to the O-Factor, Chicago, University of Chicago Press.

Sperber, D, 1975, Rethinking Symbolism, Cambridge, Cambridge University Press.

Stallybrass, P, and White, A, 1986, The Politics and Poetics of Transgression, Ithaca, NY, Cornell University Press.

Trotter, D, 2000, 'The New Historicism and the Psychopathology of Everyday Modern Life', Critical Quarterly 42, 36–58.